WRITING
WITH A
THESIS

Writing with a Thesis
A Rhetoric and Reader

ELEVENTH EDITION

Sarah E. Skwire
Liberty Fund, Inc.

David Skwire

WADSWORTH
CENGAGE Learning™

Australia • Brazil • Japan • Korea • Mexico • Singapore • Spain • United Kingdom • United States

WADSWORTH
CENGAGE Learning™

**Writing with a Thesis:
A Rhetoric and Reader,
Eleventh Edition**
Sarah E. Skwire
David Skwire

Publisher: Lyn Uhl
Acquisitions Editor:
 Margaret Leslie
Assistant Editor: Amy Haines
Editorial Assistant: Elizabeth
 Ramsey
Media Editor: Amy Gibbons
Marketing Manager: Jennifer
 Zourdos
Marketing Coordinator: Ryan
 Ahern
Marketing Communications
 Manager: Stacey Purviance
Content Project Manager:
 Aimee Chevrette Bear
Art Director: Jill Ort
Print Buyer: Susan Spencer
Permissions Editor: Katie
 Huha
Photo Manager: Jennifer
 Meyer Dare
Production Service: Ashley
 Schneider, S4Carlisle
 Publishing Services
Compositor: S4Carlisle
 Publishing Services

For product information and technology assistance, contact us at **Cengage Learning Customer & Sales Support, 1-800-354-9706**

For permission to use material from this text or product, submit all requests online at **www.cengage.com/ permissions**.Further permissions questions can be e-mailed to **permissionrequest@cengage.com**.

Library of Congress Control Number: 2009941754

Student Edition:

ISBN- 13: 978-1-428-29001-3

ISBN-10: 1-428-29001-X

Wadsworth
20 Channel Center Street
Boston, MA 02210
USA

Cengage Learning is a leading provider of customized learning solutions with office locations around the globe, including Singapore, the United Kingdom, Australia, Mexico, Brazil and Japan. Locate your local office at: **international. cengage.com/region**

Cengage Learning products are represented in Canada by Nelson Education, Ltd.

For your course and learning solutions, visit **www.cengage.com**.

Purchase any of our products at your local college store or at our preferred online store **www.ichapters.com**.

Printed in the United States of America
1 2 3 4 5 6 7 12 11 10 09

This book is for Penelope and Dinah, with love.

Contents

Guide to "What About Your Writing?"   xiii
To the Instructor   xv
To the Student   xvii
Acknowledgments   xix

Chapter 1   The Persuasive Principle   1

General Subject   1
Limited Subject   2
Thesis   3
What a Thesis Isn't   4
   A Thesis Is Not a Title   4
   A Thesis Is Not an Announcement of the Subject   5
   A Thesis Is Not a Statement of Absolute Fact   5
   A Thesis Is Not the Whole Essay   6
What a Good Thesis Is   6
   A Good Thesis Is Restricted   6
   A Good Thesis Is Unified   6
   A Good Thesis Is Specific   7
Exercises for Review   9
The Thesis at Work in the Paper   10
   Two Ads on the Community Bulletin Board   13
   Two "Personals"   14
   Two Sets of Directions   15
   Two Thank-You Notes   16
   Two Letters of Complaint   17
   Two Replies to the Second Letter of Complaint   19
Visual Prompt   21
   Two "How I Spent My Summer Vacation" Essays   21
   Two Freshman English Essays on a Literary Subject   23
The Lottery, **Shirley Jackson**   23

Chapter 1½   Basic Tools for Writers   33

Chapter 2   Narration   35

Stress the Story   36
Remember That a Good Story Has Conflict   36
Use Plenty of Convincing Realistic Details   36
Play Fair   37
   Writing Suggestions for Narration Themes   37
Readings   38
Visual Prompt   38

Student Essay: "Big Bully," **Elizabeth Hiestand**   39
Free Tibet, Man!, **Dinty W. Moore**   40
  What About <u>Your</u> Writing? (paragraph length)   41
Foul Shots, **Rogelio R. Gomez**   42
  What About <u>Your</u> Writing? (getting even, settling scores)   45
The Perfect Picture, **James Alexander Thom**   46
  What About <u>Your</u> Writing? (overwriting)   48
The Happiest Day of My Life, **Michael T. Smith**   49
Salvation, **Langston Hughes**   52
  What About <u>Your</u> Writing? (nostalgia)   55
A Cultural Divorce, **Elizabeth Wong**   55
  What About <u>Your</u> Writing? (specific details)   58
Sitting Duck, **Thomas Froncek**   58
  What About <u>Your</u> Writing? (sentence fragments)   62

Chapter 2½   Reading Around   63

Chapter 3   Description   65
  Emotional Appeal   65
    Try a Deliberately Unconventional Thesis   66
    Show Your Powers of Observation by Stressing Specific Details   66
    Use Specific Language   66
    Stress the Psychological Impact of What You Describe   66
  Organization   67
  The Persuasive Principle   67
  Writing Suggestions for Description Themes   68
  Visual Prompt   69
  Student Essay: "Master of Bad Management," **Robynn Patrick**   69
  Winstead's Best Burgers, **Sarah Bryan Miller**   71
    What About <u>Your</u> Writing? (allusion)   73
  I Was a Member of the Kung Fu Crew, **Henry Han Xi Lau**   74
    What About <u>Your</u> Writing? (pronoun agreement)   77
  My Glove: A Biography, **Stefan Fatsis**   78
    What About <u>Your</u> Writing? (citation of authority)   82
  All by Myself, **Tom Reynolds**   83
    What About <u>Your</u> Writing? (comparisons)   86
  Double Take, **Melissa Lafsky**   87
    What About <u>Your</u> Writing? (hyperbole)   89
  The Loneliness of Rose, **Jon Katz**   90
    What About <u>Your</u> Writing? (unstated thesis)   94

Chapter 3½   **Notebooks: The Writer's Savings Account**   **95**

Chapter 4   **Examples**   **97**

Are There Enough Examples to Support Your Thesis?   98
Are the Examples Fairly Chosen?   98
Have You Stuck to Your Thesis?   99
Have You Arranged Your Examples to Produce the Greatest Impact?   99
Writing Suggestions for Example Essays   100
Visual Prompt   101
Student Essay: "Broke and Bored: The Summer Job," **Ashley Hall**   102
Always Settle Scores at Noon, **Robert Fulford**   104
  What About <u>Your</u> Writing? (sentence length)   106
Couple Lies, **Adair Lara**   106
  What About <u>Your</u> Writing? ("Why didn't *I* say that?")   108
Fruitful Questions, **James Sollisch**   109
  What About <u>Your</u> Writing? (rhetorical questions)   111
Chores, **Debra Marquart**   112
  What About <u>Your</u> Writing? (intensifiers)   114
How to Speak of Animals, **Umberto Eco**   115
  What About <u>Your</u> Writing? (parallelism)   117

Chapter 4½   **Of Course They Count**   **120**

Chapter 5   **Process**   **123**

Be Sure You Are Writing About a Process   125
Follow Strict Chronological Order   125
Before Describing the First Step of the Process, Indicate Any Special
    Ingredients or Equipment That Will Be Needed   125
Be Sure the Process Is Complete   125
Try to Anticipate Difficulties   126
If You Need to Handle Many Separate Steps, Arrange Them into Groups
    When Possible   126
Define Unfamiliar Terms   127
Avoid Highly Technical Processes   127
Avoid Subjects for Which Pictures Work Better Than Words   127
Writing Suggestions for Process Essays   127
Visual Prompt   129
Student Essay: "How Not to Work Out," **Max Greene**   129
Corn Bread with Character, **Ronni Lundy**   131

What About <u>Your</u> Writing? (introductions: how do I get my reader's attention?)   134

"IT," **Stephanie Pearl-McPhee**   135
What About <u>Your</u> Writing? (repetition)   140

The Exploding Toilet and Other Embarrassments, **Patrick Smith**   141
What About <u>Your</u> Writing? (levels of usage)   146

Too Many Bananas, **David R. Counts**   147
What About <u>Your</u> Writing? (jargon)   154

The Spider and the Wasp, **Alexander Petrunkevitch**   155
What About <u>Your</u> Writing? (announcement of subject)   159

Chapter 5½   Uses and Abuses of the Computer 161

Chapter 6   Comparison and Contrast   165

Patterns   166
Block Pattern   166
Alternating Pattern   168
Which Pattern?   169
Writing Suggestions for Comparison-and-Contrast Themes   170
Visual Prompt   171
Block Pattern   172
Student Essay: "Coming in Last," **Annette P. Grossman**   172
Alternating Pattern   174
Student Essay: "Dads and Dads," **Reid Morris**   174
Lassie Never Chases Rabbits, **Kevin Cowherd**   175
What About <u>Your</u> Writing? (conclusions)   178
My Real Car, **Bailey White**   179
What About <u>Your</u> Writing? (onomatopoeia)   182
Dearly Disconnected, **Ian Frazier**   182
What About <u>Your</u> Writing? (topicality)   186
Speaking of Writing, **William Zinsser**   187
What About <u>Your</u> Writing? (thesis at end of essay)   189
Love Thy Playstation, Love Thyself, **Reihan Salam and Will Wilkinson**   189
What About <u>Your</u> Writing? (humor)   192

Chapter 6½   Revision: An Overview   193

Chapter 7   Cause and Effect   195

Do Not Oversimplify Causes   196
Do Not Oversimplify Effects   197
Distinguish Between Direct and Indirect Causes and Effects   197
Distinguish Between Major and Minor Causes and Effects   197
Do Not Omit Links in a Chain of Causes and Effects   197
Play Fair   198
Writing Suggestions for Cause-and-Effect Papers   198

Visual Prompt   199
Student Essay: "A Few Short Words," **Matthew Monroe**   199
Why We Crave Horror Movies, **Stephen King**   201
    What About <u>Your</u> Writing? (sexism: *he*)   203
Beyond Chagrin, **David Bradley**   205
    What About <u>Your</u> Writing? (elegant variation)   207
Cold Autumn, **Steve Dublanica**   208
    What About <u>Your</u> Writing? (finding a subject: work)   211
Why I Quit the Company, **Tomoyuki Iwashita**   213
    What About <u>Your</u> Writing? (qualifiers, rational tone)   216
The Best Years of My Life, **Betty Rollin**   216
    What About <u>Your</u> Writing? (comma splice)   221

Chapter 7½   Revision: Help from the Audience 223

Chapter 8   Division and Classification   225

Division   225
Classification   225
    Use Only One Principle of Classification   226
    Be Consistent   227
    Make the Classifications as Complete as Possible   227
    Acknowledge Any Complications   228
    Follow the Persuasive Principle   228
    Writing Suggestions for Classification Themes   229
Visual Prompt   230
Student Essay: "Bookworm," **Gracie Jane Watson**   231
Mother-in-Law, **Charlotte Latvala**   232
    What About <u>Your</u> Writing? (finding a subject: romantic highs and lows)   238
Take a Left Turn Onto Nowhere Street, **Anne Bernays**   239
    What About <u>Your</u> Writing? (titles)   242
The Seven-Lesson Schoolteacher, **John Taylor Gatto**   242
    What About <u>Your</u> Writing? (ironic quotation marks)   253
A Brush with Reality: Surprises in the Tube, **David Bodanis**   254
    What About <u>Your</u> Writing? (specialties of the author)   257
Three Kinds of Discipline, **John Holt**   258
    What About <u>Your</u> Writing? (alliteration)   261

Chapter 8½   Revision: The Psychology of It All   263

Chapter 9   Definition   265

A Definition Paper Can Compare and Contrast   266
A Definition Paper Can Classify   266
A Definition Paper Can Give Examples   266
A Definition Paper Can Trace a Process   267
A Definition Paper Can Study Cause-and-Effect Relationships   267

A Definition Paper Can Use Narration   267

Writing Suggestions for Definition Essays   267

Visual Prompt   268

Student Essay: "Growing Up," **Anonymous**   268

The Real Thing, **Frankie Germany**   270

    What About <u>Your</u> Writing? (comic-book punctuation, exclamation points, etc.)   271

What Is Intelligence, Anyway? **Isaac Asimov**   272

    What About <u>Your</u> Writing? (simple thesis)   274

Cheap Thrills, **Patricia Volk**   274

    What About <u>Your</u> Writing? (dialogue)   278

Sick in the Head, **Jennifer Traig**   279

    What About <u>Your</u> Writing? (puns)   286

Catachresis, **Patricia O'Hara**   287

    What About <u>Your</u> Writing? (having a gimmick)   289

Chapter 9½   Deadlines   **291**

Chapter 10   Argumentation   **293**

Go Easy on Universals–Qualify When Appropriate   295

Give Consideration to Differing Opinions   295

Be Cautious with Abuse and Ridicule   295

Devote Most of Your Attention to Supporting Your View, Not Advocating It   296

Some Common Logical Fallacies   296

    Writing Suggestions for Argumentation Essays   299

Visual Prompt   300

Student Essay: "Sing It When It Counts," **Ben Ruggiero**   300

Thanksgiving's No Turkey, **Robert W. Gardner**   302

    What About <u>Your</u> Writing? (taking sides for fun, mental exercise)   304

Distracting Miss Daisy, **John Staddon**   305

    What About <u>Your</u> Writing? (*And* at the start of a sentence)   311

The Smiley-Face Approach, **Albert Shanker**   312

    What About <u>Your</u> Writing? (passive voice)   314

Working at McDonald's, **Amitai Etzioni**   315

    What About <u>Your</u> Writing? (attack on an orthodox view)   319

Appeasing the Gods, with Insurance, **John Tierney**   320

    What About <u>Your</u> Writing? (*You*)   323

Black Athletes on Parade, **Adolph Reed, Jr.**   324

    What About <u>Your</u> Writing? (turning tables, beating opponents to the punch)   328

A Modest Proposal, **Jonathan Swift**   328

    What About <u>Your</u> Writing? (irony)   336

Chapter 10½   What About the Rest of Your Writing?   **338**

Index   341

Guide to "What About <u>Your</u> Writing?"

The "What About <u>Your</u> Writing?" entries offer comments and pointers on matters of practical concern to the student writer, as such matters turn up in the readings. For general perspectives and quick references, see the following guide.

SUBJECTS

Announcement of subject   159
Finding a subject: romantic highs and lows   238
Finding a subject: work   211
Getting even, settling scores   45
Nostalgia   55
Specialties of author   257
Taking sides for fun, mental exercise   304
"Why didn't I say that?"   108

ORGANIZATION

Attack on orthodox view in introduction   319
Conclusions   178
Introductions, getting reader's interest   94
Paragraph length   41
Thesis, at end of essay   189
Thesis, simple   274
Thesis, unstated   94
Titles   242

PERSUASIVE STRATEGIES

Citation of authority   82
Humor   192
Irony   336
Rhetorical questions   111
Topicality   186
Turning tables, beating opponents to punch   328

STYLE

Alliteration   261
Allusions   73
And at the start of a sentence   311
Announcement of subject   159
Comic-book punctuation (exclamation points, etc.)   271
Comma splices   221
Comparisons: metaphors and similes   86
Dialogue   278
Elegant variation   207
Fragmentary sentences   62
Gimmicks   289
Hyperbole   89
Intensifiers (*very, really*)   114
Jargon   154
Levels of usage   146
Onomatopoeia   182
Overwriting   48
Parallelism   117
Passive voice   314
Pronoun agreement   77
Puns   286
Qualifiers, rational tone   216
Quotation marks, ironic   253
Repetition for emphasis   140
Sentence fragments   62
Sentence length   106
Sexism: *he*   203
Short paragraphs to get attention   41
Specific details   58
You   323

To the Instructor

I love the young dogs of this age: they have more wit and humor and knowledge of life than we had; but then the dogs are not so good scholars. Sir, in my early years I read very hard.

—Samuel Johnson

In many respects, *Writing with a Thesis* tries to do a traditional job in a traditional way. Its readings are arranged according to traditional rhetorical patterns, one pattern per chapter. Each group of readings is preceded by a detailed discussion of the writing techniques appropriate to that pattern. Headnotes, explanatory footnotes, and questions on content and style accompany each reading. The book wholeheartedly accepts such traditional ideas about teaching composition as the value of omnivorous reading, the utility of close analysis of individual works, and the salutary influence of models.

In some other respects, *Writing with a Thesis* is less traditional, though its commitment to the job of improving writing skills remains constant.

First, the traditional reader or rhetoric reader tends to approach each rhetorical pattern as a separate entity requiring the development of a new set of writing skills. Chapter 1 of this book presents what it calls the *persuasive principle*: the development and support of a thesis. It goes on to demonstrate how the persuasive principle underlies almost all good writing; and subsequent chapters show how the persuasive principle functions within each of the rhetorical patterns. A major unifying theme thus runs through the entire book, with each pattern being viewed not as a separate entity, but as the application of a permanent writing principle to varying subject matter, insights, and purposes. The concept of the persuasive principle has long been stressed in some of the most popular handbooks and rhetorics. It has not ordinarily been the animating force behind a general reader.

Second, in addition to the standard apparatus, the book includes after each selection brief comments titled "What About <u>Your</u> Writing?" These comments, directly related to the selection just studied, offer quick, practical lessons that students can apply to their own work. The stress generally is on style, but the coverage is wide and by no means confined to style. Topics range from common high school superstitions—"Can I begin a sentence with *and*?"—to such broader issues of invention as finding new slants on old subjects. Every instructor knows the benefits that can come when a student raises a hand and says, "This doesn't have anything to do with the subject exactly, but I was just wondering. . . . " Just as an instructor structures a lesson and a course but builds into that structure an atmosphere that welcomes sudden, just-wondering questions, *Writing with a Thesis* uses "What About <u>Your</u> Writing?" to complement the rigorously structured elements of the rest of the book.

On page xiii a guide to "What About <u>Your</u> Writing?" provides a convenient listing of all topics.

Third are the "half-chapters" we like to call "Office Hours." These "Office Hours" offer insights and advice on the writing process that we hope will replicate the spontaneous exchanges that characterize office visits at their best. Some of the topics are familiar enough—the importance of revision, the need for careful checking of basic skills, the use of computers—but we try always for an original as well as helpful slant. Students aren't just told that they must revise, for example. They're told why they probably don't like to revise and how they can overcome their ingrained resistance to the task. Students aren't just told that spelling and grammar count; they're told a few funny stories that explain why. Students aren't just told that computers have revolutionized the writing process; they're warned of the perils, as well as the pleasures, that writing with a computer can bring. Some of the topics are more unusual. One identifies the "basic tools" that good writers need and tells students how to find some of them online. Another tries to answer the rarely spoken but commonly felt question: "What's the secret that makes good writers so good?" Another explains why experienced writers almost never need to wait for "inspiration."

Finally, one of the traditional problems with many traditional textbooks is that they bore and scare too many students. Instructors write them for other instructors, and the students suffer. *Writing with a Thesis,* with all its traditional philosophy, is written in an informal, simple, and, we hope, engaging style. The reading selections themselves, though a few are deliberately long and challenging, are generally short and easy to read. Class time can be devoted primarily to showing not what the readings mean, but what they mean for the student's writing.

To the Student

Buying textbooks is more than the dreariness of waiting in line at the bookstore. It probably also marks the only time in your life when you pay good money for books you know nothing about.

The process isn't quite as outrageous as it might seem. Your instructors already know what your courses are designed to teach and are in a solid position to decide which books will be most helpful. You can safely assume that they've spent a long time wading through piles of texts before making their final selections and that you wouldn't have enjoyed taking that drudgery on yourself. Still, in many ways your purchase of this book is an act of faith, and before committing yourself much further, you have a right to some information.

This book is designed to help you in several ways to become a better writer.

First, each section begins with a detailed, practical discussion of how to handle the writing assignments you are likely to get: comparison and contrast, classification, cause and effect, and so on. These assignments are based on highly artificial writing patterns. The patterns often overlap and are rarely encountered in their pure form. A paper devoted primarily to classification, for example, could easily spend a good deal of time comparing and contrasting each class. Most instructors find it valuable, however, to discuss and assign the patterns separately. Nobody ever played a set of tennis using only a forehand drive, but serious players may devote hours at a time to practicing that one shot. Similarly, a substantial piece of writing is likely to demand a combination of patterns, but each pattern is best practiced and mastered by being treated at the start as an independent unit.

Second, each section of the book contains at least one outlined student essay and a group of readings by professional writers designed to show effective use of the pattern under consideration. These writers put ideas together in the same pattern that will be required of you, and they went about their task in such and such a way. Studying the techniques by which they achieved their success can stimulate any writer faced with similar problems—but nobody wants you to write a barren imitation of someone else's work. A tennis player can profit from studying Serena Williams's serve without attempting to duplicate it. The writer, as well as the athlete, uses models to discover the basic principles for shaping individual strengths into an effective force, not to follow blindly some particular conception of good form.

Third, questions on each reading selection are designed to help you look closely at the means by which each writer worked. A vague impression that an essay was competently written will be of little practical benefit to your own efforts.

Fourth, to add to the practical emphasis of this book, each reading is followed by a brief comment called "What About <u>Your</u> Writing?" These comments tend to get away from the presentation of broad principles and deal instead with specific pointers and suggestions, ranging from avoiding overused words like *very* to tips on how to find a subject when your mind seems to be a complete blank.

Fifth, every chapter is followed by a shorter "half-chapter" we like to call "Office Hours," designed to resemble the informal conversations that supplement regular class meetings. Here, you'll find discussions about different parts of the writing process. You'll find suggestions for the tools that every writer should have, and we'll save you some time and money by telling you where you can find some of them online. You'll find our advice about "the secret" that all good writers know. You'll find suggestions about how to revise effectively as well as an explanation for many students' reluctance to revise at all.

Sixth, all the readings are designed to drive home a special approach to writing that runs through this book: If writing is thought of, wherever possible, as an attempt to persuade the reader of the validity of a particular point, many common problems virtually disappear or solve themselves. We call this approach the *persuasive principle*. Chapter 1 presents this principle in detail; the following chapters show how it can be applied to particular writing assignments.

That's the theory. You and your instructor are the only authorities on whether the theory works for you. If it does, this book was worth the money.

Acknowledgments

We would like to thank Ashley Hall, for her hard work and good cheer, and Darren Waschow for assistance with photograph selection. Deb Weinmann provided research assistance when it was most needed, and we cannot thank her enough. Elizabeth Hull provided useful suggestions about readings. Special thanks to Liberty Fund, Inc., for innumerable kindnesses and considerations.

Thanks also to the editorial and marketing staff at Wadsworth Cengage: Margaret Leslie, acquisitions editor; Amy Haines, assistant editor; Aimee Bear, content production manager; Jennifer Zourdos, marketing manager; Elizabeth Ramsey, editorial assistant; Jennifer Meyer Dare, image permissions manager; Katie Huha, text permissions manager.

We also want to acknowledge with gratitude the valuable reviews of:

Karen Cahill, *Southeastern Community College*
Randall Ivey, *University of South Carolina Union*
Carla Kirchner, *Southwest Baptist University*
Kirk Lockwood, *Illinois Valley Community College*
Michele Martinez, *Harvard University*
Penni Pearson, *Northern State University*
Francie Quaas-Berryman, *Cerritos College*
Scott Redmond, *Cleveland State Community College*
Clifford Weinstein, *Bergen Community College*

A NOTE ON THE ELEVENTH EDITION

Written entirely by David Skwire, the first edition of *Writing with a Thesis* was published in 1976 when Sarah Skwire was only five years old. We both remember the large world map on David's office wall becoming dotted with pins as the book sold, and David marked each state and country that had begun to use the textbook. It's a little hard for us to believe that we've all grown up so quickly! We have also changed a great deal.

Apart from many expected changes, this edition includes **three new sample student essays**, "Broke and Bored–The Summer Job," "How Not to Work Out," and "Bookworm"; and **sixteen new professional reading selections**, including "My Glove: A Biography," by Stefan Fatsis; "Chores," by Debra Marquart; "Beyond Chagrin," by David Bradley; and "Sick in the Head," by Jennifer Traig. Each selection is accompanied by post-reading questions. The most significant change to this edition are **illustrative photographs in each**

chapter that provide visual representations of the main chapter topics. The photographs are also intended to serve as inspirations for student writing–each one is accompanied by a writing prompt.

This edition continues our use of the ten "Office Hours" introduced in the ninth edition. They're short. They're practical. They replicate the real-life office hours experience. They focus on the ups and downs as well as the ins and outs of the writing process.

We can also happily report that there is much that has not changed. The *persuasive principle* remains as central to our thinking as ever. The readings continue to be short, accessible, and lively. Swift's rhetorical classic, "A Modest Proposal," remains the final piece in this edition, as it has been in every edition of the book. The discipline of success and the nearly unanimous message of user surveys not to mess with what works have made it easy to resist indulging in massive overhauls for their own sake.

Sarah E. Skwire
David Skwire

The Persuasive Principle

CHAPTER 1

This book offers you one central piece of advice: *Whenever possible, think of your writing as a form of persuasion.*

Persuasion is traditionally considered to be a separate branch of writing. When you write what's usually called a persuasion paper, you pick a controversial issue, tell your readers which side you're on, and try to persuade them that you're correct: the defense budget needs to be decreased, handguns should be outlawed, doctors must be protected against frivolous malpractice suits, required freshman English courses should be abolished. Persuasion is supposed to be based on different principles from other kinds of writing–description, narration, exposition, and so forth.

It isn't.

A description of a relative, an account of what you went through to get your first job, a comparison of two brands of dishwashers–if you can approach such assignments as an effort to persuade your reader of the validity of a particular opinion or major point, you're in business as a writer. Your paper's opinion or major point is called its *thesis*. Your thesis may be that your relative is the most boring person you have ever met, that getting your first job was easier than you thought it would be, that a Maytag dishwasher is likely to last longer than a Whirlpool. If you have a thesis and if you select and organize your material to support that thesis, a number of basic writing problems begin to solve themselves. You have built-in purpose. You have built-in organization. You have the potential for built-in interest. Aside from a few obvious exceptions, such as newspaper reports, encyclopedia articles, instruction manuals, recipes, and certain types of stories, poems, and plays, *all writing can benefit from a commitment to the persuasive principle: Develop a thesis, and then back it up.*

There is no better way to demonstrate the effectiveness of the persuasive principle than to take a close look at what goes on, or ought to go on, as a paper is being planned.

GENERAL SUBJECT

"Write something worth reading about. . . ." In essence, all writing assignments–for students, business executives, Nobel Prize winners, and everyone else–begin this way, though ordinarily, the directions aren't that frank.

Let's start from scratch and assume that your instructor has left the choice of subject mostly up to you. You may be entirely on your own, or you may have a list of general subjects from which you must make your selection. Imagine that you have to write something worth reading about one of the following topics: education, prejudice, politics, television, or sports.

You make your choice, if you're like the majority of people, by deciding what you're most interested in and informed about or what will go over best with your audience. Let's say you pick education. You now have a subject, and your troubles have now begun.

You have to write 500 words or so on a subject to which tens of thousands of books have been devoted. Where do you begin? Where do you stop? Will it ever be possible to stop? What's important? What's not important? Until you *limit your subject,* you have no way of answering any of these questions. You are at the mercy of every miscellaneous thought and scrap of information that drifts into your mind.

LIMITED SUBJECT

Narrow down your subject. Then narrow it down some more. Narrow it down until you have a subject that can be treated effectively in the assigned length. In many respects, the narrower your subject, the better off you are—as long as you still have something to say about it. With a properly limited subject, you explore only a small part of your general subject, but you explore it thoroughly.

General Subject	Limited Subject
Education	Professor X
Prejudice	Interracial marriages
Politics	People who don't vote
Television	Commercials
Sports	Baseball salaries

A paper of 500 words on education is doomed to be superficial at best. It might be possible, however, to write 500 words that are worth reading on one of your teachers, essay versus objective examinations, reasons for attending college (narrowed down to just one reason, if you have enough to say), registration procedures, fraternities, and so on.

With a sensibly limited subject, you have a chance of producing a good paper. You are no longer doomed to superficiality. If you write a description of one of your teachers, for example, you possess immensely more knowledge about your subject than do fellow students who have not taken a course from that teacher. Certainly, you are no longer at the mercy of every thought about education that you have ever had.

Your troubles are not over, though. You've limited your subject, and you've done it well—but what now? Look at the most limited of the subjects in the preceding table. You're writing a description of a teacher—Professor X. Do you tell your reader about the teacher's height, weight, age, marital status, clothing, ethnic background, religious background, educational background? Publications? Grading policy? Attendance policy? Lecture techniques? Sense of humor? Handling of difficult classroom situations? Attitude toward audiovisual aids? Knowledge of field? How, in short, do you determine what belongs in your paper and what doesn't?

The truth is that you're still at the mercy of every thought that occurs to you. This time, it's just every thought about Professor X, not every thought about education in general. But until you find a *thesis,* you still have trouble.

THESIS

Your thesis is the basic stand you take, the opinion you express, the point you make about your limited subject. It's your controlling idea, tying together and giving direction to all of the separate elements in your paper. *Your primary purpose is to persuade the reader that your thesis is valid.*

You may, and probably should, have secondary purposes. You may want to amuse or alarm or inform or issue a call to action, for instance—but unless the primary purpose is achieved, no secondary purpose stands a chance. If you want to amuse your readers by making fun of inconsistent dress codes at your old high school, there's no way to do it successfully without first convincing them of the validity of your thesis—that the dress codes *were* inconsistent and thus *do* deserve to be ridiculed.

A thesis is only a vibration in the brain until it is turned into words. The first step in creating a workable thesis is to write a one-sentence version of the thesis, which is called a *thesis statement.* For example:

Professor X is an incompetent teacher.

Professor X is a classic absentminded professor.

Professor X's sarcasm antagonizes many students.

Professor X's colorful personality has become a campus legend.

Professor X is better at lecturing than at leading discussions.

Professor X's youthful good looks have created awkward problems in class.

If you need more than one relatively uncomplicated sentence, chances are that your thesis isn't as unified as it ought to be or that it's too ambitious for a short paper. Any limited subject will still produce a wide range of possible thesis statements. Any limited subject, however, will help you keep your thesis statement focused and concise.

Limited Subject	Thesis Statement
Professor X	Professor X is a classic absentminded professor.
Interracial marriages	Hostility to interracial marriages is the prejudice least likely to die.
People who don't vote	Not voting may sometimes be a responsible decision.
Commercials	Television commercials can be great entertainment.
Baseball salaries	Many baseball players are paid far more than their abilities can justify.

Writing with a thesis gives a paper a sense of purpose and eliminates the problem of aimless drift. Your purpose is to back up the thesis. As a result, writing with a thesis also helps significantly in organizing the paper. You use only what enables you to accomplish your purpose. Weight problems and religion have nothing to do with Professor X's absentmindedness, for example, so you don't bother with them. Most of all, writing with a thesis gives a paper an intrinsic dramatic interest. You commit yourself. You have something at stake: "This is what I believe, and this is why I'm right." You say, "Professor X is absentminded." Your reader says, "Tell me why you think so." You say, "I'll be glad to." Your reader says, "I'm listening." Now all you have to do is deliver.

So far, then, we've established that a thesis is the main idea that all elements in the paper should support and that you should be able to express it in a single sentence. We've established that a thesis has several important practical benefits. That's the bird's-eye view, but the concept is important enough to demand a closer look.

WHAT A THESIS ISN'T

A Thesis Is Not a Title

A title can often give the reader some notion of what the thesis is going to be, but the title is not the thesis itself. The thesis itself, as presented in the thesis statement, does not suggest the main idea—it *is* the main idea. Remember, too, that a thesis statement will always be a complete sentence; there's no other way to make a statement.

Title: Not a Thesis	Thesis Statement
Homes and Schools	Parents ought to participate more in the education of their children.
James Cagney: Hollywood Great	James Cagney was one of the greatest actors ever to appear in movies.
Social Security and Old Age	Probable changes in the Social Security system make it almost impossible to plan intelligently for one's retirement.
A Shattering Experience	My first visit to the zoo was a shattering experience.
The Fad of Divorce	Too many people get divorced for trivial reasons.

A Thesis Is Not an Announcement of the Subject

A thesis takes a stand. It expresses an attitude toward the subject. It is not the subject itself.

Announcement: Not a Thesis	Thesis Statement
My subject is the classic absentmindedness of Professor X.	Professor X is a classic absentminded professor.
I want to share some thoughts with you about our space program.	It is time to close down our space program.
The many unforeseen problems I encountered when I went camping are the topic of this theme.	I encountered many unforeseen problems when I went camping.
This paper will attempt to tell you something about the emotions I felt on viewing the Grand Canyon.	The Grand Canyon was even more magnificent than I had imagined.
The thesis of this paper is the difficulty of solving our environmental problems.	Solving our environmental problems is more difficult than many environmentalists believe.

A Thesis Is Not a Statement of Absolute Fact

A thesis makes a judgment or interpretation. There's no way to spend a whole paper supporting a statement that needs no support.

Fact: Not a Thesis

Jane Austen is the author of *Pride and Prejudice.*

The capital of California is Sacramento.

Suicide is the deliberate taking of one's own life.

President Lincoln's first name was Abraham.

The planet closest to the Sun is Mercury.

A Thesis Is Not the Whole Essay

A thesis is your main idea, often expressed in a single sentence. Be careful not to confuse the term as it is used in this text with the book-length thesis or dissertation required of candidates for advanced degrees.

WHAT A GOOD THESIS IS

It's possible to have a one-sentence statement of an idea and still not have a thesis that can be supported effectively. What characterizes a good thesis?

A Good Thesis Is Restricted

Devising a thesis statement as you plan your paper can be a way of limiting, or restricting, your subject even further. A paper supporting the thesis that Professor X is absentminded, besides taking a stand on its subject, has far less territory to cover than a paper on Professor X in general. Thesis statements themselves, however, may not always be sufficiently narrow. A good thesis deals with restricted, bite-size issues, not with issues that would require a lifetime to discuss intelligently. The more restricted the thesis, the better the chances are for supporting it fully.

Poor	Better
The world is in a terrible mess.	The United Nations should be given more peace-keeping powers.
People are too selfish.	Human selfishness is seen at its worst during rush hour.
The American auto industry has many problems.	The worst problem of the American auto industry is unfair competition from foreign countries.
Crime must be stopped.	Our courts should hand out tougher sentences to habitual criminals.

A Good Thesis Is Unified

The thesis expresses *one major idea* about its subject. The tight structure of your paper depends on its working to support that one idea. A good thesis sometimes may include a secondary idea if that idea is strictly subordinated to the

major one. Without that subordination, the writer will have too many important ideas to handle, and the structure of the paper will suffer.

Poor	Better
Detective stories are not a high form of literature, but people have always been fascinated by them, and many fine writers have experimented with them.	Detective stories appeal to the basic human desire for thrills.
The new health program is excellent, but it has several drawbacks, and it should be run only on an experimental basis for two or three years.	The new health program should be run only on an experimental basis for two or three years. *Or* Despite its general excellence, the new health program should be run only on an experimental basis for two or three years.
The Columbus Cavaliers have trouble at the defensive end and linebacker positions, and front-office tensions don't help, but the team should be able to make the play-offs.	The Columbus Cavaliers should be able to make the play-offs. *Or* Even granting a few troubles, the Columbus Cavaliers should be able to make the play-offs.

A Good Thesis Is Specific

A satisfactorily restricted and unified thesis may be useless if the idea it commits you to is vague. "The new corporate headquarters is impressive," for example, could mean anything from impressively beautiful to impressively ugly. With a thesis statement such as "James Joyce's *Ulysses* is very good," you would prob-ably have to spend more words defining *good* than discussing *Ulysses*. Even when there's no likelihood of confusion, vague ideas normally come through as so familiar, dull, or universally accepted that the reader sees no point in paying attention to them.

Poor	Better
James Joyce's *Ulysses* is very good.	James Joyce's *Ulysses* helped create a new way for writers to deal with the unconscious.
Drug addiction is a big problem.	Drug addiction has caused a huge increase in violent crimes.

(continued)

Poor	**Better**
Our vacation was a tremendous experience.	Our vacation enabled us to learn the true meaning of sharing.
My parents are wonderful people.	Everything my parents do is based on their loving concern for the welfare of the family.

You may also extend your thesis statement to include the major points that you will discuss in the body of the paper. The previously cited thesis statements could be extended as follows:

Specific	**Extended Specific**
James Joyce's *Ulysses* helped create a new way for writers to deal with the unconscious.	James Joyce's *Ulysses* helped create a new way for writers to deal with the unconscious by utilizing the findings of Freudian psychology and introducing the techniques of literary stream of consciousness.
Drug addiction has caused a huge increase in violent crimes.	Drug addiction has caused a huge increase in violent crimes in the home, at school, and on the streets.
Our vacation enabled us to learn the true meaning of sharing.	Our vacation enabled us to learn the true meaning of sharing our time, space, and possessions.
Everything my parents do is based on their loving concern for the welfare of the family.	Everything my parents do is based on their loving concern for maintaining the welfare of the family by keeping us in touch with our past, helping us to cope with our present, and inspiring us to build for our future.

These extended thesis statements have certain virtues, but they have their drawbacks, too. They can be considered summaries or mini outlines in some respects, and therefore they can be useful because they force you to think through the entire essay before you begin to write. They may be especially helpful if you are uneasy about your organizing abilities. In short essays, on the other hand, extended thesis statements may not be necessary or desirable. They may, for example, tell readers more than you want them to know—and tell it to them too soon. After all, a summary usually belongs at the end of an essay, not at the beginning. Be sure you know whether your instructor has any preference. Remember the main point, though: It is essential that the thesis be specific.

EXERCISES FOR REVIEW

A. Write *T* next to each statement that is a thesis. Write *NT* next to each statement that is not a thesis.

_____ 1. My grandfather's memory has become very weak lately, creating major problems for him with his family, friends, and business associates.

_____ 2. In this project I will outline the three major causes of the Civil War.

_____ 3. The dessert known as "peach melba" was named for the opera singer Dame Nellie Melba.

_____ 4. Baseball players' nicknames often have interesting stories behind them.

_____ 5. Comic Books: Not Just for Kids.

_____ 6. This paper will consider the major reasons for lowering the national drinking age, namely the inconsistency the drinking age shows with the legal age for voting, for driving, and for joining the military.

_____ 7. Some students show more resourcefulness at making excuses than at getting their work done.

_____ 8. There are three main kinds of chocolate: dark, milk, and white.

_____ 9. The more sensible a parent's advice to a teenager, the more likely it is to be scorned or ignored.

_____ 10. Increasing common courtesy on the road is the best way to reduce traffic accidents.

B. Write *G* next to each statement that is a good thesis. Write *NG* next to each statement that is not sufficiently restricted, unified, or specific, and be prepared to suggest revisions.

_____ 1. During the Middle Ages, Islam was far more tolerant of other religions than was Christianity.

_____ 2. There's a sucker born every minute. *–P.T. Barnum*

_____ 3. Dieters I have known almost always regain their lost weight.

_____ 4. Obesity is a serious health problem, but the media have exaggerated the dangers, and many diets can bring about health problems of their own.

_____ 5. Stephen King's books have more literary merit than most critics want to admit.

_____ 6. The U.S. health care system is in serious trouble.

_____ 7. Raising the standard retirement age from sixty-five to sixty-seven would make a major contribution toward helping the Social Security system.

_____ 8. Learning how to make your own sushi is easier than you think.

_____ 9. Government should help citizens after natural disasters, but independence should also be encouraged, and we have to worry about government spending, too.

_____ 10. My skiing vacation was one long series of annoyances, mishaps, and disasters.

THE THESIS AT WORK IN THE PAPER

The thesis statement is a tool, not an end in itself. It has two outstanding values. First, it serves as a test of whether your main idea meets the requirements we have just discussed: whether it is a firm concept that can actually be put into words or only a fuzzy notion that is not yet ready for development. Second, the thesis statement is a constant, compact reminder of the point your paper must make. Therefore, it is an indispensable means of determining the relevancy or irrelevancy, the logic or lack of logic, of all the material that goes into the paper.

In itself, the thesis statement is a deliberately bare-bones presentation of your idea. In your paper, you will attempt to deal with the idea in a far more interesting way. The thesis statement, for example, may never appear word-for-word in your final paper. There's no special rule that in the final paper you must declare the thesis in a single sentence. In some rare cases, the thesis may only be hinted at rather than stated openly. The proper places for the bare-bones thesis statement are in your mind with every word you write, on any piece of scratch paper on which you jot down the possible ingredients of your essay, and at the beginning of a formal outline. (If you are ever required to construct such an outline, all the student papers in Chapters 2–10 begin with formal topic outlines that you can use as examples. Your instructor will give you further guidance.)

In most short papers, the thesis is presented in the first paragraph, the *introduction*. Again, no absolute rule states that this must always be the case—just as no rule demands that an introduction must only be one paragraph (the last "Sample Introduction" following, for example, is three paragraphs)—but in practice, most papers do begin that way. It's what seems to work for most people most of the time. As a general guideline, it's helpful to think of the first paragraph's job as presenting the thesis in an interesting way.

The word *interesting* is important. The introduction should not ordinarily be a one-sentence paragraph consisting solely of the unadorned thesis statement. The introduction certainly should indicate clearly what the thesis is, but it also should arouse curiosity or stress the importance of the subject or establish a particular tone of humor, anger, solemnity, and so forth.

Thesis Statement	**Sample Introduction**
Professor X is a classic absentminded professor.	I had heard about the professor who spent an entire class session looking for her glasses, when she was already wearing them. I had heard about the professor who wore mismatched sneakers to lecture. I had heard about the professor who showed up to give a final exam . . . . without the exam. I had even heard about the professor who gave an inspiring and stirring lecture on Aristotle's theory of "the good life" to a very confused calculus class. I thought the stories were the kind of creative fiction that all college students engage in to let off a little steam. Then I took a class taught by Professor X.
Hostility to interracial marriages is the prejudice least likely to die.	Progress in relations between the races often seems grotesquely slow. By looking at bundles of years instead of days, however, one can see that there has been real progress in jobs, education, and even housing. The most depressing area, the area in which there has been no progress, in which no progress is even likely, in which progress is not even seriously discussed, is the area of interracial marriages.
Not voting may sometimes be a responsible decision.	Public service ads tell us to be good citizens and make sure to vote. On election eves, the candidates tell us to exercise our sacred rights and hustle down to the polling booth, even if we're not going to cast our ballots for them. Network philosophers tell us that the country is going downhill because so few people vote for president. But my neighbor Joe is totally indifferent to politics; he knows little and cares less. My neighbor Jennifer thinks both candidates are equally foul. I believe that Joe, Jennifer, and thousands like them are making intelligent, responsible decisions when they stay home on Election Day, and I admire them for not letting themselves be bullied.
Television commercials can be entertainment.	I like television commercials. It's a terrible confession. I know I'm supposed to sneer and brood and write letters to people who want to protect me, but I like commercials. They can be great entertainment, and it's time somebody said so.

(continued)

Thesis Statement	**Sample Introduction**
Many baseball players are paid far more than their abilities can justify.	An essay in *Forbes* magazine by the late sports commentator Dick Schaap tells a story about the great Baseball Hall of Famer and Detroit Tiger of the 1930s and 1940s, Hank Greenberg, the first player to make $100,000 a year. Greenberg's son Steve was once an agent negotiating contracts. He told his father about a player he was representing whose batting average was .238. "What should I ask for?" Steve inquired.
	"Ask for a uniform," Hank replied.
	Today, unfortunately, any agent would also ask for a million dollars–and would probably get it. Baseball players' salaries have become ridiculously high and have little or nothing to do with actual athletic abilities.

The function of subsequent paragraphs–paragraphs generally referred to as the *body*–is to support the thesis. All sorts of paragraph arrangements are possible. The important consideration is that the body paragraphs, individually and as a whole, must persuade your reader that your thesis makes sense.

One of the most common paragraph arrangements is worth studying at this time, because it's the easiest to follow and because our concern here is with the essential connection between the body paragraphs and the thesis, not with fine points. This arrangement gives a separate paragraph to each supporting point and the specific evidence necessary to substantiate it. In sketchy outline form, the progression of paragraphs might look something like this:

¶ 1–Presentation of thesis: There are at least three good reasons for abolishing capital punishment.

Start of ¶ 2–First, statistics show that capital punishment is not really a deterrent. . . .

Start of ¶ 3–Second, when capital punishment is used, it is forever impossible to correct a mistaken conviction. . . .

Start of ¶ 4–Third, capital punishment has often been used in a discriminatory fashion against poor people and African Americans. . . .

Using the same form of one paragraph for each supporting idea, but abandoning the neatness of numbered points, we might find the following:

¶ 1–Presentation of thesis: Dieting can be dangerous.

Start of ¶ 2–Some diets can raise cholesterol levels alarmingly. . . .

Start of ¶ 3–In other cases, over an extended period, some diets can lead to
serious vitamin deficiencies. . . .

Start of ¶ 4–One further danger is that already existing medical problems,
such as high blood pressure, can be drastically aggravated. . . .

Most papers also have a distinct *conclusion,* a last paragraph that provides
a needed finishing touch. The conclusion can be a quick summary of your
thesis and main supporting points. It can emphasize, or reemphasize, the
importance of your thesis. It can relate a seemingly remote thesis to people's
everyday lives. It can make a prediction. It can issue a call for action. In one
way or another, the conclusion reinforces or develops the thesis; it should
never introduce a totally unrelated, new idea. The conclusion should bring
your paper to a smooth stop. Just as the introduction steers clear of direct
announcements, the conclusion should avoid the blatant "Well, that's about
it" ending. There are dozens of possible conclusions, but almost all papers
benefit from having one. (For specific examples of different kinds of conclusions, see page 178.)

The group of readings that follows shows the persuasive principle in action
by offering contrasting examples of good and not-so-good writing. From short
thank-you notes to freshman English compositions, the results of writing with
and without a thesis can be explored in detail. Later chapters will comment on
and provide examples of the techniques appropriate for particular patterns of
writing: classification, description, and so on. Patterns change depending on
subjects and approaches. Principles do not change. The basic nature of good
writing, as discussed in this chapter, remains constant.

Two Ads on the Community Bulletin Board

A.

Babysitter

Experienced high school student available, weekdays to midnight, weekends to 2 A.M. Reasonable rates. Call Sandy, 335-0000.

B.

Babysitter

A HIGH SCHOOL STUDENT WHO KNOWS *THE THREE R's*
Ready–any weekday to midnight, weekends to 2 A.M.
Reliable–four years' experience, references available.
Reasonable–$5.00 per hour, flat fee for more than five hours.
Call Sandy, 335-0000

Discussion and Questions

Even a short "position wanted" ad can use the persuasive principle to its advantage. A dozen high school students pin a dozen different typed or handwritten index cards to the bulletin board at the local library or supermarket. Most of the cards convey lifeless facts. One or two cards make the same facts come alive by using them to support an idea. Those are the cards that get a second look–and get their writers a phone call.

1. Which ad has a thesis?
2. Does the ad support its thesis?
3. Which ad uses more specific facts?

Two "Personals"

A.

Clark Kent seeks Lois Lane. I know I'm no Superman, but I'm a good guy. I'm not faster than a speeding bullet, but I love to bike and take long walks. I'm not more powerful than a locomotive, but I am in upper management at my company. I can't leap tall buildings in a single bound, but I do love to travel and just returned from a rock-climbing trip in the Southwest. Where can I find an intrepid "girl reporter" with lots of moxie who won't mind that I can't fly and that I don't wear a cape? Could you be the one?

B.

Single male, professional in an upper management position, is looking for a woman for bike rides and long walks. I also like to travel and have done a lot of it. Call if interested.

Discussion and Questions

Much like an advertisement for a babysitting business, an advertisement for yourself is most effective when, in addition to being informative, it is lively and stands out from the competition in some way. The same person describes himself in both of the previous ads, but we think that one ad is much more likely to attract interest.

1. Which ad has a thesis?
2. Which ad makes an effort to attract the reader's interest?
3. Which ad uses more specific facts?

Two Sets of Directions

A.

How to Get from Town to Camp Wilderness

Take Freeway west to Millersville Road exit. Go north on Millersville Road to Route 256. West on 256 to Laurel Lane. North on Laurel Lane until you see our sign. Turn right, and you're there.

B.

How to Get from Town to Camp Wilderness

You'll have an easy trip if you avoid three trouble spots:

1. You have to take the MILLERSVILLE ROAD exit as you go west on the Freeway, and it's a left-hand exit. Start bearing left as soon as you see the "Millersville 5 miles" sign.
2. After turning north (right) on Millersville Road, don't panic when you see Route 526. You want ROUTE 256, and that's 8 more miles.
3. Go west (left) on Route 256 to LAUREL LANE. The street signs are almost impossible to read, but Laurel Lane is the second road on the right after the Mobil station.

   Once on Laurel Lane, you're all set. Go 2 miles until you see our sign. Turn right, and you're there.

Discussion and Questions

Writing competent directions is a difficult task. When you are explaining something you know well, it's hard to put yourself in the place of a total novice. You may be excessively casual about some step—or even forget to mention it. Directions can also be hard to read; for novices, they can seem to be a series of one disconnected step after another. Writing with a thesis helps the steps come together in the readers' minds and gives them a comforting sense of security.

1. Which set of directions has a thesis?
2. Which tries to anticipate difficulties?
3. Explain the unconventional capitalization in example B.

Two Thank-You Notes

A.

July 25, 2010

Dear Aunt Molly,

"Thanks for everything" is an old, old phrase, but I've never meant it more. Thanks for your generous, great big check. Thanks for coming to the graduation ceremonies. Thanks for years of hugs and funny comments and good advice. Thanks for caring so much for me, and thanks for being Aunt Molly.

Much love,

Alice

B.

July 25, 2010

Dear Aunt Molly,

Thank you so much for your generous check. I was really happy that you could come to my graduation, and I hope you had a good time. Thank you so much again.

Much love,

Alice

Discussion and Questions

Back in the days before long-distance phone calls became routine, people wrote many more personal letters than they do now. For a good number of people today, the thank-you note is probably the only personal letter writing they do, other than a few cheerful greetings on postcards, Christmas cards, or e-mails. Graduates, newlyweds, new parents, and grieving widows and widowers all need to write thank-you notes. There's not much choice of subject, of course, and even most of the ideas are predetermined. How can the writer make a thank-you note sound like a sincere expression of emotion, not just good manners? The persuasive principle is a valuable aid.

1. Which note has a thesis?
2. How many pieces of "evidence" support the thesis?
3. How does the choice of words in the supporting evidence further reinforce the thesis?
4. Which note communicates more feeling?

Two Letters of Complaint

(in traditional and e-mail form)

A.

13 Pier Street
New York, NY 10016

Customer Complaints   July 25, 2010

Maybach Company
123 Fifth Avenue
New York, NY 10001

Subject: Defective Coffee Table

I have tried calling three different times and have not received any satisfaction, so now I am going to try writing.

I have absolutely no intention of paying any $749.60. I returned my coffee table more than a month ago. One of the legs was wobbly, and the top had a bad scratch. Two times the pickup men did not come on the day they said they would. I returned the first bill for the table, and now you just sent me another one, and all I get from people when I call the store is "We'll look into it." Also, the price was $174.96, not $749.60. I await your reply.

Yours very truly,

Augusta Briggs

Augusta Briggs

B.

Subject: Defective Coffee Table

Date: Mon, 25 July 2010 16:14:30–0500 (CDT)

From: abriggs@somedomain.com (Augusta Briggs)

To: customerservice@maybach.com

When you folks make mistakes, you don't kid around. You make big ones. Phone calls haven't done me much good, so I'm hoping that this letter can clear things up.

Early last month—probably June 9 or 10—I returned a defective coffee table. Since you had no more in stock, I canceled the order.

When the bill came for the table, I returned it with a note of explanation. Exactly one week ago, July 16, I received a second bill. To add to the fun, this second bill was for $749.60 instead of the original $174.96.

When I called the store, I was told I'd be called back by the next day at the latest. I'm still waiting.

I'm sure you agree that these are too many mistakes, and that they are big enough to be extremely annoying. Shall we get this matter settled once and for all?

Thank you for your attention.

Yours very truly,

Augusta Briggs
13 Pier Street
New York, NY 10016

Discussion and Questions

The letter to a friend may not be as common as it once was, but business writing—and business plays a role in our private lives as well as in our jobs—is as important as ever. Indeed, the advent of e-mail may have made business writing even more common. When the clear and methodical statement of ideas and facts is essential, putting it into writing, either on paper or electronically, becomes inevitable.

The writer of a letter of complaint has two special difficulties, both of which must be resolved if the letter is to be effective. On one hand, the writer must communicate the gravity of the complaint, or the complaint may be treated casually, perhaps even ignored. On the other hand, the writer must simultaneously come through as a rational human being calmly presenting a grievance. It's essential that the writer not be dismissed as a crackpot or a crank. Letters from crackpots and cranks get shown around the office, everyone has a good laugh, and then the letter goes to the bottom of the fattest pile of unanswered correspondence.

Business correspondence is increasingly done by e-mail these days. It is important to remember that although e-mail allows you to communicate with your correspondent more quickly than traditional mail, it should not be treated with any less care. It's easy, when sending an e-mail, to ignore conventions of organization, grammar, spelling, and so on. It's also easy to fall into bad habits that are unique to e-mail, such as using "emoticons" and long, self-consciously cute signature files. Don't. A sloppy piece of business e-mail is as much of an embarrassment as a sloppy piece of traditional mail. Neither one is likely to generate the response you're seeking.

1. Which letter has a thesis?
2. Does the letter support the thesis with specific evidence?
3. Does the letter have a conclusion to reinforce or develop the thesis?

4. Why does the writer of letter B say nothing specific about what was wrong with the coffee table?
5. What is the purpose of the informal phrasing ("you folks," "kid around") and humorous touches in letter B?
6. Are there elements in letter A that might allow the reader to dismiss the writer as a crank?
7. Why do business-letter paragraphs tend to be so short?

Two Replies to the Second Letter of Complaint

(in traditional and e-mail form)

A.

Maybach Company
123 Fifth Avenue
New York, NY 10001
(212) 333-3333

Customer Relations   July 28, 2010

Ms. Augusta Briggs
13 Pier Street
New York, NY 10016

Dear Ms. Briggs:

We apologize. We made a lot of mistakes, and we are truly sorry.

We tried to phone you with our apology as soon as we got your letter of July 25, but you weren't at home. Therefore, we're taking this opportunity to apologize in writing. We also want to tell you that your bill for the coffee table has been canceled once and for all, and you won't be bothered again. If something else should go wrong, please call me directly at extension 4550.

Good service makes happy customers, and happy customers are the heart of our business. We appreciate your letting us know when our service isn't so good, and we want to assure you that we've taken steps to see that these mistakes don't recur.

Again, please accept our sincere regrets. Do we dare call your attention to the storewide furniture sale all of next month, including an excellent stock of coffee tables?

Yours very truly,

Rose Alonso

Rose Alonso

B.

Subject: Defective Coffee Table

Date: Thurs, 28 July 2010 11:12:38–0500 (CDT)

From: customerservice@maybach.com

To: abriggs@somedomain.com (Augusta Briggs)

Dear Ms. Briggs:

Pursuant to your letter of July 23, please be advised that your bill for the returned coffee table has been canceled.

This department attempted to phone you immediately upon receipt of your letter, but no answer was received.

We apologize for any inconvenience you may have experienced, and we hope that we may continue to deserve your patronage in the future. There is a storewide furniture sale all of next month in which you may have a special interest.

Yours very truly,
Rose Alonso
Manager

Discussion and Questions

1. Which letter develops a thesis? Which letter is a collection of separate sentences?
2. Which letter makes the phone call seem an indication of the company's concern? Which letter makes the call seem as if the company had been inconvenienced?
3. Which letter is superior in convincing the customer that her problems are finally over?
4. Both letters express hope for the customer's continued trade. Why is letter A far better in this respect?

▎VISUAL PROMPT

Writing Prompt

Your thesis is your controlling idea, tying together and giving direction to all the separate elements in your paper. How is the broken bridge in this photograph like a paper without a thesis statement?

TWO "HOW I SPENT MY SUMMER VACATION" ESSAYS
(in-class assignment)

A.

I couldn't find a job this summer, and it's hard to write much about my summer vacation.

Every morning I would get up between 8:30 and 9:00. My breakfast would usually be juice, toast, and coffee, though sometimes I would have eggs, too.

For a couple of weeks, after breakfast I would mow some neighbors' lawns, but after a while I got bored with that, and mostly I just hung around. Usually I read the paper and then straightened up my room.

For lunch I had a sandwich and a glass of milk. I remember once my mother and I had a real argument because there wasn't anything for a sandwich.

After lunch, if my mother didn't need the car, I'd usually drive over to the big shopping center with some of my friends. We'd walk around to see what was happening, and sometimes we'd try to pick up some girls. Mostly we'd just look at the girls. Sometimes, instead of going to the shopping center, we'd go swimming.

After supper, it was usually television or a movie. Television is mostly reruns in the summer, and it was a bad scene. Some of the movies were okay, but nothing sensational.

In the middle of the summer, my older sister and her family came to visit from out of town. That was fun because I like my two little nephews a lot, and we played catch in the backyard. My brother-in-law kept asking what I was doing with my time, and my mother said at least I was staying out of trouble.

B.

I couldn't find a job this summer, and most people would probably say that I spent my summer doing nothing. In fact, I spent most of my summer practicing very hard to be a pest.

To start with, I developed hanging around the house into an art. It drove my mother crazy. After breakfast, I'd read the paper, spreading it out over the entire living room, and then take my midmorning nap. Refreshed by my rest, I'd then ask my mother what was available for lunch. Once when there was no Italian salami left and the bread was a little stale, I looked at her sadly and sighed a lot and kept opening and closing the refrigerator. She didn't take my suffering too well. As I recall, the expression she used was "no good bum" or something of that order. In the evenings, I'd sigh a lot over having to watch television reruns. When my mother asked me why I watched if I didn't enjoy myself, I sighed some more.

The other main center for my activities as a pest was at the big shopping center a short drive from home. My friends and I—we figured we needed protection—would stand in people's way in the mall and make them walk around us. We'd try on clothes we had no intention of buying and complain about the price. We'd make eyes and gestures and offensive remarks at any pretty girls. We'd practice swaggering and strutting and any other means of looking obnoxious that occurred to us.

Miscellaneous other activities during the summer included splashing people at the beach, laughing in the wrong places at movies, and honking the car horn madly at pedestrians as they started to cross the street. These are small-time adventures, I realize, but difficult to do with real style.

Basically, I had myself a good summer. It's always a pleasure to master a set of skills, and I think I've come close to being an expert pest. I wonder what new thrills lie in wait next summer.

Discussion and Questions

"How I Spent My Summer Vacation." The subject is deadly. To make matters worse, here are two students who spent a remarkably uneventful summer.

One blunders along and writes a frightful paper. The other develops a thesis, supports it, and ends with an appealing little paper. It's no candidate for a prize, but it's an appealing little paper. Enough said.

1. In paper A, is "it's hard to write much about my summer vacation" a thesis? If so, is it a good thesis? Does the writer support it?
2. If both papers have a thesis, are the theses basically the same?
3. What topics mentioned in paper A are not mentioned in paper B? Why?
4. Which paper has a conclusion? Is it effective?
5. Both papers use many specific details. Which paper uses them better? Why?
6. Which paper has better-developed paragraphs?
7. Which paragraphs in paper A do not have topic sentences? Do all the paragraphs in paper B have topic sentences?
8. Which paper handles the argument about lunch better? Why?

Two Freshman English Essays on a Literary Subject

Many freshman English courses devote part of the school year to reading, discussing, and writing about works of literature. One of the most popular and frequently anthologized American works of the twentieth century is Shirley Jackson's short story, "The Lottery." First published in 1948, it remains a subject for critical analysis and a source of controversy. We invite you to read "The Lottery" and then apply the persuasive principle to evaluating two student essays about the story.

THE LOTTERY

Shirley Jackson

1   The morning of June 27th was clear and sunny, with the fresh warmth of a full-summer day; the flowers were blossoming profusely and the grass was richly green. The people of the village began to gather in the square, between the post office and the bank, around ten o'clock; in some towns there were so many people that the lottery took two days and had to be started on June 26th, but in this village, where there were only about three hundred people, the whole lottery took less than two hours, so it could begin at ten o'clock in the morning and still be through in time to allow the villagers to get home for noon dinner.

2   The children assembled first, of course. School was recently over for the summer, and the feeling of liberty sat uneasily on most of them; they tended to gather together quietly for a while before they broke into boisterous play, and their talk was still of the classroom and the teacher, of books and reprimands. Bobby Martin had already stuffed his pockets full of stones, and the other boys soon followed his example, selecting the smoothest and roundest stones;

Bobby and Harry Jones and Dickie Delacroix–the villagers pronounced this name "Dellacroy"–eventually made a great pile of stones in one corner of the square and guarded it against the raids of the other boys. The girls stood aside, talking among themselves, looking over their shoulders at the boys, and the very small children rolled in the dust or clung to the hands of their older brothers or sisters.

3   Soon the men began to gather, surveying their own children, speaking of planting and rain, tractors and taxes. They stood together, away from the pile of stones in the corner, and their jokes were quiet and they smiled rather than laughed. The women, wearing faded house dresses and sweaters, came shortly after their menfolk. They greeted one another and exchanged bits of gossip as they went to join their husbands. Soon the women, standing by their husbands, began to call to their children, and the children came reluctantly, having to be called four or five times. Bobby Martin ducked under his mother's grasping hand and ran, laughing, back to the pile of stones. His father spoke up sharply, and Bobby came quickly and took his place between his father and his oldest brother.

4   The lottery was conducted–as were the square dances, the teen-age club, the Halloween program–by Mr. Summers, who had time and energy to devote to civic activities. He was a round-faced, jovial man and he ran the coal business, and people were sorry for him, because he had no children and his wife was a scold. When he arrived in the square, carrying the black wooden box, there was a murmur of conversation among the villagers, and he waved and called, "Little late today, folks." The postmaster, Mr. Graves, followed him, carrying a three-legged stool, and the stool was put in the center of the square and Mr. Summers set the black box down on it. The villagers kept their distance, leaving a space between themselves and the stool, and when Mr. Summers said, "Some of you fellows want to give me a hand?" there was a hesitation before two men, Mr. Martin and his oldest son, Baxter, came forward to hold the box steady on the stool while Mr. Summers stirred up the papers inside it.

5   The original paraphernalia for the lottery had been lost long ago, and the black box now resting on the stool had been put into use even before Old Man Warner, the oldest man in town, was born. Mr. Summers spoke frequently to the villagers about making a new box, but no one liked to upset even as much tradition as was represented by the black box. There was a story that the present box had been made with some pieces of the box that had preceded it, the one that had been constructed when the first people settled down to make a village here. Every year, after the lottery, Mr. Summers began talking again about a new box, but every year the subject was allowed to fade off without anything's being done. The black box grew shabbier each year; by now it was no longer completely black but splintered badly along one side to show the original wood color, and in some places faded or stained.

6   Mr. Martin and his oldest son, Baxter, held the black box securely on the stool until Mr. Summers had stirred the papers thoroughly with his hand. Because so much of the ritual had been forgotten or discarded, Mr. Summers had been successful in having slips of paper substituted for the chips of wood that had been used for generations. Chips of wood, Mr. Summers had argued, had been all very well when the village was tiny, but now that the population was more than three hundred and likely to keep on growing, it was necessary to use something that would fit more easily into the black box. The night before the lottery, Mr. Summers and Mr. Graves made up the slips of paper and put them in the box, and it was then taken to the safe of Mr. Summers' coal company and locked up until Mr. Summers was ready to take it to the square next morning. The rest of the year, the box was put away, sometimes one place, sometimes another; it had spent one year in Mr. Graves's barn and another year underfoot in the post office, and sometimes it was set on a shelf in the Martin grocery and left there.

7   There was a great deal of fussing to be done before Mr. Summers declared the lottery open. There were the lists to make up—of heads of families, heads of households in each family, members of each household in each family. There was the proper swearing-in of Mr. Summers by the postmaster, as the official of the lottery; at one time, some people remembered, there had been a recital of some sort, performed by the official of the lottery, a perfunctory, tuneless chant that had been rattled off duly each year; some people believed that the official of the lottery used to stand just so when he said or sang it, others believed that he was supposed to walk among the people, but years and years ago this part of the ritual had been allowed to lapse. There had been, also, a ritual salute, which the official of the lottery had had to use in addressing each person who came up to draw from the box, but this also had changed with time, until now it was felt necessary only for the official to speak to each person approaching. Mr. Summers was very good at all this; in his clean white shirt and blue jeans, with one hand resting carelessly on the black box, he seemed very proper and important as he talked interminably to Mr. Graves and the Martins.

8   Just as Mr. Summers finally left off talking and turned to the assembled villagers, Mrs. Hutchinson came hurriedly along the path to the square, her sweater thrown over her shoulders, and slid into place in the back of the crowd. "Clean forgot what day it was," she said to Mrs. Delacroix, who stood next to her, and they both laughed softly. "Thought my old man was out back stacking wood," Mrs. Hutchinson went on, "and then I looked out the window and the kids was gone, and then I remembered it was the twenty-seventh and came a-running." She dried her hands on her apron, and Mrs. Delacroix said, "You're in time, though. They're still talking away up there."

9   Mrs. Hutchinson craned her neck to see through the crowd and found her husband and children standing near the front. She tapped Mrs. Delacroix

on the arm as a farewell and began to make her way through the crowd. The people separated good-humoredly to let her through; two or three people said, in voices just loud enough to be heard across the crowd, "Here comes your Missus, Hutchinson," and "Bill, she made it after all." Mrs. Hutchinson reached her husband, and Mr. Summers, who had been waiting, said cheerfully, "Thought we were going to have to get on without you, Tessie." Mrs. Hutchinson said, grinning, "Wouldn't have me leave m'dishes in the sink, now, would you, Joe?," and soft laughter ran through the crowd as the people stirred back into position after Mrs. Hutchinson's arrival.

10   "Well, now," Mr. Summers said soberly, "guess we better get started, get this over with, so's we can go back to work. Anybody ain't here?"

11   "Dunbar," several people said. "Dunbar, Dunbar."

12   Mr. Summers consulted his list. "Clyde Dunbar," he said. "That's right. He's broke his leg, hasn't he? Who's drawing for him?"

13   "Me, I guess," a woman said, and Mr. Summers turned to look at her. "Wife draws for her husband," Mr. Summers said. "Don't you have a grown boy to do it for you, Janey?" Although Mr. Summers and everyone else in the village knew the answer perfectly well, it was the business of the official of the lottery to ask such questions formally. Mr. Summers waited with an expression of polite interest while Mrs. Dunbar answered.

14   "Horace's not but sixteen yet," Mrs. Dunbar said regretfully. "Guess I gotta fill in for the old man this year."

15   "Right," Mr. Summers said. He made a note on the list he was holding. Then he asked, "Watson boy drawing this year?"

16   A tall boy in the crowd raised his hand. "Here," he said. "I'm drawing for m'mother and me." He blinked his eyes nervously and ducked his head as several voices in the crowd said things like "Good fellow, Jack," and "Glad to see your mother's got a man to do it."

17   "Well," Mr. Summers said, "guess that's everyone. Old Man Warner make it?"

18   "Here," a voice said, and Mr. Summers nodded.

19   A sudden hush fell on the crowd as Mr. Summers cleared his throat and looked at the list. "All ready?" he called. "Now, I'll read the names–heads of families first–and the men come up and take a paper out of the box. Keep the paper folded in your hand without looking at it until everyone has had a turn. Everything clear?"

20   The people had done it so many times that they only half listened to the directions; most of them were quiet, wetting their lips, not looking around. Then Mr. Summers raised one hand high and said, "Adams." A man disengaged himself from the crowd and came forward. "Hi, Steve," Mr. Summers said, and Mr. Adams said, "Hi, Joe." They grinned at one another humorlessly and nervously. Then Mr. Adams reached into the black box and took out a folded paper. He held it firmly by one corner as he turned and went hastily back to his place in the crowd, where he stood a little apart from his family, not looking down at his hand.

21   "Allen," Mr. Summers said. "Anderson . . . . Bentham."

22   "Seems like there's no time at all between lotteries any more," Mrs. Delacroix said to Mrs. Graves in the back row. "Seems like we got through with the last one only last week."

23   "Time sure goes fast," Mrs. Graves said.

24   "Clark . . . . Delacroix."

25   "There goes my old man," Mrs. Delacroix said. She held her breath while her husband went forward.

26   "Dunbar," Mr. Summers said, and Mrs. Dunbar went steadily to the box while one of the women said, "Go on, Janey," and another said, "There she goes."

27   "We're next," Mrs. Graves said. She watched while Mr. Graves came around from the side of the box, greeted Mr. Summers gravely, and selected a slip of paper from the box. By now, all through the crowd there were men holding the small folded papers in their large hands, turning them over and over nervously. Mrs. Dunbar and her two sons stood together, Mrs. Dunbar holding the slip of paper.

28   "Harburt . . . . Hutchinson."

29   "Get up there, Bill," Mrs. Hutchinson said, and the people near her laughed.

30   "Jones."

31   "They do say," Mr. Adams said to Old Man Warner, who stood next to him, "that over in the north village they're talking of giving up the lottery."

32   Old Man Warner snorted. "Pack of crazy fools," he said. "Listening to the young folks, nothing's good enough for them. Next thing you know, they'll be wanting to go back to living in caves, nobody work any more, live that way for a while. Used to be a saying about 'Lottery in June, corn be heavy soon.' First thing you know, we'd all be eating stewed chickweed and acorns. There's always been a lottery," he added petulantly. "Bad enough to see young Joe Summers up there joking with everybody."

33   "Some places have already quit lotteries," Mrs. Adams said.

34   "Nothing but trouble in that," Old Man Warner said stoutly. "Pack of young fools."

35   "Martin." And Bobby Martin watched his father go forward. "Overdyke. . . . . Percy."

36   "I wish they'd hurry," Mrs. Dunbar said to her older son. "I wish they'd hurry."

37   "They're almost through," her son said.

38   "You get ready to run tell Dad," Mrs. Dunbar said.

39   Mr. Summers called his own name and then stepped forward precisely and selected a slip from the box. Then he called, "Warner."

40   "Seventy-seventh year I been in the lottery," Old Man Warner said as he went through the crowd. "Seventy-seventh time."

41   "Watson." The tall boy came awkwardly through the crowd. Someone said, "Don't be nervous, Jack," and Mr. Summers said, "Take your time, son."

42   "Zanini."

43   After that, there was a long pause, a breathless pause, until Mr. Summers, holding his slip of paper in the air, said, "All right, fellows." For a minute, no one moved, and then all the slips of paper were opened. Suddenly, all the women began to speak at once, saying, "Who is it?," "Who's got it?," "Is it the Dunbars?," "Is it the Watsons?" Then the voices began to say, "It's Hutchinson. It's Bill," "Bill Hutchinson's got it."

44   "Go tell your father," Mrs. Dunbar said to her older son.

45   People began to look around to see the Hutchinsons. Bill Hutchinson was standing quiet, staring down at the paper in his hand. Suddenly, Tessie Hutchinson shouted to Mr. Summers, "You didn't give him time enough to take any paper he wanted. I saw you. It wasn't fair!"

46   "Be a good sport, Tessie," Mrs. Delacroix called, and Mrs. Graves said, "All of us took the same chance."

47   "Shut up, Tessie," Bill Hutchinson said.

48   "Well, everyone," Mr. Summers said, "that was done pretty fast, and now we've got to be hurrying a little more to get done in time." He consulted his next list. "Bill," he said, "you draw for the Hutchinson family. You got any other households in the Hutchinsons?"

49   "There's Don and Eva," Mrs. Hutchinson yelled, "Make them take their chance!"

50   "Daughters draw with their husbands' families, Tessie," Mr. Summers said gently. "You know that as well as anyone else."

51   "It wasn't fair," Tessie said.

52   "I guess not, Joe," Bill Hutchinson said regretfully. "My daughter draws with her husband's family, that's only fair. And I've got no other family except the kids."

53   "Then, as far as drawing for families is concerned, it's you," Mr. Summers said in explanation, "and as far as drawing for households is concerned, that's you, too. Right?"

54   "Right," Bill Hutchinson said.

55   "How many kids, Bill?" Mr. Summers asked formally.

56   "Three," Bill Hutchinson said. "There's Bill, Jr., and Nancy, and little Dave. And Tessie and me."

57   "All right, then," Mr. Summers said. "Harry, you got their tickets back?"

58   Mr. Graves nodded and held up the slips of paper. "Put them in the box, then," Mr. Summers directed. "Take Bill's and put it in."

59   "I think we ought to start over," Mrs. Hutchinson said, as quietly as she could. "I tell you it wasn't fair. You didn't give him time enough to choose. Everybody saw that."

60   Mr. Graves had selected the five slips and put them in the box, and he dropped all the papers but those onto the ground, where the breeze caught them and lifted them off.

61   "Listen, everybody," Mrs. Hutchinson was saying to the people around her.

62   "Ready, Bill?" Mr. Summers asked, and Bill Hutchinson, with one quick glance around at his wife and children, nodded.

63   "Remember," Mr. Summers said, "take the slips and keep them folded until each person has taken one. Harry, you help little Dave." Mr. Graves took the hand of the little boy, who came willingly with him up to the box. "Take a paper out of the box, Davy," Mr. Summers said. Davy put his hand into the box and laughed. "Take just *one* paper," Mr. Summers said. "Harry, you hold it for him." Mr. Graves took the child's hand and removed the folded paper from the tight fist and held it while little Dave stood next to him and looked at him wonderingly.

64   "Nancy next," Mr. Summers said. Nancy was twelve, and her school friends breathed heavily as she went forward, switching her skirt, and took a slip daintily from the box. "Bill, Jr.," Mr. Summers said, and Billy, his face red and his feet overlarge, nearly knocked the box over as he got a paper out. "Tessie," Mr. Summers said. She hesitated for a minute, looking around defiantly, and then set her lips and went up to the box. She snatched a paper out and held it behind her.

65   "Bill," Mr. Summers said, and Bill Hutchinson reached into the box and felt around, bringing his hand out at last with the slip of paper in it.

66   The crowd was quiet. A girl whispered, "I hope it's not Nancy," and the sound of the whisper reached the edges of the crowd.

67   "It's not the way it used to be," Old Man Warner said clearly. "People ain't the way they used to be."

68   "All right," Mr. Summers said. "Open the papers. Harry, you open little Dave's."

69   Mr. Graves opened the slip of paper and there was a general sigh through the crowd as he held it up and everyone could see that it was blank. Nancy and Bill, Jr., opened theirs at the same time, and both beamed and laughed, turning around to the crowd and holding their slips of paper above their heads.

70   "Tessie," Mr. Summers said. There was a pause, and then Mr. Summers looked at Bill Hutchinson, and Bill unfolded his paper and showed it. It was blank.

71   "It's Tessie," Mr. Summers said, and his voice was hushed. "Show us her paper, Bill."

72   Bill Hutchinson went over to his wife and forced the slip of paper out of her hand. It had a black spot on it, the black spot Mr. Summers had made the night before with the heavy pencil in the coal-company office. Bill Hutchinson held it up, and there was a stir in the crowd.

73   "All right, folks," Mr. Summers said. "Let's finish quickly."

74   Although the villagers had forgotten the ritual and lost the original black box, they still remembered to use stones. The pile of stones the boys had made earlier was ready; there were stones on the ground with the blowing scraps of paper that had come out of the box. Mrs. Delacroix selected a stone so large she had to pick it up with both hands and turned to Mrs. Dunbar, "Come on," she said, "Hurry up."

75   Mrs. Dunbar had small stones in both hands and she said, gasping for breath, "I can't run at all. You'll have to go ahead and I'll catch up with you."

76   The children had stones already, and someone gave little Davy Hutchinson a few pebbles.

77   Tessie Hutchinson was in the center of a cleared space by now, and she held her hands out desperately as the villagers moved in on her. "It isn't fair," she said. A stone hit her on the side of the head.

78   Old Man Warner was saying, "Come on, come on, everyone." Steve Adams was in the front of the crowd of villagers, with Mrs. Graves beside him.

79   "It isn't fair, it isn't right," Mrs. Hutchinson screamed, and then they were upon her.

Essay Topic: Shirley Jackson's "The Lottery" has a long-standing reputation as a story with a powerful surprise ending. Write a 300- to 500-word essay evaluating the validity of that reputation.

A.

"The Lottery," written by the author Shirley Jackson, takes place on the morning of June 27th. June 27th is the day the lottery is always held, and everything seems normal. But the reader is in for a surprise.

The children assemble first. With school just out, they don't know what to do with themselves and start gathering stones. Then the men come telling quiet jokes. We are told that "they smiled rather than laughed." Then the women come, gossiping and summoning the children.

Finally, it is time for the head of the lottery, Mr. Summers, and we are told about the long history of the lottery: the old black box, the slips of paper, the old rituals, and the complicated procedures for drawing. Tessie Hutchinson's late arrival adds a touch of humor.

All the family names are called in alphabetical order, and there seems to be a little nervous tension in the air. Old Man Warner gets angry when told that other towns are thinking of giving up the lottery.

When the Hutchinson family is chosen, Tessie gets very upset and complains that the drawing was not fair because Bill, her husband, was not given enough time to draw. Bill had as much time as anyone else. Mrs. Delacroix tells Tessie to "be a good sport," and even Bill is embarrassed and says, "Shut up, Tessie." Then there is a second drawing where each member of the Hutchinson family draws individually. Tessie turns out to have the paper with the spot on it. She has won the lottery.

The surprise comes when we find out that Tessie has been chosen to be executed. She is going to be stoned to death, and we remember the stones from the beginning of the story. "The Lottery" by Shirley Jackson shows how people follow traditions, sometimes bad ones, without ever thinking about what they are doing.

B.

Shirley Jackson's "The Lottery" is a wonderful story, but the only thing that surprised me at the end was the stones. I admit that I had pretty much forgotten about the stones, but I knew long before the ending that something terrible was going to happen. "The Lottery" is a powerful story, certainly, but its reputation for having a "powerful surprise ending" is undeserved.

It takes no more than two pages before we realize that the annual village lottery is more mysterious and sinister than any drawing for a trip to Hawaii or a new Buick. To begin with, there's an air of mystery about the shabby black box: Shabby as it is, we are told directly that it represents a tradition of some kind, and no one wants to replace it. People nervously hesitate to hold it still while Mr. Summers mixes the paper inside it.

As if the mystery and tradition of the black box were not enough, we learn that the whole institution of the lottery goes back to the "first people" who settled the village and that it involved all sorts of mysterious ceremonies and rituals. There had been some sort of "chant," some sort of "ritual salute." We're not just at a lottery—we're practically going to church.

The sense of church-like solemnity continues when Mrs. Dunbar, whose husband has a broken leg, is asked, "Don't you have a grown boy to do it for you, Janey?" When young Jack Watson, now old enough to draw for his family, walks up to the box, he is told, "Glad to see your mother's got a man to do it." What's going on here? What is so awesome that picking up a slip of paper is considered a job appropriate only for menfolk?

As the drawing proceeds, the story stresses the tension. People wet their lips. If they grin, they do so "humorlessly and nervously."

Any surviving thoughts about the lottery being a pleasant social occasion have to disappear with Old Man Warner's hysterical reaction to the news that some villages are thinking about abandoning the lottery. He calls them a "pack of crazy fools" and virtually predicts the end of the world—"they'll be wanting to go back to living in caves." He quotes an old saying: "Lottery in June, corn be heavy soon." We're dealing with ancient rites and rituals here—famines, and gods of the harvest, and keeping the gods happy.

We're still a long way from the end, but the author keeps pouring it on. The Hutchinson family wins the drawing, and Tessie Hutchinson, instead of packing her bags for Hawaii, complains that "It wasn't fair!" She wants someone else to win because it's obvious that something bad happens to the winner. As the individual members of the

Hutchinson family participate in the second drawing, a girl's voice from the crowd says, "I hope it's not Nancy," because the girl knows what happens, too.

Any reader by this time knows from the seriousness of the reactions that we are dealing with matters of life and death. The stones are a surprise, and an important one. They fit into the story well because stoning as a means of execution is ancient, connected to religion, and involves the whole community. The stones are a surprise, but nothing else is.

Discussion and Questions

Students sometimes say that it's easy to bluff when writing an essay examination or at-home essay on a literary subject. Maybe so, but most teachers are as aware of the hazards as anyone else and make a special effort to spot bluffing.

A good, nonbluffing essay on a literary subject, especially on a "What's your opinion?" question, can go in many different directions, but it always displays the following characteristics:

A. It discusses the subject assigned, not the one the student wishes had been assigned. Inexperienced or nervous students might see the title "The Lottery" and haphazardly start writing everything they have ever heard or thought about the story. Stick to the subject.
B. It uses specific details to support its thesis. The instructor wants an essay from someone who has read and remembered and understood the story, not from someone who, from all the essay shows, has merely turned up in class and gotten the general drift of what the story must be about.
C. It does not get sidetracked into a plot summary unless the assignment specifically calls for one. Any references to the plot should support a thesis, not tell the story all over again.

1. Which essay has a thesis?
2. Is the thesis supported with specific details?
3. Which essay is mostly a plot summary?
4. Compare the first sentences of each essay. Which is more directly related to the assignment?
5. Does the writer of the essay that has a thesis keep the thesis in mind throughout, or are there some digressions?
6. Can the relative merits of both essays be determined even by a reader unfamiliar with "The Lottery"?

CHAPTER 1¹/₂
Office Hours: Basic Tools for Writers

The best do-it-yourself home repair books often include a place at the beginning of each set of instructions that tells the readers exactly what tools are needed to complete the job. These books often include pictures of necessary tools to make it easier to find them in the garage or at the hardware store even if the reader hasn't ever heard of a reciprocating saw or a table sander. Knowing exactly what tools are needed, and gathering those tools together before starting a project, means that you don't have to stop what you're doing to run to the basement and get a different kind of screwdriver or a few more nails. It means that you can get to work quickly and then stay at work until the project is done.

Having the essential tools for writing available as you begin work on a paper is as important as having the right size of washer before you start to fix a leaky faucet. To help you do this, here's a list of some of the most important and helpful basic writer's tools. Many writers keep these tools within arm's reach on their bookshelves. Nowadays, all of them are also available online.

DICTIONARY

Everyone knows that you need a dictionary when you read. How else are you supposed to figure out what zeugma or syzygy is? But a dictionary can help you when you're writing, too. It's the only way to make sure that the word you're using really means what you think it means. And it's the best way we know to make sure that you spell the word correctly.

When it comes to buying your own dictionary, we suggest that you get the best one you can afford. The pocket-sized, cheap versions won't have room for uncommon words or full definitions. Good online dictionaries are also available. You might try the one at www.dictionary.com.

THESAURUS

Too many writers think of a thesaurus as a treasure chest of fancy words. They work overtime looking for a hard way to say something easy. They prefer *asseverate* to *say, lachrymose* to *tearful,* and *perambulate* to *walk.* Using a thesaurus this way makes writers sound pretentious, not smart. This doesn't mean that thesauruses are useless. They're ideal tools, for example, when you know there's a word that means "flamboyant" and sounds a little like "floral" but you just can't quite come up with the word *florid.* That's when a thesaurus comes in most handy.

You can find a traditional thesaurus online at www.thesaurus.com. There's also a fun invention, called a *visual thesaurus,* at www.visualthesaurus.com that you might want to explore.

COLLECTIONS OF QUOTATIONS

Writers browse through collections of quotations for diversion but also for two practical reasons. First, quotations can help provide subjects by giving writers well-expressed ideas to develop with which they can agree or disagree. Second, and more specifically, quotations can provide memorable lines that can enliven a paper, especially in introductions and conclusions. (See the What About *Your* Writing? entry on citation of authority on p. 82.) One of the better websites for quotations is at www.quotationspage.com.

RANDOM FACTS

Writers can never collect enough strange facts and quirky information. They never know when they'll need Michael Jordan's stats, or the right term for the plastic gizmo at the end of a shoelace, or the birthstone for May, or the best kind of apple for making a pie, or the titles of all Willa Cather's novels. It's a helpful idea to have a couple of books of random facts near your writing desk. Almanacs, encyclopedias, and books of statistics can all come in handy when you least expect it. It's impossible to overestimate the powers of a good search engine, like www.google.com, in answering all sorts of odd inquiries, but you might also want to use www.bartleby.com, which is an online collection of reference books and other materials, some of them extremely specialized.

Add a pen, a pencil, and paper, or a computer and a printer, and you have the tools you'll need.

Narration

"Tell me a story," children say again and again. They're bored or restless, and they know the wonders a good story can perform. "Tell me another story," say the now grown-up children, still bored and restless, as they spend millions on romances, science fiction, fantasies, and whodunits. *Narration* is the telling of a story—and from the fairy tales of childhood to the parables of the New Testament, from Aesop's fables to the latest Tom Clancy novel, the shared experience of the human race suggests that a well-told story has few rivals in lasting fascination.

Telling a story is one of the patterns by which a thesis can be supported. That's by no means the only purpose of narration. Many writers of modern stories are far more interested in conveying a sense of life than in conveying ideas. "Yes," says the reader of these stories, "that's what a family argument"—or a first kiss or being a soldier or having the air conditioner break down—"is really like." A thesis, as such, either does not exist or is so subordinate to other concerns that it may as well not exist. This approach to narration has produced some great fiction, but it's not what your narration theme is about.

Chances are that your narration theme isn't going to be fiction at all. Nothing is wrong with trying your hand at fiction, but most narration themes proceed in far different ways. You'll probably be telling a story about what once really happened to you or to people you know. (Like any good storyteller, you'll emphasize some elements and de-emphasize or ignore others, depending on the point of the story.) All the reading selections in this chapter deal with authentic events in the lives of real people.

Imagine a scene in which some friends are uttering what strikes you as sentimental foolishness about the glories of jogging. You say, "I think jogging is horrible. Let me tell you what happened to me." And then you tell your story. That's the essence of the narration paper: a point and a story to back it up.

There are millions of stories and thousands of ways to tell them. *Tell your own story in your own way* is as good a piece of advice as any. As you do so, it's reasonable to remember the various bores you may have listened to or read and try to avoid their mistakes: the bores who worried about what day of the week it was when they were bitten by a snake, who constantly repeated the same phrases (*you know, and then I, you see*), who went on long after the interesting part of their story had been told. Profit from their examples, but tell your own story in your own way.

That advice has a fine ring to it, but it's certainly on the abstract side. "Your own way" will undoubtedly change from one story to another. To get less abstract, in most narration papers most of the time, you should keep the following suggestions in mind.

Stress the Story

The story must have a thesis, but the story itself is what gives life to the paper. *Write a story, not a sermon.* Your thesis is usually a sentence or two at the beginning or end of the paper. Sometimes the thesis can be so clearly part of the story itself that you may not even need to express it directly. In any event, most of your words should be devoted to the telling of your story, not to lecturing and moralizing.

Remember That a Good Story Has Conflict

Some critics would be prepared to argue that without conflict, it's impossible to have a story at all. In any event, conflict is usually the starting point for readers' interest. Three patterns of conflict are the most common. The first is *conflict between people:* You went jogging in the park with a group of friends, and while you were gasping for breath, one friend was driving you mad with lofty philosophical comments about appreciating the outdoors and feeling good about our bodies. The second is *conflict between people and their environment* (a social custom or prejudice, a religious tradition, a force of nature such as a hurricane, and so on): At the end of the jogging trail, after you managed to survive the intolerably hot weather and a killer pebble that had worked its way into one of your sneakers, your friends happily began to discuss a time and place for jogging the next day; you wanted to say "Never again," but the social pressure was too great to resist, and you went along with the crowd. The third is *conflict within a person:* All through your jogging miseries, one side of you was calling the other side a soft, overcivilized snob incapable of appreciating the simple pleasures of life. Clearly you do not need to confine your story to only one kind of conflict.

Use Plenty of Convincing Realistic Details

A good story will give a sense of having actually happened, and convincing realistic details are your best device for transmitting that sense as well as for preventing the sermon from taking over the story. Don't just mention the insect pests that kept bothering you as you jogged through the park—mention mosquitoes. Don't just mention mosquitoes—mention the huge one with blood lust that got onto your neck and summoned up dim memories of a malaria victim in an old Tarzan movie.

PLAY FAIR

Stories of pure innocence versus pure evil, of totally good guys versus totally bad guys, tend to be unconvincing because they are gross distortions of what everyone knows about the complexities of life. Support your thesis energetically, by all means, but don't neglect to show some awareness of the complexities. The paper on jogging, for example, will be more powerful and persuasive if it grudgingly concedes somewhere that the park was beautiful, after all, and that while hating every minute of your journey through it, you were able occasionally to notice the beauty.

WRITING SUGGESTIONS FOR NARRATION THEMES

Choose one of the well-known quotations or proverbs that follow, and write a narration that supports it. You will probably draw on personal experience for your basic material, but feel free to decorate or invent whenever convenient. Some of the suggestions might be appropriate for a fable or parable.

1. Oh, what a tangled web we weave / When first we practice to deceive. *—Sir Walter Scott*
2. Look before you leap.
3. It's always darkest before the dawn.
4. Nobody ever went broke underestimating the intelligence of the American public. *—H.L. Mencken*
5. Faith is believing what you know ain't so. *—Mark Twain*
6. It's better to have loved and lost than never to have loved at all.
7. The bridge between laughing and crying is not long. *—Jamaican proverb*
8. The way to a man's heart is through his stomach.
9. Few things are harder to put up with than the annoyance of a good example. *—Mark Twain*
10. Patriotism is the last refuge of a scoundrel. *—Samuel Johnson*
11. Genius is one percent inspiration and ninety-nine percent perspiration. *—Thomas A. Edison*
12. Winning isn't the most important thing. It's the only thing. *—Vince Lombardi*
13. No guts, no glory.
14. Those who do not know history are condemned to repeat it. *—George Santayana*
15. Wickedness is a myth invented by good people to account for the curious attractiveness of others. *—Oscar Wilde*
16. Rules are made to be broken.
17. The mass of men lead lives of quiet desperation. *—Henry David Thoreau*
18. The squeaky wheel gets the grease.
19. Never let a fool kiss you or a kiss fool you. *—Joey Adams*
20. Someone who hates dogs and children can't be all bad. *—W.C. Fields*

21. A thing of beauty is a joy forever. *—John Keats*
22. Everything I like is either illegal, immoral, or fattening. *—Alexander Woollcott*
23. In America, nothing fails like success. *—F. Scott Fitzgerald*
24. Luck is the residue of design. *—Branch Rickey*
25. Advice to those about to marry: Don't. *—Punch Magazine*

READINGS

Readings in this chapter, and in all remaining chapters, are intended to provide you with practical models for your own writing. The readings begin with one student-written essay (two essays in Chapter 6) together with an outline to stress the importance of careful organization. The student work is followed by a group of professional models with notes and detailed comments and questions on organization, content, and style.

VISUAL PROMPT

Writing Prompt

There are millions of stories and thousands of ways to tell them. Stories do more than just entertain us. Write your own narration essay about a time that a story taught you something important, made you ask a new question, or changed the way you think.

STUDENT ESSAY: BIG BULLY

Elizabeth Hiestand

Thesis: My friend Bethany became a big bully during a visit to the pool with her son.

    I.   Arrival at the pool

    II. The attempted lesson

    III. The baby pool

Conclusion: Bethany didn't realize she was being a big bully, but she was.

Most of the time when you think about bullies you think of big kids picking on little ones, taking away their lunch money and doing everything they can to make the little kids miserable. But it's surprising how often parents are the bullies. I was shocked to see my friend Bethany become one of those big bullies when she let her ego get in the way of her love for her son.

In mid-August, I went to visit Bethany and her two-year-old son, Troy. Needing a reprieve from the scorching Indiana sun, Bethany, Troy, and I went to the community pool in the late afternoon. I was looking forward to some pool time with a toddler—I had fond memories of the carefree, fun-filled trips to the pool of my childhood. Once there, Troy pulled on his inflatable arm bands ("floaties" to those in the know) and we all headed for the "big pool" (so much more exciting for Troy than the dinky little "baby pool"). We all jumped in—the water provided some respite from the steamy air, but without any shade nearby, it retained a lot of warmth from the day's bright rays.

Bethany and Troy began walking around the pool together, Troy floating in front with Bethany's hands firmly on his sides, supporting him. Soon, though, Bethany noticed that a little girl about Troy's age was propelling herself across the pool. The young girl looked a bit like a seahorse: She was floating vertically because "floaties" buoyed her chubby little arms up, but underneath, her little feet were churning away. The little girl's mother was trailing behind in case any assistance was needed, but for the most part, the child just happily kicked herself around the pool, exploring her surroundings and apparently enjoying a little independence. Upon seeing this, Bethany switched into competitive mode, and started showing Troy how to kick—in fact, demanding that he kick. She would take his feet in her hands and show him the motion of a flutter kick, and then try to have him copy it. Sometimes these lessons were punctuated with comments such as, "Look at that little girl kicking. Why don't you do that?" or, "Come on, can't you kick a little?"

Bethany's nagging tirade lasted something like ten minutes. By that time, Troy was a different kid. He no longer had that happy, eager smile on his face; now he looked distressed and worried. He obviously was not as caught up in this whole "learn-to-be-a-great-swimmer" business as his mom. Of course, I didn't speak up, although I was feeling that maybe Troy deserved some uncomplicated, enjoyable playtime instead of swim practice. What was going on here? I knew Bethany loved Troy, but all she seemed to be doing was tormenting him.

Finally, having given up on getting Troy to kick, Bethany suggested we go over to the baby pool. Bethany sat down with her feet in the shallowest part, while Troy went off on his own. In a few minutes he came back and sat by his mom and then started kicking! He kicked and kicked, generating that white bubbly foam that can only come from an excited toddler in a pool. My first reaction was to praise him for finally doing what his mom had been demanding. Her first response, though, was "That's enough. You're getting me all wet." Then, "Just remember to do that next time in the big pool, now that you've figured it out."

I felt so sad for Troy. I thought he deserved cheering and hugs, but instead, he got coldness and mixed messages: ten minutes of "kick," and then when he finally did kick, all he heard was "stop kicking."

I'm sure Bethany didn't realize she was being a big bully. But what was she doing? Did she want to be the mother of the best swimmer on the block? Did she think that Troy was going to grow up to compete in the Olympics? Did she think that yelling at Troy was good discipline? Good encouragement? Good teaching? I'm not sure she was thinking at all.

FREE TIBET, MAN!

Dinty W. Moore

Dinty W. Moore has published several books of nonfiction and fiction. He is the editor of *Brevity*, a journal that publishes the briefest possible creative nonfiction, and he is an editor of the journal, *Creative Nonfiction,* as well as the anthology by the same title. As you read this selection, notice how much impact Moore is able to get from the few words he uses.

✓ **Words to Check:**

fervent (paragraph 1)

1   I drive all morning, fervent and focused, finally stopping for coffee at The Waffle House, near Plain City, Ohio. My car sports a "Free Tibet" bumper sticker that I picked up in Atlanta, and as I lean against the left fender, sipping my cup of mindfulness, a young man spills out of a purple school bus and starts running toward me. He is a 1990s version of a hippie—a white kid with dreadlocks, a knit cap, probably hemp, and Grateful Dead patches on his Levi cutoffs.

2   "Hey, hey, free Tibet," he shouts, pointing to my bumper. "Free Tibet, man."

3 "Hey," I answer back.

4 "Free Tibet," he repeats. "Were you there?"

5 "Tibet?" I ask.

6 "No, man. The concert. Were you there?"

7 I realize he is talking about the Tibetan Freedom Concert in San Francisco, and that to him, the grave situation in Tibet has mainly translated into an opportunity to hear the Red Hot Chili Peppers through really big speakers. I explain that I'm not primarily a music fan, but rather heading to Bloomington, Indiana, to see His Holiness the Dalai Lama.

8 The hippie kid tells me that he and his busload of pals are on their way to Woodstock, New York, for another music festival. "It's gonna be cool."

9 His girlfriend, a 20-something, long-haired young woman in an oversized Mama Cass cotton dress and Birkenstocks, is on a pay phone about twenty feet off from us. She seems to be arguing with someone.

10 My new friend shouts to her:

11 "The Dalai Lama is in Bloomington. Wanna go?"

12 She waves and shouts back. "Free Tibet! I was there!!"

13 I give them a peace sign.

14 There is nothing else to be done.

WHAT DID THE WRITER SAY AND WHAT DID YOU THINK?

1. What is the source of the confusion between Moore and the young man he talks to in the essay? What does that confusion tell us about each of them?

2. How does the author feel about the two young people in the essay? How do you know?

3. Moore never directly states his thesis. What do you think it is?

HOW DID THE WRITER SAY IT?

1. Why, in such a short essay, do we get so many details about the appearance of the young man with whom Moore has his conversation?

2. Explain the essay's concluding sentence.

What About Your Writing?

The normal body paragraph in an essay has a topic sentence and a varying number of additional sentences that develop or support the topic sentence. Specialized one-sentence transitional paragraphs are acceptable for their own special purpose–"Now that we have finished the mixing, we are ready to bake," for example. Written dialogue, which is a large part of this essay, has its own paragraphing conventions, too (see page 278).

"Free Tibet, Man" by Dinty W. Moore has a number of short one- or two-sentence paragraphs, including the final two paragraphs of the essay—not transitional paragraphs by any stretch of the imagination. How is it that such a clearly solid, well-written essay can break, or seem to break, so many basic rules?

One part of the answer is that Moore is writing for a literary journal called *Brevity*, and its focus is on nonfiction that uses 750 words or less. Similarly, writers for newspapers often use short, snappy sentences. Newspaper paragraphs have to be kept short no matter what textbooks say. The words in a newspaper appear in narrow columns. A normal-sized paragraph in that narrow column would present readers with an excessively long, solid block of print with no convenient place for the eyes to rest. Physical reality has to take precedence over rules. Readers with eyestrain don't stay readers for long.

Another more important reason for one-sentence paragraphs in Moore's essay is that they stand out—and that's just what the author wants. Precisely because most paragraphs most of the time are much longer—and for good cause—readers will tend to pay special attention to unexpected, dramatic exceptions. Moore does not want the humorous punch of his shock and contempt at the blissful ignorance of the hipsters he encounters to be lost in the middle of a paragraph. He wants them to stand out.

Like this.

Rules let us know what works for *almost* all writers *almost* all the time. Rules can save us painful years of effort, because without them we are forced to discover all the basic truths for ourselves. Rules are not meant to enslave us, however.

Don't let them enslave you.

FOUL SHOTS

Rogelio R. Gomez

As you read this narrative about an unforgettably nasty day in the writer's high school years, ask yourself if the thesis is ever explicitly stated, and if it has to do with young men, basketball, prejudice, the power of the past, or all of these together.

✓ WORDS TO CHECK:

barrios (paragraph 2)	dictum (4)	coup (7)
sardonically (3)	reprisal (4)	retrospect (7)
acutely (3)	glib (5)	inherent (10)
cavalier (3)	quashed (6)	deft (11)
psyche (4)	fathomed (7)	

1 Now and then I can still see their faces, snickering and laughing, their eyes mocking me. And it bothers me that I should remember. Time and maturity should have diminished the pain, because the incident happened more than 20 years ago. Occasionally, however, a smug smile triggers the memory, and I think, "I should have done something." Some act of defiance could have killed and buried the memory of the incident. Now it's too late.

2   In 1969, I was a senior on the Luther Burbank High School basketball team. The school is on the south side of San Antonio, in one of the city's many barrios. After practice one day, our coach announced that we were going to spend the following Saturday scrimmaging with the ball club from Winston Churchill High, located in the city's rich, white north side. After the basketball game, we were to select someone from the opposite team and "buddy up"– talk with him, have lunch with him and generally spend the day attempting friendship. By telling us that this experience would do both teams some good, I suspect our well-intentioned coach was thinking about the possible benefits of integration and of learning to appreciate the difference of other people. By integrating us with this more prosperous group, I think he was also trying to inspire us.

3   But my teammates and I smiled sardonically at one another, and our sneakers squeaked as we nervously rubbed them against the waxed hardwood floor of our gym. The prospect of a full day of unfavorable comparisons drew from us a collective groan. As "barrio boys," we were already acutely aware of the differences between us and them. Churchill meant "white" to us: It meant shiny new cars, two-story homes with fireplaces, pedigreed dogs and mani-cured hedges. In other words, everything that we did not have. Worse, trav-eling north meant putting up a front, to ourselves as well as to the Churchill team. We felt we had to pretend that we were cavalier about it all, tough guys who didn't care about "nothin'."

4   It's clear now that we entered the contest with negative images of our-selves. From childhood, we must have suspected something was inherently wrong with us. The evidence wrapped itself around our collective psyche like a noose. In elementary school, we were not allowed to speak Spanish. The bladed edge of a wooden ruler once came crashing down on my knuckles for violating this dictum. By high school, however, policies had changed, and we could speak Spanish without fear of physical reprisal. Still, speaking our lan-guage before whites brought on spasms of shame–for the supposed inferiority of our language and culture–and guilt at feeling shame. That mixture of emo-tions fueled our burning sense of inferiority.

5   After all, our mothers in no way resembled the glamorized models of American TV mothers–Donna Reed baking cookies in high heels. My mother's hands were rough and chafed, her wardrobe drab and worn. And my father was preoccupied with making ends meet. His silence starkly con-trasted with the glib counsel Jim Anderson offered in *Father Knows Best*.

And where the Beaver worried about trying to understand some difficult homework assignment, for me it was an altogether different horror, when I was told by my elementary school principal that I did not have the ability to learn.

6   After I failed to pass the first grade, my report card read that I had a "learning disability." What shame and disillusion it brought my parents! To have carried their dream of a better life from Mexico to America, only to have their hopes quashed by having their only son branded inadequate. And so somewhere during my schooling I assumed that saying I had a "learning disability" was just another way of saying that I was "retarded." School administrators didn't care that I could not speak English.

7   As teenagers, of course, my Mexican-American friends and I did not consciously understand why we felt inferior. But we might have understood if we had fathomed our desperate need to trounce Churchill. We viewed the prospect of beating a white, northside squad as a particularly fine coup. The match was clearly racial, our need to succeed born of a defiance against prejudice. I see now that we used the basketball court to prove our "blood." And who better to confirm us, if not those whom we considered better? In retrospect, I realize the only thing confirmed that day was that we saw ourselves as negatively as they did.

8   After we won the morning scrimmage, both teams were led from the gym into an empty room where everyone sat on a shiny linoleum floor. We were supposed to mingle–rub the colors together. But the teams sat separately, our backs against concrete walls. We faced one another like enemies, the empty floor between us a no man's land. As the coaches walked away, one reminded us to share lunch. God! The mere thought of offering them a taco from our brown bags when they had refrigerated deli lunches horrified us.

9   Then one of their players tossed a bag of Fritos at us. It slid across the slippery floor and stopped in the center of the room. With hearts beating anxiously, we Chicanos stared at the bag as the boy said with a sneer, "Y'all probably like 'em"–the "Frito Bandito" commercial being popular then. And we could see them, smiling at each other, giggling, jabbing their elbows into one another's ribs at the joke. The bag seemed to grow before our eyes like a monstrous symbol of inferiority.

10   We won the afternoon basketball game as well. But winning had accomplished nothing. Though we had wanted to, we couldn't change their perception of us. It seems, in fact, that defeating them made them meaner. Looking back, I feel these young men needed to put us "in our place," to reaffirm the power they felt we had threatened. I think, moreover, that they felt justified, not only because of their inherent sense of superiority, but because our failure to respond to their insult underscored our worthlessness in their eyes.

11   Two decades later, the memory of their gloating lives on in me. When a white person is discourteous, I find myself wondering what I should do, and afterward, if I've done the right thing. Sometimes I argue when a deft comment would suffice. Then I reprimand myself, for I am no longer a boy. But my impulse to argue bears witness to my ghosts. For, invariably, whenever I feel insulted I'm reminded of that day at Churchill High. And whenever the past encroaches upon the present, I see myself rising boldly, stepping proudly across the years and crushing, underfoot, a silly bag of Fritos.

WHAT DID THE WRITER SAY AND WHAT DID YOU THINK?

1. Explain why tossing the bag of Fritos to the "barrio boys" was an insult.
2. Why does the author say the memory of the insult persists after "more than 20 years"? How has the memory adversely affected the author as an adult?
3. Comment on the meaning, or meanings, of the title.
4. How, specifically, do Anglos in the essay stereotype Mexican-Americans? Is there any evidence that Mexican-Americans do the same to Anglos?
5. "The road to hell is paved with good intentions." The coaches were apparently trying to foster better relations and only made things worse. What might they have done differently?

HOW DID THE WRITER SAY IT?

1. Why is so much background information necessary before the heart of the narration—the visit to the "north side" school—can begin?
2. What purpose is served by bringing up the diagnosis of a learning disability in paragraph 6?
3. In the last words of this essay, the author refers to the bag of Fritos as "silly." How does that word choice reflect or not reflect his current attitude?

What About Your Writing?

Many writers in search of a good subject might do well to bear in mind John F. Kennedy's reputed comment about some questionable practices of his political opponents: "Don't get mad. Get even."

Sometime when your mind is a blank and you start to believe that you have nothing to write about, you might consider revenge. Nobody would suggest that revenge is a noble emotion, but it has led to some excellent writing. In "Foul Shots," Rogelio R. Gomez presents some serious reflections on complex issues, but he is also settling old scores, getting his own back, taking revenge for twenty-year-old insults.

Think about some of your own ancient grudges as possible subjects. (They don't all need to be ancient by any means, but you may still be too overwrought by an event that happened yesterday to write about it with sufficient perspective.) Think about prejudice, romantic betrayals, and snobbish put-downs and brush-offs. Think about boring sermons and lectures. Think about the times you forced yourself or were forced by others to be polite to undeserving toads. Think about high school bullies and in-crowds. Think about unjust accusations, vicious gossip, and bad advice. Then don't get mad.

Start writing and get even.

THE PERFECT PICTURE

James Alexander Thom

James Alexander Thom has been a U.S. Marine, a reporter and columnist, a newspaper and magazine editor, and a member of the faculty at the Indiana University School of Journalism. He is the author of *Follow the River, Long Knife, From Sea to Shining Sea, Panther in the Sky, The Children of First Man,* and *The Red Heart,* among others.

✓ WORDS TO CHECK:

devastated (paragraph 3)   lapsed (4)   cherubic (5)

1   It was early in the spring about 15 years ago—a day of pale sunlight and trees just beginning to bud. I was a young police reporter, driving to a scene I didn't want to see. A man, the police-dispatcher's broadcast said, had accidentally backed his pickup truck over his baby granddaughter in the driveway of the family home. It was a fatality.

2   As I parked among police cars and TV-news cruisers, I saw a stocky white-haired man in cotton work clothes standing near a pickup. Cameras were trained on him, and reporters were sticking microphones in his face. Looking totally bewildered, he was trying to answer their questions. Mostly he was only moving his lips, blinking and choking up.

3   After a while the reporters gave up on him and followed the police into the small white house. I can still see in my mind's eye that devastated old man looking down at the place in the driveway where the child had been. Beside the house was a freshly spaded flower bed, and nearby a pile of dark, rich earth.

4   "I was just backing up there to spread the good dirt," he said to me, though I had not asked him anything. "I didn't even know she was outdoors." He stretched his hand toward the flower bed, then let it flop to his side. He lapsed back into his thoughts, and I, like a good reporter, went into the house to find someone who could provide a recent photo of the toddler.

5   A few minutes later, with all the details in my notebook and a three-by-five studio portrait of the cherubic child tucked in my jacket pocket, I went toward the kitchen where the police had said the body was.

6   I had brought a camera in with me—the big, bulky Speed Graphic which used to be the newspaper reporter's trademark. Everybody had drifted back out of the house together—family, police, reporters and photographers. Entering the kitchen, I came upon this scene:

7   On a Formica-topped table, backlighted by a frilly curtained window, lay the tiny body, wrapped in a clean white sheet. Somehow the grandfather had managed to stay away from the crowd. He was sitting on a chair beside the table, in profile to me and unaware of my presence, looking uncomprehendingly at the swaddled corpse.

8   The house was very quiet. A clock ticked. As I watched, the grandfather slowly leaned forward, curved his arms like parentheses around the head and feet of the little form, then pressed his face to the shroud and remained motionless.

9   In that hushed moment I recognized the makings of a prize-winning news photograph. I appraised the light, adjusted the lens setting and distance, locked a bulb in the flashgun, raised the camera and composed the scene in the viewfinder.

10   Every element of the picture was perfect: the grandfather in his plain work clothes, his white hair backlit by sunshine, the child's form wrapped in the sheet, the atmosphere of the simple home suggested by black iron trivets and World's Fair souvenir plates on the walls flanking the window. Outside, the police could be seen inspecting the fatal rear wheel of the pickup while the child's mother and father leaned in each other's arms.

11   I don't know how many seconds I stood there, unable to snap that shutter. I was keenly aware of the powerful story-telling value that photo would have, and my professional conscience told me to take it. Yet I couldn't make my hand fire that flashbulb and intrude on the poor man's island of grief.

12   At length I lowered the camera and crept away, shaken with doubt about my suitability for the journalistic profession. Of course I never told the city editor or any fellow reporters about that missed opportunity for a perfect news picture.

13   Every day on the newscasts and in the papers, we see pictures of people in extreme conditions of grief and despair. Human suffering has become a spectator sport. And sometimes, as I'm watching news film, I remember that day.

14   I still feel right about what I did.

WHAT DID THE WRITER SAY AND WHAT DID YOU THINK?

1. At what point in the essay does the point of the narrative become clear?
2. What elements make "the perfect picture"?
3. This essay was originally published in 1976. Is the topic still relevant?

HOW DID THE WRITER SAY IT?

1. How does the writer's statement in the first paragraph that "I was . . . driving to a scene I didn't want to see" affect our view of him? Of what happens later?
2. The author gives a number of details about the setting. How and why are these important to the point of the story?
3. Does paragraph 13 violate this textbook's rule, "Write a story, not a sermon"?

What About Your Writing?

"The Perfect Picture" is one of the most powerfully emotional essays in this textbook. No one who reads it will easily forget the story that James Alexander Thom tells or the image of the grieving grandfather bent over the body of the toddler that he killed in a horrifying accident.

Notice, though, that Thom creates all this emotion and gives his essay all this power with great restraint. Instead of *overwriting* by pouring on overwrought adjectives and tearful details, he simply writes, "A man . . . had accidentally backed his pickup truck over his baby granddaughter in the driveway of the family home. It was a fatality." And instead of preaching against media vultures who lack both honor and shame, Thom justifies his merciful decision with the few words, "I still feel right about what I did." Thom's resistance to overwriting helps him avoid the pitfall we warned you about on page 36 when we told you to "Write a story, not a sermon."

Overwriting is often a great temptation that can hamper us from communicating the honest emotions we feel when confronted with subjects such as the death of a child, the heroes of war, the rapture of romantic love. Even the best writers are not immune. Charles Dickens, one of the greatest British novelists, wrote about the death of one of his famous fictional children, Little Nell:

> For she was dead. There, upon her little bed, she lay at rest. The solemn stillness was no marvel now.
>
> She was dead. No sleep so beautiful and calm, so free from trace of pain, so fair to look upon. She seemed a creature fresh from the hand of God, and waiting for the breath of life; not one who had lived and suffered death.
>
> Her couch was dressed with here and there some winter berries and green leaves, gathered in a spot she had been used to favour. "When I die, put near me something that has loved the light, and had the sky above it always." Those were her words.
>
> She was dead. Dear, gentle, patient, noble Nell was dead. Her little bird—a poor slight thing the pressure of a finger would have crushed—was stirring nimbly in its cage; and the strong heart of its child mistress was mute and motionless for ever.

Thom certainly could have written pages of tear-jerking narrative about the tragedy of a child's death, the brutal coincidence of her grandfather's responsibility for it, and the ravening hordes of writers and photographers looking to make their professional reputations out of the tragedy. But he doesn't. He tells us, "It was a fatality." He tells us, "I still feel right about what I did." He knows that this story is so powerful that any attempt to heighten its impact by ladling on the emotionalism would be a distraction.

Beware of the dangers of overwriting. When a story truly can speak for itself, let it.

THE HAPPIEST DAY OF MY LIFE
Michael T. Smith

Michael T. Smith works in the telecommunications industry. He has published stories in several newspapers, magazines, and online publications, and will be part of the collection *From My Heart to Yours*. This story, of the happiest day in his life, focuses on two perennially popular essay topics—work and family.

✓ **WORDS TO CHECK:**

antics (paragraph 3)
composure (17)

1 It started innocently.

2 Many years ago, I worked in an office with large windows facing a busy overpass. I was standing by one of those windows one day when a woman in a passing car looked up and made eye contact. Naturally, I waved.

3 A chuckle escaped my lips and she turned and tried to identify me. It was the beginning of a year of window antics. When things were slow, I would stand in the window and wave at the passengers who looked up. Their confused looks made me laugh, and my stress evaporated.

4 Co-workers began to take an interest. They often stood just out of view so they could watch the reactions I received, and laugh along.

5 Late afternoon was the best time. Rush-hour traffic filled the overpass with cars and transit buses, and provided lots of opportunities of my end-of-day routine. It wasn't long before I had a following: a group of commuters who passed the window every day and looked up at the strange waving man.

6   There was the carpool crowd, the business lady with her children fresh from daycare, and a man with a construction truck who turned on his flashing-yellow light as he returned my wave. But my favorite was the transit bus from the docks that passed my window at 4:40 P.M. It carried the same group every day, and they became my biggest fans.

7   After a while, a simple wave became boring, so I devised ways to enhance my act. I made signs, saying, "Hi," "Hello," "Be Happy!" and posted them in the window while I waved. I stood on the window ledge in various poses, created hats from paper and file-folders, made faces, played peek-a-boo by bouncing up from below the window ledge, stuck out my tongue, and tossed paper planes in the air. Once I went into the walkway over the street and danced, while co-workers pointed in my direction to let my fans know I was there.

8   Christmas approached, and job cuts were announced. Several co-workers lost their jobs, and everyone was feeling down. Stress in the office reached a new high. We needed a miracle to repair the damage the bad news had caused.

9   While I worked a night shift, a red lab jacket attracted my attention. I picked it up and turned it over in my hands. In a back corner of the office, I found some packing material: white sheets of cloth-like foam. I cut some of it into thin strips and taped the pieces around the cuffs and collar, down the front, and around the hem of the jacket. A box of foam packing and strips of tape became Santa's beard and, when that was taped to the hat, it all slipped over my head in one piece.

10   The next working day, I hid from my co-workers and slipped into the costume. I walked bravely to my desk, sat down, held my belly, and mocked Santa's chuckle, as they gathered around me, laughing. It was the first time I had seen them smile in weeks.

11   Later my supervisor walked through the door. He took three steps, saw me, paused and shook his head, then turned and left.

12   I feared trouble. The phone on the desk rang a few minutes later. It was my supervisor.

13   "Mike, can you come to my office, please?"

14   I shuffled down the hall, the foam beard swishing across my chest with each step.

15   "Come in," the muffled voice replied to my knock.

16   He did not turn in my direction when I entered and sat down. The foam on the beard creaked briefly. A bead of sweat rolled down my forehead. The only sound was the hammering of my heart.

17   "Mike . . . " This was all he managed before he lost his composure, leaned back in his chair, and bellowed with laughter. He held his stomach, as tears formed in his eyes.

18   I sat silent and confused.

19   "Thanks, Mike!" he said, when he regained control. "With the job cuts, it has been hard to enjoy the Christmas season. Thanks for the laugh. I needed it."

20   That evening, and every evening of the Christmas season, I stood proudly in the window and waved to my fans. The bus crowd waved wildly, and the little children smiled at the strange Santa. My heart was full of the season. For a few minutes each day, we could forget the loss of jobs.

21   I didn't know it then, but a bond was forming between my fans and me. It wasn't until several months after the Santa act that I discovered how close we had become.

22   My wife and I were expecting our first child that spring, and I wanted the world to know. Less than a month before the due date, I posted a sign in the window, which said, "23 DAYS UNTIL B DAY." My fans passed and shrugged their shoulders. The next day the sign read, "22 DAYS UNTIL B DAY." Each day the number dropped, and the passing people grew more confused.

23   One day, a sign appeared in the bus. "What is B DAY?" I just waved and smiled.

24   Ten days before the expected date, the sign in the window read, "10 DAYS UNTIL BA _ _ DAY." Still the people wondered. The next day, it read, "9 DAYS UNTIL BAB_ DAY," then "8 DAYS UNTIL BABY DAY," and my fans finally knew what was happening.

25   By then, my following had grown to include twenty or thirty different buses and cars. Every night, they watched to see if my wife had given birth. Excitement grew as the number decreased. My fans were disappointed when the count reached "zero" without an announcement. The next day, the sign read, "BABY DAY 1 DAY LATE," and I pretended to pull out my hair.

26   Each day the number changed, and interest from passing cars grew. When my wife was fourteen days overdue, she finally went into labor. The next morning our daughter was born. I left the hospital at 5:30 A.M., screamed my joy into the still morning air, and drove home to sleep. I got up at noon, showered, bought cigars, and appeared at the window in time for my fans. My co-workers were ready with a banner posted in the window:

27   "IT'S A GIRL!"

28   I wasn't alone that night. My co-workers joined me in celebration. We stood and waved our cigars in the air as every vehicle that passed acknowledged the birth of my daughter. Finally, the bus from the docks made its turn onto the overpass and began to climb the hill. When it drew close, I climbed onto the window ledge and clasped my hands over my head in a victory post.

29   The bus was directly in front of me when it stopped dead in heavy traffic, and all the people on board stood with their hands in the air.

30   Emotion choked my breathing as I watched the display of celebration for my new daughter. Then it happened: a sign popped up. It filled the windows and stretched half the length of the bus. "CONGRATULATIONS!" it said, in big, bold letters.

31   There were tears in my eyes as the bus slowly resumed its journey. I stood in silence, as it pulled from view. More fans passed and tooted their horns or

flashed their lights to display their happiness, but I hardly noticed them, as I pondered what had just happened.

32   My daughter had been born fourteen days late. Those people must have carried that sign on the bus for at least two weeks. Every day they had unrolled it and then rolled it back up. They did that for me.

33   We all have a clown inside of us. We need to let it free and not be surprised at the magic it can create. For eight months, I made a fool of myself. Those people must have enjoyed the smiles I gave them, because, on the happiest day of my life, they showed their appreciation.

34   It has been more than eighteen years since that special time, but every year, on my daughter's birthday, I always remember the special gift they gave me.

WHAT DID THE WRITER SAY AND WHAT DID YOU THINK?

1. Why does Smith start his "window antics"?
2. What did the author think was going to happen when he was called into his supervisor's office? What did you think was going to happen? Why?
3. How does Smith discover the strength of the bond he has formed with the bus riders?

HOW DID THE WRITER SAY IT?

1. Elsewhere (p. 106) we've discussed the effect of varying your sentence length when writing an essay. What effect do the very short sentences in paragaph 32 have on the tone of the essay?
2. Why does Smith spend so much time telling the story of the time he dressed up as Santa?

SALVATION

Langston Hughes

Poet, playwright, short story writer, and essayist, Langston Hughes (1902–1967) is referred to by the *Encyclopedia Britannica* as "one of the foremost interpreters to the world of the black experience in the United States." Hughes achieved great popularity with readers of all races, and when he died, an astonishing twenty-seven of his books were still in print. "Salvation," from his 1940 autobiographical volume, *The Big Sea*, shows Hughes' great gift for treating essentially serious subjects with a mixture of sensitivity and humor.

✓ WORDS TO CHECK:

revival (paragraph 1)	gnarled (4)	punctuated (14)
dire (3)	knickerbockered (11)	

1 I was saved from sin when I was going on thirteen. But not really saved. It happened like this. There was a big revival at my Auntie Reed's church. Every night for weeks there had been much preaching, singing, praying, and shouting, and some very hardened sinners had been brought to Christ, and the membership of the church had grown by leaps and bounds. Then just before the revival ended, they held a special meeting for children, "to bring the young lambs to the fold." My aunt spoke of it for days ahead. That night I was escorted to the front row and placed on the mourners' bench with all the other young sinners, who had not yet been brought to Jesus.

2 My aunt told me that when you were saved you saw a light, and something happened to you inside! And Jesus came into your life! And God was with you from then on! She said you could see and hear and feel Jesus in your soul. I believed her. I have heard a great many old people say the same thing and it seemed to me they ought to know. So I sat there calmly in the hot, crowded church, waiting for Jesus to come to me.

3 The preacher preached a wonderful rhythmical sermon, all moans and shouts and lonely cries and dire pictures of hell, and then he sang a song about the ninety and nine safe in the fold, but one little lamb was left out in the cold. Then he said: "Won't you come? Won't you come to Jesus? Young lambs, won't you come?" And he held out his arms to all us young sinners there on the mourners' bench. And the little girls cried. And some of them jumped up and went to Jesus right away. But most of us just sat there.

4 A great many old people came and knelt around us and prayed, old women with jet-black faces and braided hair, old men with work-gnarled hands. And the church sang a song about the lower lights are burning, some poor sinners to be saved. And the whole building rocked with prayer and song.

5 Still I kept waiting to *see* Jesus.

6 Finally all the young people had gone to the altar and were saved, but one boy and me. He was a rounder's son named Westley. Westley and I were surrounded by sisters and deacons praying. It was very hot in the church, and getting late now. Finally Westley said to me in a whisper: "God damn! I'm tired o' sitting here. Let's get up and be saved." So he got up and was saved.

7 Then I was left all alone on the mourners' bench. My aunt came and knelt at my knees and cried, while prayers and songs swirled all around me in the little church. The whole congregation prayed for me alone, in a mighty wail of moans and voices. And I kept waiting serenely for Jesus, waiting, waiting–but he didn't come. I wanted to see him, but nothing happened to me. Nothing! I wanted something to happen to me, but nothing happened.

8 I heard the songs and the minister saying: "Why don't you come? My dear child, why don't you come to Jesus? Jesus is waiting for you. He wants you. Why don't you come? Sister Reed, what is this child's name?"

9 "Langston," my aunt sobbed.

10 "Langston, why don't you come? Why don't you come and be saved? Oh, Lamb of God! Why don't you come?"

11   Now it was really getting late. I began to be ashamed of myself, holding everything up so long. I began to wonder what God thought about Westley, who certainly hadn't seen Jesus either, but who was now sitting proudly on the platform, swinging his knickerbockered legs and grinning down at me, surrounded by deacons and old women on their knees praying. God had not struck Westley dead for taking his name in vain or for lying in the temple. So I decided that maybe to save further trouble, I'd better lie, too, and say that Jesus had come, and get up and be saved.

12   So I got up.

13   Suddenly the whole room broke into a sea of shouting, as they saw me rise. Waves of rejoicing swept the place. Women leaped in the air. My aunt threw her arms around me. The minister took me by the hand and led me to the platform.

When things quieted down, in a hushed silence, punctuated by a few 14 ecstatic "Amens," all the new young lambs were blessed in the name of God. Then joyous singing filled the room.

That night, for the last time in my life but one—for I was a big boy twelve 15 years old—I cried. I cried, in bed alone, and couldn't stop. I buried my head under the quilts, but my aunt heard me. She woke up and told my uncle I was crying because the Holy Ghost had come into my life, and because I had seen Jesus. But I was really crying because I couldn't bear to tell her that I had lied, that I had deceived everybody in the church, that I hadn't seen Jesus, and that now I didn't believe there was a Jesus any more, since he didn't come to help me.

WHAT DID THE WRITER SAY AND WHAT DID YOU THINK?

1. What is the narrative point or thesis in "Salvation"?
2. Do you think that the adults were unfair in their pressures on the children? Why, or why not?
3. How does the young Langston define *see*? Why, then, is he disappointed?
4. How is Westley's reaction different from Langston's?
5. Do you think that Hughes wants his essay to be read as a comment about adults' failure to remember the realities of childhood? Explain.

HOW DID THE WRITER SAY IT?

1. Why is Hughes' thesis implied rather than expressed directly?
2. In what order does Hughes present his narrative? Does this order create suspense for the reader? How?
3. Do you think the audience has to be acquainted with the concept of religious revivals to comprehend Hughes' narrative? If so, what details could support your answer?
4. How do the hymn lyrics contribute to the pressures the young Hughes feels?

What About <u>Your</u> Writing?

Part of the appeal of "Salvation" is its awakening of memories. While reading about the author's childhood, readers return to their own and remember the relatives, the boredom, the illusions, the ideals. Everything starts coming back.

It's hard to beat nostalgia as subject matter for papers. The friendly trivia contests at parties, the popularity of games like "Trivial Pursuit" and the "Whatever Happened to . . ." and "Remember When?" features in newspapers and magazines are only superficial signs of that appeal. In a world seemingly devoted to impermanence and the celebration of "future shock," many people find themselves drawn to keep in touch with, to keep faith with, their pasts.

The writer's age doesn't matter much with nostalgia. Our pasts may be different, but each of us has one. One person will remember Jackie Robinson and Joe DiMaggio, rationing during World War II, and *The Shadow* suspense program on radio. Another will remember the first showing of *Star Wars,* the tragic *Challenger* flight, and the attempted assassination of President Reagan. Still others may already be thinking nostalgically about the retirement of Michael Jordan, the media frenzy over the murder of JonBenet Ramsey, and the contested presidential election of 2000. There are recent and less recent memories, funny ones and tragic ones, memories to treasure and memories to fear—but no normal person ever lived without memories.

Nostalgia can work in almost any paper, but bear one warning in mind: Avoid oozing sentimentality. Don't make the mistake of assuming automatically that everything about the past was glorious and that everything about the present is terrible. With that warning, though, a nostalgic trip into your own past can often result in a surprisingly easy solution to the problem of being stuck for a subject.

A CULTURAL DIVORCE
Elizabeth Wong

Elizabeth Wong has written several plays for children as well as seven for adults, including *Letter to a Student Revolutionary* (1991), *China Doll* (1995), and *Kimchee and Chitlins* (1996). Her newest plays are *The Love Life of a Eunuch* and *Dating and Mating in Modern Times.* Wong's essay about her school days notably avoids the danger of becoming sweetly sentimental about the past: classrooms, the innocence of children, the joys of family life. After you finish this essay, consider whether it can be thought of as a story with an abrupt surprise ending or whether the surprise is anticipated earlier.

✓ **WORDS TO CHECK:**

stoically (paragraph 1)	flanked (5)	ideographs (7)
dissuade (2)	kowtow (6)	pidgin (10)

1   It's still there, the Chinese school on Yale Street where my brother and I used to go. Despite the new coat of paint and the high wire fence, the school I knew 10 years ago remains remarkably, stoically the same.

2   Every day at 5 P.M., instead of playing with our fourth- and fifth-grade friends or sneaking out to the empty lot to hunt ghosts and animal bones, my brother and I had to go to Chinese school. No amount of kicking, screaming, or pleading could dissuade my mother, who was solidly determined to have us learn the language of our heritage.

3   Forcibly, she walked us the seven long, hilly blocks from our home to school, depositing our defiant, tearful faces before the stern principal. My only memory of him is that he swayed on his heels like a palm tree, and he always clasped his impatient twitching hands behind his back. I recognized him as a repressed maniacal child killer, and knew that if we ever saw his hands we'd be in big trouble.

4   We all sat in little chairs in an empty auditorium. The room smelled like Chinese medicine, an imported faraway mustiness. Like ancient mothballs or dirty closets. I hated that smell. I favored crisp new scents. Like the soft French perfume that my American teacher wore in public school.

5   There was a stage far to the right, flanked by an American flag and the flag of the Nationalist Republic of China, which was also red, white and blue but not as pretty.

6   Although the emphasis at the school was mainly language—speaking, reading, writing—the lessons always began with an exercise in politeness. With the entrance of the teacher, the best student would tap a bell and everyone would get up, kowtow, and chant, "Sing san ho," the phonetic for "How are you, teacher?"

7   Being ten years old, I had better things to learn than ideographs copied painstakingly in lines that ran right to left from the tip of a *moc but*, a real ink pen that had to be held in an awkward way if blotches were to be avoided. After all, I could do the multiplication tables, name the satellites of Mars, and write reports on *Little Women* and *Black Beauty*. Nancy Drew, my favorite book heroine, never spoke Chinese.

8   The language was a source of embarrassment. More times than not, I had tried to disassociate myself from the nagging, loud voice that followed me wherever I wandered in the nearby American supermarket outside Chinatown. The voice belonged to my grandmother, a fragile woman in her seventies who could outshout the best of the street vendors. Her humor was raunchy, her Chinese rhythmless, patternless. It was quick, it was loud, it was unbeautiful. It was not like the quiet, lilting romance of French or the gentle refinement of the American South. Chinese sounded pedestrian. Public.

9   In Chinatown, the comings and goings of hundreds of Chinese on their daily tasks sounded chaotic and frenzied. I did not want to be thought of as mad, as talking gibberish. When I spoke English, people nodded at me, smiled sweetly, said encouraging words. Even the people in my culture would cluck and say that I'd do well in life. "My, doesn't she move her lips fast," they would say, meaning that I'd be able to keep up with the world outside Chinatown.

10   My brother was even more fanatical than I about speaking English. He was especially hard on my mother, criticizing her, often cruelly, for her pidgin speech—smatterings of Chinese scattered like chop suey in her conversation. "It's not 'What it is,' Mom," he'd say in exasperation. "It's 'What is it, what is it, what is it!'" Sometimes Mom might leave out an occasional "the" or "a," or perhaps a verb of being. He would stop her in midsentence: "Say it again, Mom. Say it right." When he tripped over his own tongue, he'd blame it on her: "See, Mom, it's all your fault. You set a bad example."

11   What infuriated my mother most was when my brother cornered her on her consonants, especially "r." My father had played a cruel joke on Mom by assigning her an American name that her tongue wouldn't allow her to say. No matter how hard she tried, "Ruth" always ended up "Luth" or "Roof."

12   After two years of writing with a *moc but* and reciting words with multiples of meanings, I finally was granted a cultural divorce. I was permitted to stop Chinese school.

13   I thought of myself as multicultural. I preferred tacos to egg rolls; I enjoyed Cinco de Mayo[1] more than Chinese New Year.

14   At last, I was one of you; I wasn't one of them.

15   Sadly, I still am.

WHAT DID THE WRITER SAY AND WHAT DID YOU THINK?

1. What is Wong's thesis? Does she state it directly? Does she need to?
2. What are the implications of the last sentence of this reading?
3. When the author was a child, she hated speaking Chinese. Why?
4. What are Wong's current feelings about being forced to attend Chinese school?
5. What is the "cruel joke" of the author's mother's name?

HOW DID THE WRITER SAY IT?

1. What specific details does the author use to emphasize her childhood distaste for all that was Chinese and her love for all that was American?
2. What does the phrase "a cultural divorce" mean?
3. How and where does Wong indicate that her childhood attitudes have changed?

[1] May 5, a holiday celebrating the defeat of French troops in Mexico at the Battle of Puebla, 1862.

What About Your Writing?

Once writers are ready to go beyond the obvious ingredients of grammar, mechanics, and organization, they frequently find themselves working hardest on specific details. That's what they should be doing. Writing that lacks effective specific details is almost always dull and is sometimes unclear. Writing that uses effective specific details has energy, character, and conviction. Of course, writers must generalize; a thesis statement is a generalization, after all. To a great extent, however, it's by specific details that the writing lives or dies. Without them, no matter how sensible or important or even brilliant the ideas, a paper is likely to perish from malnutrition.

In "A Cultural Divorce," Elizabeth Wong uses specific details to bring her subject to life. She does not settle for writing accurately but ploddingly, "I was proud of my American schooling and contemptuous of my Chinese schooling." Instead, she makes the same general point with specific details—and the writing becomes twice as interesting, twice as forceful, and twice as convincing: "After all, I could do the multiplication tables, name the satellites of Mars, and write reports on *Little Women* and *Black Beauty.* Nancy Drew, my favorite book heroine, never spoke Chinese." Wong does not tell us in general terms that her mother had trouble speaking English. Instead, we see Wong's mother unable to pronounce her own name, and we share some of the pain and embarrassment. We start to care, and we care intensely. And that's why specific details are so important.

SITTING DUCK

Thomas Froncek

Thomas Froncek was an editor for *Reader's Digest* for twenty-five years. He has written books on a wide range of subjects. His most recent book, *A Splendid Madness: A Man, a Boat, a Love Story,* explores his rediscovery of the joys and frustrations of sailing.

✓ Words to Check:

dawdle (paragraph 2)	Audubon (21)	fraudulent (27)
lavishly (4)	existential (24)	transience (28)
refuge (17)	chagrined (25)	scenario (28)
demise (19)	ersatz (26)	

1 The ice was our first surprise. The duck was the second. We knew the cold snap had set in even before we left the house. We'd heard it coming the night before, when the wind fluted in the chimney and banged percussion on the storm windows. Through the night the furnace droned a steady bass in the cellar, and in

the morning when we pulled up the shades, we found the windows etched with frost. It was our first inkling of winter in Maine.

2   Having moved up from the Hudson Valley in June, my wife, Ellen, and I had savored every minute of our first full summer around Casco Bay. Newly retired, we were free to linger in places we'd barely sampled during our too-brief vacations in the area. Finally we had all the time in the world to visit beaches and take boat trips out to the islands. We could dawdle in galleries, antique shops, and bookstores. In the evenings we had any number of con-certs and theater events to choose from within a few minutes of our Brunswick home. And if we missed one, well, we knew there would always be another next week or the week after that.

3   Now, in late November, we were happily anticipating our first winter in Maine. Hard-core natives, we'd heard it said, believe that "if you can't stand the winters in Maine, you don't deserve the summers." Eager to earn our stripes, we donned mittens, parkas, and heavy socks on that chilly morning and headed out the door.

4   A short drive brought us to one of our favorite country roads: a pretty lane that wandered through meadows and pastures before rolling down to the head of an inlet, where it offered a broad view of Middle Bay and its island. Back in June, when we'd first walked here, the surrounding fields had been lavishly gowned in purple, pink, and blue lupines. A few weeks later the whites and yellow were showing their stuff: daisies, buttercups, and Queen Anne's lace. By now, though, the bright summer frocks had been packed away. The fields wore tweedy shades of brown, bordered by the muted greens of the distant pine forest.

5   I parked on the shoulder. As soon as we opened our doors we were hit by a frigid blast of north wind. We laughed, pulled our caps down over our ears, and began walking. This was what we had come for after all.

6   We were perhaps a quarter mile along when we saw the sheet of ice lying just off the road. Ice? So soon? Two days earlier a pretty little pond had filled this spot, blue water reflecting a fringe of dried grasses and cattails, which glowed golden in the afternoon sun. Now that pond was as hard and brittle as porcelain. The freeze had set in fast.

7   Just how fast became brutally clear when we walked a few steps farther and spotted the duck. Fat and gray, its feathers puffed up against the cold, it sat perfectly still in the middle of the frozen pond. It did not make a move as we approached, did not even turn its head to give us a look.

8   "Do you think he's stuck?" Ellen asked.

9   "Or asleep," I suggested. "It's hard to tell from here."

10   The duck was perhaps fifty feet away: beyond a marshy drainage ditch, across a barbed wire fence, and a good ten feet out into the ice. The distance and the gray light from the overcast sky made it difficult to make out the details, and the wind in my eyes didn't help either. A small patch of open water

seemed to encircle the duck, which could mean his body still held some heat. But I couldn't be sure.

11   We clapped our mittened hands, yet even this evoked no reaction. The poor creature seemed as solidly frozen as the water around him.

12   I thought if I'd had a stick I might prod a response out of him, or even pry him free. But the nearest tree was a good quarter-mile away. "Maybe I can get closer," I said, and I stepped off the road and jumped over the ditch.

13   I didn't know what I hoped to accomplish. Rescue him? Take him home and wrap him in a blanket until he was warm enough to fly away?

14   I eased a leg over the wire, then realized that the ground was still soft and my boots were sinking into the muck. This was not a good idea. Time to retreat.

15   I scrambled back to the road, resigned to the fact that there was no way I could help the little guy. Nature would have to take its course. No doubt some hungry crow or animal would come along to finish what the ice had started.

16   Reluctantly we turned our backs on him and went on our way. But in the days that followed I could not shake the pathetic image of that duck caught in the ice. It puzzled me. I had always assumed that keen survival instincts protected animals from such calamities. Surely a duck knew better than to fall asleep in still water on a freezing night.

17   Was he old and sick? Had he gone off alone to die? Or had he simply been too tired to wake up? I imagined him landing on the pond at sunset, drawn to the familiar element that had been his safe harbor throughout his life—a resting place, a source of food, a refuge from predators. I thought of him drifting into sleep as the night grew colder, oblivious to the hard sheen that slowly crept over the surface: sleeping on even as the waters hardened around him, until it was too late and he was stuck fast.

18   Did he wake in the night? Did he know he was caught? Did he die in fear, knowing his end was at hand? Or did he merely slip deeper into sleep because sleep felt so good on a cold, dark night with morning far away?

19   The melancholy scene kept replaying itself in my mind. I found myself telling friends and family about it, even as I wondered why I was so obsessed. Later it occurred to me that the duck's demise perhaps touched something deep within me, stirring anxieties about my new stage of life, when I could no longer rely on the familiar rituals of work and career to make me forget the advancing years, the relentless creep of mortality.

20   I was almost relieved, then, when Susan, a new friend, suggested that Ellen and I may not have seen what we thought we'd seen.

21   "Are you sure it wasn't a decoy?" Susan replied after I had emailed her about the sorry sight. "My husband and I were fooled the same way a couple of years back. We saw three ducks frozen in a pond and we mentioned it to some Audubon birders who were passing through. When they informed us of our mistake we felt quite silly."

22   A decoy? Could it be? I drove back to check. This time I took binoculars.

23   Parking again on the shoulder. I walked to the pond and turned the lenses toward that dark shape on the ice.

24   What I saw left me feeling oddly deflated. Sure enough, in close-up I could make out the sheen of plastic feathers, the dull black of plastic eyes. My fine existential metaphor was a fraud. Never mind deep meditations on nature's cruel indifference and the cold realities of man's fate—my fate. A plastic duck stuck in the ice was only litter, the leavings of a forgetful hunter.

25   But as I stood there feeling chagrined at being duped, I saw something that offered a measure of consolation: proof that sharper senses than mine had been fooled.

26   Since our last visit a light snow had fallen, dusting the ice, and there, stitched across that white carpet, was a trail of tiny footprints. Some four-footed critter—a fox, perhaps, or a raccoon—had passed this way and its tracks told a story. Stepping out onto the pond, the animal had made a beeline for the far shore, trotting along to who knows where. But halfway across it had been distracted. Like a hungry shopper catching sight of a cake in a bakery window, the animal had made a sharp left turn toward the ersatz duck. It had come close enough to take a sniff and to check whether those feathers were real. Then it had done a U-turn back to its original route and continued on.

27   I imagined that critter was even more disappointed than I was to discover that fraudulent fowl. I was missing only a metaphor. He was missing a tasty snack.

28   Yet as I headed back to the car I found my own spirits lifting. I felt as if I had been granted a reprieve. I had let myself be decoyed into melancholy musings on age and the transience of life. But why get stuck there? Sure, the future held uncertainties. For some creature the coming months would bring hard times. Survival itself might well depend on finding a duck trapped in the ice. Yet others would thrive and bear new life in the spring. There was no way to tell how each small scenario would play out. All I knew was that a new season was upon us, and for however long it lasted, I would be foolish indeed if I did not take every opportunity to enjoy it.

WHAT DID THE WRITER SAY AND WHAT DID YOU THINK?

1. Where is the thesis? Is it stated directly?
2. The writer says they go for a walk "to earn our stripes." What does this mean? Given the results of that walk, has he succeeded in earning his stripes?
3. What does the trapped duck represent to the narrator? Does this change throughout the narrative?
4. Is there any conflict in this story? If so, what is its nature?

HOW DID THE WRITER SAY IT?

1. What do the first two paragraphs of this essay accomplish?
2. Locate passages where the author provides descriptive details. How do these contribute to the narrative?
3. The author uses several questions in paragraphs 13, 17, and 18. What's the purpose of these questions, and are they effective?
4. Is the ending to this story satisfactory?

What About *Your* Writing?

"The duck was the second." Isn't that a sentence fragment? "Time to retreat." Isn't that another sentence fragment? Aren't sentence fragments illegal? The answers to these questions are *yes, yes,* and *sort of.*

Look at it this way: There's a sensible speed limit on the road. One night you're driving well over the limit. A police officer who is worth anything would stop you to give you a ticket. This night an officer stops you and finds that you're speeding to get a pregnant woman to the hospital in time or a badly beaten man to the emergency ward. If the officer is worth anything now, you get a siren escort that enables you to break the law more safely and efficiently.

Your instructor, in some respects, is the police officer. By and large, sentence fragments are not standard written English, and your instructor rightly gives you a ticket for them. Every once in a while, a situation turns up when a fragment can be justified. You want a special dramatic effect, a sudden note of breeziness or informality, perhaps, that a grammatically complete sentence could not achieve as well. In that case, your instructor usually tries to be cooperative.

You don't speed to the emergency ward often, however, and sentence fragments, too, should be saved for special occasions. The burden of proof is on you: The officer wants to see the pregnant woman or beaten man, and the instructor wants to be convinced that the sentence fragment was justified by the demands of your paper. Finally, just as the officer wants assurance that you knew you were speeding and were in constant control, the instructor wants assurance that your sentence fragment was a deliberate stylistic device, not a simple grammatical error.

CHAPTER 2¹/₂
Office Hours: Reading Around

Two students. Both have read, understood, and successfully applied the lessons of this textbook, and probably of others. Both are competent writers, and both deserve—and get—plenty of credit from their instructor. But one student goes beyond mere competence. You know the one we mean: not just clear, but brilliant; not just solid, but dazzling. Where did that person get that way with words, that feel for language, that magic touch? How does he do it? What's her secret? What vitamins do these people take?

When it comes to magic pills for writing excellence, most people confess their ignorance. Genetics? Parental upbringing? Great teachers? Sensitivity? Divine gifts? Maybe. Maybe not. There may be many elements of writing at the highest levels that can't be taught any more than that amazing bridge or poker player ever took lessons in "card sense." But there are ways to learn what can't be taught. There *is* a vitamin pill. Writers with the special spark differ as much as any other group of people, but they have one characteristic in common: They all love to read. And they *read around*.

If you want to increase your prospects of catching fire as a writer, start reading around. Read what you enjoy and what interests you—we're not dealing with assigned drudgery here. You're not trying to impress your instructor. Read around. Lives of famous generals, gangsters, movie stars, scientists. The history of aviation, of baseball, of totem poles, of furniture, of postage stamps. Horror novels, science fiction, and suspense thrillers are fine if you are so inclined. Read magazines. Read newspapers. Your college and public libraries are major sources for this sort of reading. There are also some excellent online databases that will allow you to access thousands of articles right from your computer.

You will be reading the work of professional writers, and you will start experiencing one of the most effective forms of education—learning without lessons. It doesn't happen overnight, but you start to pick things up, often not even realizing that you are doing so. You begin to sense what a good sentence or paragraph looks like, sounds like, feels like. Words come more easily. You find you can make distinctions between language and ideas that are fresh and those that are stale. And all this happens while you're not really paying that much attention. You're just reading what you like—and the absorption process goes on.

Reading around won't make everyone a magnificent writer, of course, but magnificent writers all do a great deal of reading around. Why not? It's fun. It's pain-free education. And it's an easy pill to swallow.

Description

Description is nothing new. You undoubtedly noted the descriptions you encountered in the previous narration chapter. Narrative writing draws much of its life from descriptive details. In "Foul Shots," when Rogelio R. Gomez writes, "My mother's hands were rough and chafed, her wardrobe drab and worn," and in "Salvation," when Langston Hughes writes of a friend "swinging his knickerbockered legs and grinning down at me, surrounded by deacons and old women on their knees praying," these authors are using descriptive details to help the reader see a specific image. If you have already written a narrative essay, you too probably relied on description to help bring the narration to life. In your essays to come, you will also find that description is essential. Description is not new, but devoting an entire paper to it is new and demands separate consideration.

Some descriptions can be completely *objective*: They can describe the size and color of measles spots, the size and speed of a missile. Objective descriptions make no judgments about the ugliness of the spots or the morality of the missile. Ordinarily intended to meet special needs, objective descriptions are not within the province of this chapter.

Here, the *impressionistic* or *interpretive* description paper is our basic concern. The writer of this type of paper uses description to convey an attitude. Any objective description of measles spots, for instance, is subordinate to convincing the reader of the ugliness or triviality or seriousness of the spots.

Rules, guidelines, and handy hints are of less practical value than usual when writing the comparatively freewheeling description paper. Only three major points need to be stressed, and none of them is especially restrictive.

EMOTIONAL APPEAL

Description papers tend to rely more than others on a direct appeal to the reader's emotions. A description of a room will more probably have a thesis such as *The room was frightening* than *The room was big.* To make their emotional appeal, description papers also tend to concentrate more than others on using colorful language. Such hard-to-pin-down elements as mood and tone tend to be major concerns. These generalizations don't apply to all description papers, and they certainly shouldn't be interpreted as implying that other patterns of writing can't or shouldn't appeal to emotions, use colorful language, and so on.

As a whole, however, good description papers do receive praise more for their insight and sensitivity than for their masterful logic.

Nobody can teach you how to make your writing tingle with deep perceptions. Insight and sensitivity come from within. It might help, however, to suggest a few approaches that can give your writing a push in the right direction toward attaining the lively emotional appeal of good description.

Try a Deliberately Unconventional Thesis

If a room would strike ninety-nine people out of a hundred as ugly, try pointing out its hidden beauties. If everyone agrees that a young woman is painfully shy, try showing that she really has a superiority complex. Don't lie, and don't attempt to support a thesis you believe is idiotic. Do see if you can make a case for an unconventional idea.

Show Your Powers of Observation by Stressing Specific Details

Virtually all good writing uses specifics, lots of them. A description paper absolutely depends on them. Try to take a seemingly trivial detail and show its surprising relevancy. Demonstrate that you had the ability to notice the detail in the first place and then to have its significance register on your mind. If you write a paper attempting to show that a certain man pays no attention to his appearance, don't just say that he looks messy; bring up the bread crumbs in his moustache and the toe protruding through the hole in his sneaker. Too trivial? Not at all. As long as the details support the thesis, they add life to the paper.

Use Specific Language

Another principle of most good writing is of particular importance in description. The effect of a specific detail can be weakened if the language used to present that detail is not itself specific. *There were bread crumbs in his mustache* shows observation of specific details. *Forgotten bread crumbs, slowly hardening in his mustache, had the same revolting inappropriateness as mustard stains on a silk blouse* shows observation of specific details dramatized by specific language.

Stress the Psychological Impact of What You Describe

A good description will be accurate, but it will be exciting, too. Your description of a dusty old room won't convey a sense of immediacy by itemizing the locations of all the clumps of dust. Your reader should have not only a picture of what the room looks like but also a strong sense of how depressed or indignant or philosophical the room made you feel.

So much for emotional appeal.

ORGANIZATION

Choose an appropriate organizing principle and stick to it. Some authorities suggest that in describing the appearance of a person, the writer might start with the head and go down to the toes (or vice versa). In describing a landscape, the writer might start with objects farthest away and progress to those closest. Many writers should be able to do better. The authorities want to achieve order but sometimes seem to invite rigidity.

Still, the authorities have a case, and cautious agreement with them is the only reasonable course. Nobody wants rigidity, but chaos is even worse. Certainly, a writer needs enough of a predetermined organizing principle to decide which descriptive details come first and which come last. It's easy to understand hesitation about the cut-and-dried mathematics of top-to-bottom or far-to-near, but not all the formulas need to be that definite. Some description papers may be organized on a looser principle, such as attractive features/ unattractive features, first impressions/second impressions, impact on senses like sight, touch, and hearing. Structure of some kind is necessary. In addition, even the top-to-bottom and far-to-near principles seldom turn out to be as dreary as they sound. A good writer, after all, doesn't ordinarily make formal announcements such as "moving down from the forehead, I shall now discuss the nose" or "The next closest object is. . . ." Don't adopt an organizing principle that makes a prisoner of you and your reader, but do adopt a principle. There's freedom of choice, but you have to make a choice.

THE PERSUASIVE PRINCIPLE

The description paper must commit itself to the discipline of the persuasive principle. With all this material on freedom and emotional appeal, this last point is particularly important. It's precisely because of the relatively free-form nature of much descriptive writing that the persuasive principle has to be insisted on so strongly. Freedom and sloppiness are not the same. Thesis and support of thesis are the main ingredients for holding the description paper together. Without a thesis, a process paper (see Chapter 5) can still trace a process. Without a thesis, a description paper goes off in all directions and disintegrates into a shapeless mass. It doesn't describe; it simply takes inventory. Without a thesis, a description paper has no backbone and, like a body without a backbone, has no freedom to do or be anything.

There's not much this book can say about the general nature of the persuasive principle that it hasn't already said. Throughout much of Chapter 1, the book showed how a paper on education was narrowed down to a description of Professor X with the thesis "Professor X is a classic absentminded professor."

On page 11, a sample opening paragraph showed how such a paper might begin. A description paper doesn't merely benefit from a thesis. It needs one in order to exist.

WRITING SUGGESTIONS FOR DESCRIPTION THEMES

Some of the suggested topics that follow are more specific than usual, but don't feel hemmed in. Use them only as starting points for your own ideas. Notice that many topics can be treated in two different ways. You can write a description of a general or composite type of airline flight attendant or lifeguard or hospital waiting room, having no one specific person, place, or thing in mind. You can also write a description of an *individual* person, place, or thing: lifeguard Susan Early, the waiting room at St. Luke's, the antique mirror from the yard sale.

1. Street musicians
2. Know-it-all car mechanics
3. Traffic jams
4. Lifeguards
5. Spoiled children
6. Garage sales
7. People eating lobster or corn on the cob
8. Thunderstorms
9. Librarians
10. Animals in the zoo
11. Bus drivers
12. Airline flight attendants
13. Video game fanatics
14. Normally busy places, now deserted
15. People waiting in line
16. Disadvantaged children
17. Intoxicated people
18. Campus hangouts
19. The contents of a pocketbook
20. Overcommercialized tourist attractions
21. Housing developments
22. Amusement parks
23. SUVs
24. Sports stadiums

VISUAL PROMPT

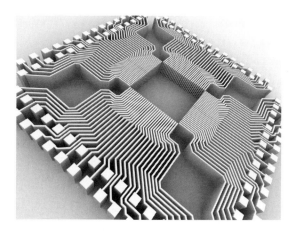

Writing Prompt

Demonstrate that you have the ability to notice detail and to have its significance register. The computer chip in this photograph is a tiny detail with enormous significance. Describe something small that has a huge impact.

STUDENT ESSAY: MASTER OF BAD MANAGEMENT

Robynn Patrick

Thesis: In the course of the average evening, my manager displays every trait of a bad boss.

    I. Initial image
        A. tacky clothes

    II. Greeting
        A. insults
        B. cursing

    III. Pre-shift meeting
        A. abuse
        B. double-standard
        C. yelling

    IV. The shift
           A. lack of assistance
           B. more insults
           C. laziness

    V. End of shift
           A. accepting bribes

They come in many shapes and sizes. They can be immature, unfair, vindictive, unhelp-ful, or lazy. They might show favoritism, fail to recognize a job well done, sexually harass employees, belittle, neglect, or manipulate. They sometimes drive you to despair, and sometimes make you furious. One special member of this varied breed is my current manager, Mike Joyce. He can flaunt almost every trait of a bad boss in just a single night at the restaurant where we work.

    At five foot nine, Mike is not physically imposing, but his sleazy tackiness assaults you. His tangerine shirt paired with its crisp Miami Vice white jacket is blinding. He accessorizes with a huge belt buckle and a mammoth boar's tusk necklace. When I arrive at work, I can't avoid noticing him; it's like involuntarily slowing down for a car wreck.

    As soon as I walk through the door, not yet clocked in, he spots me. Immediately he slithers toward me, his slicked back hair leaving a trail of grease in his wake. "You forgot to clock out last night, shit-for-brains!" My night, like every night, begins with yelling and insults.

    "I'm sorry, the computers were down, and I couldn't."

    "No one else seemed to have a problem," he retorts.

    "Well, I was the last one here and the system crashed before I could. . . ." I'm still trying to explain as he dismissively waves his hand and slides off with a huff and smirk.

    I arrive at the mandatory pre-shift meeting with the other servers, the bussers, and the bartenders. The chef tries to go through the menu, and the managers are supposed to make the staff aware of important news. But, since I'm cursed to work for Mike Joyce, the meeting serves up a hot steaming cup of negativity soup. "You are the laziest staff I have ever worked with!" I can smell putrid cigarette smoke seething from his mouth as he berates the group. "At lunch today there were fifteen dirty tables and not one server bothered to help the bussers." In silence I wonder why he would count the number of dirty tables, but not help the bussers *himself*. "I went in the back and saw three servers eating soup! Fifteen dirty tables, and three servers eating soup! You are all pathetic!" As he pounds his fist on the table and shouts, tiny drops of spit shower the employees sitting nearby. "Unacceptable!" he barks, as the wine glasses bounce like scared children during an earthquake.

    The shift is doomed from the start, and Mike makes a special effort to send the night further into the pits. The kitchen is slow, we are out of the wines that guests are ordering, and I get all my tables at once. I limp and scrimp by most of the night, but eventually I get overwhelmed and make the mistake of asking Mike for help. I plead,

"Can you help me? Table thirty-one needs another napkin." I haven't even finished my request when he shrugs and says, "You can't handle it, huh?" As he swaggers off, his Payless Shoe Source shoes squeak every other step and he says, to no one in particular, "Robynn has a hard time selling bread and water to tables." (These items are complementary.) When I finish gathering the items my guests need and head back out to the dining room, I spy Mike lounging against the bar, coolly sipping a drink while telling a joke to some of his friends.

He completes his master's class in bad management with a little bribery and favoritism. At the end of shift, I see another server handing Mike a fifty dollar bill and saying, "Thanks for the hook-up, bro. Keep it coming and I'll keep it flowing." Mike winks and says, "You know I take care of my squad." I quickly review the evening in my head. Bribing Server's tables were filled to capacity with guests drinking expensive wine, whereas my tables had empty chairs and notoriously stingy customers. I quickly understand: The manager has absolute control over the seating of the restaurant and Mike takes bribes to give "his squad" better tips and money making opportunities.

Mike Joyce, Master of Sleaze, ruins every night I have to work for him. Petty, corrupt, and mean, he takes pleasure in inflicting misery. I know there are other bad bosses out there, but I sincerely hope that he's one of a kind.

WINSTEAD'S BEST BURGERS

Sarah Bryan Miller

Classical music critic Sarah Bryan Miller shows the wide range of her tastes and lets a new generation in on an old pleasure by celebrating in mouthwatering detail the continuing excellence of a Kansas City institution.

✓ WORDS TO CHECK:

colloquially (paragraph 3)	aesthetic (5)	repast (7)
Elysian (3)	in situ (5)	brusque (8)
extraneous (4)		

1 They do not sell their hamburgers by the billion. You cannot "supersize" your meal. They are a household word only in Kansas City. But Calvin Trillin was right:[1] Winstead's has the world's best hamburgers.

2   Mr. Trillin, the famed foodie, made his claim nearly 30 years ago, but time has not diminished its essential truth. Winstead's makes a hamburger (or, more properly, steakburger) that is blessedly pure in its simplicity: Fresh ground high-quality lean beef–no additives!–is grilled, greaselessly, and placed upon a plain toasted bun. You may choose between a single ($1.65), a double ($2.75)

[1] Calvin Trillin's many articles about food have been collected in the books *American Fried*; *Alice, Let's Eat*; and *Third Helpings*. Trillin fans can feast on all three books in *The Tummy Trilogy* (1994).

or a triple ($3.25), cheese and lettuce extra; the patties are thin, the double is recommended. The steakburger does not come automatically loaded with slop, but ask and you shall receive. It is served half-wrapped in paper, the better to consume it without soiling one's hands, upon a sturdy china plate.

3   But the steakburger is not quite complete without its perfect complement, "the exclusive Winstead drink you eat with a spoon." Known officially as the "special chocolate malt" and colloquially as a "frosty"—a name that predates the Wendy's chain by a generation or two—the frosty is thick, chocolaty and delicious. Take a bite of steakburger; follow it with a spoonful of frosty, alternating the salty and textured with the sweet and smooth. The cholesterol police will swoon, but the sensation is Elysian.

4   The menu is limited, and not much changed since Winstead's opened in 1940. They now serve breakfast, and you can get what my 11-year-old daughter, a connoisseur of fast food, assures me is the best grilled cheese sandwich of her ample experience. The french fries, served in a boat-shaped china dish, are respectable and the onion rings highly thought of by those who cherish such things; the dessert menu seems extraneous to one in post-frosty bliss. Green stuff has also been added to the menu, but going to Winstead's and ordering a salad is like going to a microbrewery and ordering a Coke.

5   Winstead's original restaurant, topped by its distinctive art deco spire, sits just north of the Country Club Plaza and conveniently near another of Kansas City's centers of aesthetic excellence, the Nelson-Atkins art gallery. When Winstead's first opened, the brainchild of Katherine Winstead and her sister and brother-in-law, Nelle and Gordon Montgomery, the emphasis was on the drive-in. Drivers would pull into empty spaces, flash their lights for service, and carhops would come up and take their orders, which were then consumed in situ. "When it opened, it immediately became a gathering spot," recalls my father, Tom Miller, a third-generation Kansas Citian who as a student at nearby Southwest High School was present at the creation.

6   "We went on 'good-time' dates—a group of us would go to a movie and sit in the cheaper seats; then we'd head over to Winstead's and get a steakburger and a frosty. It was 'see and be seen'; people would go from car to car and visit, and then everybody would pull out with a grand squeal of tires. During the war, if you were lucky enough to get a furlough, the first thing you did was head for Winstead's. In spite of the wartime regulations, they kept up the quality."

7   I was introduced to the joy of frosties at the age of eight months, I am reliably informed, and never looked back; throughout childhood, a meal at Winstead's was a special treat, invariably consumed in the car, a repast dispensed from a metal tray hanging on the driver's side window. When my father decided that we would not partake of a single hamburger on a marathon car trip to and from California—just to prove that it could be done, and, perhaps, from a bit of simple cussedness—we marked the end of our journey with a celebratory feast at Winstead's. "And during the years we lived in Chicago,"

notes my father, who returned to Kansas City from his northern exile upon taking early retirement, "we always came to Winstead's when we were back on visits–and we always saw somebody we knew."

8   The original restaurant (Winstead's is now a chain, with a total of 12 outlets; the quality is most reliable at the flagship) has been remodeled and enlarged; the yellow tile exterior remains, along with the spire. The old convenience of the drive-in is gone, replaced by an office building and the new convenience of a drive-through window. But the current owners, the Haddad Restaurant Group, have kept standards up. The feel of the place is much the same, from the booths to the deco light fixtures; the jukebox still offers Glenn Miller, albeit on compact disc. The lunchtime crowd includes high school kids, older folks (my father, true to form, spots a classmate), construction workers, mothers with toddlers. The waitresses still wear pastel uniform dresses with white trim and little caps, and they are still brusque and prone to wisecracking.

9   Connie Llamas started as a carhop at the age of 18; she's been at Winstead's for 25 years. "I had more fun at the curb; you could flirt with the boys. But the place is pretty much the same. It just got bigger. People who retired and moved away come back on vacations–they think Winstead's is the place to be. And it is."

WHAT DID THE WRITER SAY AND WHAT DID YOU THINK?

1. In addition to the hamburgers, what menu items make Winstead's so outstanding?
2. Is the author's enthusiasm about the food limited in any way?
3. What does Winstead's offer beyond excellent food?
4. Are there any suggestions that Winstead's, good as it is, may no longer be all that it used to be?

HOW DID THE WRITER SAY IT?

1. Who are the "cholesterol police" in paragraph 3?
2. Why is Chicago described as a place of "northern exile" in paragraph 7?
3. How does the author make a reference to the Nelson-Atkins art gallery relevant to the rest of the essay?

What About Your Writing?

An allusion is a reference, usually brief and often indirect, to a character, event, activity, work of art, and so on, distinct from what is being discussed. In paragraph 2 of Sarah Bryan Miller's hymn of praise to Winstead's, Miller alludes to the New Testament when she writes, "The steakburger does not come automatically loaded with slop, but ask and you shall receive." In the next paragraph, she alludes to the Elysian Fields, the paradise of Greek mythology, to describe the combined taste of a burger and frosty. These references purposefully suggest an amusing connection between true divinity and the truly divine food at Winstead's. Well-managed allusions, employed sparingly—don't use them for mere showing off—can add depth to a writer's style and thought. They can reveal unsuspected resemblances, relate unfamiliar material to material the reader knows, make abstract subjects seem more specific, and help establish confidence in a writer's range of knowledge. You don't need to be an expert in any particular field to add an occasional allusion to your writing; anyone with ordinary education and some experience of life has a rich fund on which to draw:

Television: My father reminds me of Jerry Springer. Whenever I see him, he's talking.

History: The instructor gave unannounced quizzes throughout the term. Every week was another Pearl Harbor.

Movies: The stranger had Antonio Banderas eyes, an Orlando Bloom smile, and a Woody Allen physique.

Famous quotes: It's true that nothing is more powerful than an idea whose time has come, but saving the environment through recycling is an idea whose time has gone.

Sports: The administration has given up. Its game plan can be summed up in one word: Punt.

Literature: The lawyers indicated at first that we would be entitled to a beautiful tax deduction. Then they told us about Catch-22.

Advertisements: The senator can't help being embarrassed. He hasn't exactly broken his promises, but voters are starting to ask, "Where's the beef?"

I WAS A MEMBER OF THE KUNG FU CREW
Henry Han Xi Lau

Henry Han Xi Lau was a student at Yale when his article about the Kung Fu Crew was published in the *New York Times*. A later article by Lau in the online journal *Macrocosm* notes his frustration with the fact that many of the people who read his article misunderstood his definition of "ghetto." They thought he meant "gangster." What do you think?

✓ **Words to Check:**

karaoke (paragraph 3)	bok choy (4)	stalemate (8)
amble (4)	assess (4)	

1 Chinatown is ghetto, my friends are ghetto, I am ghetto. I went away to college last year, but I still have a long strand of hair that reaches past my chin. I need it when I go back home to hang with the K.F.C.–for Kung Fu Crew, not Kentucky Fried Chicken. We all met in a Northern Shaolin kung fu class years ago. Our *si-fu* was Rocky. He told us: "In the early 1900s in China, your grand master was walking in the streets when a foreigner riding on a horse disrespected him. So then he felt the belly of the horse with his palms and left. Shortly thereafter, the horse buckled and died because our grand master had used *qi-gong* to mess up the horse's internal organs." Everyone said, "Cool, I would like to do that." Rocky emphasized, "You've got to practice really hard for a long time to reach that level."

2   By the time my friends and I were in the eighth grade, we were able to do twenty-plus pushups on our knuckles and fingers. When we practiced our crescent, roundhouse, and tornado kicks, we had 10-pound weights strapped to our legs. Someone one remarked, "Goddamn–that's a freaking mountain!" when he saw my thigh muscles in gym class.

3   Most Chinatown kids fall into a few general categories. There are pale-faced nerds who study all the time to get into the Ivies. There are the recent immigrants with uncombed hair and crooked teeth who sing karaoke in bars. There are the punks with highlighted hair who cut school and the gangsters, whom everyone else avoids.

4   Then there is the K.F.C. We work hard like the nerds, but we identify with the punks. Now we are reunited, and just as in the old days we amble onto Canal Street, where we stick out above the older folks, elderly women bearing laden bags of bok choy and oranges. As an opposing crew nears us, I assess them to determine whether to grill them or not. Grilling is the fine art of staring others down and trying to emerge victorious.

5   How the hair is worn is important in determining one's order on the streets. In the 1980s, the dominant style was the mushroom cut, combed neatly or left wild in the front so that a person can appear menacing as he peers through his bangs. To gain an edge in grilling now, some kids have asymmetrical cuts, with long random strands spouting in the front, sides, or back. Some dye their hair blue or green, while blood red is usually reserved for gang members.

6   Only a few years ago, examination of the hair was sufficient. But now there is a second step: assessing pants. A couple of years ago, wide legs first appeared in New York City, and my friends and I switched from baggy pants. In the good old days, Merry-Go-Round in the village sold wide legs for only $15 a pair. When Merry-Go-Round went bankrupt, Chinatown kids despaired. Wide-leg prices at other stores increased drastically as they became more popular. There are different ways of wearing wide legs. Some fold their pant legs inward and staple them at the hem. Some clip the back ends of their pants to their shoes with safety pins. Other simply cut the bottoms so the fuzzy strings hang out.

7   We grill the opposing punks. I untuck my long strand of hair so that it swings in front of my face. Nel used to have a strand, but he chewed it off one day in class by accident. Chu and Tom cut their strands off because it scared people at college. Jack has a patch of blond hair, while Tone's head is a ball of orange flame. Chi has gelled short hair, while Ken's head is a black mop. As a group, we have better hair than our rivals. But they beat us with their wide legs. In our year away at college, wide legs have gone beyond our 24-inch leg openings. Twenty-six to 30-inch jeans are becoming the norm. If wide legs get any bigger, they will start flying up like a skirt in an updraft.

8   We have better accessories, though. Chi sports a red North Face that gives him a rugged mountain-climber look because of the jungle of straps sprouting in the back. Someone once asked Chi, "Why is the school bag so important to one's cool?" He responded, "Cuz it's the last thing others see when you walk away from them or when they turn back to look at you after you walk past them." But the other crew has female members, which augments their points. The encounter between us ends in a stalemate. But at least the K.F.C. members are in college and are not true punks.

9   In the afternoon, we decide to eat at the Chinatown McDonald's for a change instead of the Chinese bakery Maria's, our dear old hang-out spot. "Mickey D's is good sit," Nel says. I answer: "But the Whopper gots more fat and meat. It's even got more bun." Nel agrees. "True that," he says. I want the Big Mac, but I buy the two-cheeseburger meal because it has the same amount of meat but costs less.

10   We sit and talk about ghettoness again. We can never exactly articulate what being ghetto entails, but we know the spirit of it. In Chinatown toilet facilities we sometimes find footprints on the seats because F.O.B.'s (fresh off the boats) squat on them as they do over the holes in China. We see alternative brand names in stores like Dolo instead of Polo, and Mike instead of Nike.

11   We live by ghettoness. My friends and I walk from 80-something Street in Manhattan to the tip of the island to save a token. We gorge ourselves at Gray's Papaya because the hot dogs are 50 cents each. But one cannot be stingy all the time. We leave good tips at Chinese restaurants because our parents are waiters and waitresses, too.

12   We sit for a long time in McDonald's, making sure that there is at least a half-inch of soda in our cups so that when the staff wants to kick us out, we can claim that we are not finished yet. Jack positions a mouse bite of cheeseburger in the center of a wrapper to support our claim.

13   After a few hours, the K.F.C. prepares to disband. I get in one of the no-license commuter vans on Canal Street that will take me to Sunset Park in Brooklyn, where my family lives now. All of my friends will leave Chinatown, for the Upper East Side and the Lower East Side, Forest Hills in Queens and Bensonhurst in Brooklyn. We live far apart, but we always come back together

in Chinatown. For most of us, our homes used to be here and our world was here.

WHAT DID THE WRITER SAY AND WHAT DID YOU THINK?

1. What does this essay describe? Does it have a stated thesis?
2. Explain what "grilling" and "opposing crew" mean. How are encounters judged?
3. The author says, "We live by ghettoness." Does the description of the group's dispersal contradict that statement in any way?
4. What groups do you have in your culture? How would you describe them to an outsider?

HOW DID THE WRITER SAY IT?

1. Why doesn't the author define *si-fu* and *qi-gong* in the first paragraph?
2. In paragraph 7, the writer introduces his crew by describing their hairstyles. Is this enough introduction, or does the essay need more information about the crew in order to make its point?
3. Several sentences in this selection begin with "We." What's the effect of this repetition?
4. What's the organizational principle for this description?

What About Your Writing?

Henry Han Xi Lau writes with great detail, thoughtfulness, and humor. He does so many hard things so well that it's startling to find him committing a common grammatical error in pronoun agreement.

In paragraph 7, Xi Lau writes, "Nel used to have a strand, but he chewed it off one day in class by accident. Chu and Tom cut their strands off because it scared people at college." "Strands" is a plural noun. "It" is a singular pronoun; they don't go together.

It's easy to see how Xi Lau wrote himself into this particular corner. He wants to avoid writing, "Chu and Tom cut their strands off because they scared people at college," because he wants to make it clear that it is the gangster-style strands of hair–not Chu and Tom–that people find frightening. The problem is that by trying to avoid that kind of confusion, he has fallen into another kind of confusion–a problem in *pronoun agreement*. He could have avoided the difficulty by phrasing his sentence in another way:

> Chu and Tom cut their strands off because their hair scared people at college. When Chu and Tom discovered that people at college were scared by their strands, they cut them.

Another common version of the problem is when you have a noun that is grammatically singular but, in meaning, could refer to vast numbers. That gives us a reason for the error, but it's still an error. Watch out for similar errors:

Every home owner is required to recycle their trash.

No one in the theater knew what they should expect.

Each business must meet their responsibilities to the community.

See page 201 for related comments on sexist language.

MY GLOVE: A BIOGRAPHY
Stefan Fatsis

Stefan Fatsis is the author of *Word Freak* and *A Few Seconds of Panic,* about his adventures in the worlds of Scrabble and the National Football League. He talks about sports on National Public Radio and Slate.com, and writes for a variety of publications.

✓ WORDS TO CHECK:

curmudgeonly (paragraph 2)	capillary (11)
notational (2)	parabolic (12)
gruff (8)	palpable (16)
bromides (8)	discernible (21)
bon mots (8)	

1   "I'll tell you what. It's sure broken in perfect."

2   In my forty-three years on Earth, this ranks among the highest compliments I have received. Right up there, definitely top five, maybe number one. So tell me more, Bob Clevenhagen, you curmudgeonly craftsman extraordinaire, you seen-it-all, stitched-'em-all Boswell of the baseball glove, you notational archive of five-fingered leather, historical facts and figures, you Ravel of Rawlings Sporting Goods.

3   "It's broken in as well as any I ever get," Bob says. On the other end of the telephone line, I smile so hard that blood vessels threaten to pop in my cheeks. After all, Bob has been making and repairing gloves for current and future Hall of Famers for three decades. "The target for you is the base of your index finger, not the web. That's the way the pro player would do it. Not the retail market. Not a softball player."

4   Hell no! Not the retail market! Not a softball player!

5   "This looks like a major-league gamer."

6   I move from happiness to rapture. In fact, I might just cry.

7   "That's high praise," I manage to say, filling dead air when what I really want to do is drop the phone and dance.

8   "Yes, it is," Bob replies, curt, gruff, no nonsense, Midwestern. He's just the third person in the one-hundred-nineteen-year history of Rawlings to hold the exalted title of Glove Designer, not a man given to bromides and bon mots, which of course makes his words all the sweeter. "Yours looks like—well, look in the Hall of Fame."

9   I may spontaneously combust.

10   "Those gloves probably look just like yours. Same color, same shape, same faded-out look," he says. "It's just a nice-looking glove."

11   My glove isn't just broken in perfect, to quote Bob. I believe it is stunningly perfect, consummately perfect, why-would-anyone-use-anything-else? perfect. To play baseball well, you have to consider your glove an ideal; if not, it will let you down. A glove has to feel like an extension of your hand, something over which you have the motor control of a surgeon repairing a capillary. But my glove is more than just a piece of equipment that works for me. I really think it is empirically flawless.

12   Let's start with its shape: parabolic from the top of the thumb to the tip of the pinkie. This is the result of years of pushing those two fingers toward the middle; there's a slight break about three inches from the end of each digit. No ball is leaving my glove because it bent back one of the outermost fingers.

13   When I put the glove on, the first thing I inevitably do is press down the index finger. This transforms the parabola into a circle. Open your palm and spread your fingers wide. Now curl your fingertips forward. That's what my stationary glove looks like.

14   My glove is soft. It collapses of its own accord when set down. But, thanks to its aforementioned shape, it never falls completely flat, full thumb atop full pinkie. Instead, the tip of the thumb and the tip of the pinkie touch delicately, like God reaching out to Adam on the ceiling of the Sistine Chapel. I've never understood gloves that open to a V and shut like a book. The idea is to catch a round ball, not a triangular block. Roundness is essential. Softness is, too. The trick is to create a glove pliable enough to respond to your slightest movement. To bend to a player's will, a glove needs to bend. Mine does.

15   The index finger of my left hand—I throw right-handed—lies on the exterior of the glove's back, the only digit not tucked inside. This technique provides bonus protection when catching hard-hit or fast-thrown balls. I believe it also helps me better control the glove's behavior. And it looks cool.

16   Each finger curves gently, like a suburban cul-de-sac. The adjustable loops surrounding the pinkie and thumb aren't tied too tightly, but their existence is palpable. The web isn't soft and deep so that a ball might be lost, but rather follows the natural curvature from the top of the index finger to the top of the thumb. The heel of my glove aligns with the heel of my palm. The shearling beneath the wrist strap is matted but still recognizable. There are no garish

personal adornments, just my first initial and last name written meticulously in black ink letters three-eighths of an inch tall just above the seam along the thumb. It looks as if I used a ruler to line the letters up.

17   Then there's the smell: leather, dirt, grass, saliva, sun, spring, childhood, summer, hope, skill, anticipation, achievement, fulfillment, memory, love, joy.

18   I bought my glove in the spring of 1977. I was about to turn fourteen, out of Little League and over my head in the ninety-feet-to-first-base Senior League in the inner suburb of Pelham, New York. A wall of leather graced the sporting goods store in a nearby town, soft porn in my baseball-centric world. I had to have a Rawlings—it would be my third or fourth Rawlings, one of them royal blue—because that's what major leaguers wore. And it had to be a good one because, while every other kid pined for his turn at bat, I happily chased grounders until dark. Five feet tall and under a hundred pounds, I was a typical prepubescent second baseman: all field, no hit. An adult size glove would make me feel bigger, and play bigger.

19   My choice, the XPG6, was expensive. I remember the price as $90, though old Rawlings catalogues tell me it was probably $70 (or we were ripped off). I didn't know it then, but it was the fourth-priciest glove in the Rawlings line. Thanks, Mom, for not blinking.

20   Not insignificantly, the XPG6 reminded me of the glove my eight-years-older brother wore when he was in high school. Virtually all of my decisions at that age were influenced by my brother, who had taught me how to calculate my batting average when I was in the second grade. (At age nine, clearly my athletic prime, I hit .750, aided, no doubt, by some generous scoring.) He played shortstop and, like me, was a competent but unexceptional player. But his glove was just right: round and bendable. I didn't want his, just one like it.

21   So the XPG6 it was. It bore Rawlings's famous trademarks: HEART OF THE HIDE written inside a snorting steer stamped in the "DEEP WELL" POCKET. The TRIPLE ACTION web with a *Spiral Top* (in grade school cursive). Along the thumb, Rawlings's familiar bright-red Circle R. Next to it, another classic, the EDGE-U-CATED HEEL. Below that the patent number, 2,995,757. (And below that, my first initial and last name. And a single, mysterious, black dot.) Along the glove's heel, XPG6 stamped just above the handsome Rawlings script, with a long swooping tail on the R, itself resting atop the letters U.S.A Only the U and the top of the S are discernible today.

22   Two other marks cemented my love. Explanation is unnecessary as to why, arcing along the pinkie, FOR THE *Professional* PLAYER was so seductive. The signature's allure was less obvious. My glove was endorsed by Willie Stargell, who (a) threw left-handed, and (b) played one hundred eleven games at first base in 1976. Why his autograph—which looked fake, with penmanship-class loops and flourishes—was on what I assumed was a middle infielder's glove was incomprehensible, but I loved its cocktail-conversation quality. When you're fourteen, weird sometimes is good.

23   It's not a stretch to say that I've had a longer (and closer) relationship with my baseball glove than anyone or anything, apart, maybe, from my immediate family and a couple of childhood pals. I broke it in in the manner of the times: a couple of baseballs, string, the underside of my mattress, ceaseless play. It carried me through my last two years of organized ball, on a team sponsored by the local American Legion post.

24   A black and white team photo hangs framed on my office wall now. It's from the end of the 1977 season, and of the eighth grade. I sit smiling in the front row of wooden bleachers along the first-base line at Glover Field with my friends Peter Derby (shortstop), John McNamara (left field), and Chuck Heaphy (right field, coach's son), and a younger kid whose name I can't remember. My wavy hair wings out from under the two-tone cap with the too-high crown. Black block felt letters spell LEGION across the chests of our double-knit uniforms. We wear what are essential Detroit Tigers period road grays: black, orange, and white piping along the neck and sleeves of the buttonless jerseys, black stirrups with orange and white stripes stretched as high as possible to reveal as much of our white sanitary socks as possible. The '70s rocked.

25   The XPG6 rests on my left knee. My index finger pokes out, pointing directly at the camera lens. The leather is dark and rich. I am young and small. The twelve-inch XPG6 is new and large—much too large for me, a glove worn, I have since learned, by big league outfielders and third base-men. Joe Morgan used a ten-inch glove at second base at the time. But what did I know? (More relevant: what did the salesman know?) All that matters is that, in that photograph, the XPG6 and I look like we're starting life, which, of course, we are.

26   How did it do for me? Records of my glove's rookie year are lost to his-tory. But my 1978 Legion season is preserved on a single piece of lined white loose-leaf paper, folded inside a schedule, stored with other keepsakes in the basement. It reveals that I played in thirteen games—with nine appearances at second base, four at shortstop, and a few innings at third base and in right field—and committed five errors, two of them in our 9–4 championship-game loss to Cornell Carpet. (The stat sheet also shows that I totaled just four hits in twenty-three at-bats, an average of, ouch, .175. But that I walked sixteen times and had a robust on-base percentage of .404. Billy Beane would have given me a chance.)

27   I can still see and feel the ball rolling under the XPG6, and through my legs, during tryouts for the junior varsity the next spring, ending my competi-tive hardball career. But my glove's best years were yet to come. In college on fast but artificial turf at the University of Pennsylvania's historic Franklin Field, my glove snared line drives, grabbed one-hoppers to the shortstop side, shielded me from screaming bullets, and stated more 1–6–3 double plays than you'd expect. My team won back-to-back intramural championships, and my glove was one of the stars. Later, it performed well on the pitcher's mound

again in New York City softball leagues. It shagged hundreds of baseball fungoes[1] lofted heavenward on lazy afternoons by my best friend Jon.

28   As I aged–knee surgeries, work, a wife and daughter–my glove lay dormant most springs and summers, its color fading and leather peeling: wan, weathered, cracked. But it's always remained in sight, not stashed in a closet or buried in a box of mouldering sports equipment. Single, on a couch, in Brooklyn, the Yankees on TV–married, in Washington, in the attic, at a desk–I put on the XPG6 and whip a ball into its still-perfect pocket. My glove is a comfort.

WHAT DID THE WRITER SAY AND WHAT DID YOU THINK?

1. Why does Fatsis repeat Bob Clevenhagen's comments in paragraph 4 ("Not the retail market!" "Not a softball player!")?
2. Fatsis carefully describes how his name is printed on his glove. Why does this matter to him?
3. Why is it unnecessary for the author to explain why the words "For the professional player" were "so seductive"?
4. Are you persuaded that Fatsis' glove is perfect?

HOW DID THE WRITER SAY IT?

1. Fatsis often uses alliteration in this essay. Find and mark as many examples as you can.
2. How does Fatsis organize the many specific details he uses to describe his baseball glove?
3. Why does Fatsis add, "to quote Bob" at the end of the first sentence of paragraph 11?

What About Your Writing?

When Stefan Fatsis begins his essay with Bob Clevenhagen's assessment of his baseball glove as "broken in perfect" he is counting on his readers to appreciate Clevenhagen's status as the "Boswell of the baseball glove," and the "third person in the one-hundred-nineteen-year-history of Rawlings to hold the exalted title of Glove Designer." It's a fine quotation. It fits with Fatsis' thesis, and dialogue is always a good way to make a reader take notice, but Fatsis is doing something more important than just attracting our attention.

Fatsis is backing up his thesis by *citation of authority.* This is the term used when a writer reinforces a point by quoting or referring to sources whose view the reader must take seriously. A writer on religion quotes the Bible. A writer

---

[1] Hits made so that a fielder can practice catching.

on psychoanalysis quotes Freud. A writer on art quotes Picasso. A writer on food quotes the world's first epicure. A writer researching his baseball glove quotes the Glove Designer for the biggest glove-making company in America. "The people who should know agree with me," says the writer, no longer an isolated voice but a voice with authority. In addition, the writer conveys the valuable impression of having done a certain amount of serious research before arriving at an opinion.

The citation of authority must be combined with taste and judgment. An authority in one special field, removed from that field, is no longer an authority. Picasso's endorsement of an aftershave lotion would be of limited worth. A former star quarterback's comments about a football coach merit attention, but his feelings about instant tea or shampoos are another matter.

Comments of authorities must also be kept in context. Quoting a Supreme Court decision that the Supreme Court itself reversed ten years later is flatly irresponsible.

Finally, assuming that even within the proper field and context the authority must always be right is another danger. Most people agree that Thomas Jefferson was a great president, but his decision to make the Louisiana Purchase without consulting Congress was not necessarily correct. Citations of authority can strengthen a point; they can't prove it.

With all these necessary warnings, your own writing can profit from an occasional citation of authority. In Emerson's words, "Next to the originator of a good sentence is the first quoter of it."

ALL BY MYSELF
Tom Reynolds

Tom Reynolds has been a country music DJ, a training film and television commercial producer, and technical director for The Groundlings comedy theater. He has also produced reality television shows and cable documentaries. He claims that writing his book on depressing music was a cathartic experience and that he's currently happy—for now.

✓ WORDS TO CHECK:

errant (paragraph 1)	formative (3)	Acadian (6)
machete (1)	pastiche (5)	cataclysms (6)
vivisects (1)	modulations (6)	apocalyptic (6)
concerto (1)	clavichord (6)	tectonic (7)
bathos (1)	induce (6)	maelstroms (7)
deranged (2)	Visigoth (6)	
reminisces (3)	histrionics (6)	

Performed by Celine Dion
Released 1996 (No. 6 in the United Kingdom, no. 4 in the United States)
Originally written and performed by Eric Carmen
Released 1976 (No. 12 in the United Kingdom, no. 2 in the United States)

1 There is a stock device used in slasher films known as the "false relief." It's when the stalked and terrified heroine hears a scratching noise at a window and raises up the blind only to find an errant tree branch banging against the glass. Sighing with relief, the girl thinks she's in the clear until the machete-wielding killer crashes through an adjacent window a few seconds later and vivisects her. With this in mind, let us revisit the recorded history of "All by Myself." To whit: Eric Carmen leaves the Raspberries to pursue a solo career, and writes a really long ballad about loneliness entitled "All by Myself" based on Rachmaninoff's really long "Third Piano Concerto." That's the sound of something scratching on the window. The song becomes an unexpected top-ten hit in 1976. That's the terrified heroine raising the blind. Yet despite its bathos and faux-Russian misery, Carmen's "All by Myself" inflicts no lasting harm on the listener. That's the heroine finding a tree branch banging on the glass and sighing with relief.

2   Celine Dion doing a remake of "All by Myself" is the deranged killer crashing through the adjacent window.

The Song

3   At first Celine Dion follows Carmen's song more or less faithfully. "All by Myself" begins with a pinging piano, a device shamelessly used in that other vein-opener, Bette Midler's "The Rose." Celine reminisces about wild younger days when she never needed anybody and how "making love was just for fun." That nobody in their right mind would ever believe Celine Dion spent her formative years deflowering guys indiscriminately is beside the point. Her delivery has already sucked you in, holding you fast until there's nothing to do but wait for the moment when you know she's going to totally lose it. She laments for long-gone friends who are never home when she calls them (Trust me, Celine, they're home. It's just that with caller ID, they know it's you calling). On the song's Rachmaninoff-cursed chorus, she mournfully declares: "All by myself, don't want to live all by myself anymore. . . ."

4   Celine confesses to being racked with insecurity while considering love to be "distant and obscure," an emotion that is her only salvation yet remains out of reach. Again; "Allll byyyy myyyy-selll-elf. . . ." The chorus, repeated several times throughout the song, is so unrelenting that you can't imagine things getting any worse. But they do, because like any good horror move, Celine is building the suspense.

5   In the original version of "All by Myself," Eric Carmen adds a musical "interlude," reworking elements of Rachmaninoff's second piano concerto into a pastiche of Romantic exercises that sound like the 11 P.M. show at the Beethoven Lounge. Celine Dion skips all the classical nonsense, opting instead for the keyboard to work its way through the bridge while she gears up for the surprise assault, beginning with the dreaded BCM.

6   BCMs, or brain concussion modulations, are a standard element in most 1990s power love ballads and nobody changes key with the force of a hurricane better than Celine Dion. Modulations have been around since Bach was tempering his clavichord, but are used to add color to a composition. Celine's BCMs induce whiplash while letting her demonstrate her ability to shatter tank armor from three miles away. In "All by Myself," Celine nods to the orchestra, then launches into a BCM that sounds like a DC10 crashing into your house. From this point on, it's Visigoth time and she takes no prisoners, her vocal histrionics surpassing the blood-soaked psychic fury that slaughters the prom-goers at the end of the movie *Carrie:* "DON'T WANNA LIVE ALL BY MYSELF, BY MYSELF, ANYMOOOOOORRRRRRRRRRRE!!!" she shrieks in her Acadian wail, triggering cataclysms everywhere. By the time the song fades out, the carnage left behind is apocalyptic: Walls have buckled, foundations have crumbled, locusts are unleashed, worlds have collapsed, universes have imploded. Plus, the cable's out.

Why It's Depressing

7   Celine Dion makes the fatal error of many uber-vocalists by not performing "All by Myself" in its proper context. When recording his original version, Eric Carmen instinctively knew that he wasn't retelling the death of Socrates. Though he overstuffs it with neo-Romantic bloat, Carmen sings with a world-weary timbre that belies any attempt at overt melodrama. Ms. Dion's version, on the other hand, resembles two tectonic plates battling over a continent. Listening to her wrap her Wagnerian pipes around "All by Myself" is like watching a Huey helicopter being used on a fox hunt; it's so out of proportion to the task at hand, it's beyond criminal. True, Celine Dion made her career transforming assembly line power ballads into maelstroms of sound and fury, but her remake of Carmen's song is the audio equivalent of the firebombing of Dresden. In fact, had she been around in 1944, the Allies could've skipped the D-Day invasions and just dropped her off at Omaha Beach with a PA system so she could sing "All by Myself" until the German infantry bayoneted themselves.

WHAT DID THE WRITER SAY AND WHAT DID YOU THINK?

1. Explain what the author means when he compares the history of this song to "false relief."

2. What is the "BCM," and why is it so horrifying to the author?
3. In what way does the author find this song depressing? Is this what you usually think of as depressing music?

HOW DID THE WRITER SAY IT?

1. What techniques does Reynolds use to describe the song, given that he never specifically discusses the melody and only includes a few of the lyrics?
2. Does Reynolds do anything to placate Celine Dion fans who might be offended by this description?
3. Why does the essay end with the hyperbolic suggestion that this song, and Dion herself, could be used as a weapon?

What About Your Writing?

Tom Reynolds begins his essay with an extended comparison between a song recorded by Celine Dion and the kind of psycho-killer attack found in horror movies. The comparison is startling, but Reynolds takes us through it step-by-step until we wind up nodding our heads and thinking, "You know, he's right. The song *is* like that!" His use of this comparison works well on several levels. Its humor sets the tone for the rest of the funny piece. It associates something the reader may not be familiar with—the particular recording about which he is complaining—with something that most readers will recognize—the classic "slasher" movie. Finally, its focus on the aural qualities of the slasher movies, like trees scraping against windows and shattering glass, parallels the essay's horrified focus on the almost indescribable sounds of Dion's recording.

Comparisons can sometimes add a spark to your own writing. Instead of settling for "I was embarrassed," for example, you might try to finish off the thought with a comparison:

I was as embarrassed as a pool-room hustler hitting the cue ball off the table.

I hadn't been so embarrassed since I was six and my mother caught me playing doctor with Jimmy Fisher next door.

I was so embarrassed it was like having a simultaneous attack of dandruff, noisy stomach, and underarm perspiration.

The two most common kinds of comparisons are similes and metaphors. *Similes* make the comparison explicit by using *like* or *as*. A few words by George Orwell describe a man trampled by an elephant:

The friction of the great beast's foot had stripped the skin from his back as neatly as one skins a rabbit.

Metaphors are sometimes defined as similes without the *like* or *as*. The simile "The moon was like a silver dollar" becomes a metaphor when expressed "The moon was a silver dollar." A metaphor can be more sophisticated than that, however, and the term is best defined as a word or phrase ordinarily associated with one context that is transferred to another. Some metaphors have become part of the language—so much so that they are either hopelessly trite or barely recognizable as metaphors:

Life is a rat race.

He ought to come down from his ivory tower.

Keep your paws off me.

She has a good nose for news.

. . . branches of knowledge

. . . key to the problem

. . . legs of a table

. . . hit below the belt

Other metaphors are waiting to be created to add impact, originality, and excitement to your writing:

Cautiously, the psychiatrist started to enter the haunted castle of his patient's mind.

It was the same thing all over again. My whole life had turned into a summer rerun.

Don't ever let your dreams of scaling Mount Everest some day keep you from facing the practicalities of daily life here in Death Valley.

Two cautions are necessary. First, use comparisons in moderation; otherwise, your style, instead of becoming enlivened, will become bogged down by excess baggage. Second, don't be tempted into using the ready-made, trite comparisons that fill the language: "as easy as pie," "so hungry I could eat a horse," "like taking candy from a baby," "like a bolt out of the blue," and so on. Trite phrases, by definition, are dead, and good comparisons are intended to be life-giving.

DOUBLE TAKE
Melissa Lafsky

Melissa Lafsky is a writer and former lawyer who lives in New York City. She has been an editor at the Huffington Post, the Freakonomics blog, and she founded the blog Opinionistas.com. This essay came from that blog and was chosen for inclusion in an anthology of creative nonfiction.

✓ **WORDS TO CHECK:**

saccharine (paragraph 1)   halcyon (2)   ubiquity (2)

1 Nothing drives home the viral power of American culture like seeing it on the other side of the world. Step off a bus in the South China Sea coast, snap a picture of jutting cliffs stretching into lush forests, turn around to nab an action shot of the rustic seaside village and BAM! there's Mariah Carey writhing across a 20-foot billboard, her airbrushed cheekbones towering over roadside vendors peddling pork buns and cuttlefish balls. "In Hong Kong for One Night, Her Only Concert in Asia!" screams the English headline beneath her pillowy breasts. Walk into a Wan Chai pharmacy and you'll hear Justin Timberlake squawking and thumping over the loudspeakers. Turn on the TV and see MTV Asia's gelled veejays gushing over Leo's latest look and Paris Hilton's love life–"Does she still love Stavros? Or has she moved on?" It's enough to turn one mid-afternoon Tsingtao into a three-digit bar tab (in Hong Kong dollars, of course). Nine thousand miles of travel to new continents, and here it is, the same old saccharine carbonated crap shoved down into our gullets. Though I'll admit, there's something transcendent about watching a pasty British pop star in a plaid jumpsuit blurt, "Right, let's pimp my ride, shall we?"

2   At last we reach Vietnam, where the culture and halcyon landscape are still untouched by KFCs and Body Shops. We're in a car heading south to Cu Chi and I sigh with relief, safe at last from Pepsi and Lancôme and Tag Hauer and the cagey emptiness of pop culture ubiquity. After two hours of cruising along a dirt road, we pull through a village consisting of a few aluminum-topped houses, a crafts shop leaning heavily to one side and an open-air restaurant. A handful of patrons lounge on stools just shy of the road, drinking black coffee in clear glasses.

3   I gaze out the car window wishing I could freeze-frame moments, giving me time to absorb it all; barefoot children waving and giggling at our Western faces pressed against the windows; a small but muscular man whizzing by on a motor scooter with four feet of sugar cane packed behind his seat, all held in place with twine; rice fields stretching for miles, broken up by occasional ponds where boys gather to fish with bamboo rods; stray dogs, bored cows and mud-coated water buffalos wandering along the side of the road, oblivious to the scooters and occasional car. It's different and perfect; finally, a place that exists without the More-is-More doctrine worshipped so unequivocally in Western culture.

4   I rub my eyes, watery from the lash-singeing sunlight that doesn't seem to bother anyone but Westerners. When I open them, I see an older man (though it's impossible to guess his age–he could be 40 or 70) squatting on a patch of grass, his feet just clear of a mud puddle. He's extending an arm to point to his wares: portraits of faces on rough parchment, done in stunning detail. "LOW PRISES" boasts a cardboard sign nailed to a wooden stake. I glance at the row

of pictures depicting smiling babies, local children, farmers, a few sweating tourists and, . . .wait, what the hell?

5   "Hey guys, stop the car a sec. Look at that!" I point to the largest portrait, propped up against a bush in a prominent position. "You have got to be kidding me."

6   We sit gaping for a second at the unmistakable image—blond hair, carefully lined blue eyes, pert ski-slope nose, a set of culture-embodying features branded into our gray matter: Britney Spears.

7   "Holy crap, that's either hilarious or really sad," says one travel companion. "Please don't let that be the only example these people have of American culture."

8   "Why shouldn't it be? I'd say it's pretty accurate," I respond as he restarts the car. "Deeply and incurably depressing, maybe, but still accurate."

WHAT DID THE WRITER SAY AND WHAT DID YOU THINK?

1. Does Lafsky exaggerate her case against American culture? What evidence do you have?
2. The author begins her essay with a different image of Vietnam than the one she has at the end. Explain the difference.
3. What is the double meaning contained in Lafsky's reference to "saccharine, carbonated crap" in her first paragraph?
4. In what ways, according to this essay, is American culture "viral"?

HOW DID THE WRITER SAY IT?

1. Why does Lafsky leave the misspelling on the painter's sign uncorrected when she tells us about it?
2. What details of Vietnamese culture does the author use to support her initial impression that it is free from American influence? How would you characterize this view of a culture?

What About Your Writing?

"Step off a bus in the South China Sea coast, snap a picture of jutting cliffs stretching into lush forests, turn around to nab an action shot of the rustic seaside village and BAM! there's Mariah Carey writhing across a 20-foot billboard, her airbrushed cheekbones towering over roadside vendors peddling pork buns and cuttlefish balls," writes Melissa Lafsky in paragraph 1. The author is using *hyperbole,* deliberate exaggeration for dramatic or humorous impact. Lafsky's intent is to draw her readers' attention to the striking contrast between the glorious natural scenery of the South China Sea coast and the glorious artificiality of American popular culture. Both she and her readers are well aware that the juxtaposition of the scenery, the billboard and the peddlers, may not have been that extreme. The hyperbole helps to intrigue Lafsky's readers, persuading them to read further, and to engage their interest in the contrasts and cultural clashes that she records.

Hyperbole has been around a long time. Shakespeare uses it, for example, when Macbeth, after murdering the king of Scotland, expresses his horror and shame with these words:

> Will all great Neptune's ocean wash this blood / Clean from my hand? No, this my hand will rather / The multitudinous seas incarnadine [turn red, redden] / Making the green one red.

Stylistically, hyperbole is showy and loud; it should not be used frequently. For *occasional* special effects, though, hyperbole might sometimes help liven up your writing:

- Beware of Professor Reeves. That man eats students for breakfast and picks his teeth with their bones.
- Cynthia was hungry enough for a lunch of fifty Big Macs and two dozen chocolate shakes.
- Offer him a tax-free deal at a guaranteed 10 percent return, and he would gladly sell his mother and sister into lives of slavery.

THE LONELINESS OF ROSE

Jon Katz

Jon Katz is a journalist and technology writer, best known for his work for *Hotwired* and *Slashdot*. He has published a successful series of murder mysteries and several books about dogs, including *A Good Dog: The Story of Orson, Who Changed My Life* (2006). His articles on dogs now also appear regularly on Slate.com.

✓ **WORDS TO CHECK:**

livelihood (paragraph 2)	prerequisite (4)
citations (2)	belligerent (19)
pulverize (3)	

1   The phone rang a bit before midnight. The caller was a farmer from North Hebron, who said calmly that he had a "bit of a problem. I've got goats, sheep and cows out of the fence and onto Route 31. One of the goats has been hit by a car. I need to get the animals back in. My fence is broke in two places, at least, and I want to get them off the road. I hear you got a working dog there. I'll pay for your time."

2   Even though he was calm and conversational, I understood that there was an urgency to the call. His livelihood was wandering around on the road. More of his animals could be killed or injured, as well as the people who hit them. Fences could be torn up and damaged, citations and lawsuits to follow.

3   But I had Rose, a 34-pound, 2-year-old border collie. Rose was supremely confident and experienced around sheep. They flocked together when she appeared. But she had never herded goats and cattle, especially in the middle of the night in a strange place on a busy road. One kick from a dairy cow would pulverize her, and goats were notoriously smart and aggressive. She didn't know the farmer and she didn't know his dog, a feisty farm mutt, he said.

4   Still, I started dressing right away. I am not a farmer, but I have a farm. I have seen all of my animals pour through an open gate and into the woods. It is not a feeling I could go back to sleep and forget about. In 15 minutes, we pulled up to the farm, a sprawling old place with the prerequisite giant barns, rotting tractors and trucks, and cannibalized cars. A dead goat and a damaged car were in the middle of the road. Cows, sheep, goats, and trucks were all over the place.

5   "Good luck, girl," I said. No time to lose. Rose first charged the farmer's dog, who was barking excitedly, chasing him under a truck. Then she took on three goats, who each tried to butt her. She backed them up, nipping and charging, until they went into a pen, and the farmer locked them in.

6   She circled around behind the cows—who do not flock like sheep, but do get nervous around strange animals—and nipped at one or two from the rear, staying well behind their legs. They started to move. I called her off, and the farmer got behind them—his son out in front with a bucket of grain—and they started moving toward the barn. Rose stayed behind, barking, nipping, and charging, while I yelled, "Barn, barn!" a command we use on my farm when I wanted animals brought to the barn.

7   There were also about 25 Tunis ewes and rams, and I could see they were not "dog broke"—that is, not used to being herded by dogs. But they did flock together, a few of them coming forward to challenge Rose. This was no problem. She may be cautious around cows, but there is no sheep alive that Rose fears. She did her practiced rope-a-dope, charging and retreating. The sheep became convinced of her determination and turned and ran to the safest place—in this case, an open pasture gate held by the farmer. In a few minutes they were all inside. Two cows bellowed from across the road but Jim hopped into his pickup and honked and rattled them back across the road.

8   "Good girl," I shouted, and gave the command "Truck, up," which means get back into the car. She had brought order in less than 10 minutes. The farmer gave me a crisp $10 bill—double our usual fee—and we headed home and went to sleep. A remarkable thing to see, at least to me. No big deal for Rose.

9   I have four dogs—two border collies, two yellow Labs—and sometimes, as a student of the human-animal bond, I ask friends and acquaintances which dog, if any, they might want.

10   Three of my dogs are what you might call cute–they are pretty, love people, enjoy being held or scratched. Pearl has big brown eyes and swoons onto her back when she meets a dog-lover. Clementine adores anyone who will give her a biscuit. Izzy, my other border collie, will herd sometimes but he would rather cuddle with people, given the choice.

11   Rose is not cute. She is a working dog, a farm dog. She herds sheep, keeps the donkeys apart from the other animals during graining, alerts me when lambs are born, watches my back when the ram is around. She battles the donkeys, the ewes who protect their lambs, and stray dogs who approach the farm. She and I take the sheep out to graze two or three times a day. On Sundays, we sometimes march the flock down to the Presbyterian Church to hear the organ music and present ourselves through the big windows. "Hey, Rose," the kids sometimes shout after the service is over. With Rose, we don't need fences. As my friend Peter Hanks said, Rose is the fence.

12   Rose is a bit scrawny and ungainly looking, though quite beautiful to me. She is not like any dog I have had. She has few people skills. She does not cuddle or play. She tolerates kids, but is not fond of them. She is rarely in the same room with me, going from window to window of my farmhouse to scan for her flock. Every morning around sunrise, she hops onto my bed, gives me about 50 licks, and then disappears into a secret lair. I do not know where she sleeps. She checks on me constantly but rarely stays in the same room with me.

13   When I go to the back door, she watches to see which boots I am putting on. If I put on my barn boots, she joins me. If I put on my walking shoes, she stays in the house. When I had spinal troubles, Annie, my farm manager, walked the dogs for me. All of them went eagerly, except Rose. She sat on the foot of my bed day and night, going out only if I hobbled to the back door to let her out. She will take the sheep out for me, sitting in the meadow across the street watching them for hours.

14   I could not live on my farm without Rose. When the shearer came, Rose escorted the shorn sheep out of the barn one by one. When the vets come, they ask Rose to hold animals in a corner until they can grab them and tie them down. "Rose is the most useful dog I know," the vet told me.

15   Rose is on call 24/7 for farmers who don't have the money to buy a dog like her or the time to train one. We have rounded up many cows, stray goats, and sheep. Last winter, when a gate broke, a desperate farmer with 400 dairy cows called me in the middle of the night. He heard I had a working dog and we rushed to his farm. Rose stood at the open gate, facing down the herd of 1,200-pound cows for two hours. Some of the cows nosed up to Rose, curious. They got nipped. She was not their friend, she seemed to be saying. Not a one made it through.

16   A widow in Cossayuna was surprised by a blizzard and couldn't get her sheep in to the barn in time. Rose rushed to the scene and did it in five minutes. We usually charge $5 for these emergency calls for the pride of the farmers and

the honor of Rose. She has earned $240, which sits in a basket. Most of the money will go to a border collie rescue group I belong to. The rest will buy a big steak bone for Rose.

17   Last year, Rose was kicked by Lulu, one of my donkeys. She sent the dog flying, bounding off the barn wall. I thought Rose was dead. She wasn't. Since that day, Rose has never entered the pasture without nipping Lulu in the butt. Lulu considered another kick, but could never get the right angle.

18   I worry about Rose. She has been torn up by barbed wire, impaled herself on posts and sharp rocks, slid and rolled down steep hills. I often see her limping (never for long), licking an unseen wound, or nursing torn paw pads, or I find scabs covered by her fur. When she lets me, I stroke and brush her and tell her how much I love and appreciate her. She will softly lick my hand and face. Sometimes, at night, even though she fights it, I see her eyes close as she slips into a deep sleep.

19   A few weeks ago, a breeding ram was delivered. He was reportedly assertive and belligerent, as rams are expected to be. We brought him through a gate with the other sheep and my donkeys: Lulu, her sister Fanny, and grumpy Jeannette, who had just unexpectedly given birth to Jesus, a baby boy, and was ferociously protective of him.

20   Rose had to maneuver through the donkeys–two of which were dying to clobber her. She had to deal with the ram, too, who came off the trailer charging at her. She raced around and grabbed his privates, and when he groaned and grunted, ran around and nipped him on the nose. She spun him around and around for five minutes–keeping an eye on the donkeys and the sheep– until he ran into the middle of the flock of ewes and hid. Then she ran over and nipped Lulu on the butt, staying away from Jeannette and the baby. She gathered the sheep and the ram and moved them into the next pasture. In a few minutes, everyone was calmly munching on hay or grass.

21   Rose comes from Colorado, from a herding line. Her favorite spot–when she is not working, which is her favorite thing–is to sit in the garden, rain, cold, snow, or sun, and watch her sheep. She sometimes seems lonely to me. I think there is perhaps a price to pay for letting a working dog work: A working dog can't be a pet, at least not in the conventional sense of the term. She does the things I need, but few of the things that often please us most about dogs– snuggling, playing, tagging along, making friends with dogs and people.

22   Often, I will look out and see her blanketed in snow and ice. When I drive the ATV, the other dogs like to hop in the back rack and ride with me. Rose always runs ahead. When we walk in the woods, she is always in front, alert for chipmunks, birds, squirrels, or deer. When kids walk up the road from school, they line up to pet the dogs. Rose never comes up to say hello, and they never look for her.

23   I have asked about 200 people which of my dogs they would like to have. Only two have mentioned Rose.

WHAT DID THE WRITER SAY AND WHAT DID YOU THINK?

1. On which of Rose's characteristics does the essay focus?
2. Explain the conclusions you draw from paragraphs 12 and 13, which describe Rose's habits.
3. At the end of the essay, Katz says that only two people have ever said they'd choose Rose out of his pack of dogs. Is this essay designed to change anyone's mind?
4. Does the description persuade you that Rose is lonely? In what way?

HOW DID THE WRITER SAY IT?

1. The essay begins with a narrative passage about a specific job that Rose did. Why does the author include this lengthy story?
2. Katz ends the opening story with two sentence fragments: "A remarkable thing to see, at least to me. No big deal for Rose." What's the effect of these fragments?
3. Why does the author baldly state that "Rose is not cute"?
4. Locate some specific sentences or phrases designed for emotional appeal. What emotions do these descriptions appeal to?

What About Your Writing?

When you read Katz's essay "The Loneliness of Rose," it's clear that Katz's thesis is that Rose is the best dog he owns, and that her talents, loyalty, and work ethic are underrated by those who prefer cuddlier, more outgoing dogs. But Katz never says so. At no point in this essay does Katz ever state his thesis.

Sometimes the thesis of an essay—like this one—is so obvious to the reader that it doesn't matter much whether an author specifically states it. Every piece of evidence, every supporting detail, every bit of description that Katz puts into the piece makes his thesis clear. He doesn't need to underline it for you any more than a mother who says, "The baby's been coughing, sniffling, and running a fever all day. I'm calling the doctor," needs to state her thesis: "The baby is sick." Any reasonable person would reach the same conclusion. It doesn't need saying.

For an unstated thesis to work, though, it has to be that apparent. When it isn't, it leaves your reader asking, "What's the point of this essay? Why is this guy so interested in a dog?" So, before you even think of experimenting with an unstated thesis, you should be positive that you know how to write a good paper with a traditional, stated thesis. Then you should let your instructor know that you'd like to experiment with an unstated thesis. Only then should you try it—with caution.

CHAPTER 3½

Office Hours: Notebooks: The Writer's Savings Account

Professional writers rarely, if ever, start the day hoping that they will find something to write about. They certainly don't spend time sighing and waiting for what nonprofessionals call "inspiration." They sit down and write. One reason they can get straight to it, of course, is that if they don't write, they and their families will go hungry. Another reason is that they all keep *notebooks*. You don't need to have aspirations to be a professional writer to benefit from their examples. A notebook is any writer's savings account, and when you need to do some writing, it's smart to have plenty of goodies tucked away in the bank.

Don't confuse notebooks with journals. Some instructors, aware that serious writers write every day, not just when they're in the mood, encourage or require the keeping of journals. Students are told not to worry about organization, spelling, grammar, and style but simply to write down what is on their minds every day. One page recites the day's events, another a complaint about cafeteria food, another a romantic misadventure, another a few words about the weather. Journal-keeping certainly helps foster the habit of writing every day, but opinions vary greatly on what else they actually do—or don't do—to improve a student's work.

A notebook is not a record of the comings and goings of your passing thoughts. It is your major resource for future writing. The basic idea is that when something useful or potentially useful to your writing pops into your mind, *write it down*. Write it down or you'll forget it. Write it down even though you have no idea at the time if you'll ever do anything with it. Write it down often enough and you'll rapidly develop a large savings account, ready for withdrawals at any time. Your writing problem, should you have one, will not be having a blank mind but having to decide which writing opportunity to choose from the many available.

You'll write down possible topics, of course. The important difference is that such topics normally pop into our heads unannounced and then disappear forever five or ten seconds later. When you write them down, they stay there. And remember that few topics come to us full grown. You see something or feel something sad or funny or beautiful, and—who knows?—it could grow into a topic someday. Write it down.

Don't forget ideas for titles, an overheard wisecrack, a moving quotation, an original phrase that suddenly comes to you. They all belong in your notebook. So do all the other things that will have meaning only to you but that might become the heart of a fine paper someday: the name of a treasured relative, a hated food, a favorite song. Remember that you won't be worrying any more than in a journal about correctness or even coherence for anyone other than yourself. You may only need to write down two or three words for many of the entries. In a notebook, you're not trying to share your thoughts. You're trying to save them. For example:

tribute to Uncle Ernie

worst movie ever?

behavior of people in traffic jams

more help for foreign students

vegetables I hate? love?

"Nothing so became him in his life as his leaving of it."

between-meal snacks—my downfall

We close with a few practical suggestions: Make your notebook something you can always carry around with you. A small spiral pad that can fit in a pocket is fine. Don't use index cards—they're too easy to lose. Keep your notebook at your bedside. Ideas can turn up at night, and they will always vanish by morning. Finally, when one cheap pad is filled, buy another. You'll be certain to enjoy looking through the old one. It's like rich people counting their money.

Examples

An example is a single item drawn from a larger group to which it belongs. An example also is often viewed as one of a number of specific cases in which a generalization turns out to be true. Smog is one of many possible examples of pollution. Chicken pox is an example of a childhood disease. The egg yolk on Bill's necktie is an example of his sloppy eating habits. The bald eagle is an example that backs up the generalization that endangered species can sometimes be preserved. The French Reign of Terror is an example that supports the idea that violent revolutions often bring about further violence. (The preceding five sentences are examples of examples.)

It's hard to write a good paper of any kind without using at least some examples. Examples *clarify* a writer's thought by bringing remote abstractions down to earth:

> The American Civil War was not all the romantic valor we read about in story-books. It was the horrors of trench warfare, the medical nightmare of wholesale amputations, and for the South, at least, the agony of slow starvation.

Examples also *add interest*. The most humdrum generalization can take on new life if supported by effective examples. Specific details described in specific language are at the heart of almost all good writing, and examples by their very nature are specific:

> My father is probably the most dangerous cook in the world. He burns toast. He burns scrambled eggs. He burns water. When he puts leftovers in the freezer—you guessed it—they get freezer burn. Dad even managed, on one memorable occasion, to lose control of the kitchen so badly that he burned the bottom of a pan, the side of his hand, and the cookbook he was using, all at once.

Examples help *persuade*. Without the help of examples, many perfectly valid statements can be perceived as dismal echoes of ideas the author has heard somewhere but never thought about seriously. If the writer of the following paragraph had omitted the examples, there would be no way to evaluate the merits of the complaint:

> Routine city services are in a terrible state. The freeway from West 50th Street to the Downtown exit has been filled with gaping chuckholes since early spring. Rat-infested, condemned, and abandoned buildings still line

Water Street despite three-year-old promises to tear them down. Last week the papers reported the story of a man who called the police about a burglar entering his home—and got a busy signal.

An example essay is one that relies entirely on examples to support its thesis. The ordinary pattern for an example essay is elementary, though bear in mind that no pattern should be followed blindly. A first paragraph presents the thesis. A varying number of paragraphs—depending on the subject, complexity of thesis, and material available to the writer—then establishes through examples the validity of the thesis. A concluding paragraph reinforces or advances the thesis. The pattern seems simple, and it is.

What isn't quite so simple is seeing to it that all the examples are relevant and persuasive.

Are There Enough Examples to Support Your Thesis?

Three examples may sometimes be enough. A hundred may be too few (and in that case you've made a poor choice of thesis for an example essay). Common sense is your best guide. Three in-depth examples of overly sentimental deathbed scenes from a Dickens novel may be enough to establish that Dickens had trouble with deathbed scenes. A hundred examples of middle-aged men with protruding stomachs will not even begin to establish that most middle-aged men have potbellies. As a general rule for a paper of 500 or so words, choose a thesis that can be supported adequately with no more than fifteen examples, unless your instructor tells you otherwise. Don't use fewer than three examples unless you're extremely confident about the virtues of your paper. Remember, too, that the fewer the examples, the more fully each one needs to be developed.

Are the Examples Fairly Chosen?

Your reader must be convinced that the examples represent a reasonable cross section of the group with which you are dealing. Choose typical examples; anyone can load the dice. You may have an imposing number of dramatic examples showing that the downtown business area of a city is deserted and dying, but if you drew all the examples from only one street or from visiting the area on a Sunday afternoon, you would not have played fair. Plan your paper with the notion of a cross section constantly in mind. If you're generalizing about teachers in your school, try to pick examples from different departments, age groups, sexes, and so on. If you're attacking television commercials, make sure your examples include significantly different products; otherwise, you might wind up convincing your reader that only ads for soaps and detergents are bad.

Have You Stuck to Your Thesis?

One way to lose sight of your thesis has just been described. Poorly selected examples, besides creating an impression of unfairness, may support only part of the thesis; one writer demonstrates that only a single block is deserted and dying, not the whole downtown area, and another shows that commercials about laundry products are offensive, not commercials in general.

A second, but equally common, way of drifting off is to forget you are writing an example paper. A writer starts out well by providing examples establishing the idea that "routine city services are in a terrible state." Halfway through the paper, however, the writer gets sidetracked into a discussion of the causes for this condition and the steps the average citizen can take to remedy it. The writer thus manages to produce a paper that is 50 percent irrelevant to the declared thesis.

Have You Arranged Your Examples to Produce the Greatest Impact?

In planning your paper, you've limited your subject, developed a thesis, and jotted down many examples. You've also eliminated irrelevant and illogical examples. Now how do you handle those that are left? Which comes first? Which comes last?

Unless you're superhuman, some of the examples you're going to use will be clearly superior to others. As a general principle, try to start off with a bang. Grab the attention of your reader as soon as possible with your most dramatic or shocking or amusing or disturbing example. If you have two unusually effective examples, so much the better. Save one for last: Try to end with a bang, too.

A large number of exceptionally strong examples can also lead to a common variation on the orthodox pattern of devoting the first paragraph to a presentation of the thesis. Use the first paragraph instead to present one of the strongest examples. (Humorous anecdotes often work particularly well.) Stimulate curiosity. Arouse interest. Then present the thesis in the second paragraph before going on to the other examples.

Paragraphing in itself is important throughout the essay to help the reader understand the nature of your material and the logic of your argument. With a few well-developed examples, there's no problem. Each should get a paragraph to itself. With a great number of examples, however, there's some potential for difficulties. Each example will probably be short—one or two sentences, let's say—because you're writing an essay of only a few hundred words, not a term paper. If each of these short examples gets a separate paragraph, the paper is likely to be extremely awkward and choppy to read. Even without that burden, the physical appearance alone of the page can bother most readers: Before getting to the actual reading, they will have thought of the paper as a collection of separate sentences and thoughts rather than as a unified composition.

The solution to this paragraphing problem is to gather the many examples into a few logical groups and write a paragraph for each group, not for each example. Suppose you have fifteen good examples of declining city services. Instead of writing fifteen one-sentence paragraphs, you observe that four examples involve transportation; five, safety; three, housing; and the rest, pollution and sanitation. Your paragraphing problems are over.

¶ 1 Thesis: *Routine city services are in a terrible state.*

¶ 2 *Transportation*

   Example 1–Higher fares for same or worse service

   Example 2–No parking facilities

   Example 3–Poor snow removal

   Example 4–Refusal to synchronize traffic lights downtown

¶ 3 *Safety*

   Example 1–Unrepaired chuckholes

   Example 2–Unrepaired traffic lights

   Example 3–Busy signals at police station

   Example 4–Slow response when police do come

   Example 5–Releasing of dangerous criminals because of overcrowding
        at city jail

¶ 4 *Housing*

   Example 1–Decaying public projects

   Example 2–Abandoned buildings not torn down

   Example 3–Housing codes not enforced in some neighborhoods

¶ 5 *Pollution and sanitation*

   Example 1–Flooded basements

   Example 2–Litter in public parks

   Example 3–Increase in rats

¶ 6 *Conclusion*

WRITING SUGGESTIONS FOR EXAMPLE ESSAYS

Write an example essay supporting one of the following statements or a related statement of your own.

1. Life in [your town] is not as bad as it's cracked up to be.
2. Some teachers try too hard to identify with their students.
3. Junk food has many virtues.
4. Corruption is part of the American way of life.

5. Teenage marriages are likely to end unhappily.
6. People express their personalities through the clothes they wear.
7. Baby boomers are obsessed with staying young.
8. Children's television programs display too much violence.
9. A student's life is not a happy one.
10. Members of the clergy are complex human beings, not plaster saints.
11. You can tell a lot about people from their table manners.
12. Student government is a farce.
13. Apparent nonconformists are sometimes the worst conformists.
14. Everyone loves to gossip.
15. Many people never learn from their mistakes.
16. The effort to succeed is more satisfying than success itself.
17. Even at their best, most people are basically selfish.
18. The road to hell is paved with good intentions.
19. Taking care of a pet can be a great educational experience for children.
20. Newspapers rarely bother to report good news.

VISUAL PROMPT

Writing Prompt

An example is a single item drawn from a group to which it belongs. Cupcakes are an example that helps to support our thesis that everything that tastes good is bad for you. Can you think of a few more examples that support or argue against this thesis?

STUDENT ESSAY: BROKE AND BORED: THE SUMMER JOB
Ashley Hall

Thesis: Summer jobs are a low-paying and tedious waste of time.

    I.   Bussing Tables

   II.   Tutoring Math Students

  III.   Babysitting

  IV.   Newspaper Reporting

   V.   Trimming Christmas Trees

 VI.   Serving Food Samples

Conclusion: The only summer jobs that are worthwhile come with snacks.

My parents were committed to showing their kids the value of a hard earned dollar. At the end of each school year, immediately following final exams, my siblings and I were quickly shoved out the front door to earn our keep. Grinning tightly, our parents directed us to find an acceptable summer job, and then they shut and locked the door behind us. While my sister managed to stick with the same employer year after year, I never found a job I wanted to go back to. As a result, I've had many summer jobs, all of which have taught me that summer jobs are usually a low-paying and tedious waste of time.

My first summer job was bussing tables at Bob's Big Boy where the average tip from the local patrons typically never reached beyond 26 cents. I was usually tasked with the absurdly dull and messy job of combining the contents of the ketchup containers when any of them were low. Inevitably I splashed my clean white shirt with a smattering of ketchup which was often mistaken for blood by the customers. Incidentally, Big Boy restaurants are all equipped not only with buffets, germ cesspools, and blue hair, but also with very slippery tile floors. Together with my natural clumsiness, I could never seem to keep my feet underneath me for an entire shift. The unfortunate events happened when this would coincide while I was holding a tray of food. Dumping a full tray of food into a customer's lap was a great way to get sent home early though!

Reprinted with permission from the author.

One summer I tutored middle school students in math after school. Unsurprisingly this looked a great deal like mandatory detention. From 2:30 pm–4:30 pm three times a week, while all the other kids were outside playing flag football or softball, my students were trapped inside a sterile classroom with sticky desktops, florescent bulbs burning an orange-yellow hue into their retinas, and continuous interruptions from the school secretary demanding that Rick Sczykutowicz report to the office immediately or face unthinkable consequences. Until they had mastered each painful step of long division, my students were imprisoned with me for six hours a week in what was referred to as the *Math Recovery* program. At least once every day, the inevitable question was asked, "Why do I have to know this when my calculator can do it a lot faster?" Even now I don't have a good answer.

I had countless summer jobs babysitting when I was in high school. Each time desperate parents called me to watch their kids, I wondered how many others turned them down. There was one family who asked me to watch their three rambunctious boys for a few hours. While there, the boys talked me into loading raw eggs into a sling shot and launching them at the neighbor's dog. We were too busy aiming to notice their parents driving up behind us. Needless to say this job, like most of my babysitting, was a one-time gig.

My first summer during college, I took a job as a newspaper reporter, which often required posing as an experienced photographer in addition to writing the article. Armed with my very own disposable camera, I would drive for hours tracking down the resident farmer whose grandson had just won the blue ribbon at the county fair for growing the largest squash. At twenty cents per word, and following severe cuts from my editor, my longest article barely produced a paycheck large enough to cover the gas I'd used, and none of my articles ever saw a page number lower than 9.

I spent a summer working with my brother trimming evergreen trees at one of the many Christmas tree farms in town. My brother and I could hardly believe our good fortune on the first day when the owners equipped each of us with a machete, a water bottle and a box lunch, and sent us off to shape trees into the perfect triangular shape we were shown during training. Instead we staged sword fights and hosted free samurai training for our fellow soldiers. This would have been a great job, but the occasional shock of swinging a machete into a hidden bee's nest was always enough to ruin my week, especially when coupled with the requirement of long sleeves and pants. Hot and itchy makes for a long summer.

The only summer job I ever really liked was serving food samples at Costco. Reporting for duty, the cuisine sampling queens would line up in the back supply room to receive our daily assignments. I caught on early that the food sample assignments were typically given towards the end of the line. While my counterparts, who were easily triple my age, were given *Spot Shot Carpet Cleaner* or *Oxy Clean Laundry Detergent* to sample, I was assigned lobster ravioli and imported cheese.

Summer jobs are useless and tedious. But every now and again there is one that comes with something that makes it worthwhile—like gourmet snacks. I'm not sure that's the lesson my parents intended to teach me, but it's the one I learned. Next summer I'll be working at the local candy store, dipping strawberries into chocolate for the tourists. I'm sure I'll manage to sample one or two along the way.

ALWAYS SETTLE SCORES AT NOON
Robert Fulford

Robert Fulford is a Toronto author, journalist, broadcaster, and editor who writes a weekly column for the *National Post.* He is the author of several books on film, culture, and Canada.

✓ WORDS TO CHECK:

garret (paragraph 1)   mandatory (15)
incriminating (11)   hysterical (16)
suave (14)

1 The great thing about Paris is that you can always see the Eiffel Tower from your room, whether you're an artist in a tiny garret or a millionaire in a first-class hotel. Just look out the window and there it is. We who have spent much of our lives at the movies know this to be a fact, having seen it demonstrated on many occasions.

2   That's a perfect example of Movie Wisdom, the information we absorb inadvertently while sitting in the dark. We may go to the movies to enjoy the actors and the stories, but the experience also enlarges our view of the world. In early autumn, when the Toronto International Film Festival comes around again, it reminds me of how much the movies have taught me.

3   Fans of traditional western movies, for example, know that the gunmen on the American frontier settled their disputes fair and square, meeting in one-on-one main-street pistol duels, ideally at noon. I was shocked when Elmore Leonard said he made it a rule to omit that scene from the western books and movies he wrote. He claims no one would ever be so foolish as to do that.

4   While his opinion may seem reasonable on the surface, it appears overly literal to me. I'm sticking with the Movie Wisdom version. It has tradition behind it.

5   Over the last 25 years or so the movies have also taught me that there's no such thing as a good man who is also rich. Years ago, a rich man of good character would occasionally show up in a movie, though always in disguise. If several young women working in a department store met by accident a man who appeared to be poor, he would later turn out to be the store's owner. But since stores are now owned by giant corporations, it's been many years since the movies depicted a capitalist with admirable qualities. Today rich men spend most of the time hiring lawyers to save their drug-dealing, murdering sons from justice.

6   As for corporations, we know they never follow their own stated principles. What they do, mainly, is poison the public with industrial waste.

7   It's not hard to follow the plot of a movie, once you have a little practice.

8   For instance, you can be sure that the nicest, sweetest, most helpful character who appears in the early scenes will likely die before the end (providing he or she is not a star).

9   As soon as we identify someone as a CIA agent, we know he's concocting an evil plot. He's almost certainly the member of a rogue faction in the agency, scheming to place its candidate in the presidency.

10   If we are watching a movie about people in Biblical times, we can expect that they will sometimes wear ragged clothes but their teeth will always be perfect.

11   If a baseball player goes up to bat in Yankee Stadium, he can always spot his girlfriend, sitting somewhere in the crowd, so that they can exchange loving glances before he wins the game with a home run. If a detective disregards his superior's order and sneaks illegally into an office in search of incriminating information, he will almost certainly find it in the first file drawer he opens.

12   Chauncey Gardiner, played in 1979 by Peter Sellers in Jerzy Kosinski's film *Being There*, had the same problem. A simple-minded gardener employed by a rich man, he knew nothing of life except what he learned by watching television during his free hours. When he was fired and forced to live on his own, he became famous for his wise sayings ("Spring is a time for planting") but had trouble managing personal relations. When Shirley MacLaine tried to interest him in a love affair, he found it impossible to meet her expectations. Films on television had not shown him how.

13   Even so, it's in the matter of romance and courtship that Movie Wisdom provides the most helpful guide to life. It teaches us that if a man and a woman intensely dislike each other when they meet, they will soon fall in love and marry. It warns us that if a girl has sex just once, she'll for sure get pregnant, particularly if she's only 16. When a baby is about to be born, the important thing is to boil a lot of water. Who could do without this information?

14   The late Pauline Kael, many years ago, was asked how movies affected political opinions. They had no influence on politics, she said, but in private life they were crucial. She could remember when the first great performances of Cary Grant in the 1930s transformed the behavior of boys. By his example, Grant taught boys the essence of suave behavior on a date. No one ever did anything nicer for girls. "Every boy became a better date," as Kael recalled.

15   When screen directors began to choose elegant restaurants as the favorite setting for emotional encounters, they instructed us on proper conduct in public. We learned that it is permissible, in fact it is sometimes mandatory, to order a big meal and eat almost none of it. Certainly it is a fast rule, obeyed by all movie characters, that no one ever finishes a drink unless they are ordering another one. We also discovered that when two male friends have a beer together, at least one of them, after his first gulp, will wipe his mouth on his sleeve.

16   Emotional difficulties will often arise between men and women, and Movie Wisdom can help us there, too. For instance, if a woman becomes hysterical, you slap her, for her own good, and that quickly straightens her out. I know all that. I learned it at the movies.

WHAT DID THE WRITER SAY AND WHAT DID YOU THINK?

1. Do any of Fulford's examples of Movie Wisdom strike you as inaccurate?
2. In paragraph 14, Fulford includes an anecdote about a real influence that the movies have had over real life. Why do you think he does that in an essay that shows how movies get it wrong?
3. Why does Fulford say he relies on Movie Wisdom even when there is evidence against it?
4. The final paragraph is one that some readers will find funny and others will find shocking or offensive. What do you think? Why?

HOW DID THE WRITER SAY IT?

1. Does Fulford organize his examples in any way?
2. How seriously does the author take Movie Wisdom? How do you know?
3. How does Fulford demonstrate to his readers the incompleteness of Movie Wisdom about love and sex?

What About Your Writing?

To avoid monotony, the good writer varies sentence length. Long and short sentences are neither good nor bad in themselves. Variety is the key.

In the Fulford selection, notice how paragraph 1, beginning with a sentence of thirty-three words, is followed by a very brief sentence of only nine words. Notice how those sentences are then followed by a twenty-four-word sentence. Again, the final paragraph, beginning with two sentences of seventeen and twenty-one words ends with sentences of a mere four and six words each.

Mathematical formulas are inapplicable, of course. There's no magic number of words at which a sentence ceases to be short and suddenly becomes long. There's no special point, for that matter, at which readers suddenly cease to be interested and become bored. Monotonous sentence length, however, contributes to boredom, and variety can often contribute to interest. So try to vary sentence length.

COUPLE LIES

Adair Lara

Domestic tranquility in the nation sometimes requires the U.S. government, according to the Constitution, but for domestic tranquility in marriage, "couple lies" often come in handy. Has Adair Lara, a columnist for the *San Francisco Chronicle,* discovered a new kind of lie, found a new name for an old lie, or merely dramatized a harmless aspect of human relations into seeming like a lie? Whatever the answer, married students among Lara's readers may find themselves checking the coffee and laundry in new and different ways.

✓ WORDS TO CHECK:

abashed (paragraph 1)	chronically (7)
lapse (4)	squeamish (8)

1 I discovered one morning that my husband, Bill, who buys and brews the beans for our morning coffee, had switched to decaf months ago. He had the grace to look abashed when I stormed into his bathroom and confronted him. "I didn't think you'd notice," he said, blushing.

2 The night before, I was feeling tired just as a late meeting was about to start and had the inspiration of getting a coffee bean to chew on. To my surprise, all three of our white bags of beans were marked decaf: Swiss, Columbian, Hazelnut Creme. "When were you planning to tell me?" I asked.

3 "Well, never," he said. He admitted he had reduced the amount of caffeine we were drinking gradually, over months, before cutting it out completely. "You never make the coffee, so how would you know? I had no idea you'd do a crazy thing like eat a coffee bean. I was afraid if I did tell you, you'd want the caffeine back, and I've been feeling so much better since I stopped drinking it. You're not mad, are you?"

4 Mad? Me? Of course not! I'm just glad to have an explanation for all those puzzling health problems I've been experiencing–like pounding headaches and a tendency to lapse into unconsciousness before noon.

5 It's easy to see how this sort of thing can happen. As couples march in lockstep toward the boneyard, disagreements are bound to arise. You can't agree on everything, and maybe one of you wants to give up coffee but the other either might not be ready to or hasn't thought about it. So while the two of you drink out of the same pot, one stealthily reduces the caffeine yet doesn't tell the other. As Oscar Wilde said, "If one tells the truth, one is sure, sooner or later, to be found out."

6 This is marital lying. It's not a white lie, meant to spare your feelings. It's a pink lie, a couple lie. It means: I'll make the decisions, Angelface; you just drink the coffee.

7 Everybody tells couple lies. A woman I know fills the Mountain Valley bottles with tap water when they're empty and puts them back in the fridge. Her husband never catches on. Another friend, Donna, exasperated that her mate, Michael, kept absentmindedly walking off with the Papermate she kept next to the grocery list in the kitchen, now hides the pen in the silverware drawer. And my friend Dirk tells his chronically late girlfriend they have to be everywhere a half hour before they actually do.

8 I myself used to slip polyester shirts in my then-boyfriend's wardrobe to make the ironing easier. I must say, despite his contention that he could wear

only pure cotton, I didn't see him tearing off his button-downs in the middle of the morning, swearing he couldn't breathe. He also claimed he was allergic to garlic, but I figured he meant he was squeamish about the smell or that he associated garlic with a three-day beard–I added it anyway, and the food tasted so much better.

9   A couple lie is, in reality, close to an omission. Bill didn't actually tell me an untruth. I never said to him, "Morning, Sweetie, coffee have caffeine in it today?" Michael never said to Donna, as he searched futilely for the pen that used to be there, "You aren't by any chance hiding it in the silverware drawer, are you, Honeybunch?"

10   Since we're all guilty, sooner or later, of a little pink omission, I've decided I'm not mad about the coffee. And I know Bill won't mind if I admit that sometimes, after I do the laundry and discover one of the socks still behind the hamper–and wanting to keep the pair together but unwilling to wash the clean one all over again–I let him go off to work wearing one dirty sock and one laundered one. It's not lying. He didn't, after all, ask me if both his socks were clean.

WHAT DID THE WRITER SAY AND WHAT DID YOU THINK?

1. What is a *couple lie*? Does Lara ever explicitly define the term?
2. What is the difference between a white lie and a couple lie?
3. What is the thesis? Is it ever directly stated?
4. What seems to motivate most couple lies?
5. What kept Lara from getting even angrier than she did about the coffee episode?
6. Are couple lies necessarily limited to married couples?

HOW DID THE WRITER SAY IT?

1. Are there enough examples? Do they represent a "reasonable cross section" (see page 98)
2. The couples in this essay use several supersweet terms of endearment such as "Honeybunch" and "Angelface." Does Lara mean this dialogue to be realistic?
3. Why does the essay begin with a story about a couple lie rather than with a definition of the term or a thesis statement?

What _Your_ Writing?

"Couple Lies" is a good example of why-didn't-I-think-of-saying-that writing. Now that the author mentions it, who doesn't know how often married couples–or parents and children, brothers and sisters, even best friends–make life easier by not telling the "truth"? Who hasn't distinguished between telling direct lies and simply not volunteering information? What does this author know that we don't know? Many readers probably see in the Lara essay a main idea that has occurred to them, read insights that they themselves have probably had, and mutter, "Why didn't I think of saying that?" Maybe they didn't think of it because they were too busy lamenting that they didn't have anything to write about. More likely, they had drifted into the habit of not taking their own ideas seriously.

In "Self-Reliance," Ralph Waldo Emerson presents this moral more memorably when he complains of the person who "dismisses without notice his thought, because it is his. In every work of genius we recognize our own rejected thoughts: they come back to us with a certain alienated majesty." You don't have to believe that Lara's article is a work of genius to agree with Emerson's conclusion: We "should learn to detect and watch that gleam of light which flashes across the mind. . . .Else, tomorrow a stranger will say with masterly good sense precisely what we have thought and felt all the time, and we shall be forced to take with shame our own opinion from another."

FRUITFUL QUESTIONS

James Sollisch

James Sollisch is an advertising copywriter and a freelance writer. Here, with examples ranging from children in a food fight to one of the world's greatest astronomers, he helps explain the nature of creative thinking and issues a call for more of it.

✓ Words to Check:

paradigm (paragraph 1)	parameters (1)	critique (10)
linear (1)	potent (9)	

1 The other night at the dinner table, my three kids—ages 9, 6 and 4—took time out from their food fight to teach me about paradigm shifts, and limitations of linear thinking and how to refocus parameters.

2 Here's how it happened: We were playing our own oral version of the Sesame Street game, "What Doesn't Belong?," where kids look at three pictures and choose the one that doesn't fit. I said, "OK, what doesn't belong, an orange, a tomato or a strawberry?"

3 The oldest didn't take more than a second to deliver his smug answer: "Tomato because the other two are fruits." I agreed that this was the right answer despite the fact that some purists insist a tomato is a fruit. To those of us forced as kids to eat them in salads, tomatoes will always be vegetables. I was about to think up another set of three when my 4-year-old said, "The right

answer is strawberry because the other two are round and a strawberry isn't."
How could I argue with that?

4   Then my 6-year-old said, "It's the orange because the other two are red."
Not to be outdone by his younger siblings, the 9-year-old said, "It could also
be the orange because the other two grow on vines."

5   The middle one took this as a direct challenge. "It could be the strawberry
because it's the only one you put on ice cream."

6   Something was definitely happening here. It was messier than a food fight
and much more important than whether a tomato is a fruit or vegetable. My
kids were doing what Copernicus did when he placed the sun at the center of
the universe, readjusting the centuries-old paradigm of an Earth-centered system. They were doing what Reuben Mattus did when he renamed his Bronx
ice cream Häagen-Dazs and raised the price without changing the product.
They were doing what Edward Jenner did when he discovered a vaccination
for smallpox by abandoning his quest for a cure.

7   Instead of studying people who were sick with smallpox, he began to study
people who were exposed to it but never got sick. He found that they'd all con-
tracted a similar but milder disease, cow pox, which vaccinated them against
the deadly smallpox.

8   They were refocusing the parameters. They were redefining the problems.
They were reframing the questions. In short, they were doing what every scientist who's ever made an important discovery throughout history has done,
according to Thomas Kuhn, in his book, *The Structure of Scientific Revolutions.*
They were shifting old paradigms.

9   But if this had been a workbook exercise in school, every kid who didn't
circle tomato would have been marked wrong. Every kid who framed the question differently than "Which is not a fruit?" would have been wrong. Maybe
that explains why so many of the world's most brilliant scientists and inventors
were failures in school, the most notable being Albert Einstein, who was perhaps this century's most potent paradigm-shifter.

10   This is not meant to be a critique of schools. Lord knows, that's easy enough
to do. This is, instead, a reminder that there are real limits to the value of information. I bring this up because we seem to be at a point in the evolution of our
society where everyone is clamoring for more technology, for instant access to
ever-growing bodies of information.

11   Students must be online. Your home must be digitally connected to the
World Wide Web. Businesses must be able to download volumes of data instan-
taneously. But unless we shift our paradigms and refocus our parameters, the
super information highway will lead us nowhere.

12   We are not now, nor have we recently been, suffering from a lack of information. Think how much more information we have than Copernicus had four
centuries ago. And he didn't do anything less Earth-shattering (pun intended)
than completely change the way the universe was viewed. He didn't do it by

uncovering more information—he did it by looking differently at information everyone else already had looked at. Edward Jenner didn't invent preventive medicine by accumulating information; he did it by reframing the question.

13   What we need as we begin to downshift onto the information highway is not more information but new ways of looking at it. We need to discover, as my kids did, that there is more than one right answer, there is more than one right question and there is more than one way to look at a body of information. We need to remember that when you have only a hammer, you tend to see every problem as a nail.

WHAT DID THE WRITER SAY AND WHAT DID YOU THINK?

1. Sollisch humorously uses elevated language in paragraph 1: His children taught him about "paradigm shifts, and limitations of linear thinking and how to refocus parameters." Express the same idea or ideas in everyday language. Does the author ever attempt to do this himself?
2. Why does the author believe the Häagen-Dazs founder belongs in the same group as Copernicus and Jenner? What did Sollisch's children do to deserve membership in this group?
3. What diseases other than smallpox have been conquered by abandoning the quest for a cure and instead finding ways to prevent them?
4. What is the author's main complaint about schools and computers?
5. Can the kind of thinking Sollisch wants actually be taught, or is it an inborn gift or talent?

HOW DID THE WRITER SAY IT?

1. Why is the title particularly effective?
2. What makes the elevated language in paragraph 1 especially amusing?
3. How does the last sentence relate logically to the rest of the essay?

What About Your Writing?

At the end of his third paragraph, as he considers the surprising variety of answers his children develop in response to what he thinks is a simple query, James Sollisch asks a *rhetorical question*: "How could I argue with that?"

A rhetorical question is a question that either expects no reply or clearly calls for one desired reply. It is not a genuine inquiry, like "Who was the thirteenth president of the United States?" or the questions that Sollisch asks his children at the dinner table. Sollisch is confident he has proven his point that the diversity and creativity of his children's responses can't be quarreled with. Nevertheless, a flat statement to this effect may simply sound too flat— a dull summary, a bit of needless repetition. Rhetorical questions, in this case, can help remind us of the main point without needing to repeat it.

As long as they are not overused, rhetorical questions can also be a powerful device for establishing a dramatic atmosphere, particularly in conclusions. Rhetorical questions of this kind must be handled with restraint or they become forced and artificial, but a good writer should feel free to use them.

Can all these blunders really be honest mistakes? Isn't it possible that we've let ourselves be duped again? And isn't it time to act?

Doctors get paid only for their patients' being ill, not for their patients' staying healthy. Is that practical? Is that smart? Is that even sane?

Is life so dear, or peace so sweet, as to be purchased at the price of chains and slavery? Forbid it, Almighty God! I know not what course others may take; but as for me, give me liberty, or give me death.

CHORES

Debra Marquart

A poet, English professor, and creative writing teacher, Debra Marquart grew up on a farm near Napoleon, North Dakota, near the Missouri River. Her experiences there inspired this essay. She performs with a jazz-poetry, rhythm and blues project, "The Bone People" with whom she has produced two CDs. She is working on a novel and her memoir, *The Horizontal World: Growing Up Wild in the Middle of Nowhere* was published in 2006.

✓ **WORDS TO CHECK:**

sanctum sanctorum (paragraph 3)	stanchions (9)
centrifugal (3)	culled (9)
gyration (3)	docile (10)
spigots (3)	

1 My three older sisters had made their rapid getaways after high school—the two oldest to college, the third to marriage and children in town. One by one, their belongings were packed into cars that disappeared down the gravel road. Their old bedrooms became my pick of bedrooms. Pretty soon I had the top floor of the house to myself, and I was left along with my parents on that farm with so many chickens to feed, so many cows to milk, and so much land to work.

2 From sunup to sundown, my parents ran frantically from place to place trying to perform all the chores that kept the farm afloat. Because I was a teenager, and none of this had been my idea, I determined to make myself as useless as possible. The most my father could do was assign me small jobs from season to season.

3 One of my early chores was running the DeLaval cream separator, a machine that worked its transforming magic in a cozy closet off the milk room. In this sanctum

sanctorum ordinary milk was poured into a large stainless-steel bowl on top of the whirring, spinning separator. By some alchemy, the liquid filtered through the layers of the machine. After a great deal of noise and centrifugal gyration, the separator brought forth cream that flowed like gold from one of the spigots below.

4   From the second spigot appeared the now-skimmed milk, which was quickly mixed back in with the whole milk in the pot-bellied bulk cooler. Every few days, a driver arrived in our yard with a refrigerated tanker truck capable of siphoning from the cooler the many gallons of milk we extracted from our cows. This was taken to Wishek Cheese, a factory in a town about twenty-five miles to the southeast.

5   But the cream had choicer destinations. It was collected in pint and quart jars, each marked with the name of people in town who had ordered fresh farm cream. Mother hand-delivered the jars next day.

6   Of all the chores I had to do on the farm, I liked running the separator the best. The milk room was warmer than the rest of the barn, and my primary responsibility was to keep the cats away from the cream. I took a book and read as the noisy machine churned and shook the life from the milk. Around me, things were filled and emptied; cream poured from spouts; jars were whisked away; and I was left to read my book hunched over in the dim light.

7   At my feet, tabbies and tomcats, tuxedos and calicos, milled and meowed. They craned their necks and howled with tortured voices. They tried to scale my pant legs, their claws out, just to get a quick paw, a stretched tongue, anything, into that golden stream. I would shoo and bat them away, absorbed in thought, clutching my book and reading all the while about all the strange places and marvelous people in the outside world.

8   Perhaps separation became my special talent, because at thirteen my father put me in charge of separating the calves from the cows when it was time to wean them from their mothers' milk.

9   On this day, the cows are herded into the barn, their udders heavy with milk. As usual, they file in and put their necks through the stanchions lining the barn. The slats are closed around their necks to hold them in place during milking. But as they enter the barn, their calves are culled away and taken by me to a separate pen I have prepared for them with fresh straw in another part of the barn.

10   At first the cows don't realize what's happening. They move through the enclosures and gates in their docile way. They eat the oats put in place for them inside the stanchions. But once outside the barn, after milking, they begin to look around, to sniff, as if trying to recall something they've forgotten. They turn their long necks; they swish their tails. Nothing.

11   Then they begin to call out, low mooing, until the calves answer. The cows moo and moo in the direction of the calves' voices, and the calves bleat back. This goes on for hours. The crying becomes unbearable. The calves look so small in their holding pen. They stick their heads through the fence, their bodies shaking as they wail. They push their hungry voices toward their mothers' frantic calling: "Where are you? Where are you?"

12   "Here I am. Here I am."

13   The separation of an offspring from a parent. It's the most unnatural event. You feel cruel when you're the one enforcing it. On those days, I will myself not to think about it. I only know that it's my job to feed them. I step into the holding pen with buckets of the warm milk I've mixed from powder. Our farm depends upon the real milk the mothers produce. I must convince the calves to accept the substitute.

14   One by one I take the bawling face of a calf into my hands; I dip my fingertips into the milky liquid in the bucket that rests hard-edged and shiny silver between my legs; I slip my wet fingers into the mouth of the crying calf. One by one they begin to suck, from exhaustion and hunger and instinct—the soft sandpaper tongue, the little pricks of new teeth on my fingertips, the slurping as they finally dip their snouts into the bucket of milk.

15   As they drink, the calves cry and hiccough. I stroke the curls on their soft foreheads. One by one they lie down in their new straw beds, stretch their long downy necks, and sleep.

16   They quiet this way, one after the other, until all is silent in the calf shed, but the crying in the mother's holding pen doesn't stop. It goes on through the night and into the next day, sometimes for hours, sometimes for days.

WHAT DID THE WRITER SAY AND WHAT DID YOU THINK?

1. This book recommends being sure that you have enough examples to support your thesis strongly. How many does Marquart have? Are they sufficient? Why?
2. What is the significance of Marquart's introduction?
3. Why does the author like running the cream separator?
4. Why do the calves need to be separated from their mothers? Do you think this is cruel? Does Marquart?

HOW DID THE WRITER SAY IT?

1. Marquart's example essay uses other rhetorical patterns as well. Find and mark at least two other passages where she uses other rhetorical patterns.
2. Does anything about Marquart's essay suggest that she now disagrees with her teenaged assessment of life on the farm?

What About Your Writing?

Watch out for *very, really,* and *pretty.* Of all the troublemaking words in the language, these have possibly contributed most to sloppy writing. *Very, pretty,* and *really* are intensifiers. You can smack them in front of nearly any adjective and strengthen—intensify—the meaning: *very smart, pretty silly, really funny,* and so forth. The trouble is that the strengthening tends to be so generalized and imprecise that usually little of any substance is actually added to the meaning. Sometimes the meaning is even diminished or confused.

Few readers will object to Debra Marquart saying that she had the top floor of the house to herself "pretty soon," but wasn't she perhaps settling for convenient writing rather than effective writing? Tossing in *pretty* takes a tenth of a second. Finding a more precise term, however, may be worth the extra time and bother, particularly in an essay that is so filled with careful observations and specific details. What about *As soon as they could say goodbye? In less time than it took them to drive off?* Nobody suggests that these words be outlawed, but in your own writing you'd do well to avoid them whenever you can. Start by looking for one-word synonyms: Instead of *very smart,* try *brilliant;* instead of *pretty silly,* try *goofy.* If you can't think of one, try leaving out the intensifier entirely. Would Marquart's essay have lost anything if she'd said, "Soon I had the top floor of the house to myself" instead of "Pretty soon"?

Really is an especially overused intensifier, particularly when intended as the equivalent of *very.* Though *very* may not mean much, at least it means itself. *Really* doesn't even have that much going for it in the following sentences:

- They ate a really fine dinner.
- The stairs are really steep.
- The new furniture was really expensive.

So watch out for *really,* too. Its only legitimate use occurs when the writer has in mind a distinction between what is factual or real in opposition to what is false or imaginary:

- The seemingly bizarre accusations of child abuse were really accurate.
- When she says tomorrow, she doesn't mean next week. She really means tomorrow.

HOW TO SPEAK OF ANIMALS
Umberto Eco

Umberto Eco, respected scholarly writer and lecturer, is the author of numerous popular novels, such as *The Name of the Rose* (1983), *Foucault's Pendulum* (1989), *The Island of the Day Before* (1995), *Baudolino* (2002), and *The Mysterious Flame of Queen Loana* (2005). Here, Eco considers the problems of "toyifying" nature and its creatures.

✓ **Words to Check:**

subproletariat (paragraph 2)   benevolent (5)
sporadic (4)   lemming (6)
per se (5)   viper (6)
carnivorous (5)   equilibrium (6)

1 Central Park. The zoo. Some kids are playing near the polar bear tank. One dares the others to dive into the tank and swim alongside the bears; to force them to dive in, the challenger hides the others' clothes; the boys enter the water, splashing past a big male bear, peaceful and drowsy; they tease him, he becomes annoyed, extends a paw, and eats, or rather chomps on, two kids, leaving some bits lying around. The police come quickly, even the mayor arrives, there is some argument about whether or not the bear has to be killed, all admit it's not his fault; some sensational articles appear in the press. It so happens that the boys have Hispanic names: Puerto Ricans, perhaps black, perhaps newcomers to the city, in any event, accustomed to feats of daring, like all slum kids who hang out in packs.

2   Various interpretations ensue, all fairly severe. The cynical reaction is fairly widespread, at least in conversation: natural selection, if they were stupid enough to mess with a bear, they got what they deserved; even when I was five, I had enough sense not to jump into a bear tank. Social interpretation: areas of poverty, insufficient education, alas, the subproletariat has a tendency to act on impulse, without thinking. But, I ask you, what's all this talk about insufficient education? Even the poorest child watches TV, or has read a schoolbook in which bears devour humans and hunters therefore kill bears.

3   At this point I began to wonder if the boys didn't venture into the pool precisely because they do watch TV and go to school. These children were probably victims of our guilty conscience, as reflected in the schools and the mass media.

4   Human beings have always been merciless with animals, but when humans became aware of their own cruelty, they began, if not to love all animals (because, with only sporadic hesitation, they continue eating them), at least to speak well of them. As the media, the schools, public institutions in general, have to explain away so many acts performed against humans by humans, it seems finally a good idea, psychologically and ethically, to insist on the goodness of animals. We allow children of the Third World to die, but we urge children of the First to respect not only butterflies and bunny rabbits but also whales, crocodiles, snakes.

5   Mind you, this educational approach is *per se* correct. What is excessive is the persuasive technique chosen: to render animals worthy of rescue they are humanized, toyified. No one says they are entitled to survive *even* if, as a rule, they are savage and carnivorous. No, they are made respectable by becoming cuddly, comic, good-natured, benevolent, wise, and prudent.

6   No one is more thoughtless than a lemming, more deceitful than a cat, more slobbering than a dog in August, more smelly than a piglet, more hysterical

than a horse, more idiotic than a moth, more slimy than a snail, more poisonous than a viper, less imaginative than an ant, and less musically creative than a nightingale. Simply put, we must love—or, if that is downright impossible, at least respect—these and other animals for what they are. The tales of earlier times overdid the wicked wolf, the tales of today exaggerate the good wolves. We must save the whales, not because they are good, but because they are a part of nature's inventory and they contribute to the ecological equilibrium. Instead, our children are raised with whales that talk, wolves that join the Third Order of St. Francis, and, above all, an endless array of teddy bears.

7   Advertising, cartoons, illustrated books are full of bears with hearts of gold, law-abiding, cozy, and protective—although in fact it's insulting for a bear to be told he has a right to live because he's only a dumb but inoffensive brute. So I suspect that the poor children in Central Park died not through lack of education but through too much of it. They are the victims of our unhappy conscience.

8   To make them forget how bad human beings are, they were taught too insistently that bears are good. Instead of being told honestly what humans are and what bears are.

WHAT DID THE WRITER SAY AND WHAT DID YOU THINK?

1. Before presenting his own explanation for the boys' behavior, the author rejects some other explanations. Summarize those other explanations.
2. Who are the main culprits in misleading the boys about the nature of animals?
3. What do the animals listed at the start of paragraph 6 have in common?
4. Express the thesis in your own words.

HOW DID THE WRITER SAY IT?

1. Define the invented word *toyified* in paragraph 5.
2. In paragraph 4, why is *bunny rabbits* a better choice of words than *bunnies* or *rabbits*?

What About Your Writing?

One of the fundamental ingredients of English style is parallelism: using the same (parallel) grammatical forms to express elements of approximately the same (parallel) importance. This definition may seem more formidable than it really is. Parallelism is so fundamental that we use it all the time.

Three parallel adjectives:

The man was *tall, dark,* and *handsome.*

Four parallel nouns:

We have to buy a *rug,* a *sofa,* two *chairs,* and a *lamp.*

Three parallel prepositional phrases:

. . . *of the people, by the people, for the people.*

Three parallel independent clauses:

I want you. I need you. I love you.

Two parallel imperatives:

Sit down and relax.

Four parallel infinitives:

To strive, to seek, to find, and not *to yield.*

The parallel grammatical forms point to and reinforce the parallels in thought and importance. Moreover, parallelism is what readers normally expect; it's the normal way that words are put together. Notice how a break-down in expected parallelism adversely affects these sentences:

The man was tall, dark, and an athlete.

. . . of the people, by the people, and serving the people.

To strive, to seek, to find, and we must not yield.

We can find frequent and effective use of parallelism throughout "How to Speak of Animals." We find parallel nouns in paragraph 4: "whales, croc-odiles, snakes." We find parallel adjectives in paragraph 5: "cuddly, comic, good-natured, benevolent, wise, and prudent." Take a special look at the long list beginning paragraph 6. The parallel phrasing here is not just a technicality. It reinforces the idea that the animals *are* parallel in their behavior, that they all have undesirable characteristics that many people would rather ignore.

Bear three points in mind for your own writing:

1. Parallelism isn't just a matter of sterile correctness. It can contribute to genuine stylistic distinction. Some of the most memorable phrases in the language draw much of their strength from parallelism:

   Friends, Romans, countrymen. . . .
   I have nothing to offer but blood, sweat, toil, and tears.
   . . . life, liberty, and the pursuit of happiness.
   I came, I saw, I conquered.
   . . . with malice toward none, with charity for all.

2. Occasional modifying words do not break the basic parallelism and can sometimes help avoid the danger of monotony. These sentences still show parallelism:

> He was tall, dark, and astonishingly handsome.
> We have to buy a rug, a sofa, two chairs, and most of all a fancy new lamp.

3. Parallelism works only when each member of the parallel series is roughly equivalent in importance. It leads to absurdity in the following cases:

> My teacher has knowledge, enthusiasm, concern, and sinus trouble.
> We must protect society from murderers, sexual predators, kidnappers, and litterbugs.

CHAPTER 4¹/₂
Office Hours: Of Course They Count

Do spelling and grammar and other basic skills count? A recent e-mail claims to be a report on a scientific study at Cambridge University about human language, reading, spelling, and communication. It's not, really. No such study took place at Cambridge, and the e-mail is a fabrication. But the e-mail, fake or not, is interesting. It reads:

> Aoccdrnig to a rscheearch at Cmabrigde Uinervtisy, it deosn't mttaer in waht oredr the ltteers in a wrod are, the olny iprmoetnt tihng is taht the frist and lsat ltteer be at the rghit pclae. The rset can be a total mses and you can sitll raed it wouthit porbelm. Tihs is bcuseae the huamn mnid deos not raed ervey lteter by istlef, but the wrod as a wlohe.

The clever person who created this e-mail certainly has a point. You can read it. It may give you a headache. But you can read it. An idea is communicated.

Someone is guaranteed to point to this e-mail and say, "I've known it all along. Spelling and grammar don't matter. As long as my ideas are good and people can understand me, I should do fine."

The problem with this point of view is that writing involves more than communication at the "Me Tarzan, You Jane" level. If all that we needed to do was to communicate in this most basic way, we would require nothing more than some grunts and maybe a few nouns. But no one wants people to think he grunts because he doesn't know how to talk. No one wants people to think she makes grammatical and other errors because she doesn't know any better.

Think about it this way. You could send out a cover letter and résumé to a prospective employer that looked like the e-mail mentioned previously. It would probably be understood. But why would anyone bother to try to understand it when, right next to it, is a foot-high stack of correctly spelled résumés from other job candidates? Whatever you may want to communicate in a paper for class, think about what you've already communicated if you begin by misspelling the instructor's name. Being careless with language in important situations—job applications, papers for classes, letters to the editor—tells the reader that you don't really care about what you're saying or about the person you're saying it to. That's probably not what you're hoping to communicate.

Taking care of the basics is important for all these reasons, but also because errors *can,* in fact, lead to a complete lack of communication. Think about the difference between these two sentences:

Let's eat, Grandpa!

Let's eat Grandpa!

One sentence is a grisly invitation to cannibalism. The other is an invitation to dinner.

And don't forget the gentleman who told his sweetheart after their first kiss, "Darling, I've wanted to kiss you so badly." "And you just did," she replied.

Spelling counts. Grammar counts. It may seem easier and faster to be careless, but it's never worth it.

Process

In its most familiar form, writing about a process provides instructions. This kind of process paper tells readers the series of steps they must perform to achieve a particular result. At its simplest level, the process paper is a how-to-do-it paper: how to cook beef Wellington, how to drive from town to Camp Wilderness (see page 15), how to install wall paneling, how to operate a home computer, how to put together a child's bike on Christmas morning. Writing simple, clear instructions makes many demands on a writer, and people who are good at it often earn excellent salaries. Ask those parents struggling with that bike on Christmas morning how many dollars they would offer for easy-to-read and easy-to-follow instructions.

The conventional how-to paper sometimes can lend itself to humor, as when a writer deliberately gives instructions on what no one wants to learn: how to flunk out of school, how to have a heart attack, and so forth. Besides drawing on the appeal of humor, such papers can also have serious instructional purposes by telling the reader, between the lines, how to do well in school or how to avoid coronaries. Other humorous pieces give instructions on what many people *do* want to learn but don't usually want to acknowledge: *How to Succeed in Business Without Really Trying* and *Gamesmanship, or the Art of Winning Games Without Actually Cheating* are titles of two famous books.

Several other variations on the how-to paper are also fairly common. A how-it-works paper explains the functioning of anything from an electric toothbrush to the system for ratifying a new Constitutional amendment. A how-it-was-done paper might trace the process by which Stonehenge or the pyramids were built or of how the chase scenes in the old *Keystone Kops* movies were filmed. A how-not-to-do-it paper might trace the process by which the writer did everything wrong in reshingling the roof or buying a used car.

At a more advanced level, process papers can study the course of social, political, scientific, and cultural developments: the process that led to the discovery of the polio vaccine, the decision of Napoleon to invade Russia, the spread of Christianity, or Franklin D. Roosevelt's proposal to increase the membership of the Supreme Court. Process writing can also be a powerful instrument of literary analysis: the process by which Frederic Henry in *A Farewell to Arms* comes to desert the army, Captain Ahab in *Moby Dick* associates the white whale with evil, or Iago persuades Othello that Desdemona has been unfaithful.

How does the persuasive principle apply to process writing? If you're writing a straightforward how-to paper, for example, why not simply list the steps and forget about a thesis? You don't have a point to make as such, do you? Aren't you saying only that these are the things one must do to paint a room or change a flat tire or study for an exam? Why not just list them?

These questions are legitimate, and it's certainly possible to write a process paper without a thesis. In most cases, though, the paper won't be as good as it could be—and as it ought to be. Apart from the advantages of writing with a thesis as described in Chapter 1, you're writing a how-to paper, after all, for people who don't yet know "how to do it." (If they knew, they'd have no reason to read the paper.) A long list of things to do, with each step considered separately, can both bore and confuse readers. A thesis helps readers get solidly oriented at the outset and enables them to see each separate step as part of a coherent pattern.

But what kind of thesis makes sense in the humble little paper on how to paint a room? All kinds.

Painting a room is much easier than it seems.

Painting a room is much harder than it seems.

Painting a room is great fun.

Painting a room is horrible drudgery.

Painting a room is easy compared to preparing the room to be painted.

Painting a room takes less time than most people suppose.

Painting a room takes more time than most people suppose.

Any one of these ideas, not to mention many more imaginative ones, could give unity and interest to a how-to paper. The writer, in addition to making each step convey the necessary raw information, would connect each step or group of related steps to the thesis.

1—Presentation of thesis: Painting a room is much easier than it seems.

Start of ¶2—To prepare the room, you need only a dust cloth, lots of masking tape, spackling paste . . .

Start of ¶3—If preparing the room was easy, the painting itself is child's play . . .

Start of ¶4—Cleaning up is the easiest part of all . . .

With the desirability of a thesis in mind, it's no massive project to think up promising theses for some other subjects:

- Every step of the way, Napoleon's decision to invade Russia was based on foolish overconfidence.
- Franklin D. Roosevelt's proposal to pack the Supreme Court came in response to a long series of legislative frustrations.
- Frederic Henry's desertion of the army in *A Farewell to Arms* is the last step in a gradually accelerating process of disillusionment.

- The dramatic discovery of the polio vaccine came as the result of a fiercely competitive race to be first.
- The seemingly spontaneous, mad chase scenes in *Keystone Kops* movies were actually the product of careful planning of every detail.
- The process by which the pyramids were built shows an astonishing knowledge of the laws of modern physics.

Once you set up a thesis, the significant issues are the mechanics of writing about the process itself.

Be Sure You Are Writing About a Process

The words *How to* or *How* in your title guarantee nothing. A process is a series, a sequence, an orderly progression. One step or event follows another: first this, then that, then something else. A happy-go-lucky collection of handy hints is not a process. Chapter 1 of this book followed a necessary sequence in the description of the process of *first* starting with a general subject, *then* limiting the subject, *then* devising a thesis and thesis statement, *then* incorporating the thesis into the whole paper. Chapter 4, on the other hand, while telling "how to" write an example paper, presented a bundle of miscellaneous suggestions on what to think about in looking over the examples; the suggestions followed no particularly rigid order and therefore did not constitute a real process.

Follow Strict Chronological Order

The need to follow strict chronological order seems obvious, but in fact it is unique to process writing. In other patterns, you try to begin with your most important or dramatic or amusing material. In process writing, you begin with step one. You try to make all the steps of the process as interesting as possible to your reader, but you have no choice about the order in which you discuss them.

Before Describing the First Step of the Process, Indicate Any Special Ingredients or Equipment That Will Be Needed

Recipes, for example, almost always begin with a list of ingredients.

Be Sure the Process Is Complete

In a how-to paper, you're describing a process that you probably can do automatically, and it's easy to omit some obvious steps because you don't consciously think about them at all. They are not so obvious to your reader. If you're telling the reader how to stop a leak in the kitchen sink, for instance, don't forget to have the poor soul shut off the water supply before removing the faucet and replacing the washer.

TRY TO ANTICIPATE DIFFICULTIES

First, warn the reader in advance if a notably tough step is coming up:

Now comes the hard part.

The next step is a bit tricky.

Be extremely careful here.

Second, advise the reader of what can be done to make the process easier or more pleasant. You're an insider, and you have an insider's information. The process of changing a flat tire does not require anyone to put the lugs into the inverted hubcap so they won't get lost, but it's a technique insiders use to head off trouble before it starts. Painting a room does not require anyone to wear an old hat, but your mentioning the advisability of an old hat might be appreciated by anyone who prefers paint-free hair.

Third, tell the reader what to do if something goes wrong. Don't terrify the reader, but be frank about common foul-ups:

If any paint should get on the window. . . .

If the hubcap is hard to replace. . . .

IF YOU NEED TO HANDLE MANY SEPARATE STEPS, ARRANGE THEM INTO GROUPS WHEN POSSIBLE

Even a simple process may involve a large number of steps. The process paper is far less intimidating if the steps are presented in manageable bunches. Earlier, we divided the process of painting a room into preparation, painting, and cleaning up. Each division received a paragraph, and the reader got the impression of having only three major areas to worry about instead of fifty separate steps. Even as uninspired a grouping of steps as Phase I, Phase II, Phase III—or Beginning, Middle, End—is preferable to none at all. The more steps in the process, the more essential it becomes to collect them into groups.

DEFINE UNFAMILIAR TERMS

Definitions of unfamiliar terms are needed in all writing. They're especially important in the how-to paper, because the instructions are for an audience that must be assumed to know nothing about the subject.

Two final recommendations about your choice of topics are worth brief notes.

AVOID HIGHLY TECHNICAL PROCESSES

Because you must define all unfamiliar terms, you don't want to choose an obscure scientific subject with such a specialized vocabulary that most of your energy will be spent providing definitions rather than presenting a process.

AVOID SUBJECTS FOR WHICH PICTURES WORK BETTER THAN WORDS

Some processes, often but not always the highly technical ones, can best be explained with a few diagrams and almost as few words. Consider instructions on how to tie shoelaces. Pictures are the only way to go.

Depending solely or almost solely on words would create pointless trouble for the writer and confusion for the reader. Since you are in a writing class, not an art class, you should avoid such processes.

WRITING SUGGESTIONS FOR PROCESS ESSAYS

Many topics have already been mentioned in this chapter. The suggestions here are meant to provide some further inspiration. Suggestions have been grouped into two categories: General Areas for Exploration (with examples) and Specific Topics.

General Areas for Exploration
1. Do-it-yourself repairs: bikes, cars, radios, television sets, broken windows.
2. Routine chores: gardening, cooking, shopping.
3. School and business: studying, taking notes, registering, applying to colleges, applying for jobs, creating a good impression at job interviews.
4. Sports, games, and other recreational activities: how to win at poker, bridge, Monopoly, *Grand Theft Auto*; how to watch a football game, throw Frisbees, water ski; how to plan a trip.

5. Finances: budgeting, borrowing, investing.
6. Hobbies: how to start a stamp, coin, tropical fish collection; how to work at a particular art or craft; how a magic trick is performed.
7. Children and pets: babysitting, toilet training, safety, housebreaking, traveling.
8. Personal care: grooming, breaking a bad habit, treating a cold, curing a hangover.
9. Humor: how to be a bore, worrywart, nag; how to get out of housework, butter up teachers, call in sick; how to die at thirty.
10. How it works: power steering, air conditioning, CD players, zippers.
11. The past: how a battle was fought, a crime was committed, a structure was built, a law was passed, a disease was conquered.
12. Literature: how an author prepares the reader for a surprise ending, how a character makes a crucial decision.

Specific Topics
1. What to do if arrested.
2. What to do if in a car accident.
3. How to find a rich husband or wife.
4. How to diet.
5. How to exercise.
6. How to drive defensively.
7. How to apply first aid for snake bites.
8. How to protect oneself in a natural disaster: tornado, hurricane, flood.
9. How to waste time.
10. How to plan for a holiday or other special occasion: Thanksgiving dinner, Passover seder, birthday party, bar mitzvah or confirmation party, Easter egg hunt, wedding.
11. How to live on nothing a year.
12. How to pack a suitcase.
13. How to stop smoking.
14. How to hitch a ride.
15. How to give oneself a perfect shave.

VISUAL PROMPT

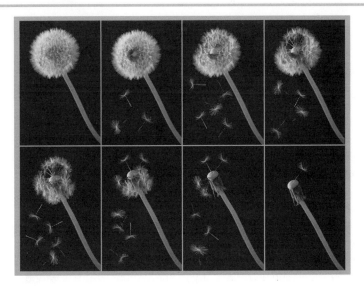

Writing Prompt

A process is a sequence, a series, an orderly progression. This time-lapse photograph of dandelion seeds being blown away reminds us that processes can be about destruction as well as about creation. Write your own process essay about taking something apart, breaking something, or tearing something down.

STUDENT ESSAY: HOW NOT TO WORK OUT
Max Greene

Thesis: Learning to not work out is a complex procedure, but it can be broken down into a few simple steps.

    I. Set Goals
        A. Tell everyone you're going to work out
        B. Do everything else first

    II. Dress Appropriately
        A. Find your workout gear
        B. Find all the problems with your workout gear

    III. Wait for the Laundry

    IV. Take Care of Technical Issues
        A. Update your iPod
        B. Update your fitness equipment

    V. Eat Well
        A. Have a healthy snack
        B. Listen to your body
        C. Don't workout too soon

    VI. Take a Rest

Conclusion: Rest up. You've earned it!

There are 24-hour fitness channels. There are DVDs for yoga, pilates, weightlifting, abdominal work, aerobics, something called "The Crunch," something else called "The Firm," and something called "Zumba." Every celebrity has a workout video. Every magazine has an article about how to tighten this, tone that, or reduce the other thing. Nike has a website that lets you track your running mileage. If you want to learn how to work out, there are millions of options for you.

You can also find endless discussions in all these places about how to avoid injury, about "The Top Ten Fitness Mistakes to Avoid," or "The One Exercise You Should Never Do." You can turn on the talk shows and hear all about the fitness myths we should ignore, or how everything you thought you knew about sit-ups is wrong. If you want to learn how not to work out, there are thousands of people to help you.

But what if you're lazy? What if you're terrified of the danger of being caught up in the fitness craze? What if, everywhere you turn, people are urging you to get up off the couch, increase your heart rate, and count the number of steps you take? What if you just want them to leave you alone? What if all you want is to learn how to not work out?

Not working out is not as simple as just sitting on the couch in front of the television. It is a complex procedure, involving mental effort and serious commitment from you. Fortunately, it can be broken down into just a few simple steps.

In order to not work out properly, you have to set goals. This means that you must state loudly and emphatically that you are, in fact, planning to work out. It is, you know, vitally important that you work out. You would be doing it right now, actually, except that you have to do a little homework, feed the dog, and get the oil changed in the car first. But as soon as these crucial tasks are fulfilled, you're definitely going to work out today.

Next, you must dress appropriately for not working out. Find your workout clothes and begin to get dressed. Discover that your lucky t-shirt is missing, that your sports bra doesn't fit anymore, or that you've lost the drawstring to your running shorts. Discover that you don't have any clean white socks. Who can work out without clean white socks?

Resolve to work out just as soon as the laundry load of clean white socks is done. Until then, continue not working out.

While you wait for the laundry to finish, look for your iPod. It's probably not charged, so be sure to take the hour or so that it takes to charge the battery. While you're at it, you might want to make sure that you have sufficiently energetic and inspiring music loaded onto it. You can't work out without the right tunes. This is also a good time to fiddle with your DVD player and the settings on your treadmill. Taking care of these technical issues will help you to not work out.

You have to eat well in order to have fuel to not work out. Have a healthy and nutritious snack. Remember to listen to your body. It will tell you what nutrients it needs. Most people find that, in order to not work out efficiently, their bodies require chips, Cheetos, and chocolate. Of course, you'll want to wait a few hours after eating before exercising. You wouldn't want to feel sick.

The final step in learning to not work out is to check your watch. Surprisingly, you'll find that it's time for bed, or at least for the latest episode of *American Idol.* Have a seat. Put your feet up.

You've earned it. You've been not working out all day. You must be exhausted.

CORN BREAD WITH CHARACTER

Ronni Lundy

Ronni Lundy works as a feature writer for Louisville, Kentucky's *The Courier-Journal* where her special interests in bluegrass and traditional music often appear in her commentary. She has published several cookbooks, the most recent of which is *Butterbeans to Blackberries: Recipes from the Southern Garden* (1999), and a book on crafts called *Crafts for the Spirit* (2003). She has also done freelance writing for such national magazines as *Esquire* in which "Corn Bread with Character" was first published.

✓ WORDS TO CHECK:

homogenized (paragraph 2)	impart (7)	pulverize (11)
cracklings (2)	improvise (7)	scotch (11)
forebear (3)	heady (8)	instinctive (12)
wield (3)	throes (8)	facsimile (14)
facet (5)		

1 There are those who will tell you that real corn bread has just a little sugar in it. They'll say it enhances the flavor or that it's an old tradition in the South. Do not listen to them. If God had meant for corn bread to have sugar in it, he'd have called it cake.

2 Real corn bread is not sweet. Real corn bread is not homogenized with the addition of flour or puffed up with excessive artificial rising agents. Real corn bread rises from its own strength of character, has substance, crust, and texture. Real corn bread doesn't depend on fancy cornmeal, buttermilk, or cracklings for its quality. Real corn bread is a forthright, honest food as good as the instincts of its cook and the pan it is baked in.

3 That pan had best be a cast-iron skillet, preferably one inherited from a forebear who knew how to wield it. My mother, who made real corn bread almost every day of my growing-up life, has a great pan, a square cast-iron skillet given by a great aunt. She also has an eight-slot corn stick pan I would be satisfied to find as

my sole inheritance someday. In the meantime, I bake corn bread in a nine-inch round cast-iron skillet I grabbed up in a secondhand store because it already had a black, nasty crust on the outside and the proper sheen of seasoning within.

4   If you have to start with a pan fresh from the store, season it according to the instructions for cast iron, then fry bacon in it every morning for a month to add a little flavor. Pour the leftover bacon grease into an empty one-pound coffee can and refrigerate it. Wipe your pan clean with a paper towel and don't ever touch it with anything as destructive as soap and water. When the inside starts to turn black and shiny, you're ready to start making corn bread.

5   It's not enough to have the right pan, however; you also need to know how to heat it properly. Heating right is the most important facet of the art of making corn bread, because if you have your skillet and drippings just hot enough, you'll consistently turn out corn bread with a faultless brown and crispy crust.

6   "Just what are drippings?" you may ask here, thereby revealing that you have never been closer than a pig's eye to a country kitchen.

7   In my family, drippings were the bacon grease my mother saved every morning in coffee cans. If you've followed the directions for seasoning a new pan, you're in good shape here. But what if you've inherited a well-seasoned pan and want to start baking corn bread before your next breakfast? Or what if you've never eaten bacon in your life? Don't despair. You will learn, as I did during a brief flirtation with vegetarianism, that while bacon drippings impart a distinctive taste to corn bread cooked with them, they aren't essential to baking great corn bread. You can improvise a lot with grease.

8   If you feel extravagant, you can use half a stick of butter, but if you need to conserve, you can use some not too flavorful oil with a teaspoon or two of butter for effect. If you like the taste, you can use peanut oil or the thick, golden corn oil sold in health food stores that tastes like Kansas in the heady throes of late August. But you can't use olive oil or sesame oil (too strong and foreign), and margarine won't heat right.

9   To heat the pan correctly, you must leave it in the oven until it and the drippings are really hot but not smoking. Knowing just how long that takes is a trick you'll learn with time. A good rule of thumb: Leave the pan in the oven while you mix the other ingredients, but don't stir too slowly. A good precaution, in the early stages of making corn bread, is to check the pan frequently.

10   A final secret on the art of heating: It does not work to heat the corn bread skillet on top of the stove. Doing so may save you from setting off the smoke alarm, but the burner will create circular hot spots in your skillet and when you flip it to get the corn bread out, the middle crust will stay behind, clinging to those spots.

11   You will need cornmeal, of course. You may want to invest in a sturdy little grinder and pulverize the kernels yourself at home. Or you may want to cultivate a dark and narrow little store somewhere that sells only stone-ground cornmeal in expensively priced brown paper bags. Either method is fine. Both will bake up just as nicely as the commercially ground white cornmeal you can find in bags on any supermarket shelf. That's what my mother always used,

and years of sampling gourmet grinds have given me no reason to scotch her preference.

12 In my mother's kitchen, where I learned to make corn bread, there were two kinds of measurements: enough and not enough. If we owned anything as fancy as a measuring cup, I'm sure it was not taken down for an occurrence so everyday as the baking of dinner corn bread. I do know that we had a set of four measuring spoons in primary colors, because it made a dandy toy for visiting children, but I don't remember ever seeing it in my mother's hand as she sprinkled salt, baking powder, or soda into the corn bread mixing bowl. In the interest of science, however, and for those unable to visit my mother's kitchen, her instinctive art is converted here to teaspoons, tablespoons, and cups. What follows is a recipe for real corn bread, enough to accompany dinner for six:

13 Turn on your oven to 450 degrees.

14 In a nine-inch round cast-iron skillet or a reasonable facsimile thereof, place four tablespoons of the grease of your choice. Place the skillet in the oven and heat it until the grease pops and crackles when you wiggle the pan.

15 While the grease heats, mix together in a medium-sized bowl two cups of fairly finely ground white cornmeal with one teaspoon of salt, one-half teaspoon of baking soda, and one-half teaspoon of baking powder. Use your fingers to blend them together well.

16 Crack one big egg or two little ones into the meal mixture.

17 Add one and a half cups of milk or buttermilk.

18 Stir until just blended.

19 Remove the skillet from the oven and swirl it carefully so the grease coats most of the inside edges of the pan but not your hand. Pour the grease into the corn bread mixture, and if everything is going right, it will crackle invitingly. Mix together well with a big wooden spoon, using about twenty-five strokes.

20 Pour the mixture back into the hot skillet and return it to the oven for twenty minutes. Run the pan under the broiler for a few seconds to get a light-brown top crust, then remove it from the oven and turn it upside down onto a large plate. If your skillet is seasoned right, the bread will slide out in a hot brown slab. If not, then just serve it straight from the pan. It will taste every bit as good. (This recipe can also be baked in a corn stick pan, but the baking time is cut in half.)

21 Serve the bread with fresh sweet butter, or crumble it in a bowl and cover with hot pinto beans, a green onion, and sweet pickle on the side. Now, that's real corn bread.

WHAT DID THE WRITER SAY AND WHAT DID YOU THINK?

1. What is Lundy's thesis?
2. How does this recipe differ from most recipes?
3. How does the author's use of personal background affect the essay?
4. Why does Lundy devote so much attention to the seasoned skillet?
5. Why does Lundy use the overworked phrase "If God had meant . . . " in paragraph 1?

HOW DID THE WRITER SAY IT?

1. How do the essay title and paragraph 2 relate?
2. Are the obvious repetitions in paragraph 2 effective? Why, or why not?
3. What is the overall tone of the essay? Is it unusual for a recipe? Explain.
4. Is Lundy's conclusion typical for a recipe? Why, or why not?
5. Where does Lundy begin presenting the actual recipe? Why so late?

What About Your Writing?

Your instructors are captive audiences. They may often enjoy their captivity and be eager to read your work, but in fact they have no choice. In the mood or not, they have to read it. That's their job. Fret all you want about their grading–you'll never find such soft touches again. Your future, noncaptive audiences will be infinitely tougher. They don't use red ink, but they don't need any. All they need is a wastebasket. And every good writer respects and fears wastebaskets.

Like Ronni Lundy in "Corn Bread with Character," the professional writer of a magazine article or advertisement suffers from–and benefits tremendously from–one problem that more writers ought to feel. *How do I get my reader's attention?* Nobody starts to read a magazine wondering what Lundy or the Jones and Smith Company has to say that day. The author or the company has to make the reader stop turning the pages. The soft-touch instructor may sometimes comment, "This essay starts slowly but gets better as it goes along." The other folks out there just keep turning the pages.

Think about your readers. They're rooting strongly for you, if only because they want their own reading experience to be pleasurable, but they need your help. Here are three specific suggestions for making a good start.

First, try for a strong title. You don't normally personify food as Lundy does in her title, "Corn Bread with Character." But it is original and catchy, a title that can easily stimulate a reader's curiosity. (For a more detailed discussion of titles, see page 242.)

Second, spare the reader such unpromising first sentences as "In this composition I will try to show . . . " or "My paper has as its thesis . . . " or "According to *Webster's Dictionary*. . . ." You needn't go overboard–there's no virtue in being self-consciously cute or eccentric. (Lundy's opening sentence, for example, is mostly a simple, straightforward statement.) Still, a well-calculated touch of showbiz now and then never hurt anyone and can sometimes work miracles. Consider these first sentences from three essays by George Orwell:

- As I write, highly civilised human beings are flying overhead, trying to kill me.
- Soon after I arrived at Crossgates (not immediately, but after a week or two, just when I seemed to be settling into the routine of school life), I began wetting my bed.
- In Moulmein, in Lower Burma, I was hated by large numbers of people—the only time in my life that I have been important enough for this to happen to me.

Third, and most important, remember that there's a real person reading what you've written. Writing isn't just self-expression—it's communication. If self-expression were the whole story, you'd be better off doodling or singing in the shower or making funny noises while you run through the nearest meadow. Whenever you can—and that will be most of the time—give your reader an immediate reason for paying attention to you. In "Corn Bread with Character," the author employs the oldest—and still most effective—technique in the writer's trade: From the first sentence on, she appeals to the reader's self-interest. "Do what I tell you, and you will soon be enjoying the world's best corn bread." Not all of your writing will deal with life and death issues, but you can almost always give your reader a reason to care—even about family recipes.

A writer is at one end and a reader at the other, and unless the reader is your instructor, that reader has a wastebasket.

───────────────

"IT"

Stephanie Pearl-McPhee

Stephanie Pearl-McPhee writes the well-known blog www.yarnharlot.ca. She has published several books of knitting essays and instructions, and she and her blog readers have raised over $600,000 for Doctors Without Borders. This essay first appeared in her book, *Yarn Harlot: The Secret Life of a Knitter,* and provides a humorous portrait of what happens when a person obsessed with a craft tries to make everything in time for the holidays.

✓ **WORDS TO CHECK:**

bane (paragraph 2)	maniacal (10)	prioritizing (19)
delusion (7)	perilous (17)	continuum (19)
strategically (8)		

1 Once again, it's Christmastime. How I can be completely blindsided by a holiday that happens on the same day each year is absolutely beyond me. You'd swear that they only announce the date for Christmas in November and I have maybe three weeks to cope with the news. Once again I am nowhere near ready, and once again my family has turned its back on me.

2   I can't really blame the poor embattled souls; they have been down this road with me before and they know how it ends. I know how it ends too. "IT" is the bane of our holidays. Every year I swear that "IT" will never happen again, that I will learn from my experience. It seems I can't be taught.

3   Even as I write, I don't believe that "IT" will happen to me this year. This year will be different. This year I can do it.

4   Here's how "IT" begins. Sometime in the fall, when the weather gets crisp and wearing wool starts to make sense again, I realize that Christmas is coming and I'd better get started on the holiday knitting. (Mind you, if everyone pitched in and did something about global warming I might get more of a heads-up but never mind.) Usually I voice this happy concern as I begin taking apart the stash, leaving stacks of patterns and yarn around the house, and further neglecting housework and my real job. Every year I am convinced that this time, I have started early enough to avoid "IT." I plan all kinds of things. Little sweaters for babies I know, hats for quick gifts, socks to keep darling feet warm and afghans for new homes. (That's right–afghans. Hope springs eternal.)

5   Thus we enter Phase 1. Phase 1 is a happy time. I am planning; I love my wool and patterns; I am full of good ideas; I bask in the pleasure of expressing my love through wool. Christmas is far enough away. Phase 1 is joy.

6   Phase 2 involves detailed planning and casting on. During Phase 2, I start making lists. What exactly do I plan on knitting before Christmas? Here is this year's list:

- Four pairs of felted clogs (brother, sister-in-law, aunt, and uncle)
- One afghan (brother with new house)
- One throw (sister with new house)
- Three hoodie sweaters (daughters)
- One shawl (mother-in-law)
- Two sets of hats and mittens (nieces)
- Three sweaters (nephew, goddaughter, friend's baby)
- Hat and scarf (daughter's tutor)
- Five washcloths (daughters' teachers)
- Two pairs of socks (mate, best friend)
- Elegant copper and gold wrap (myself, to go with my little black dress)

7   This last item marks the depths of my delusion. Not only does it rest on the illusion that I will be invited somewhere where this is appropriate attire, but it assumes that I will get through the mountain of knitting I've planned with enough time not just to knit the wrap but to go out wearing it.

8   Then I go through the stash and to the yarn store and cast on all of these projects (usually in one day), place them strategically around the house so that I have the right kind of knitting in each room, and happily begin knitting.

Phase 2 is when my family starts laughing and shaking their heads. Phase 2 is when I tell them that this year will be different.

9   Phase 3 is when it starts to get ugly. Phase 3 is when I look at the projects scattered around the house and start to feel the first pangs of concern. It dawns on me that this may be a fairly large (read "impossible") enterprise. This is the phase in which my family stops laughing and starts the nervous giggling as it slowly dawns on them that "IT" is going to happen again. I handle Phase 3 by rationalizing and planning. Some common rationalizations are "Well, I know it looks like a lot, but the afghan is on big needles" or "I've never knit felted clogs, but they can't take more than an hour a pair." The planning is more vague. I'll knit on the bus; my mate will do the laundry to free up time; I'll knit for thirty minutes on each thing, and it will all go so quickly. I can do it. It will be fine. I'm a fast knitter and this is reasonable . . . .Right?

10   Phase 4 is when the support of my family goes out the window. Phase 4 is when it finally occurs to me that I might have a knitting crisis. Being the hopeful type, I'm still fairly positive. I know I have a problem, but I believe that with a serious commitment I can get out of it. It is in this phase that my family starts to express concern for my physical health and mental wellbeing. They begin to talk about how "IT" was last year. Phase 4 strategies include the following:

1. Carefully assess project status and estimate how many hours of knitting remain. Divide this number by the number of days until Christmas. (When figuring the number of knitting days available to you, allow every day between now and Christmas, even though you know that you will have to spend some days doing other things. Denial is a powerful Phase 4 tool.) This gives you the KHPD (Knitting Hours Per Day) that you must knit to meet your Christmas goal. (Tip: Make sure that you underestimate the number of hours it will take you to knit your items; you don't want to scare yourself.)
2. Neglect housework. This can increase knitting time substantially, but you must remember to deduct one day from your total number of days until Christmas to clean up for the guests.
3. Deduct sleeping time. Minor sleep deprivation is okay here. People with new babies miss all kinds of sleep. It won't kill you. I find that I can convert one hour of sleep to knitting time every night without any real consequences.
4. Make sure your family knows that you are going to be knitting full time. Make known the gravity of the situation. My personal technique for this consists of showing everyone the list repeatedly and explaining in a maniacal tone of voice that I am going to need some extra help and con-sideration. Ignore their pleas for sanity. If they beg you to stop and ask you please, for the love of God, not to let "IT" happen this year, ask them if they are trying to ruin Christmas.

11   Some holiday knitters never make it to Phase 5. Phase 5 is the final stage before "IT" overwhelms a knitter. In Phase 4, there is the lurking knowledge that this may not be possible, but during Phase 5 this concern becomes outright terror. Phase 5 is the first time that you actually think "Oh-oh, I might not make it."

12   What are some Phase 5 symptoms?

1. You have decided, calmly and reasonably, that it makes total sense to deduct another three hours of sleep per day to increase your knitting time.
2. You have decided that having all your meals delivered is a smart move.
3. You have canceled your attendance at the Christmas party because it will reduce knitting time. Not because you can't knit at the party, but because you can't justify losing the knitting time to take a shower and put on a dress.
4. You aren't entirely sure where your children are, and you may be losing touch with caring about it.
5. You start calculating how many stitches per minute you need to knit if you are going to make it.

13   The most profound symptom of Phase 5 is project modification. Scarf and hat sets become just scarves, or just hats, whatever I have done. Sweaters become vests, afghans become throws—you get the picture. Knitters in Phase 5 do not give up completely; they just work out what needs to be knit smaller or out of chunky yarn on bigger needles.

14   Each year during Phase 5 my family makes their last appeal. They beg me not to lose touch. They tell me that there is more to life than knitting and that people would rather I was well rested and happy than making them socks. They tell me that the sooner I give up, the sooner I can enjoy some of the holiday. They tell me that I am on the brink of "IT." My husband rubs my back and tells me that it really isn't as important as I think to finish all this knitting.

15   I ignore their lies. They are not on my side; I can tell.

16   And then I enter "IT."

17   "IT" is a far and perilous place known only to the most determined and obsessive knitters. I don't know for sure how many knitters have experienced "IT," but no matter how many of us there are, "IT" still feels like a dark and lonely place. The difference between "IT" and regular holiday deadlines is like the difference between a stress headache and having your head squeezed in a drill press.

18   "IT" questions go like this:

1. How many hours will it be before people open their gifts? ("IT" usually takes place only in the three days before Christmas; anything before that gives you enough time to save yourself and is therefore still Phase 5.)

2. How many things are left unknit? ("IT" always has multiple items. If you are just trying to finish one gift . . . well, good for you.)

3. Does your KHPD (Knitting Hours Per Day) required to finish in time for Christmas now exceed twenty-four?

19   If you are truly experiencing "IT," the following will also be true:

1. Despite having calculated your KHPD, and realizing that you cannot possibly finish in time, you are still knitting instead of sleeping.

2. You have actually not slept since you entered "IT," and depending on your type, you have also given up eating, or you have only eaten chocolate and leftover pizza crusts for the last several days.

3. The children will be up in forty-five minutes to see what Santa brought them and you are sitting wild-eyed in the darkened house frantically knitting the hats you want to put in their stockings.

4. You are prioritizing the knitting according to when you will see the recipient. For example: You don't see your aunt until the evening of the twenty-fifth, but you see your mother in the afternoon. Therefore, since it is only the twenty-fourth you are working on your husband's sock because you will see him first thing on Christmas morning. You have actually come to believe that this means that you have *lots of time* until you need your aunt's present.

5. You are planning to sew your nephew's sweater together in the basement while everyone else opens gifts. You are pretty sure that as long as they all go first you can make it.

6. Finally, you have vowed that next year you will start sooner, do less, and be more realistic about your knitting goals. You have vowed that you will not ruin Christmas by dedicating your life to the pursuit of woolen gifts for everyone. You admit that it may be possible to buy your aunt's dog a gift next year instead of knitting it a sweater. Furthermore, you have admitted that while this plan looked like fun when you started, you are not having much fun now. You admit that your refusal to go skating with the children, because tying skates up cuts into kitting time, may be affecting their happiness as well. You have also agreed with your spouse that it is reasonable to expect that you would have time for "marital relations" at least once during the month of December, and you know that this means you will have to knit less. You have also admitted that you cannot warp the time-space continuum, despite the persistent belief and occasional proof that it is possible.

20   In short you have promised that next year you will not do "IT." Never again.

21   But you will, and I will be here for you. I promise.

WHAT DID THE WRITER SAY AND WHAT DID YOU THINK?

1. What is the stated thesis? What's the purpose of this essay? What's the relationship between these two?
2. What is "IT"? How much of "IT" is exaggeration?
3. The author suggests that "IT" is an inevitable meltdown, for her and for the audience. What seems to cause one phase to advance to the next?
4. Is this process relevant to any activities or situations other than knitting Christmas gifts?

HOW DID THE WRITER SAY IT?

1. The process is narrated in first person, but when the author reaches her description of Phase 4, she begins to use "you." What's the effect of using second person?
2. This book suggests that you define unfamiliar terms. Does this essay make the meaning of all its terminology clear? How does the author do this, or where does she fail to do it?
3. The author uses several lists within the essay. What's the function of these lists?
4. The last sentence contradicts the paragraph immediately before it. Why does the author do this?

What About <u>Your</u> Writing?

Effective repetition of words and phrases—sometimes exact repetition, sometimes repetition with slight variations—is one of a writer's most direct means of driving home a point and achieving a touch of stylistic power. In her description of Phase 5 of "IT," Stephanie Pearl-McPhee uses repetition to emphasize the eternal cycle of hope, despair, and madness that characterizes her holiday knitting and the ritualistic quality of her family's comments about it. "They beg me not to lose touch. They tell me that there is more to life than knitting and that people would rather I was well rested and happy than making them socks. They tell me that the sooner I give up, the sooner I can enjoy some of the holiday. They tell me that I am on the brink of 'IT.'" Notice also the repeated use of the phrasing "Phase 2 is when . . . Phase 3 is when . . . Phase 4 is when . . ." as a unifying detail throughout the essay.

Repetition can be abused, of course. Handled poorly, it can become monotonous and irritating. If *every* sentence in Pearl-McPhee's essay began with "They tell me that . . . " for example, her readers would lose their patience and their minds. Used properly, however, repetition has produced some of the most memorable phrases in the English language:

- Gentlemen may cry peace, peace—but there is no peace.
- We have nothing to fear but fear itself.
- It was the best of times, it was the worst of times.
- We shall fight on the beaches, we shall fight on the landing grounds, we shall fight in the fields and in the streets, we shall fight in the hills; we shall never surrender.
- Good bread, good meat, good God, let's eat!

THE EXPLODING TOILET AND OTHER EMBARRASSMENTS

Patrick Smith

Author of the weekly "Ask the Pilot" column at Salon.com, Patrick Smith is an airline pilot and freelance writer. He has flown passenger and cargo jets and has visited more than fifty countries.

✓ WORDS TO CHECK:

bromidic (paragraph 1)	adrenaline (10)	camaraderie (20)
adage (1)	pylon (15)	disgorging (20)
void (2)	cataract (16)	detritus (21)
mesmerized (3)	boisterous (17)	mystique (21)
cleaved (3)	scenarios (19)	ionosphere (23)
ruminations (3)	psychedelic (19)	scatological (23)
emanate (10)		

1　An old bromidic adage defines the business of flying planes as long stretches of boredom punctuated by moments of sheer terror. Moments of sheer ridiculousness, maybe, are equally as harrowing. One young pilot, when he was 22 and trying to impress the pretty Christine Collingworth with a sightseeing circuit in a friend's plane, highlighted the seduction by whacking his forehead into the jutting metal pitot tube hanging from the wing. Earning a famous "Cessna dimple," so he chose to think, would be the stupidest thing he'd ever do in or around an airplane.

2　That was a long time ago, and a long way from this same pilot's mind during a late-night cargo flight. It's eleven p.m. and the airplane, an old DC-8 freighter loaded with pineapples, is somewhere over the Bermuda Triangle, bound from San Juan, Puerto Rico, to Cincinnati. The night is dark and quiet, void of moonlight, conversation, and for that matter worry. The crew of three is tired, and this will be their last leg in a week's rotation that has brought them from New York to Belgium and back again, onward to Mexico, and now the Caribbean.

3　They are mesmerized by the calming drone of high-bypass turbofans and the deceptively peaceful noise of 500 knots of frigid wind cleaved along the cockpit windows. Such a setting, when you really think about it, ought to be enough to scare the living shit from any sensible person. We have no business, maybe, being up there, participants in such an inherently dangerous balance between naïve solitude and instant death, distracted by paperwork and chicken sandwiches while screaming along, higher than Mount Everest and at the speed of sound in a 40-year-old assemblage of machinery. But such philosophizing is for poets, not pilots, and also makes for exceptionally bad karma. No mystical ruminations were in the job description for these three airmen, consummate professionals who long ago sold their souls to the more practical-minded muses of technology and luck.

4   Our pilot, whose name is Patrick Smith, born Patrick R Santosuosso of Revere, Massachusetts, a fourth-generation descendant of Neapolitan olive growers, is one of these consummate professionals. Now 34, he has seen his career stray oddly from its intended course. His ambitions of flying gleaming new passenger jets to distant ports-of-call have given way to the coarser world of air cargo, to sleepless, back-of-the-clock timetables, the greasy glare of warehouse lights and the roar of forklifts—realities that have aroused a low note of disappointment that rings constantly in the back of his brain. He is the second officer. His station, a sideways-turned chair and a great, blackboard-sized panel of instruments, is set against the starboard wall.

5   He stands up from the second officer's seat and walks out of the cockpit, closing the door behind him. Here he enters the plane's only other accessible zone during flight, the small entryway vestibule adjacent to the main cabin door. It contains a life raft, oven, cooler, some storage space and the lavatory. His plan is simple enough—to get himself a Diet Coke. The soft drinks are in a cardboard box on the floor, in a six-pack strapped together with one of those clear plastic harnesses so threatening to sea turtles and small children. These plastic rings are banned at home, but apparently perfectly legal in the Caribbean, where there are, of course, lots of sea turtles and small children. The pilot thinks about this as he reaches for a can, weighing the injustices of the world, philosophizing, daydreaming, ruminating—things that, again, his manuals neither command nor endorse, for perhaps good reason.

6   He unstraps a Coke and decides to put the remaining ones in the cooler to chill. The cooler, a red, lift-top Coleman that you'd buy in Sears, sits in front of the lavatory and is packed with bags of ice. He drops in the cans, but now the cooler will not close.

7   There's too much ice. One of the bags will have to go. So he pulls one out and shuts the lid. Decisions, decisions. Which checklist do I initiate? Which valve do I command closed? Which circuit breakers do I pull? How do I keep us alive and this contraption intact? And what to do, now, with an extra, sopping wet bag of ice?

8   Well, the pilot will do what he always does with an extra bag of ice. He will open the bag and dump it down the toilet. This he has done so often that the sound of a hundred cubes hitting the metal bowl is a familiar one.

9   This time, though, for reasons he hasn't realized yet, there are no cubes. More accurately, there is one huge cube. He rips open the bag, which is green-ish and slightly opaque, and out slides a long, single block of ice, probably two pounds' worth, that clatters off the rim and splashes into the bowl. There it is met, of course, by the caustic blue liquid one always finds in airplane toilets—the strange chemical cocktail that so efficiently and brightly neutralizes our organic contributions. The fluid washes over the ice. He hits the flush and it's drawn into the hole and out of sight. He turns, clutching the empty bag and worrying still about the dangers of plastic rings and turtles, picturing some poor endangered hawksbill choking to death. It's just not fair.

10   And it's now that the noise begins. As he steps away, the pilot hears a deep and powerful burble, which immediately repeats itself and seems to emanate from somewhere in the bowels of the plane. How to describe it? It's similar to the sound your own innards might make if you've eaten an entire pizza or, perhaps swallowed Drano, amplified many times over. The pilot stops and a quick shot of adrenaline pulses into his veins. What was that? It grows louder. Then there's a rumble, a vibration passes up through his feet, and from behind him comes a loud swishing noise.

11   He turns and looks at the toilet. But it has, for all practical purposes, dis-appeared, and where it once rested he now finds what he will later describe only as: a vision. In place of the commode roars a fluorescent blue waterfall, a huge, heaving cascade of toilet fluid thrust waist-high into the air and splashing into all four corners of the lavatory. Pouring from the top of this volcano, like smoke out of a factory chimney, is a rapidly spreading pall of what looks like steam. He closes his eyes tightly for a second, then reopens them.

12   He does this not for the benefit of unwitnessed theatrics, or even to create an embellishment for later use in a story. He does so because, for the first time in his life, he truly does not believe what is cast in front of him.

13   The fountain grows taller, and he sees that the toilet is not actually spraying, but bubbling—a geyser of lathering blue foam topped with a thick white fog. And suddenly he realizes what's happened. It was not a block of ice, exactly, that he fed to the toilet. It was a block of dry ice.

14   To combine dry ice with liquid is to initiate the turbulent, and rather unstoppable, chemical reaction now underway before our unfortunate friend. The effect, though in our case on a much grander scale, is similar to the mixing of baking soda with vinegar, or dumping water into a Fryolator, an exciting experiment those of you who've worked in restaurants have probably expe-rienced: the boiling oil will have nothing to do with the water, discharging its elements in a violent surge of bubbles. Normally when the caterers use dry ice, it's packed apart in smaller, square-shaped bags you can't miss. Today, though,

an extra-large allotment was stuffed into a regular old ice cube bag–two pounds of solid carbon dioxide now mixing quite unhappily with a tankful of acid.

15   Within seconds a wide blue river begins to flow out of the lav and across the floor, where a series of tracks, panels, and gullies promptly splits it into several smaller rivers, each leading away to a different nether-region beneath the main deck of the DC-8. The liquid moves rapidly along these paths, spilling off into the crevices. It's your worst bathroom nightmare at home or in a hotel–clogging up the toilet at midnight and watching it overflow. Except this time it's a Technicolor eruption of flesh-eating poison, dribbling into the seams of an airplane, down into the entrails to freeze itself around cables or short out bundles of vital wiring. Our pilot once read a report about a toilet reservoir somehow becoming frozen in the back of a 727. A chunk of blue ice was ejected overboard and sucked into an engine, causing the entire thing, pylon and all, to tear away and drop to earth.

16   And the pilot knows his cataract is not going to stop until either the CO_2 is entirely evaporated or the tank of blue death is entirely drained. Meanwhile the white steam–the evaporating carbon dioxide–is filling the cabin with vapor like the smoke show at a rock concert. He decides to get the captain.

17   Our captain tonight, as fate would have it, is a boisterous and slightly crazy Scandinavian. Let's call him Jens. Jens is a tall, square-jawed Norwegian with graying, closely cropped curls and an animated air of imperious cocksure. Jens is one of those guys who makes everybody laugh simply by walking into a room, though whether or not he's trying to is never clear. He is sitting in the captain's chair. The sun has set hours ago but he is still wearing Ray-Bans.

18   "Jens, come here fast. I need your help."

19   Jens nods to the first officer and unbuckles his belt. This is an airline captain, a confident four-striper trained and ready for any variety of airborne calamity–engine failures, fires, bombs, wind shear. What will he find back there? Jens steps into the entryway and is greeted not by any of a thousand different training scenarios, but by a psychedelic fantasy of color and smoke, a wall of white fog and the fuming blue witch's cauldron, the outfall from which now covers the entire floor, from the entrance of the cockpit to the enormous nylon safety net that separates the crew from its load of pineapples.

20   Jens stares. Then he turns to his young second officer and puts a hand on his shoulder, a gesture of both fatherly comfort and surrendering camaraderie, as if to say, "Don't worry son, I'll clean all this up," or maybe, "Down with the ship we go." He sighs, nods toward the fizzing, disgorging bowl and says, with a tone of surprisingly unironic pride: "She's got quite a head on her, doesn't she?"

21   But what can they do? And in one of those dreaded realizations pilots are advised to avoid, that insulation between cockpit calm and atmospheric anarchy looks thin indeed. An extrapolated vision of horror: the riveted aluminum planks bending apart, the wind rushing in, explosive depressurization, death, the first airliner–no, the first vehicle–in history to crash because of an

overflowing toilet. Into the sea, where divers and salvage ships will haul up the wreckage, detritus trailing from mauled, unrecognizable pieces while investigators shake their heads. At least, the pilot thinks, odds are nobody will ever know the truth, the cold ocean carrying away the evidence. He's good as dead, but saved, maybe, from immortal embarrassment. A dash of mystique awaits him, the same that met Saint-Exupéry at the bottom of the Mediterranean, another lousy pilot who got philosophical and paid the price. Maybe he blew up the toilet too: Probable cause: unknown.

22   "Call flight control," commands Jens, hoping a dose of authority will interject some clarity into a scene that is obviously and hopelessly absurd. "Get a patch with maintenance and explain what happened."

23   The pilot rushes back to the cockpit to call the company's maintenance staff. He fires up the HF radios, small black boxes that can bounce the human voice, and any of its associated embarrassments, up off the ionosphere and halfway around the world if need be. He will announce his predicament to the mechanics, and also to any of dozens of other crews monitoring the same frequency. Even before keying the mike he can see the looks and hear the wisecracks from the Delta and United pilots in their state-of-the-art 777s, Mozart soothing their passengers through Bose headsets, flight attendants wiping down the basins while somewhere in the night sky three poor souls in a Cold War relic are trapped in a blue scatological hell.

24   "You say the toilet exploded?" Maintenance is on the line, incredulous but not particularly helpful. "Well, um, not sure. Should be okay. Nothing below the cabin there to worry about. Press on, I guess." Thanks. Click.

25   Jens has now grabbed the extension wand for the fire extinguisher—a hollow metal pole the length of a harpoon—and is shoving it down into the bowl trying to agitate the mixture to a stop. Several minutes have passed, and a good ten gallons have streamed their way onto the floor and beyond. Up front, the first officer has no idea what's going on. Looking behind him, his view mostly blocked by the circuit breaker panels and cockpit door, this is what he sees: a haze of white odorless smoke, and his captain yelping with laughter and thrusting at something with a long metal pole.

26   The pilot stands aside, watching Jens do battle. This was the same little kid who dreamed of becoming a 747 captain, the embodiment of all that was, and could still be, glamorous and exciting about aviation. And poor Jens, whose ancestors ploughed this same Atlantic in longboats, ravenous for adventure and conquest, a twenty-first century Viking jousting with a broken toilet.

27   So it goes, and by the time the airplane touches down, its plumbing finally at rest, each and every employee at the cargo hub, clued in by the amused mechanics who received our distress call, already knows the story of the idiot who poured dry ice into the crapper. His socks and hundred-dollar Rockports have been badly damaged, while the walls, panels and placards aboard aircraft 806 are forever dyed a heavenly azure.

28   The crew bus pulls up to the stairs, and as the pilots step on board the driver looks up and says excitedly, "Which one of you did it?"

WHAT DID THE WRITER SAY AND WHAT DID YOU THINK?

1. What are the "other embarrassments" referred to in the title?
2. Smith's adventure ends safely, if humiliatingly. Where does he show the reader that there were some real dangers involved?
3. We've put this essay in the "Process" chapter, and it does explain the process of accidentally blowing up a toilet. What other chapters might it have fit in?
4. Why does Smith tell us the anecdote about the "Cessna dimple"?

HOW DID THE WRITER SAY IT?

1. This subject is one that some readers will find hilarious and others will find disgusting. How does Smith try to communicate the unpleasant details of the exploding toilet without revolting his readers? Does he succeed?
2. What effect do the quiet, almost philosophical introductory paragraphs have on the rest of the essay?
3. Why does Smith, in paragraph 26, talk about his childhood dreams and about Jens' Viking ancestry?

What About _Your_ Writing?

Smith makes frequent use of words that belong far more to formal English than to the everyday English more familiar to most people. He writes _bromidic_ instead of _unoriginal, harrowing_ instead of _scary, void_ instead of _empty_. Isn't this language too fancy? Is fancy writing good English?

The best reply to those questions is that they need to be rethought. It's like asking if tuxedos and evening gowns are good dress. They're good dress for formal dances, but they're bad dress for mowing the lawn. Shorts and a T-shirt are good dress for mowing the lawn, but bad dress for a formal dance. There's no one kind of good dress. A good dresser is someone who knows what kind of clothes to wear for different occasions.

There's no one kind of good English, either. It varies. It's what's appropriate to the subject, situation, and audience. As these elements change, the nature of what's appropriate will change. Tuxedo English is appropriate for ceremonial occasions, serious studies of specialized subjects, and so on. Lincoln's Gettysburg Address is written in formal English. If it had been written in a chatty, conversational style with folksy anecdotes about Lincoln's childhood, it would have been written in bad English and bad taste. On the other hand, shorts-and-T-shirt English is good English for much conversation and the dialogue of certain characters in works of fiction. A quarterback in a huddle says, "Play 32. Left tackle. Let's get the bums"—or something like that. It would be bad English for him to say, "Let us, my teammates, utilize Play 32 to assault the left tackle position of our adversaries."

Most freshman English papers should probably be written at the coat-and-tie or skirt-and-sweater level. A tuxedo is absurd. Even a business suit might sometimes be a bit stiff for the subject, situation, and audience. But shorts and a T-shirt are also out of place. Grammar still counts. Organization still counts. There aren't as many rules to worry about as in tuxedo English, but there are still plenty of rules.

In "The Exploding Toilet and Other Embarrassments," Smith is probably writing what could be called business-suit English. The subject is a comic one, and Smith heightens the comedy by using very formal English to deal with the hilariously informal subject matter of an exploding airplane toilet. And his piece is all the funnier for it. Good English changes all the time—and it doesn't have much to do with avoiding words like *ain't* or *desuetude*.

TOO MANY BANANAS

David R. Counts

David R. Counts is a professor of anthropology who has written, with his wife Dorothy Ayers Counts, on a range of topics from aging in Pacific cultures, to creation theology in New Guinea, to the culture of RVers in America.

✓ **WORDS TO CHECK:**

disgruntled (paragraph 3)   acquiesced (10)
gauche (6)   deference (18)

No Watermelon at All

1   The woman came all the way through the village, walking between the two rows of houses facing each other between the beach and the bush, to the very last house standing on a little spit of land at the mouth of the Kaini River. She was carrying a watermelon on her head, and the house she came to was the government "rest house," maintained by the villagers for the occasional use of visiting officials. Though my wife and I were graduate students, not officials, and had asked for permission to stay in the village for the coming year, we were living in the rest house while the debate went on about where a house would be built for us. When the woman offered to sell us the watermelon for two shillings, we happily agreed, and the kids were delighted at the prospect of watermelon after yet another meal of rice and bully beef. The money changed

hands and the seller left to return to her village, a couple of miles along the coast to the east.

2   It seemed only seconds later that the woman was back, reluctantly accompanying Kolia, the man who had already made it clear to us that he was the leader of the village. Kolia had no English, and at that time, three or four days into our first stay in Kandoka Village on the island of new Britain in Papua New Guinea, we have very little Tok Pisin. Language difficulties notwithstanding, Kolia managed to make his message clear: The woman had been outrageously wrong to sell us the watermelon for two shillings and we were to return it to her and reclaim our money immediately. When we tried to explain that we thought the price to be fair and were happy with the bargain, Kolia explained again and finally made it clear that we had missed the point. The problem wasn't that we had paid too much; it was that we had paid at all. Here he was, a leader, responsible for us while we were living in his village, and we had shamed him. How would it look if he let guests in his village buy food? If we wanted watermelons, or bananas, or anything else, all that was necessary was to let him know. He told us that it would be all right for us to give little gifts to people who brought food to us (and they surely would), but no one was to sell food to us. If anyone were to try—like this woman from Lauvore—then we should refuse. There would be plenty of watermelons without us buying them.

3   The woman left with her watermelon, disgruntled, and we were left without two shillings. But we had learned the first lesson of many about living in Kandoka. We didn't pay money for food again that whole year, and we did get lots of food brought to us . . . but we never got another watermelon. That one was the last of the season.

4   *Lesson 1: In a society where food is shared or gifted as part of social life, you may not buy it with money.*

Too Many Bananas

5 In the couple of months that followed the watermelon incident, we managed to become at least marginally competent in Tok Pisin, to negotiate the construction of a house on what we hoped was neutral ground, and to settle into the routine of our fieldwork. As our village leader had predicted, plenty of food was brought to us. Indeed, seldom did a day pass without something coming in—some sweet potatoes, a few taro, a papaya, the occasional pineapple, or some bananas—lots of bananas.

6   We had learned our lesson about the money, though, so we never even offered to buy the things that were brought, but instead made gifts usually of tobacco to the adults or chewing gum to the children. Nor were we so gauche as to haggle with a giver over how much of a return gift was appropriate, though the two of us sometimes conferred as to whether what had been brought was a "two-stick" or a "three-stick" stalk, bundle, or whatever. A "stick" of tobacco was a single large leaf, soaked in rum and then twisted into a ropelike form. This,

wrapped in half a sheet of newsprint (torn for use as cigarette paper), sold in the local trade stores for a shilling. Nearly all of the adults in the village smoked a great deal, and they seldom had much cash, so our stocks of twist tobacco and stacks of the *Sydney Morning Herald* (all, unfortunately, the same day's issue) were seen as a real boon to those who preferred "stick" to the locally grown product.

7   We had established a pattern with respect to the gifts of food. When a donor appeared at our veranda we would offer our thanks and talk with them for a few minutes (usually about our children, who seemed to hold a real fascination for the villagers and for whom most of the gifts were intended) and then we would inquire whether they could use some tobacco. It was almost never refused, though occasionally a small bottle of kerosene, a box of matches, some laundry soap, a cup of rice, or a tin of meat would be requested instead of (or even in addition to) the tobacco. Everyone, even Kolia, seemed to think that arrangement had worked out well.

8   Now, what must be kept in mind is that while we were following their rules—or seemed to be—we were really still buying food. In fact we kept a running account of what came in and what we "paid" for it. Tobacco as currency got a little complicated, but since the exchange rate was one stick to one shilling, it was not too much trouble as long as everyone was happy, and meanwhile we could account for the expenditure of "informant fees" and "household expenses." Another thing to keep in mind is that not only did we continue to think in terms of our buying the food that was brought, we thought of them as selling it. While it was true they never quoted us a price, they also never asked us if we needed or wanted whatever they had brought. It seemed clear to us that when an adult needed a stick of tobacco, or a child wanted some chewing gum (we had enormous quantities of small packets of Wrigley's for just such eventualities) they would find something surplus to their own needs and bring it along to our "store" and get what they wanted.

9   By late November 1966, just before the rainy season set in, the bananas were coming into flush, and whereas earlier we had received banana gifts by the "hand" (six or eight bananas in a cluster cut from the stalk), donors now began to bring bananas, "for the children," by the stalk! The Kaliai among whom we were living are not exactly specialists in banana cultivation—they only recognize about thirty varieties, while some of their neighbors have more than twice that many—but the kinds they produce differ considerably from each other in size, shape, and taste, so we were not dismayed when we had more than one stalk hanging on our veranda. The stalks ripen a bit at the time, and having some variety was nice. Still, by the time our accumulation had reached four complete stalks, the delights of variety had begun to pale a bit. The fruits were ripening progressively and it was clear that even if we and the kids ate nothing but bananas for the next week, some would still fall from the stalk onto the floor in a state of gross overripeness. This was the situation as, late one afternoon, a woman came bringing yet another stalk of bananas up the steps of the house.

10   Several factors determined our reaction to her approach: one was that there was literally no way we could possibly use the bananas. We hadn't quite reached the point of being crowded off our veranda by the stalks of fruit, but it was close. Another factor was that we were tired of playing the gift game. We had acquiesced in playing it–no one was permitted to sell us anything, and in turn we only gave things away, refusing any circumstances to sell tobacco (or anything else) for money. But there had to be a limit. From our perspective what was at issue was that the woman wanted something and she had come to trade for it. Further, what she had brought to trade was something we neither wanted nor could use, and it should have been obvious to her. So we decided to bite the bullet.

11   The woman, Rogi, climbed the stairs to the veranda, took the stalk from where it was balanced on top of her head, and laid it on the floor with the word, "Here are some bananas for the children." Dorothy and I sat near her on the floor and thanked her for her thought but explained, "You know, we really have too many bananas–we can't use these; maybe you ought to give them to someone else. . . ." The woman looked mystified, then brightened and explained that she didn't want anything for them, she wasn't short of tobacco or anything. They were just a gift for the kids. Then she just sat there, and we sat there, and the bananas sat there, and we tried again. "Look," I said, pointing up to them and counting, "we've got four stalks already hanging here on the veranda–there are too many for us to eat now. Some are rotting already. Even if we eat only bananas, we can't keep up with what's here!"

12   Rogi's only response was to insist that these were a gift, and that she didn't want anything for them, so we tried yet another tack: "Don't your children like bananas?" When she admitted that they did, and that she had none at her house, we suggested that she should take them there. Finally, still puzzled, but convinced that we weren't going to keep the bananas, she replaced them on her head, went down the stairs, and made her way back through the village toward her house.

13   As before, it seemed only moment before Kolia was making his way up the stairs, but this time he hasn't brought the woman in tow. "What was wrong with those bananas? Were they no good?" he demanded. We explained that there was nothing wrong with the bananas at all, but that we simply couldn't use them and it seemed foolish to take them when we had so many and Rogi's own children had none. We obviously didn't make ourselves clear because Kolia then took up the same refrain that Rogi had–he insisted that we shouldn't be worried about taking the bananas, because they were a gift for the children and Rogi hadn't wanted anything for them. There was no reason, he added, to send her away with them–she would be ashamed. I'm afraid we must have seemed as if we were hard of hearing or thought he was, for our only response was to repeat our reasons. We went through it again–there they hung, one, two, three, four stalks of bananas, rapidly ripening and already far beyond our capacity to eat–we just weren't ready to accept any more and let them rot (and, we added to ourselves, pay for them with tobacco, to boot.)

14   Kolia finally realized that we were neither hard of hearing nor intentionally offensive, but merely ignorant. He stared at us for a few minutes, thinking, and then asked: "Don't you frequently have visitors during the day and evening?" We nodded. Then we asked, "Don't you usually offer them cigarettes and coffee or milk?" Again, we nodded. "Did it ever occur to you to suppose," he said, "that your visitors might be hungry?" It was at this point in the conversation, as we recall, that we began to see the depth of the pit we had dug for ourselves. We nodded, hesitantly. His last words to us before he went down the stairs and stalked away were just what we were by that time afraid that they might be. "When your guests are hungry, feed them bananas!"

15   *Lesson 2: Never refuse a gift, and never fail to return a gift. If you cannot use it, you can always give it away to someone else—there is no such thing as too much—there are never too many bananas.*

Not Enough Pineapples

16 During the fifteen years between that first visit in 1966 and our residence there in 1981 we had returned to live in Kandoka village twice during the 1970s, and though there were a great many changes in the village, and indeed for all of Papua New Guinea during that time, we continued to live according to the lessons of reciprocity learned during those first months in the field. We bought no food for money and refused no gifts, but shared our surplus. As our family grew, we continued to be accompanied by our younger children. Our place in the village came to be something like that of educated Kaliai who worked far away in New Guinea. Our friends expected us to come "home" when we had to leave, but knew that our work kept us away for long periods of time. They also credited us with knowing much more about the rules of their way of life than was our due. And we sometimes shared the delusion that we understood life in the village, but even fifteen years was not long enough to relieve the need for lessons in learning to live within the rules of gift exchange.

17   In the last paragraph I used the word friends to describe the villagers intentionally, but of course they were not all our friends. Over the years, some really had become friends, others were acquaintances, others remained consultants or informants to whom we turned when we needed information. Still others, unfortunately, we did not like at all. We tried never to make an issue of these distinctions, of course, and to be evenhanded and generous to all, as they were to us. Although we almost never actually refused requests that were made of us, over the long term our reciprocity in the village was balanced. More was given to those who helped us the most, while we gave assistance or donations of small items even to those who were not close or helpful.

18   One elderly woman in particular was a trial for us. Sara was the eldest of a group of siblings and her younger brother and sister were both generous, informative, and delightful persons. Her younger sister, Makila, was a particularly

close friend and consultant, and in deference to that friendship we felt awkward in dealing with the elder sister.

19   Sara was neither a friend nor an informant, but she had been, since she returned to live in the village at the time of our second trip in 1971, a constant (if minor) drain on our resources. She never asked for much at a time. A bar of soap, a box of matches, a bottle of kerosene, a cup of rice, some onions, a stick or two of tobacco, or some other small item was usually all that was at issue, but whenever she came around it was always to ask for something—or to let us know that when we left, we should give her some of the furnishings from the house. Too, unlike almost everyone else in the village, when she came, she was always empty-handed. We ate no taro from her gardens, and the kids chewed none of her sugarcane. In short, she was, as far as we could tell, a really grasping, selfish old woman—and we were not the only victims of her greed.

20   Having long before learned the lesson of the bananas, one day we had a stalk that was ripening so fast we couldn't keep up with it, so I pulled a few for our own use (we had only one stalk at the time) and walked down through the village to Ben's house, where his five children were playing. I sat down on his steps to talk, telling him that I intended to give the fruit to his kids. They never got them. Sara saw us from across the open plaza of the village and came rushing over, shouting, "My bananas!" Then she grabbed the stalk and went off gorging herself with them. Ben and I just looked at each other.

21   Finally it got to the point where it seemed to us that we had to do something. Ten years of being used by her was long enough. So there came the afternoon when Sara showed up to get some tobacco—again. But this time, when we gave her the two sticks she had demanded, we confronted her.

22   First, we noted the many times she had come to get things. We didn't mind sharing things, we explained. After all, we had plenty of tobacco and soap and rice and such, and most of it was there so that we could help our friends as they helped us, with folktales, information, or even gifts of food. The problem was that she kept coming to get things, but never came to talk, or to tell stories, or to bring some little something that the kids might like. Sarah didn't argue—she agreed. "Look," we suggested, "it doesn't have to be much, and we don't mind giving you things—but you can help us. The kids like pineapples, and we don't have any—the next time you need something, bring something—like maybe a pineapple." Obviously somewhat embarrassed she took her tobacco and left, saying that she would bring something soon. We were really pleased with ourselves. It had been a very difficult thing to do, but it was done, and we were convinced that either she would start bringing things or not come. It was as if a burden had lifted from our shoulders.

23   It worked. Only a couple of days passed before Sara was back, bringing her bottle to get it filled with kerosene. But this time, she came carrying the biggest, most beautiful pineapple we had seen the entire time we had been there.

We had a friendly talk, filled her kerosene container, and hung the pineapple up on the veranda to ripen just a little further. A few days later we cut and ate it, and whether the satisfaction it gave came from the fruit or from its source would be hard to say, but it was delicious. That, we assumed, was the end of that irritant.

24   We were wrong, of course. The next afternoon, Mary, one of our best friends for years (and no relation to Sara), dropped by for a visit. As we talked, her eyes scanned the veranda. Finally she asked whether we hadn't had a pineapple there yesterday. We said we had, but that we had already eaten it. She commented that it had been a really nice-looking one, and we told her that it had been the best we had eaten in months. Then, after a pause she asked, "Who brought it to you?" We smiled as we said, "Sara!" because Mary would appreciate our coup—she had commented many times in the past on the fact that Sara only got from us and never gave. She was silent for a moment, and then she said, "Well, I'm glad you enjoyed it—my father was waiting until it was fully ripe to harvest it for you, but when it went missing I thought maybe it was the one you had here. I'm glad to see you got it. I thought maybe a thief had eaten it in the bush."

25   *Lesson 3: Where reciprocity is the rule and gifts are the idiom, you cannot demand a gift, just as you cannot refuse a request.*

26   It says a great deal about the kindness and patience of the Kaliai people that they have been willing to be our hosts for all these years despite our blunders and lack of good manners. They have taught us a lot, and these three lessons are certainly not the least important things we learned.

WHAT DID THE WRITER SAY AND WHAT DID YOU THINK?

1. Counts doesn't state his thesis until the end of the essay. Even then it is not directly stated. How would you put his thesis into words?
2. What does Sara teach Counts about gifts?
3. Counts calls this essay, "Too Many Bananas," which refers to only one step in his process of learning about gift exchange. Can you think of a better title?
4. In paragraph 8, the author says that his family was still buying food, despite no longer using money to do so. Is he? What are the differences in the ways that he and the villagers think about buying food?

HOW DID THE WRITER SAY IT?

1. Counts uses an unusual approach to process writing here. What structures his essay instead of the traditional progression of small steps leading to a completed process?
2. What other rhetorical patterns are present in this essay?
3. Are any of Counts' steps unclear? Which one or ones?

What About <u>Your</u> Writing?

David R. Counts' essay about his experiences as an anthropologist in Papua, New Guinea, deftly avoids a grave danger that can arise when writing about such specialized subject matter. By explicitly defining such terms as *stick* and by clearly contextualizing the definitions of words and phrases like *taro, rest house,* and *Tok Pisin,* Counts avoids causing his readers the confusion, tedium, and annoyance that result from reading an essay that is filled with jargon.

Jargon is the specialized language and trade talk–the technical vocabulary–that insiders use to communicate with each other. Psychology, sociology, education, government, economics, the armed forces, virtually every area of human activity has its own jargon. Jargon is sometimes necessary, of course. No one can logically object when nuclear physicists or brain surgeons, addressing themselves or their colleagues, use the restricted vocabulary of their own field. There isn't any synonym in everyday English for *medulla oblongata.* So much material, however, allegedly written for general audiences, has been filled with jargon that, in addition to its original meaning, the word has now come to refer to pompous double-talk, offensive to outsiders and insiders alike. Jargon of this kind gives the impression that the author is unable to tolerate simplicity. Sometimes it gives the even more objectionable sense of being deliberately designed to give commonplace ideas a bogus air of dignity, presumably to impress all the ignorant peasants–like us.

You will be writing for a general audience in your composition course. It's almost always possible to turn the high-sounding mumbo jumbo of jargon into everyday English. Be extremely careful about picking subjects for your essays in which it is not possible: tuning an engine, programming a computer, performing a chemical analysis, or operating a forklift. If you decide to go ahead anyway, be sure to follow Counts' model and provide simple definitions for all the unfamiliar terms.

Offensive Jargon	**Everyday English**
Maximum utilization of vehicular resources. . . .	Making the best use of transportation. . . .
Furtherance of interpersonal communications between disparate socioeconomic units. . . .	Getting people of different backgrounds to talk more with each other. . . .
Bilateral accommodation is imperative.	Both sides will have to compromise.
The classroom situation is geared to the fostering of meaningful, democratic decision-making opportunities by the student population.	Students have a voice in determining what happens in class.

THE SPIDER AND THE WASP

Alexander Petrunkevitch

Alexander Petrunkevitch (1875–1964) was one of the world's leading authorities on spiders. Born in Russia, he taught at various American universities. His wide range of skills and interests is suggested by his translation of English (to Russian) and Russian (to English) poetry and by such titles as *Index Catalogue of Spiders of North, Central, and South America* (1911), *Choice and Responsibility* (1947), and *Principles of Classification* (1952).

✓ **Words to Check:**

progeny (paragraph 1)	nectar (9)	secretion (13)
archenemy (1)	pungent (9)	olfactory (14)
unwittingly (1)	chitinous (9)	simulating (15)
tactile (8)	girth (11)	

1 In the feeding and safeguarding of their progeny insects and spiders exhibit some interesting analogies to reasoning and some crass examples of blind instinct. The case I propose to describe here is that of the tarantula spiders and their archenemy, the digger wasps of the genus *Pepsis*. It is a classic example of what looks like intelligence pitted against instinct–a strange situation in which the victim, though fully able to defend itself, submits unwittingly to its destruction.

2 Most tarantulas live in the tropics, but several species occur in the temperate zone and a few are common in the southern U.S. Some varieties are large and have powerful fangs with which they can inflict a deep wound. These formidable looking spiders do not, however, attack man; you can hold one in your hand, if you are gentle, without being bitten. Their bite is dangerous only to insects and small mammals such as mice; for a man it is no worse than a hornet's sting.

3 Tarantulas customarily live in deep cylindrical burrows, from which they emerge at dusk and into which they retire at dawn. Mature males wander about after dark in search of females and occasionally stray into houses. After mating, the male dies in a few weeks, but a female lives much longer and can mate several years in succession. In a Paris museum is a tropical specimen which is said to have been living in captivity for 25 years.

4 A fertilized female tarantula lays from 200 to 400 eggs at a time; thus it is possible for a single tarantula to produce several thousand young. She takes no care of them beyond weaving a cocoon of silk to enclose the eggs. After they hatch, the young walk away, find convenient places in which to dig their burrows and spend the rest of their lives in solitude. The eyesight of tarantulas is poor, being limited to a sensing of change in the intensity of light and to the

perception of moving objects. They apparently have little or no sense of hearing, for a hungry tarantula will pay no attention to a loudly chirping cricket placed in its cage unless the insect happens to touch one of its legs.

5   But all spiders, and especially hairy ones, have an extremely delicate sense of touch. Laboratory experiments prove that tarantulas can distinguish three types of touch: pressure against the body wall, stroking of the body hair, and riffling of certain very fine hairs on the legs called trichobothria. Pressure against the body, by the finger or the end of a pencil, causes the tarantula to move off slowly for a short distance. The touch excites no defensive response unless the approach is from above where the spider can see the motion, in which case it rises on its hind legs, lifts its front legs, opens its fangs and holds this threatening posture as long as the object continues to move.

6   The entire body of a tarantula, especially its legs, is thickly clothed with hair. Some of it is short and wooly, some long and stiff. Touching this body hair produces one of two distinct reactions. When the spider is hungry, it responds with an immediate and swift attack. At the touch of a cricket's antennae the tarantula seizes the insect so swiftly that a motion picture taken at the rate of 64 frames per second shows only the result and not the process of capture. But when the spider is not hungry, the stimulation of its hairs merely causes it to shake the touched limb. An insect can walk under its hairy belly unharmed.

7   The trichobothria, very fine hairs growing from disclike membranes on the legs, are sensitive only to air movement. A light breeze makes them vibrate slowly, without disturbing the common hair. When one blows gently on the trichobothria, the tarantula reacts with a quick jerk of its four front legs. If the front and hind legs are stimulated at the same time, the spider makes a sudden jump. This reaction is quite independent of the state of its appetite.

8   These three tactile responses–to pressure on the body wall, to moving of the common hair, and to flexing of the trichobothria–are so different from one another that there is no possibility of confusing them. They serve the tarantula adequately for most of its needs and enable it to avoid most annoyances and dangers. But they fail the spider completely when it meets its deadly enemy, the digger wasp *Pepsis*.

9   These solitary wasps are beautiful and formidable creatures. Most species are either a deep shiny blue all over, or deep blue with rusty wings. The largest have a wing span of about four inches. They live on nectar. When excited, they give off a pungent odor–a warning that they are ready to attack. The sting is much worse than that of a bee or common wasp, and the pain and swelling last longer. In the adult stage the wasp lives only a few months. The female produces but a few eggs, one at a time at intervals of two or three days. For each egg the mother must provide one adult tarantula, alive but paralyzed. The mother wasp attaches the egg to the paralyzed spider's abdomen. Upon hatching from the egg, the larva is many hundreds of times smaller than its living but helpless victim. It eats no other food and drinks

no water. By the time it has finished its single Gargantuan meal and become ready for wasphood, nothing remains of the tarantula but its indigestible chitinous skeleton.

10   The mother wasp goes tarantula-hunting when the egg in her ovary is almost ready to be laid. Flying low over the ground late on a sunny afternoon, the wasp looks for its victim or for the mouth of a tarantula burrow, a round hole edged by a bit of silk. The sex of the spider makes no difference, but the mother is highly discriminating as to species. Each species of *Pepsis* requires a certain species of tarantula, and the wasp will not attack the wrong species. In a cage with a tarantula which is not its normal prey, the wasp avoids the spider and is usually killed by it in the night.

11   Yet when a wasp finds the correct species, it is the other way about. To identify the species the wasp apparently must explore the spider with her antennae. The tarantula shows an amazing tolerance to this exploration. The wasp crawls under it and walks over it without evoking any hostile response. The molestation is so great and so persistent that the tarantula often rises on all eight legs, as if it were on stilts. It may stand this way for several minutes. Meanwhile the wasp, having satisfied itself that the victim is of the right species, moves off a few inches to dig the spider's grave. Working vigorously with legs and jaws, it excavates a hole 8 to 10 inches deep with a diameter slightly larger than the spider's girth. Now and again the wasp pops out of the hole to make sure that the spider is still there.

12   When the grave is finished, the wasp returns to the tarantula to complete her ghastly enterprise. First she feels it all over once more with her antennae. Then her behavior becomes more aggressive. She bends her abdomen, protruding her sting, and searches for the soft membrane at the point where the spider's legs join its body—the only spot where she can penetrate the horny skeleton. From time to time, as the exasperated spider slowly shifts ground, the wasp turns on her back and slides along with the aid of her wings, trying to get under the tarantula for a shot at the vital spot. During all this maneuvering, which can last for several minutes, the tarantula makes no move to save itself. Finally the wasp corners it against some obstruction and grasps one of its legs in her powerful jaws. Now at last the harassed spider tries a desperate but vain defense. The two contestants roll over and over on the ground. It is a terrifying sight and the outcome is always the same. The wasp finally manages to thrust her sting into the soft spot and holds it there for a few seconds while she pumps in the poison. Almost immediately the tarantula falls paralyzed on its back. Its legs stop twitching, its heart stops beating. Yet it is not dead, as is shown by the fact that if taken from the wasp it can be restored to some sensitivity by being kept in a moist chamber for several months.

13   After paralyzing the tarantula, the wasp cleans herself by dragging her body along the ground and rubbing her feet, sucks the drop of blood oozing

from the wound in the spider's abdomen, then grabs a leg of the flabby, helpless animal in her jaws and drags it down to the bottom of the grave. She stays there for many minutes, sometimes for several hours, and what she does all that time in the dark we do not know. Eventually she lays her egg and attaches it to the side of the spider's abdomen with a sticky secretion. Then she emerges, fills the grave with soil carried bit by bit in her jaws, and finally tramples the ground all around to hide any trace of the grave from prowlers. Then she flies away, leaving her descendant safely started in life.

14   In all this the behavior of the wasp evidently is qualitatively different from that of the spider. The wasp acts like an intelligent animal. This is not to say that instinct plays no part or that she reasons as man does. But her actions are to the point; they are not automatic and can be modified to fit the situation. We do not know for certain how she identifies the tarantula—probably it is by some olfactory or chemo-tactile sense—but she does it purposefully and does not blindly tackle a wrong species.

15   On the other hand, the tarantula's behavior shows only confusion. Evidently the wasp's pawing gives it no pleasure, for it tries to move away. That the wasp is not simulating sexual stimulation is certain, because male and female tarantulas react in the same way to its advances. That the spider is not anesthetized by some odorless secretion is easily shown by blowing lightly at the tarantula and making it jump suddenly. What, then, makes the tarantula behave as stupidly as it does?

16   No clear, simple answer is available. Possibly the stimulation by the wasp's antennae is masked by a heavier pressure on the spider's body, so that it reacts as when prodded by a pencil. But the explanation may be much more complex. Initiative in attack is not in the nature of tarantulas; most species fight only when cornered so that escape is impossible. Their inherited patterns of behavior apparently prompt them to avoid problems rather than attack them. For example, spiders always weave their webs in three dimensions, and when a spider finds that there is insufficient space to attach certain threads in the third dimension, it leaves the place and seeks another, instead of finishing the web in a single plane. This urge to escape seems to arise under all circumstances, in all phases of life, and to take the place of reasoning. For a spider to change the pattern of its web is as impossible as for an inexperienced man to build a bridge across a chasm obstructing his way.

17   In a way the instinctive urge to escape is not only easier but often more efficient than reasoning. The tarantula does exactly what is most efficient in all cases except in an encounter with a ruthless and determined attacker dependent for the existence of her own species on killing as many tarantulas as she can lay eggs. Perhaps in this case the spider follows its usual pattern of trying to escape, instead of seizing and killing the wasp, because it is not aware of its danger. In any case, the survival of the tarantula species as a whole is protected by the fact that the spider is much more fertile than the wasp.

WHAT DID THE WRITER SAY AND WHAT DID YOU THINK?

1. A primary thesis tells why the process is worth discussing. What is the primary thesis, and where does it appear?
2. A secondary thesis tries to explain why the process happens as it does. What is the secondary thesis, and where does it appear?
3. Does the author acknowledge alternate explanations?
4. What makes the behavior of the spider so puzzling?
5. Where does the author suggest his own emotional reaction to the process?
6. Is the reader meant to take sides, to root for the spider or the wasp?
7. People who think they are totally indifferent to nature and science often become deeply involved in "The Spider and the Wasp." Can you suggest why?
8. Can you think of certain types of human beings whose behavior corresponds to the spider's? To the wasp's?

HOW DID THE WRITER SAY IT?

1. Who is the intended audience for this selection?
2. The description of the process does not begin until paragraph 10, though paragraph 9 presents a summary of the process. What has the author been doing until then?
3. Are all obscure scientific terms defined?
4. Consult the table of contents. What patterns of writing are in this selection in addition to *process*?
5. Does the author gather the many separate steps into groups? If so, into how many?
6. "The mother wasp goes tarantula-hunting . . . " Does this phrase seem too informal, almost slangy, for a scientific article? Are there other unusually informal words or phrases? Are they justified?

What About <u>Your</u> Writing?

"The Spider and the Wasp" is a very specific kind of writing. Although the essay can be read and enjoyed by a wide audience, it is also a highly technical piece of scientific writing. This means that Petrunkevitch follows the conventions, or traditional ways of doing things, for his field. He uses more technical vocabulary and more specialized knowledge (see the What About Your Writing on specialized knowledge on page 257) than most essays in this book. He also writes in paragraph 1, "The case I propose to describe here is that of the tarantula spiders and their archenemy, the digger wasps of the genus *Pepsis*." That's an *announcement* of his subject, and it's both accepted and expected in scientific writing.

While the conventions of science writing encourage announcements, we've specifically warned you against them (page 5). For most of the writing you will do, in most of the classes you will take, and for most of the instructors you will have, we stand by our advice. It is best, in general, to avoid making an announcement unless you want your instructor to reach for the red pen. If you think that an assignment that you're working on is so technical that it needs an announcement of its subject, check with your instructor to make sure.

CHAPTER 5½
Office Hours: Uses and Abuses of the Computer

One of the most remarkable changes since the first edition of this textbook was published over thirty years ago is the immense growth in the use of personal computers. We've gone from a time when a single computer took up a whole room to a time when we can put a computer into a briefcase and have space left over. We've gone from a time when a personal computer was the stuff of science fiction to a time when nearly everyone either owns or has access to one.

And what are people doing with all these computers? Most of the time, they're writing. Whether they're sending instant messages to their friends, writing e-mail to their bosses or their grandmothers, creating web pages, or using their favorite word-processing program to compose a paper or an article, they're using their computers to write.

Lots of books give lots of advice about writing with a computer. Computers, they often argue, have revolutionized the writing process and have created almost a whole new set of rules for good writing. We think they're wrong.

Don't misunderstand. Computers are indispensable. They make parts of the writing process much easier. However, having an impressive set of high-tech tools doesn't mean that all the advice in this book and others is obsolete. The good old advice and the brand-new technology can work together to help you produce good writing more efficiently. You just have to remember that if you aren't careful, all this brand-new technology can cause you some brand-new problems.

POTENTIAL ABUSES

Spell Checker

Spell checkers help us catch the silly typographical mistakes and occasional mental slips that every writer makes. They save writers from the tedium of having to check every word of every sentence for correctness. Spell checkers are a blessing, right?

Not quite. The problem with spell checkers is not with the technology. A spell checker will always let you know if you type *Wendsday* instead of *Wednesday*. But spell checkers can't make judgment calls. For example, if you type "I need to buy some flower to make a cake," a spell checker has no way of knowing that you meant to type *flour*. All it knows is that you've spelled *flower* correctly. So you won't get your warning, and you won't correct an embarrassing mistake. (Your cake won't be very good, either.) A similar problem showed up when a student used a spell checker on a paper about Shakespeare's comic character Falstaff. The computer corrected the name "Falstaff" to "Flagstaff" through the whole essay. Suddenly, the student's paper was about a city in Arizona and not about Shakespeare at all. (Her instructor was not impressed.)

So what's the solution? You simply have to remember that spell checkers do some things very well, but they can't think for you. Instead of letting your spell checker do a brainless "auto correct" to instantly fix all the errors it thinks it has found, use it to help *you* go through your paper sentence by sentence and word by word, alerting you every time it suspects an error. Then *you* make the decision about what to change. You'll catch more mistakes, and you'll be using your spell checker and your computer as they were meant to be used—as extra support for your brain, not as substitutes.

Grammar Checker

Grammar checkers, like spell checkers, should be used in conjunction with your brain, not instead of it. The more advanced and distinctive your writing becomes, the less useful grammar checkers are. They just aren't up to the task of knowing that sometimes sentence fragments, or sentences that begin with *And* or end with a preposition, or any of a number of other variations, can be justifiable violations of traditional writing rules. Those are the kinds of decisions that only you can make. Sometimes you know more than your computer thinks you do.

Thesaurus

We discuss the misuse of a thesaurus on page 34. But a computer thesaurus is far more likely to be misused because you don't even have to walk over to your bookshelf to use it. It makes it much too easy to look for a long, impressive, gold-plated word when a simpler word will do.

The other worry about computer thesauruses is that while they do their best to list synonyms, they often list words that are close in meaning but aren't precisely right. For example, when we ran our computer's thesaurus function on the word *precisely* in the previous sentence, it listed the following words as acceptable synonyms: *exactly, accurately, specifically, in particular, correctly, just,* and *quite*. You can easily see that only two or three of those would work as reasonable substitutes.

Just remember to use your brain as well as your computer's when you use your thesaurus and you'll be fine. Forget, and you'll pick the wrong word and lose your reader.

Decorations

One of the temptations of writing with a computer is the ease of pushing a few buttons and making everything pretty. It doesn't take any time at all to dress up an essay with a picture or change to a font that's eye-catching or even colorful, or to emphasize a word with **boldface** type or *italics* or underlining, even ***all three.*** Sometimes, writers try to make the bells and whistles of graphics, pretty colors, and exotic fonts do all their work for them. You can use your computer to make your paper catch your reader's eye, but if you don't have anything interesting to say, all the decorations in the world won't help.

POTENTIAL USES

Cut and Paste

When preparing the earliest editions of this textbook, if we wanted to move a paragraph around before the book went to press, it had to be cut and pasted– with scissors and glue. Really. It took forever. For this edition, though, because it's prepared on a computer, it's easy to rearrange a whole paragraph, a whole chapter, or even the whole book, just by highlighting the text that needs to be moved, "cutting" it from its old position, and "pasting" it somewhere new. And it can be moved over and over again until it's right.

This is good news for your papers, too. Suppose you've finished your essay for class tomorrow, and as you're rereading it, you decide that you've put your strongest supporting point much too late in the essay, where it might lose its impact. In the old days, you had no choice but to retype the whole paper. Today, ten seconds of cutting and pasting can solve the whole problem.

Storage

Personal computers help writers be thrifty. You can save anything and everything that you want to save. Have some notes you didn't use for your essay this week? Hang onto them. They may come in handy for the next essay you write or the next class you take. Have to cut a section from a paper because it doesn't fit? Save it. It may work in another draft later in the semester or in another paper for another class. You can even use your computer to supplement the traditional writer's notebook (see Chapter 3½).

Research

When you need to write a research paper, computers can work wonders. Taking notes is a pleasure. You can sit in the library or at home with a newspaper article or book and simply type notes right into the computer. Who needs index cards and pens that run out of ink?

Best of all is the moment when you're ready to put those notes into a paper. You just use the cut and paste functions to drop the quotation you want, along with all its relevant bibliographical information, right into your paper. Instead of carefully retyping a whole passage after tediously copying it onto an index card, you're done in seconds.

There are plenty of other ways that computers are useful tools for writing. They make it easier to share papers with friends and colleagues if you're looking for suggestions about your writing. They help save paper by allowing you to e-mail your essays to your instructors (assuming the instructors don't mind). They let you save all your records for a particular class or a particular semester in a neat and organized fashion.

The most important thing to remember about computers is that they are just tools. Fountain pens replaced quills and inkwells. Then came ballpoint pens and typewriters. Now computers are replacing them all. But people are still the same. You are still the same, and your audience is still the same. This means that the principles of good writing that this textbook has insisted on since its first edition—the Persuasive Principle and all that it involves—are still vital. No matter how great your computer is, and no matter how skillful you are with it, nothing will ever replace careful planning, clear thinking, and imaginative writing.

Comparison and Contrast

CHAPTER 6

A comparison-and-contrast paper is one of the most common kinds of writing assignments because it reflects one of the most common kinds of thinking—the kind of thinking on which most practical decisions are based. Comparison and contrast often dominate thought in choosing a college, a major, a career, a job. We compare and contrast doctors and dentists; husbands and wives (actual and potential) and children; homes, neighborhoods, and cities; breakfast foods, pizza joints, and brands of bottled water. The comparison-and-contrast assignment on an essay exam or composition in an English class is not a remote intellectual exercise but a natural extension of the role played by comparison and contrast in human life.

Just as comparison-and-contrast thinking aims at a decision or judgment—the school I attend, the job offer I accept, the horse I bet on, the toothpaste I buy—comparison-and-contrast writing must add up to something. Without a thesis, comparison-and-contrast writing is a pointless game in a never-never land where the only activity people engage in is devising elaborate lists of similarities and differences or advantages and disadvantages. The comparison-and-contrast paper must commit itself firmly to the persuasive principle:

- Late novels by Dickens express a far more pessimistic view of life than early novels by Dickens.
- Spike's Java Joint is a better place for a cup of coffee than the Starstruck Café.
- The community college can sometimes offer a number of benefits unknown at the four-year college.
- The dream and the reality of owning a car are seldom the same.
- Sexual discrimination is harder to fight than racial discrimination.

Three quick pointers:

1. As a matter of common sense and convenience, stick to two units for comparison and contrast. No regulation prohibits three or more units, but two are far easier to manage.
2. Avoid vague, what-else-is-new theses like "There are many similarities between Smith and Jones." The same statement could be made of any two human beings and is therefore worthless.
3. Don't feel that you need to pay equal attention to comparisons and contrasts. In practice, most papers give much greater weight to similarities

(comparisons) or to differences (contrasts). Some papers may deal entirely with one or the other; their whole point may be that two seemingly similar items are, in fact, very different, or that two seemingly different items are very similar. Check with your instructor whether an all-contrast or all-comparison paper is acceptable. In any event, theses like "Despite obvious differences, drug addiction and alcoholism present strikingly similar psychological problems" are both common and workable. In a paper with that thesis, the "obvious differences" could be taken care of in the introduction, and the rest of the paper would deal solely with the similarities.

PATTERNS

Comparison-and-contrast papers can use one of two patterns, both highly structured. A long paper can sometimes shift patterns from one distinct division of the paper to another, but most papers should stick to one pattern.

Block Pattern

In the first pattern, the writer discusses one unit in its entirety before going on to the other.

Thesis Statement: Spike's Java Joint is a better place for a cup of coffee than the Starstruck Café.

I. Spike's Java Joint
    A. Price
    B. Quality
    C. Service
    D. Atmosphere

II. Starstruck Café
    A. Price
    B. Quality
    C. Service
    D. Atmosphere

Thesis Statement: The community college can sometimes offer a number of benefits unknown at the four-year college.

I. Community college
    A. Cost
    B. Convenience
    C. Instructors
    D. Training for a vocation

II. Four-year college
   A. Cost
   B. Convenience
   C. Instructors
   D. Lack of training for a vocation

Notice that in these sample outlines we could easily reverse the order of the major topics. Rather than concluding with negative comments about the Starstruck Café or four-year colleges, some writers may want to stress the positive by ending with praise of Spike's Java Joint or community colleges. Which comes first is up to the writer.

The danger built into the block pattern is that the writer can end up with two separate essays instead of one unified comparison-and-contrast essay. To ensure unity, take note of the following guidelines:

Each Subtopic in Part I Must Also Be Discussed in Part II: Bring up the atmosphere at Spike's Java Joint only if you have something to say about the Starstruck Café's atmosphere—or lack of it. The atmosphere at Spike's Java Joint must be compared with or contrasted to something; in comparison-and-contrast writing, it is not significant in itself.

Subtopics Should Be Discussed in the Same Order in Both Parts: If cost and convenience are the first two subtopics you consider for community colleges, they should be the first two subtopics when you turn to four-year colleges.

Paragraphing Should Be Similar in Both Parts: A paper with only one or two sentences for each subtopic under Spike's Java Joint will probably gather the subtopics together into one good-sized paragraph. A paper with a lot to say on each of Spike's subtopics will probably give a separate paragraph to each. Whatever paragraph arrangement is appropriate for Spike's Java Joint should usually be maintained for the Starstruck Café.

Subtopics in Part II Should Generally Include Reminders of the Point Made About the Same Subtopic in Part I: In the block pattern, you consider the first unit (Spike's Java Joint, community colleges) before moving on to the second (the Starstruck Café, four-year colleges), so your readers may experience some memory lapses by the time they finally reach Part II. Their memories need refreshing. Above all, they should not be allowed to forget that they are reading a single comparison-and-contrast paper rather than two separate essays. In the paragraph outlines that follow, note the italicized reminders:

¶ 1—Presentation of thesis: Spike's Java Joint is a better place for a cup of coffee than the Starstruck Café.

Start of ¶ 2—First, and most surprising, Spike's prices are genuinely low.

Start of ¶ 3–The quality of Spike's coffee is also outstanding: dark, rich, and always hot.

Start of ¶ 4–Unlike the service at all too many coffeehouses, Spike's service is fast and friendly.

Start of ¶ 5–Finally, when it comes to atmosphere, Spike's is a surprising delight to the eye. . . .

Start of ¶ 6–When we consider the Starstruck Café, *far from finding low prices,* we find prices that are probably the highest in town.

Start of ¶ 7–The coffee itself at Starstruck's also suffers *when compared to Spike's tasty blends.*

Start of ¶ 8–*A long way from fast and friendly,* the service at Starstruck's tends to be slow and uninterested.

Start of ¶ 9–Even with its elegant atmosphere, Starstruck's *does not outdo Spike's funky charm.*

¶ 1–Presentation of thesis: The community college can sometimes offer a number of benefits unknown at the four-year college.

Start of ¶ 2–First, community colleges are cheap. . . .

Start of ¶ 3–Second, they are incredibly convenient. . . .

Start of ¶ 4–Third, most instructors are likely to be experienced and readily available. . . .

Start of ¶ 5–Last, community colleges offer the practical education most students want. . . .

Start of ¶ 6–At many four-year colleges, the cost of attending is so *much greater than at community colleges that.* . . .

Start of ¶ 7–*Contrasting dramatically to the convenience of a community college,* a four-year college. . . .

Start of ¶ 8–*Instead of meeting full-time, professional teachers,* the beginning student at a four-year college will more probably. . . .

Start of ¶ 9–Finally, many four-year colleges are still fighting *against the vocational trends in education that the community colleges have welcomed.* . . .

Alternating Pattern

This pattern can be thought of as a seesaw. It swings back and forth between its two subjects.

Thesis Statement: Spike's Java Joint is a better place for a cup of coffee than the Starstruck Café.

I. Price
   A. Spike's Java Joint
   B. Starstruck Café

II. Quality
   A. Spike's Java Joint
   B. Starstruck Café

III. Service
   A. Spike's Java Joint
   B. Starstruck Café

IV. Atmosphere
   A. Spike's Java Joint
   B. Starstruck Café

Thesis Statement: The community college can sometimes offer a number of benefits unknown at the four-year college.

I. Cost
   A. Community college
   B. Four-year college

II. Convenience
   A. Community college
   B. Four-year college

III. Instructors
   A. Community college
   B. Four-year college

IV. Training for a vocation
   A. Community college
   B. Four-year college

Most of the principles applicable to the block pattern still hold. You still say something about both subjects for each issue considered. You still use a consistent order (observe how "Spike's Java Joint" and "Community college" always come first). You still make a consistent arrangement of paragraphs. The major difference is that reminders are not nearly as important as in the block pattern. Instead of getting to the Starstruck Café's atmosphere one or two pages after dealing with Spike's atmosphere, you'll be getting to them in the very next sentences.

Which Pattern?

Both patterns enable you to write what you want. Both patterns cover the same territory, though in different order. In many cases, you can probably do a good job with either pattern, so your decision may be more a matter of taste than anything else. It is possible, however, to make some distinctions between patterns, and for whatever the distinctions are worth, here are a couple to keep in mind:

- *The block pattern tends to work better for short papers, the alternating pattern for long papers.* In short papers, the alternating pattern can sometimes bounce back and forth between subjects too frequently to let anything settle in the reader's mind. In long papers, the block pattern can put too much of a burden on the reader's memory: The reader should not have to wonder on page 7 what it was that you said on page 2, and you may be forced to spend a disproportionate amount of time and words on reminders.
- *The block pattern tends to work better with few subtopics, the alternating pattern with many.* With only a few subtopics, the reader should have no difficulty keeping track of them. You can safely make your four points about Spike's and then go on to the Starstruck Café. The seesaw, back-and-forth movement of alternating could be somewhat distracting. With many subtopics, the alternating pattern is probably safest; if you had a dozen or more elements to consider about Spike's and the Starstruck Café, for example, discussing each coffeehouse one after the other within each element would make the comparison-and-contrast relationship immediately clear. The block pattern could again put a fierce strain on the reader's memory and patience.

WRITING SUGGESTIONS FOR COMPARISON-AND-CONTRAST THEMES

Comparison-and-contrast writing offers almost endless variation in choice of subject. The subjects listed here may be less valuable for themselves than for bringing other subjects to your mind. In any event, don't forget the necessity of a thesis and for sticking to one of the two patterns of organization.

1. Two household chores.
2. Life in a city versus life in a suburb; life in two cities or two suburbs.
3. Two commercial products: razor blades, hair sprays, tires, breakfast foods.
4. Two department stores or discount stores.
5. Contrasting fates of two married couples.
6. Two sports or two athletes: baseball versus football, football versus soccer, Maria Sharapova versus Justine Henin-Hardenne.
7. Two clergymen or two churches.
8. Two movies or television programs (should be of same basic type: science fiction, horror movies, sitcoms).
9. Two politicians.

10. Two musicians or singers.
11. Conflicting viewpoints on a controversial subject: capital punishment, abortion, immigration.
12. Two character traits or emotions that can be confused: courage and recklessness, love and infatuation.
13. Two high schools or two colleges; high school versus college.
14. Two teachers with contrasting educational philosophies.
15. Dogs versus cats.
16. An attitude you had as a child versus an attitude you have now toward parents, religion, sex, and so on.
17. Contrast between advertising claims and reality.
18. Two blind dates.
19. Two tourist attractions.
20. Two employers.

VISUAL PROMPT

Writing Prompt:

Comparison and contrast writing aims at a decision or a judgment. You can compare and contrast any two things, as long as you are willing to make some sort of judgment between the two. Write a comparison and contrast essay about two decisions or judgments you have made.

BLOCK PATTERN

STUDENT ESSAY: COMING IN LAST
Annette P. Grossman

Thesis: The huge contrast between the runners at the beginning and end of the Chicago Marathon taught me a lot about what it means to be a sports hero.

    I.   Runners at the head of the marathon
        A. Look like runners
        B. Dress like runners
        C. Focus intensely

    II. Runners at the back of the marathon
        A. Don't look like runners
        B. Don't dress like runners
        C. Have poor focus but more fun

Conclusion: The real sports heroes are the second set, who look nothing like real runners but who run marathons anyway.

I am not an athlete. So when a couple of my more active friends asked me to get up at 7 A.M. with them and go cheer for the runners in this year's Chicago Marathon I almost refused. I'm still not sure what convinced me to go, but I went. I stood on the sidewalk for about six hours, passing out cups of water, or banging on a pot with a wooden spoon, or just yelling my head off to cheer on complete strangers. In between the cheering and the banging and the jumping about, though, I had a chance to do something I'd never done before: Watch a marathon. It was fascinating. I'd always thought that all runners were pretty much the same, but as I watched the 29,000 people who ran this year, I realized that there are huge differences between the runners at the beginning of the race and the runners at the end. This contrast even taught me a little bit about what it means to be a sports hero.

The runners at the head of the pack in a marathon look like runners. Their bodies are built for running and little else. These are people who have carefully trained for peak performance. They're lean, with corded muscles in places that I never knew could have muscles. Their legs are long and hard with strength enough to run more than 26 miles in a day but not slow them down with extra bulk.

The runners at the front of the marathon dress like runners too. They wear t-shirts they've gotten for participating in previous marathons. They wear clothes made from materials invented for the space program—materials with names like Neotex and Gorprene. They wear really short shorts, and really tight tights. These frontrunners carry impressive accessories as well. They start with gloves and hats and extra layers, but they shed them as the race heats up and their bodies get warm. By the end of the race, their only accessories are watches, sports goo, and shoes. The watches are marvels of modern sports technology that let them track their heart rate and their pace for every quarter mile as well as letting them figure a projected finish time, all of this while running, of course. The goo is contained in small foil packets of a jelly-like mess that's all carbohydrates and caffeine. They suck on these packets for energy as the race wears on. They wear shoes that cost half a month's rent. Everything about their running gear is serious.

The runners at the front of the pack have one more special quality: focus. They run with an intensity that blocks out everything. When we passed these people cups of water they didn't speak, smile, or glance our way. They didn't even slow down. The cups just went from our hands to theirs, mid-stride. These runners don't seem to hear the cheering or see the signs and people lining the streets. Their running takes them away from the outside world to someplace deep inside themselves that's made of work, determination, strength, and will. They don't need cheering to help them along.

Back at the end of the race, trailing about five hours behind the people at the front, are the other runners. These people don't look like runners. They look like lawyers, and plumbers, and administrative assistants, and people who never pass up a dessert or a french fry. They look as if running is an extremely rare activity for them, as if they'd feel much more natural in a recliner, watching a football game. They limp a lot.

The runners at the end of the race don't dress like runners either. They wear old gym shorts and baggy t-shirts with funny sayings on them. They carry signs that say things like, "59 years old, first marathon. Cheer for me!" and "I'm running in memory of my mother." They wear clown wigs and pigs' noses and antennae with stars on them. They don't wear watches because they don't really care how much time this is taking. They carry sports goo, too, but they want a ham sandwich. They wear expensive shoes, like the runners at the front of the race, but you can tell that their feet hurt anyway.

The real difference, though, is that the runners at the back don't have the focus that the others do. They need the music and the pot banging and the enthusiastic cheering more than the real runners because they're doing something that's hard for them. It's hard for everyone, of course, but it simply has to be harder for an overweight accountant to finish his first marathon than it is for a dedicated runner to finish her tenth, even with a personal best time. These runners at the end of the race need the cheering sections, and they show their appreciation. They wave back and give exhausted "thumbs up" signs. Once in a while, one will slow down for long enough to say "Thanks," and one man who must have been at least 75 actually stopped to dance with me for a minute or two before he turned and ran off to finish the final stretch of the course. These runners have at least as much determination as the runners at the front of the race, but they need to know that somebody cares about them, too, and not just about the people who can run the marathon in under three hours.

Everyone I saw that day impressed me, all 29,000 complete lunatics who finished the race. The athletic skill of the front runners, their devotion to their sport, was humbling. Even more humbling was hearing that the winner of the race set a world's record, running the marathon in 2:05. The newspapers called him a sports hero. For me, though, the real sports heroes were the people at the end of the race, the ones who didn't look or dress or act a thing like "real runners," but who ran anyway. I cheered for them the loudest.

ALTERNATING PATTERN

STUDENT ESSAY: DADS AND DADS
Reid Morris

Thesis: There are a few things that set my dad apart from my friends' dads.

    I. Cooking
        A. Other dads
        B. My dad

    II. Style
        A. Other dads
        B. My dad

    III. Money
        A. Other dads
        B. My dad

Conclusion: My dad might be a little different, but he taught me an important lesson.

There has always been something just a little bit different about my father. He isn't like any of the other dads on the block. He is friendly like the other dads are, and he will fix my car when something is wrong like the other dads do for their kids, but there are a few very special things that set my dad apart from the others.

Most of my friends' dads don't do a lot of cooking. Some of them specialize in scrambled eggs and anything that can be grilled outdoors. Others mostly stick to sandwiches. The dads that do cook often take it very seriously indeed, creating gourmet meals that require special appliances and pots, several trips to gourmet groceries, and use every dish in the kitchen.

If my Dad makes dinner it is of one variety and one variety only: fried fish. He perfected his recipe when he was in his twenties, and I suppose he never saw any reason to change. When I was five years old, I completely agreed. I thought my dad was the greatest cook on the face of the earth. It was a real treat when my mom went out of town and we could enjoy the heavily battered, deep fried, golden brown, fish dinner. Every night. Monday through Sunday. Until Mom came home. As a teenager, I started inviting myself over to friends' homes whenever my mom went out of town for extended periods of time.

Most of my friends' dads dress for work with a certain care and attention. The dads who work in offices look great in suits and interesting ties. The dads who get to wear jeans to work take pride in finding ways to look casual, yet professional. Even the dads who are stuck wearing company uniforms wear them with a certain style and panache.

For my dad, though, style is not a strong point. As a football coach, if he isn't walking around with a whistle around his neck, warm-up pants and jogging shoes I would scarcely recognize him. I counted recently, and he owns more than thirty t-shirts and sweatshirts with his team's name, mascot, and victories on the front. It's a signature look, certainly, but I'm a little worried about what he might wear to my graduation.

My friends have told me tales, though I'm still not sure I believe them, about dads who hand out gas money, or who find a way to slip their kids a little extra money when there's an important date or dance coming up. I've even heard about kids who are paid to do standard household chores or who get an allowance, "just because."

The money my dad gives out is what he likes to call "walkin' around money." Using a standard for prices that I think must have been set in the 1960s the sum is limited, at best, to four dollars. At an early age I learned to stop asking for anything more since it would inevitably lead into the old familiar "when I was your age" sermon. Even without my begging for spare change, my dad is more than willing to let us know how much he had spent on us already that week. "Do you know how much it costs me just to light this house?" He actually tried to train my siblings and myself to use specified numbers of squares of toilet paper for specified bodily functions.

Last week instead of purchasing a tire pump from the store for fifteen dollars, I chose to walk my bike almost 2 miles to the gas station to fill the tires. It was somewhere in the middle of my walk when I realized I had turned into my father. I was cutting costs while wearing jogging pants, and I was filling up my bike tires so I could go to the local fish fry for dinner. And it occurred to me that, while I might wish for a dad with a better cooking repertoire and a snappier fashion sense, I'd never find one who knew more about how to live on a tight budget, or who loved me enough to teach me.

LASSIE NEVER CHASES RABBITS

Kevin Cowherd

Kevin Cowherd is a columnist for the *Baltimore Sun*. As you read this good-natured, seemingly freewheeling set of humorous complaints, notice how carefully the author follows one of the formal comparison-and-contrast patterns outlined in this chapter.

✓ **WORDS TO CHECK:**

grizzled (paragraph 26)

1   Look, I am the last person in the world who would rip Lassie or speak unkindly about a dog that has accomplished so much over the years, rescued so many terrified children from swollen rapids, fought off so many enraged coyotes, etc.

2   But my kids just dragged me to see the new "Lassie" movie. And it occurred to me that many of the things that bugged me about Lassie 30 years ago still bug me today.

3   For instance, how did everyone around Lassie always know what she was saying when she barked?

4   When I was a kid, it seemed like every "Lassie" episode on TV had a scene like this:

5   Lassie: "Woof, woof!"

6   Mr. Martin: "What's that, girl? You say Timmy's down by the power plant?"

7   Lassie: "Woof, woof!"

8   Mr. Martin: "And he's clinging to a vine while trapped in 30 feet of oozing quicksand?"

9   Lassie: "Woof, woof!"

10   Mr. Martin: "And the bad guys who pulled that bank job are heading north out of town?"

11   Lassie: "Woof, woof!"

12   Now, I have a dog myself. And my dog barks at me all the time.

13   But whenever my dog barks at me, my first reaction is: What the heck is he saying?

14   In fact, most of our conversations (if you want to call them that) go something like this:

15   My dog: "Woof, woof!"

16   Me: "What? You wanna go out?"

17   (I open the screen door. The dog just sits there.)

18   My dog: "Woof, woof!"

19   Me: "What?! Food? I gave you food!"

20   My dog: "Woof, woof!"

21   Me: "What, a dog biscuit?"

22   (I hold out a dog biscuit. The dog doesn't move. The dog looks at me like I'm holding a fistful of sand.)—The point is, all I get out of that "woof, woof!" stuff is, well, woof, woof.

23   When my dog barks at me, it never occurs to me to say: "What's that? You say a bolt of lightning from the electrical storm just hit the garage? You say we better get out of here pronto before the whole place goes up in flames?" Because if anybody heard me say that, they'd be hustling me into an ambulance and shooting me up with 250 milligrams of Thorazine.

24   You know another thing that irritates me about Lassie? She never, ever makes a mistake.

25 Just once I'd like to see Lassie mess up big-time. Instead of jumping into a raging river to rescue a 5-year-old, I'd like to see her, I don't know, start chasing a rabbit or something.

26 Or instead of leading the grizzled old-timer out of the collapsed mine shaft, I'd like to see Lassie start digging for bones.

27 Understand, it's not that I want to see anyone get hurt.

28 But it would be neat to have someone else rescue the kid in the river or the old-timer in the mine for a change.

29 Then everyone could turn to Lassie and say: "Where the heck were you? You're vastly overrated, you know that?" I guess what I'm saying is: I'd like to see Lassie act more like a real dog.

30 Let's put it this way: If I were clinging to a vine while trapped in 30 feet of oozing quicksand, you know what my dog would do? I'll tell you what he'd do: nothing. My dog would find a nice comfortable place under the nearest tree and fall asleep. Because that's all my dog ever does: sleep.

31 Believe me, it would be a total waste of time to scream: "Pudgie, go get help!"

32 In fact, my dog would be so mad at me for waking him up that he'd start chewing the vine. Just so I'd sink into the quicksand faster and shut up. Lassie, of course, is far too busy to sleep. Everything is always go, go, go.

33 In the course of this new movie, she leads her sullen 13-year-old master to his late mom's long-lost diary, rescues a kid in the familiar raging river, battles a coyote in a cave, herds sheep, gently helps the 13-year-old adapt to his new surroundings, hooks him up with a babe and does everything else but join O.J. Simpson's defense team. For my dog, a big day is moving from one side of the couch to the other.

34 Believe me, if I ever fell into a raging river, my dog would never even know it—unless someone moved the couch down to the river.

35 Even then his philosophy would be: Hey, it's nap time. You're on your own, pal.

36 He's not exactly a go-getter, if you catch my drift.

WHAT DID THE WRITER SAY AND WHAT DID YOU THINK?

1. Which does the author emphasize more—his own dog's worthlessness or the unrealistic glorification of Lassie?
2. To what extent could this essay be considered a humorous treatment of the issue dealt with seriously in Eco's "How to Speak of Animals" (page 115)?

HOW DID THE WRITER SAY IT?

1. Where is the thesis stated most directly?
2. Which comparison-and-contrast pattern does the author use?
3. The title may strike some readers as needing improvement. Why is it misleading in some ways? Any suggestions for better titles?

What About <u>Your</u> Writing?

"Lassie Never Chases Rabbits" ends with a body paragraph, a comment on the laziness of the author's dog. Many readers and instructors may feel that the essay should have had an additional paragraph, a normal concluding paragraph designed in one way or another to remind readers of the main point of the whole essay.

Ordinarily, your paper needs a concluding paragraph. Without one, your paper usually ends with the last small detail of supporting evidence, and your reader is all too likely to forget about or neglect your main point—in this case, the absurdity of Hollywood's fantasy of a perfect dog.

Your conclusion must be related to, must grow out of, what has come before. It is your last chance to remind your reader of your thesis and to drive home its importance. It is not the place to introduce irrelevant or trivial new topics. It is not the place to worry about being under or over any assigned number of words. The words of your conclusion are the last ones your reader will see, and they ought to be good words.

Beyond these observations, unfortunately, there are no tidy rules governing the writing of conclusions. Too many different kinds of conclusions exist to be wrapped into one neat package. Your best bet for writing a good conclusion is to keep the various choices in mind so they'll be available when you need them—and then to trust your instincts and common sense.

The following list suggests a few of the most useful kinds of conclusions:

Summary: We can see, then, that for many people divorce has become the preferred method of settling marital problems. Liberalized grounds for divorce, the increased social acceptance of those who have been divorced, and the loosening of religious taboos have all contributed to the dramatic increase in the divorce rate.

Note: Summaries run the risk of dullness. If your conclusion is a summary, try not to make it a word-for-word repetition of language used earlier in the paper. Summaries work best in long papers. The shorter the paper, the more you should consider another kind of conclusion.

Call for Action: As this paper has shown, the divorced man gets sympathy and attention and lots of dinner invitations. The divorced woman generally just gets propositioned. It's time she got some sympathy, too. She's not asking for special favors, but it's time to stop treating her like a social outcast.

Prediction: And so it goes. Divorce becomes more common every day. Eventually it may become so common that it will stop mattering much. Then, perhaps, we will find people boasting about their former marriages the way our quaint old grandparents used to boast about shipping on a tramp steamer, or winning first prize for apple pie at the county fair, or with voices soft with pride and joy and love, staying happily married for forty or fifty years.

Question: The increasing divorce rate is not merely a colorful statistic. It raises disturbing questions. How great is the damage done to children? Does divorce solve a problem or only run away from it? Is marriage itself a dying institution? Can a society of broken homes be a healthy society? These and other questions will trouble this nation for years to come.

Quotation: All in all, there seems little any one person or group can do about the increasing number of broken marriages except to start taking seriously the century-old wisecrack of *Punch* magazine: "Advice to those about to marry: Don't."

Anecdote: Yes, everybody's doing it. The tragedy has gone from divorce. It's now an official part of the natural cycle. Last week one of the churches in my town had a divorce service. It was a big dress-up occasion. Friends and relatives got invited. Music. Prayers. Lots of lofty sentiments about change and growth and stages. It was just like getting married. It was just like dying.

Restatement of the Importance of the Topic: At a time when news magazines and television specials go into weekly panics about gas mileage and electric bills, about the balance of payments and inflation, about deficits and dictatorships, it may seem almost frivolous to start brooding about how many people are getting divorced. In an age of revolution, it may seem almost irresponsible to create a new panic by studying statistics at the county courthouse. In the long run, however, nothing may be less frivolous or more thoroughly revolutionary for American civilization than the frightening basic truths revealed by the divorce figures of our turbulent society.

MY REAL CAR

Bailey White

Bailey White has published stories and essays in many magazines, but she is perhaps best known as a storyteller on National Public Radio. Her books include *Mama Makes Up Her Mind and Other Dangers of Southern Living* (1993), *Sleeping at the Starlight Motel* (1995), and *Quite a Year for Plums* (1998). "My Real Car" was originally published in *Smithsonian Magazine* in 1991.

✓ WORDS TO CHECK:

premiums (paragraph 1)	ominous (9)	acrylic (11)
disintegrated (5)	carburetor (9)	concerto (11)
odometer (5)	internal combustion (10)	

1   It really makes you feel your age when you get a letter from your insurance agent telling you that the car you bought, only slightly used, the year you got out of college is now an antique. "Beginning with your next payment, your premiums will reflect this change in classification," the letter said.

2   I went out and looked at the car. I thought back over the years. I could almost hear my uncle's disapproving voice. "You should never buy a used car," he had told me the day I brought it home. Ten years later I drove that used car to his funeral. I drove my sister to the hospital in that car to have her first baby, and I drove to Atlanta in that car when the baby graduated from Georgia Tech with a degree in physics.

3   "When are you going to get a new car?" my friends asked me.

4   "I don't need a new car," I said. "This car runs fine."

5   I changed the oil often, and I kept good tires on it. It always got me where I wanted to go. But the stuffing came out of the backseat and the springs poked through, and the dashboard disintegrated. At 300,000 miles the odometer quit turning, but I didn't really care to know how far I had driven. A hole wore in the floor where my heel rested in front of the accelerator, and the insulation all peeled off the fire wall. "Old piece of junk," my friends whispered. The seat belt catch finally wore out, and I tied on a huge bronze hook with a fireman's knot.

6   Then one day on my way to work, the car coughed, sputtered and stopped. "This is it," I thought, and I gave it a pat. "It's been a good car."

7   The mechanic laughed at me. "You know what's wrong with that car?" he asked. "That car is out of gas." So I slopped some gas in the tank and drove ten more years.

8   The fuel gauge never worked again after that, but I got to where I could tell when the gas was low by the smell. I think it was the smell of the bottom of the tank. There was also a little smell of brake fluid, a little smell of exhaust, a little smell of oil and after all the years, a little smell of me. Car smells.

9   And sounds. The wonderful sound when the engine finally catches on a cold day, and an ominous *tick tick* in July when the radiator is working too hard. The windshield wipers said, "Gracie Allen Gracie Allen Gracie Allen." I didn't like a lot of conversation in the car, because I had to keep listening for a little skip that meant I needed to jump out and adjust the carburetor. I kept a screwdriver close at hand, and a pint of brake fluid and a new rotor, just in case. "She's strange," my friends whispered. "And she drives so slow."

10   I don't know how fast I drove. The speedometer had quit working years ago. But when I would look down through the hole in the floor and see the pavement, a gray blur, whizzing by just inches away from my feet, and feel the tremendous heat from the internal-combustion engine pouring back through the fire wall into my lap, and hear each barely constrained explosion, just as a heart attack victim is able to hear her own heartbeat, it didn't feel like slow to me. A whiff of brake fluid would remind me just what a tiny thing I was relying

on to stop myself from hurtling along the surface of the Earth at an unnatural speed. When I arrived at my destination, I would slump back, unfasten the seat belt hook with trembling hands and stagger out. I would gather up my things and give the car a last look. "Thank you sir," I would say. "We got here one more time."

11   But after I received that letter I began thinking about buying a new car. I read the newspaper every night. Finally I found one that sounded good. It was the same make as my car, but almost new. "Call Steve," the ad said. I went to see the car. It was parked in Steve's driveway. It was a fashionable wheat color. There was carpet on the floor and the seats were covered with soft, velvety-feeling stuff. It smelled like acrylic, and vinyl, and Steve. I turned a knob. Mozart's Concerto for Flute and Harp poured out of four speakers. "But how can you listen to the engine with music playing?" I asked Steve.

12   I turned the key. The car started instantly. I fastened my seat belt. Nothing but a click. Steve got in the passenger seat, and we went for a test drive. We floated down the road. I couldn't hear a sound, but I decided it must be time to shift gears. I stomped around on the floor and grabbed Steve's knee before I remembered the car had automatic transmission.

13   "You mean you just put it in 'Drive' and drive?" I asked. Steve scrunched himself against his door and clamped his knees together. He tested his seat belt. "Have you ever driven before?" he asked.

14   I bought it. I rolled all the windows up by mashing a button beside my elbow, set the air-conditioning on "Recirc" and listened to Vivaldi all the way home.

15   So now I have two cars. I call them my new car and my real car. Most of the time I drive my new car. But on some days I go out to the barn and get in my real car. I shoo the rats out of the backseat and crank up the engine. Even without daily practice my hands and feet know just what to do. My ears perk up, and I sniff the air, I add a little brake fluid, a little water. I sniff again. It'll need gas next week, and an oil change. I back it out and we roll down the road. People stop and look. They smile. "Neat car!" they say.

WHAT DID THE WRITER SAY AND WHAT DID YOU THINK?

1. Which car does the author prefer? Why?
2. Does the author ever state her preference directly?
3. Do any of the author's statements about her old car strike you as difficult to believe?

HOW DID THE WRITER SAY IT?

1. Which comparison-and-contrast pattern is used in this reading selection?
2. Why does the author not devote equal time to both cars?

What About <u>Your</u> Writing?

Bailey White's windshield wipers say "Gracie Allen Gracie Allen Gracie Allen." The radiator says "tick tick" when it's working too hard. To help us learn to love and understand her car the way that she does, White tells us how it smells, how it feels, and, most effectively, how it sounds. The evocative and sometimes funny words she uses to tell us about the sounds of her car work so well because the words she uses sound like the noises that her car makes. This tuneful writing technique is called *onomatopoeia*.

We use onomatopoeia more than we think. Every time we sing the "parum-pum-pum-pum" chorus of "The Little Drummer Boy," or ask a friend to give us a "buzz," or mention the bug we "squished" in the shower the other night, we're using onomatopoeia. In "The Secret Life of Walter Mitty" James Thurber uses it, like Bailey White, to describe an engine that says "ta-pocketa-pocketa-pocketa-pocketa-pocketa." When the television chef and restaurant owner Emeril Lagasse shouts "Bam!" as he adds a handful of spices to the gumbo on the stove, he's using onomatopoeia, too. It grabs his audience's attention, and it can liven up your writing just as Emeril's spices liven up his cooking.

Use onomatopoeia too often, though, and you'll risk sounding like a character from an old superhero comic. Don't shout "wham," "kapow," and "kablooey" in every sentence. If your windshield wipers don't want to say "Gracie Allen Gracie Allen Gracie Allen," don't force them. Just wait, listen, and try a little onomatopoeia when you want to give your writing a bit of a bang.

DEARLY DISCONNECTED

Ian Frazier

Comedy writer Ian Frazier was born in Cleveland, Ohio. He was on the staff of *The Harvard Lampoon*, and wrote for *The New Yorker* for twenty-one years. He has published several books, including *Coyote v. Acme*, and *Dating Your Mom*.

✓ WORDS TO CHECK:

nondescript (paragraph 3)	undifferentiated (6)	proliferate (13)
vestibule (3)	transience (10)	infinitude (13)
mundane (6)	sentient (11)	

1 Before I got married I was living by myself in an A-frame cabin in northwestern Montana. The cabin's interior was a single high-ceilinged room, and at the center of the room, mounted on the rough-hewn log that held up the ceiling

beam, was a telephone. I knew no one in the area, or indeed the whole state, so my entire social life came to me through that phone. The woman I would marry was living in Sarasota, Florida, and the distance between us suggests how well we were getting along at the time. We had not been in touch for several months; she had no phone. One day she decided to call me from a pay phone. We talked for a while, and after her coins ran out I jotted the number on the wood beside my phone and called her back. A day or two later, thinking about the call, I wanted to talk to her again. The only number I had for her was the pay phone number I'd written down.

2   The pay phone was on the street some blocks from the apartment where she stayed. As it happened, though, she had just stepped out to do some errands a few minutes before I called, and she was passing by on the sidewalk when the phone rang. She had no reason to think that a public phone ringing on a busy street would be for her. She stopped, listened to it ring again, and picked up the receiver. Love is pure luck; somehow I had known she would answer, and she had known it would be me.

3   Long afterwards, on a trip to Disney World in Orlando with our two kids, then aged six and two, we made a special detour to Sarasota to show them the pay phone. It didn't impress them much. It's just a nondescript Bell Atlantic pay phone on the cement wall of a building, by the vestibule. But its ordinariness and even boringness only make me like it more; ordinary places where extraordinary events have occurred are my favorite kind. On my mental map of Florida that pay phone is a landmark looming above the city it occupies, and a notable, if private, historic site.

4   I'm interested in pay phones in general these days, especially when I get the feeling that they are about to go away. Technology, in the form of sleek little phones in our pockets, has swept on by them and made them begin to seem antique. My lifelong entanglement with pay phones dates me; when I was young they were just there, a given, often as stubborn and uncongenial as the curbstone underfoot. They were instruments of torture sometimes. You had to feed them fistfuls of change in those pre-phone-card days, and the operator was a real person who stood maddeningly between you and whomever you were trying to call. And when the call went wrong, as communication often does, the pay phone gave you a focus for your rage. Pay phones were always getting smashed up, the receivers shattered to bits against the booth, the coin slots jammed with chewing gum, the cords yanked out and unraveled to the floor.

5   You used to hear people standing at pay phones and cursing them. I remember the sound of my own frustrated shouting confined by the glass walls of a phone booth—the kind you don't see much anymore, with a little ventilating fan in the ceiling that turned on when you shut the double-hinged glass door. The noise that fan made in the silence of a phone booth was for a while the essence of romantic, lonely-guy melancholy for me. Certain specific pay

phones I still resent for the unhappiness they caused me, and others I will never forgive, though not for any fault of their own. In the C concourse of the Salt Lake City airport there's a row of pay phones set on the wall by the men's room just past the concourse entry. While on a business trip a few years ago, I called home from a phone in that row and learned that a friend had collapsed in her apartment and was in the hospital with brain cancer. I had liked those pay phones before, and had used them often; now I can't even look at them when I go by.

6   There was always a touch of seediness and sadness to pay phones and a sense of transience. Drug dealers made calls from them, and shady types who did not want their whereabouts known, and otherwise respectable people planning assignations, and people too poor to have phones of their own. In the movies, any character who used a pay phone was either in trouble or contemplating a crime. Pay phones came with their own special atmospherics and even accessories sometimes–the predictable bad smells and graffiti, of course, as well as cigarette butts, soda cans, scattered pamphlets from the Jehovah's Witnesses, and single bottles of beer (empty) still in their individual, street-legal paper bags. Mostly, pay phones evoked the mundane: "Honey, I'm just leaving. I'll be there soon." But you could tell that a lot of undifferentiated humanity had flowed through these places, and that in the muteness of each pay phone's little space, wild emotion had howled.

7   Once, when I was living in Brooklyn, I read in the newspaper that a South American man suspected of dozens of drug-related contract murders had been arrested at a pay phone in Queens. Police said that the man had been on the phone setting up a murder at the time of his arrest. The newspaper story gave the address of the pay phone, and out of curiosity one afternoon I took a long walk to Queens to take a look at it. It was on an undistinguished street in a middle-class neighborhood, by a florist's shop. By the time I saw it, however, the pay phone had been blown up and/or firebombed. I had never before seen a pay phone so damaged; explosives had blasted pieces of the phone itself wide open in metal shreds like frozen banana peels, and flames had blackened everything and melted the plastic parts and burned the insulation off the wires. Soon after, I read that police could not find enough evidence against the suspected murderer and so had let him go.

8   The cold phone outside a shopping center in Bigfork, Montana, from which I called a friend in the West Indies one winter when her brother was sick; the phone on the wall of the concession stand at Redwood Pool, where I used to stand dripping and call my mom to come and pick me up; the sweaty phones used almost only by men in the hallway outside the maternity ward at Lenox Hill Hospital in New York; the phone by the driveway of the Red Cloud Indian School in South Dakota where I used to talk with my wife while priests in black slacks and white socks chatted on a bench nearby; the phone in the old wood-paneled phone booth with leaded glass windows in

the drugstore in my Ohio hometown—each one is as specific as a birthmark, a point on earth unlike any other. Recently I went back to New York City after a long absence and tried to find a working pay phone. I picked up one receiver after the next without success. Meanwhile, as I scanned down the long block, I counted half a dozen or more pedestrians talking on their cell phones.

9   It's the cell phone, of course, that's putting the pay phone out of business. The pay phone is to the cell phone as the troubled and difficult older sibling is to the cherished newborn. People even treat their cell phones like babies, cradling them in their palms and beaming down upon them lovingly as they dial. You sometimes hear people yelling on their cell phones, but almost never yelling at them. Cell phones are toylike, nearly magic, and we get a huge kick out of them, as often happens with technological advances until the new wears off. Somehow I don't believe people had a similar honeymoon period with pay phones back in their early days, and they certainly have no such enthusiasm for them now. When I see a cell-phone user gently push the little antenna and fit the phone back into its brushed-vinyl carrying case and tuck the case inside his jacket beside his heart, I feel sorry for the beat-up pay phone standing in the rain.

10   People almost always talk on cell phones while in motion—driving, walking down the street, riding on a commuter train. The cell phone took the transience the pay phone implied and turned it into VIP-style mobility and speed. Even sitting in a restaurant, the person on a cell phone seems importantly busy and on the move. Cell-phone conversations seem to be unlimited by ordinary constraints of place and time, as if they represent an almost-perfect form of communication whose perfect state would be telepathy.

11   And yet no matter how we factor the world away, it remains. I think this is what drives me so nuts when a person sitting next to me on a bus makes a call from her cell phone. Yes, this busy and important caller is at no fixed point in space, but nevertheless I happen to be beside her. The job of providing physical context falls on me; I become her call's surroundings, as if I'm the phone booth wall. For me to lean over and comment on her cell-phone conversation would be as unseemly and unexpected as if I were in fact a wall; and yet I have no choice, as a sentient person, but to hear what my chatty fellow traveler has to say.

12   Some middle-aged guys like me go around complaining about this kind of thing. The more sensible approach is just to accept it and forget about it, because there's not much we can do. I don't think that pay phones will completely disappear. Probably they will survive for a long while as clumsy old technology still of some use to those lagging behind, and as backup if ever the superior systems should temporarily fail. Before pay phones became endangered I never thought of them as public spaces, which of course they are. They suggested a human average; they belonged to anybody who had a couple of coins. Now I

see that, like public schools and public transportation, pay phones belong to a former commonality our culture is no longer quite so sure it needs.

13   I have a weakness for places—for old battlefields, car-crash sites, houses where famous authors lived. Bygone passions should always have an address, it seems to me. Ideally, the world would be covered with plaques and markers listing the notable events that occurred at each particular spot. A sign on every pay phone would describe how a woman broke up with her fiancé there, how a young ballplayer learned that he had made the team. Unfortunately, the world itself is fluid, and changes out from under us; the rocky islands that the pilot Mark Twain was careful to avoid in the Mississippi are now stone outcroppings in a soybean field. Meanwhile our passions proliferate into illegibility, and the places they occur can't hold them. Eventually pay phones will become relics of an almost-vanished landscape, and of a time when there were fewer of us and our stories were on an earlier page. Romantics like me will have to reimagine our passions as they are—unmoored to earth, like an infinitude of cell-phone messages flying through the atmosphere.

WHAT DID THE WRITER SAY AND WHAT DID YOU THINK?

1. Why is Frazier so fond of pay phones?
2. Are any of the things the author likes about pay phones surprising?
3. What is the point of the long list of phones in paragraph 8? How does it connect to Frazier's conclusion?
4. Is the romantic story in the introduction only possible with pay phones?
5. The "What About Your Writing" for this selection addresses topicality. Are any of Frazier's details out of date, or dangerously close to being so?

HOW DID THE WRITER SAY IT?

1. Is Frazier's essay in the block pattern or the alternating pattern of comparison-and-contrast writing?
2. The author doesn't state his thesis until paragraph 10. Why does he wait so long?
3. Why does Frazier say about himself that "middle-aged guys like me go around complaining about this kind of thing"? What is he hoping to accomplish with this remark?

What About Your Writing?

Ian Frazier's extended meditation on the demise of pay phones and their replacement by cell phones is a fine example of an essay that uses topical subject matter. Topical subject matter is essay material that relates specifically to current events or culture. A topical reference is a briefer version of this—a moment within an essay where the author refers to current events, personalities, problems, culture, and so on. Topicality presents some obvious opportunities for any writer—together with some not-so-obvious dangers.

Topical references, by their very nature, are specific references, and specific writing adds to the prospects for reader interest. Moreover, any writer may want to strike readers as being well informed and up-to-date. Frazier's original readers, certainly, will have had their vivid memories of the change from pay phones to cell phones. Topical references, too, may be more readily understood than more obscure references and allusions (see page 73). Your reference to a current hit song, a television show, a politician, a sports figure, a trial can enliven your writing and impress your audience.

While topicality, then, can help your writing from time to time, remember that it also has its dangers. It can give a bogus contemporary feel that distracts a reader's attention from the real subject. It can date the essay and the ideas—sometimes overnight. How long will the demise of the pay phone be a topic that readers will care about, or even understand? Today's college students may be the last generation to have ever used a pay phone at all. Topical references are tricky. Tastes in music change; television shows are canceled; politicians retire or get defeated; athletes become newscasters. Today's recognition becomes tomorrow's puzzled stare. Today's fad becomes tomorrow's footnote. Don't be afraid of topical subject matter or topical references, but do be careful.

SPEAKING OF WRITING
William Zinsser

A distinguished newspaper editor and critic, teacher, and author of many books, William Zinsser is perhaps best known for his writing about writing. The following selection is from *On Writing Well,* an established classic that celebrated its thirtieth anniversary in 2006.

✓ **WORDS TO CHECK:**

vocation (paragraph 1)	bohemian (2)	gusto (11)
avocation (1)	arduous (3)	

1   A school in Connecticut once held "a day devoted to the arts," and I was asked if I would come and talk about writing as a vocation. When I arrived I found that a second speaker had been invited—Dr. Brock (as I'll call him), a surgeon who had recently begun to write and had sold some stories to magazines. He

was going to talk about writing as an avocation. That made us a panel, and we sat down to face a crowd of students and teachers and parents, all eager to learn the secrets of our glamorous work.

2   Dr. Brock was dressed in a bright red jacket, looking vaguely bohemian, as authors are supposed to look, and the first question went to him. What was it like to be a writer?

3   He said it was tremendous fun. Coming home from an arduous day at the hospital, he would go straight to his yellow pad and write his tensions away. The words just flowed. It was easy. I then said that writing wasn't easy and it wasn't fun. It was hard and lonely, and the words seldom just flowed.

4   Next Dr. Brock was asked if it was important to rewrite. Absolutely not, he said. "Let it all hang out," he told us, and whatever form the sentences take will reflect the writer at his most natural. I then said that rewriting is the essence of writing. I pointed out that professional writers rewrite their sentences over and over and then rewrite what they have rewritten.

5   "What do you do on days when it isn't going well?" Dr. Brock was asked. He said he just stopped writing and put the work aside for a day when it would go better. I then said that the professional writer must establish a daily schedule and stick to it. I said that writing is a craft, not an art, and that the man who runs away from his craft because he lacks inspiration is fooling himself. He is also going broke.

6   "What if you're feeling depressed or unhappy?" a student asked. "Won't that affect your writing?"

7   Probably it will, Dr. Brock replied. Go fishing. Take a walk. Probably it won't, I said. If your job is to write every day, you learn to do it like any other job.

8   A student asked if we found it useful to circulate in the literary world. Dr. Brock said he was greatly enjoying his new life as a man of letters, and he told several stories of being taken to lunch by his publisher and his agent at Manhattan restaurants where writers and editors gather. I said that professional writers are solitary drudges who seldom see other writers.

9   "Do you put symbolism in your writing?" a student asked me.

10   "Not if I can help it," I replied. I have an unbroken record of missing the deeper meaning in any story, play or movie, and as for dance and mime, I have never had any idea of what is being conveyed.

11   "I *love* symbols!" Dr. Brock exclaimed, and he described with gusto the joys of weaving them through his work.

12   So the morning went, and it was a revelation to all of us. At the end Dr. Brock told me he was enormously interested in my answers—it had never occurred to him that writing could be hard. I told him I was just as interested in *his* answers—it had never occurred to me that writing could be easy. Maybe I should take up surgery on the side.

13   As for the students, anyone might think we left them bewildered. But in fact we gave them a broader glimpse of the writing process than if only one of

us had talked. For there isn't any "right" way to do such personal work. There are all kinds of writers and all kinds of methods, and any method that helps you to say what you want to say is the right method for you.

WHAT DID THE WRITER SAY AND WHAT DID YOU THINK?

1. What is the thesis? Where is it stated?
2. Summarize in your own words the main difference between the two men's approaches to writing.
3. Apply the approaches to writing of Zinsser and Dr. Brock to areas such as cooking, sports, and driving an automobile. Do you agree that the proper approach is really up to the individual?

HOW DID THE WRITER SAY IT?

1. Which comparison-and-contrast approach does Zinsser use—alternating or block?
2. Why are we given details about Dr. Brock's clothing?
3. Is Zinsser's quip, "Maybe I should take up surgery on the side," a harmless wisecrack, or does it make a serious point beneath the humor?

What About Your Writing?

Just because writers of short essays usually present their theses by the end of their first paragraph doesn't mean they always do. Or always should. William Zinsser lets us wait until the last paragraph before directly presenting his thesis that any approach to writing is valid as long as it works for the writer. Had he presented the thesis in the first paragraph, some of the humor of the contradictory statements might have been lost as the story became too much like a sermon. If the formula that usually works doesn't turn out to work this time, it's too bad for the formula.

LOVE THY PLAYSTATION, LOVE THYSELF

Reihan Salam and Will Wilkinson

Washington, DC writers Salam and Wilkinson use this essay to explore a complicated economic concept through the lens of popular culture. Originally published at *Slate.com,* the essay was written to appeal to a wide audience of readers, with and without backgrounds in economics.

✓ **Words to Check:**

sociologists (paragraph 1)	habituation (2)	nuptials (4)
hedonic (2)	endorphins (3)	dopamine (6)
marginal utility (2)	incalculably (4)	pixilated (6)

1   As summer approaches, millions of Americans busily plan their weddings, full of hope for the future. That is understandable. In recent years, a number of economists and sociologists, including Christopher Jenks, David Ellwood, Kathryn Edin, Daniel Hamermesh, and David Popenoe, have stressed the benefits of marriage. But before you tie the knot, pause for a moment and consider whether a spouse is what you really need. Could it be that you'd be happier if you shacked up with the Sony PlayStation 3?

2   Economists David Blanchflower and Andrew Oswald have suggested that a lasting marriage produces as much happiness as an extra $100,000 a year in salary. This might sound like a strong case for getting hitched. But many economists have shown that happiness is expensive–$100,000 will buy you only a small amount of joy. Studies like these also hide individual variation. Marriage isn't worth $100,000 to just anybody. A recent German study found that matrimony's hedonic gains go disproportionately to couples who have similar education levels but a wide income gap. Worse yet, on average, people adapt very quickly and completely to marriage. As anyone who's ever consumed seven pumpkin pies in one sitting knows, we quickly get used to our favorite new things, and we just as quickly tire of them. As Harvard psychologist Dan Gilbert artfully puts it, "Psychologists call this habituation, economists call it declining marginal utility, and the rest of us call it marriage."

3   We submit that a relationship with a PlayStation 3 is worth at least $100,000 a year in happiness for all individuals. Unlike a nagging spouse, the PS3 doesn't care about your income or your level of education–it loves you just the way you are. It is true that you will eventually become accustomed to your sleek new PS3, but this will take an extremely long time. The PS3, after all, has been built expressly to keep mind-blowing novelty coming and coming and coming. Periodic infusions of novelty–new games–will keep the endorphins flowing.

4   Even if you assume that a good marriage is worth $100,000, you can't discount the vast amount of money it takes to woo a spouse. The costs of daily grooming–calculated at the minimum wage–run into the tens of thousands of dollars over a lifetime, not counting the costs of soap, water, Gillette Fusion cartridges, and Old Spice. Then there are the birthday presents, the anniversary presents, and the occasional meals at popular chain restaurants, not to mention the incalculably expensive psychic toll of accommodating your schedule to the increasingly unreasonable demands of your "partner." Compare with the PS3, which does not demand that you bathe or slather yourself in cologne and is

available for guilt-free sensual pleasures 24 hours a day. Admittedly, you will have to purchase new games to keep the romance alive with your PS3. This, however, is vastly less expensive than renewing your nuptials, the tack taken by human couples such as Kevin Federline and Britney Spears.

5   Some weak-kneed gamers will object to paying the PS3's high price tag: $500 for the "cheap" version, $600 for a souped-up model. This reluctance is understandable. Amusements like the PS2, the Xbox 360, and the Turbo Grafx 16 were never an adequate substitute for human companionship. Keep in mind, however, that none of these platforms could play Blu-ray DVDs, a fatal flaw rectified by the PS3. Life with the primitive PS2 is best understood as a loveless marriage, a source of stress and anxiety rather than true happiness.

6   And really, how expensive is $500? According to the U.S. Census Bureau, the median household income in America in 2003 was $43,318. Gamers skew young, so let's be conservative and cut that number in half. That's $21,659. The Organisation for Economic Co-Operation and Development says Americans worked an average of 1,792 hours in 2003. That comes to $12.09 an hour for those making half the median. At that rate, a $500 PS3 can be had for a little more than 41 hours of work–about half of which you will spend reading blog posts about Lindsay Lohan. That 41 hours of work will earn you how many hours of dopamine-pumping PS3 action? The Entertainment Software Association informs us that the average American gamer spends about seven-and-a-half hours per week, or 390 hours annually, riding the video tiger. Let's again make a conservative estimate and assume that PS3 users will log twice that amount: 780 hours a year of gaming time. Now suppose your PS3 explodes in a dazzling shower of sparks after exactly one year. In that tragic circumstance, each hour of pixilated joy will have cost you about three minutes on the job. If it makes you feel better, you can spend that three minutes in the bathroom.

7   The Bush administration's "Healthy Marriage Initiative," an innovative effort to encourage stable marriages among the poor, has been one of the hallmarks of compassionate conservatism. Wouldn't it make more sense, though, to establish a "PlayStation 3 Initiative" that will put video game consoles in the hands of the neediest?

WHAT DID THE WRITER SAY AND WHAT DID YOU THINK?

1. What's the thesis of this essay?
2. What is the main standard for the evaluation the authors are making about the ability to attain happiness?
3. The authors argue that marriage is expensive and a PS3 is relatively cheap. Do their statistics and logic seem valid to you? Why or why not?

4. What does the authors' attitude toward marriage seem to be? Does it affect the credibility of their essay?

HOW DID THE WRITER SAY IT?

1. How is this essay organized? Is the organization consistent and effective?
2. The authors mention some of the sources for the figures they use. Does this make their information credible?
3. Who is the audience for this essay? Identify some specific examples or word choices that help you determine who the intended audience is.
4. The essay ends by suggesting a "PlayStation 3 Initiative." Is this a serious suggestion? How can you tell?

What About Your Writing?

According to Mary Poppins, "A spoonful of sugar makes the medicine go down." Think of humor as sugar. When you are dealing with stodgy material—or sometimes presenting a point of view that many readers may find discomforting or hotly controversial—nothing can get your audience on your side faster than a few touches of humor. Who enjoys technical discussions of fine points of economics? Whose eyelids don't get heavy at the very sight of terms like *marginal utility*? Salam and Wilkinson use humor effectively to make their economic discussion more pleasant to read. Details, like their reference to the PS3 as something "which does not demand that you bathe or slather yourself in cologne and is available for guilt-free sensual pleasures 24 hours a day," not only make us smile but help support their thesis that marriage is a poor economic decision compared to buying a PS3. For humor, readers will pardon a stretch of dullness, accept—or at least bear with—a point they strongly oppose, and generally let the writer get away with more than the writer would ever think of asking for.

There are dangers, of course. You don't want your readers to feel that your point isn't important, that beneath the humor you yourself don't take it seriously. You don't want to distract your reader from the significant intellectual content of your work. You don't want to come through as a crude smart aleck. With all these warnings, however, humor is a major resource for many good writers. Be cautious with it, but don't be shy.

CHAPTER 6½

Office Hours: Revision: An Overview

There is no good writing, only good rewriting.
—Justice Louis D. Brandeis

Easy writing's vile hard reading.
—Richard Brinsley Sheridan

Every student knows it, because every instructor says it at least a thousand times a semester: To write well, you must revise. Sometimes it's hard. Sometimes it's boring. And it requires that you pick up a piece of writing that you had hoped was done, and that you work on it some more.

Nothing can make revising as much fun as ignoring it and going to a movie, but there are some steps you can take to make the work of revising pay off:

1. Always let your first draft sit overnight, or even longer. Do some other homework. Make dinner. Go to the gym. Once you've blown the cobwebs out of your mind, you're ready to take another look at the work you've done.
2. Think about your thesis. Is it as clear as it should be? Now that you're done with the paper, is the thesis that you started with really the thesis for the paper that you've just finished? Perhaps you began by arguing that people should never buy anything on credit. Then you thought about cars and houses and student loans and realized that there could be some exceptions. That's fine, but be sure to change your thesis to reflect the change in your argument.
3. Think about logic. Do your main ideas truly support your thesis? Are they clear? Are they important? Do they do the work you intended? Would they be more effective if you put them in a different order? How can you make your argument flow most naturally?
4. Concentrate on clarity. You're the writer, and you know what you meant to say. Naturally everything makes sense to you, but what about your

reader? Are there specialized terms that need to be defined for the general reader? Could another example or two help your reader understand a complex point? Have you omitted a step in a process because it seems so obvious? You might take this opportunity to consult another writer. Someone who isn't as immersed in your topic as you can often point out places where your reader might not be able to follow you.

5. Now think about details of organization and style. Take another look at that introduction and conclusion. Make sure they've done their jobs. Make sure they don't feel "tacked on" to your paper. Have you been too wordy, used too much fancy language, or been too casual? Did you write a paragraph or sentence thinking, "I can come back and fix that later"? Now is the time. Fix it.

6. Don't forget that proofreading is different from revising. Once you like your paper's structure and details, once you're happy with its style, go over it again for spelling, grammar, and possible errors in other basics. You've worked hard on this paper, too hard to let your efforts be undone by neglecting the fundamentals.

7. Finally, a word of cheer. Don't torture yourself with dreams of perfection. You've got to finish sometime. Yes, revise. No one should ever tell you not to. But don't get stuck there. Don't overdo it. Don't worry your writing to death. Make it as solid and clear and lively as you can, check it over, and then send it on its way. You can sleep well, or head out to see that movie, knowing that you've done the best you can.

> A poem is never finished, only abandoned.
> —*Paul Valery*

> There are two kinds of people, those who finish what they start and so on.
> —*Robert Byrne*

Cause and Effect CHAPTER

7

The school board of a suburban town near Denver has decided to ask the voters to approve a large increase in property tax assessments to construct a new high school. The board knows that, at best, its request will be unwelcome. It launches a vigorous campaign to make the voters more favorably inclined. Part of the campaign is a pamphlet setting forth the board's case. The pamphlet, of necessity, presents a study of cause-and-effect relationships.

The board first states the *causes* for its request. Student enrollment has more than doubled. Three years ago, the board tried to cope with this problem by going to two sessions, but the classrooms are still too crowded for basic physical comfort as well as for optimum learning conditions. Moreover, the situation is not temporary; current enrollment in the junior high and elementary schools assures continued increases in the student population. Finally, the building is in poor physical condition: The roof leaks, the basement floods, the boiler is on its last legs. The board has investigated the possibility of remodeling and expanding the old building and has found that costs for that project would mean an average of only $135 a year less in taxes per family than if a completely new school were built.

Next, the board discusses the results, or *effects*, of voter approval. The town's leading eyesore will be replaced by a beautiful new structure in which everyone can take pride. New facilities for the most modern teaching devices will improve the quality of education. Experienced teachers will be more inclined to stay than to seek new employment. The strength of the town's educational system will be a selling point for new residents and consequently will increase property values.

The school board's pamphlet, in short, presents a thesis—the proposal for a new high school should be approved—and supports it with cause-and-effect writing.

It's worth noting here that cause-and-effect relationships can sometimes shift. In the first part of the pamphlet, for example, the proposal to build a new school is the effect that was caused by overcrowding and a decaying building. In the second part of the pamphlet, however, the approved proposal becomes the cause of such beneficial effects as beauty and improved education. A cause creates an effect, but that effect, in turn, can become the cause of another effect. No problems are likely to arise as long as the writer keeps any shifting relationships clearly in mind.

Many classroom papers are not lengthy enough to give equal weight to cause and effect, so they emphasize one over the other. "Cause" papers might have theses like these:

- The rioting at last week's rock concert was mostly the fault of the police.
- The growth of interest in coin collecting is attributable to practical financial considerations.
- Government policies penalize savers and reward borrowers.
- Iago plots against Othello because of an accumulation of petty resentments.

The introduction of the cause paper will usually contain a brief description of the *effect*–the rioting that resulted from police actions, the decrease in bank deposits that resulted from government policies–and then the entire body of the paper will analyze the causes, giving a paragraph, perhaps, to each.

"Effect" papers might have theses like these:

- Passage of a national health insurance program would result in heavy burdens on doctors.
- Fear of germs made me a nervous wreck as a child.
- The invention of the cotton gin helped perpetuate slavery in the South.
- Rigid enforcement of holding penalties in professional football has made the sport less exciting than it used to be.

The introduction to an effect paper will naturally reverse the procedure of a cause paper. It will briefly describe or discuss the *cause*–the health insurance program, the cotton gin, and so on–and the rest of the paper will then be devoted to the effects.

As you plan your paper, try to remember a few logical requirements.

Do Not Oversimplify Causes

Most subjects worth writing about have more than one cause. Sometimes particular combinations of causes have to be present at the same time and in certain proportions to bring about a particular result. Attributing a young man's delinquency solely to the poverty of his family oversimplifies what everyone knows about life. Poverty may have been a contributing cause, but there had to have been others as well: Plenty of poor children do not become delinquents, and plenty of rich ones do.

Beware especially of the *post hoc ergo propter hoc* fallacy: "after this, therefore because of this." After Herbert Hoover was elected president, America had a depression; therefore, America had a depression because Herbert Hoover was elected. An argument like this depends purely on an accident of time; the writer must point out, if possible, actual policies of the Hoover administration that brought about the depression. Otherwise, the argument has no more logical validity than "I lost my job after a black cat crossed my path; therefore, I lost my job because a black cat crossed my path."

Do Not Oversimplify Effects

Uncontrolled enthusiasm is probably the biggest danger here. A writer may be able to present a strong case that an ill-conceived national health insurance program might have adverse effects on medical care. If the writer predicts that millions of people will die of neglect in waiting lines in the doctor's office, however, the writer's case—and common sense—is sure to be viewed skeptically. The school board's pamphlet said that a new high school would be an additional selling point to attract new residents; if it had said that property values would triple within five years, it would have oversimplified the effects in an irresponsible and hysterical fashion.

Distinguish Between Direct and Indirect Causes and Effects

Don't treat all causes and effects equally. Some are more remote than others, and the distinctions need to be made clear.

Bad design and incompetent management were direct causes of the Soviet nuclear disaster at Chernobyl in 1986. The centuries-old desire for cheap sources of energy was an indirect cause. Though indirect causes and effects can sometimes be important, you need to set limits on how many of them you can deal with, or nearly every cause-and-effect essay will turn into a history of the world.

Distinguish Between Major and Minor Causes and Effects

The Confederacy's firing on Fort Sumter was a direct cause of the Civil War, but not nearly as important as the issues of secession and slavery. Although it should acknowledge minor causes and effects, a paper should naturally spend most of its time on major ones.

Do Not Omit Links in a Chain of Causes and Effects

As previously noted, you may not always be faced with a set of separate causes for a particular effect or separate effects from a particular cause. One cause leads to another, the second to a third, and so on—and only then is the given effect brought about. Unless you carefully discuss each part of the sequence, your reader may get lost. One effect of television, for example, may be a growing number of discipline problems in elementary and high school classrooms, but before you can persuade your reader of that point, you will have to examine many intermediate effects.

Play Fair

Give some attention, where appropriate, to causes and effects that opponents of your thesis may point to. You may justifiably want to pin the rioting at the rock concert on the police, but your case will be strengthened, not weakened, if you concede that the promoters' selling of more tickets than there were seats and the attempt of a few fans to rush the stage and tear the clothes off the performers' backs also contributed to the disaster. You don't need to make a lavish production of these arguments on the other side; just show that you're aware of them and have given them serious consideration.

WRITING SUGGESTIONS FOR CAUSE-AND-EFFECT PAPERS

All the subjects in the following list offer good opportunities for a cause-and-effect, cause-only, or effect-only paper. Explore each cause and effect thoroughly; don't just write a list.

1. A personal, unreasonable fear (your own or someone else's).
2. A personal, unreasonable irritation (your own or someone else's).
3. A personal habit or mannerism (your own or someone else's).
4. Outlawing of prayers in public schools.
5. Violence on children's television programs.
6. A personal experience with racial or religious discrimination.
7. Your first romantic attachment.
8. The quality of food at the school cafeteria.
9. The popularity or decline in popularity of a hairstyle or clothing style.
10. High school graduates who still can't read.
11. Your like or dislike of a particular book, writer, movie, painter, musician, television program.
12. Children's lack of respect for parents.
13. Sexual harassment in high school or college.
14. A minor invention (Scotch tape, electric toothbrushes, Post-it Notes, parking meters).
15. Your interest or lack of interest in a sport.
16. Your passionate like or dislike of a food.
17. Your decision to continue your education.

18. Being overweight or underweight.
19. Swearing.
20. Gossip.

VISUAL PROMPT

Writing Prompt:

Uncontrolled enthusiasm is probably the biggest danger here. Write a cause-and-effect essay that details either the cause of the effect of someone's exuberant behavior.

STUDENT ESSAY: A FEW SHORT WORDS

Matthew Monroe

Thesis: My height seems to bring out the worst in everyone.

    I. Stupid jokes
        A. When accepting an award
        B. From my girlfriend's dad

    II. Rudeness
        A. When trying to buy a suit
        B. When shopping for cars
        C. From total strangers

    III. Being overlooked
        A. In bars
        B. For sports
        C. By women

Conclusion: Although people assume I don't mind the abuse I take because of my
height, it really does make me angry.

I am short. How short? Suffice it to say that for a man of almost twenty-two years of age, I am very short indeed. Now, I am comfortable with my height. I've lived with it for years, and it just doesn't bother me anymore. It is the effect that my height has on other people that I just can't stand. My height seems to bring out the worst in everyone.

People seem to see my height as an excellent excuse to try to be funny. Stupid jokes follow me wherever I go. When I had to accept an award for perfect high school attendance, some jerk at the back of the room waited until I was about to say a gracious thank you, and then he hollered, "Stand up, pal. We can't see you!" There was, of course, much laughter, just as there was when my girlfriend's dad told her to "Throw the boy back. He's too small to keep!"

The jokes, though, are easier to handle than outright rudeness. There was the time I was trying to buy a suit and was told that not even the "very best" cut could disguise my height. There was the car salesman who refused to show me anything but sub-compacts, insisting that anything else would be far too big for such a little fellow. And then I cannot forget the random strangers who feel compelled to walk up to me and say "Wow! You're really short." Thanks guys, I hadn't noticed.

The worst part, though, is being overlooked because of my height. I'm the last to get served at any bar, because the bartender can't see me. I'm never chosen for any pick-up sports teams, even though being short doesn't mean I can't run as fast or throw as straight as any other guy. Women look right past me and right into the eyes of the six-foot-tall idiot at the other end of the room. Sometimes they pat me on the head as they pass by.

People assume that my height makes me nothing more than a target for their dumb wisecracks, their insensitive rudenesses, or their complete disregard. They assume that because I can laugh it off, I just don't care. One day I will surprise them by taking a stand, making a statement, walking right up to them, and punching them in the kneecaps.

WHY WE CRAVE HORROR MOVIES
Stephen King

It's a reasonable guess that if asked to "name a writer" most average citizens would name Stephen King. In 1996, King achieved the unprecedented feat of having five books on the best-seller list at the same time. With total sales comfortably above 20 million copies, King's horror tales seem to have achieved a popularity unrestricted by education or social class. Among his books are *Carrie* (1974), *Salem's Lot* (1975), *The Shining* (1977), *The Dead Zone* (1979), *Firestarter* (1980), *Christine* (1983), *Pet Sematary* (1983), *The Girl Who Loved Tom Gordon* (1999), *Hearts in Atlantis* (1999), *From a Buick 8* (2002), *Lisey's Story* (2006), and the lengthy and popular *Dark Tower* series. Many of these titles, as well as others, have been made into films, and King can write with considerable authority on the subject of horror movies.

✓ **WORDS TO CHECK:**

grimaces (paragraph 1)	voyeur (6)	sanctions (10)
depleted (3)	penchant (7)	remonstrance (10)
innately (4)	status quo (9)	anarchistic (11)

1 I think that we're all mentally ill; those of us outside the asylums only hide it a little better–and maybe not all that much better, after all. We've all known people who talk to themselves, people who sometimes squinch their faces into horrible grimaces when they believe no one is watching, people who have some hysterical fear–of snakes, the dark, the tight place, the long drop . . . and, of course, those final worms and grubs that are waiting so patiently underground.

2   When we pay our four or five bucks and seat ourselves at tenth-row center in a theater showing a horror movie, we are daring the nightmare.

3   Why? Some of the reasons are simple and obvious. To show that we can, that we are not afraid, that we can ride this roller coaster. Which is not to say that a really good horror movie may not surprise a scream out of us at some point, the way we may scream when the roller coaster twists through a complete 360 or plows through a lake at the bottom of the drop. And horror movies, like roller coasters, have always been the special province of the young; by the time one turns 40 or 50, one's appetite for double twists or 360-degree loops may be considerably depleted.

4   We also go to re-establish our feelings of essential normality; the horror movie is innately conservative, even reactionary. Freda Jackson as the horrible melting woman in *Die, Monster, Die!* confirms for us that no matter how far we may be removed from the beauty of a Robert Redford or a Diana Ross, we are still light-years from true ugliness.

5   And we go to have fun.

6   Ah, but this is where the ground starts to slope away, isn't it? Because this is a very peculiar sort of fun, indeed. The fun comes from seeing others menaced—sometimes killed. One critic has suggested that if pro football has become the voyeur's version of combat, then the horror film has become the modern version of the public lynching.

7   It is true that the mythic, "fairy-tale" horror film intends to take away the shades of gray. . . . It urges us to put away our more civilized and adult penchant for analysis and to become children again, seeing things in pure blacks and whites. It may be that horror movies provide psychic relief on this level because this invitation to lapse into simplicity, irrationality and even outright madness is extended so rarely. We are told we may allow our emotions a free rein . . . or no rein at all.

8   If we are all insane, then sanity becomes a matter of degree. If your insanity leads you to carve up women like Jack the Ripper or the Cleveland Torso Murderer, we clap you away in the funny farm (but neither of those two amateur-night surgeons was ever caught, heh-heh-heh); if, on the other hand, your insanity leads you only to talk to yourself when you're under stress or to pick your nose on your morning bus, then you are left alone to go about your business . . . though it is doubtful that you will ever be invited to the best parties.

9   The potential lyncher is in almost all of us (excluding saints, past and present; but then, most saints have been crazy in their own ways), and every now and then, he has to be let loose to scream and roll around in the grass. Our emotions and our fears form their own body, and we recognize that it demands its own exercise to maintain proper muscle tone. Certain of these emotional muscles are accepted—even exalted—in civilized society; they are, of course, the emotions that tend to maintain the status quo of civilization itself. Love, friendship, loyalty, kindness—these are all the emotions that we applaud, emotions that have been immortalized in the couplets of Hallmark cards and in the verses (I don't dare call it poetry) of Leonard Nimoy.

10   When we exhibit these emotions, society showers us with positive reinforcement; we learn this even before we get out of diapers. When, as children, we hug our rotten little puke of a sister and give her a kiss, all the aunts and uncles smile and twit and cry, "Isn't he the sweetest little thing?" Such coveted treats as chocolate-covered graham crackers often follow. But if we deliberately slam the rotten little puke of a sister's fingers in the door, sanctions follow—angry remonstrance from parents, aunts and uncles; instead of a chocolate-covered graham cracker, a spanking.

11   But anticivilization emotions don't go away, and they demand periodic exercise. We have such "sick" jokes as, "What's the difference between a truck-load of bowling balls and a truckload of dead babies?" (You can't unload a truckload of bowling balls with a pitchfork . . . a joke, by the way, that I heard originally from a ten-year-old.) Such a joke may surprise a laugh or a grin

out of us even as we recoil, a possibility that confirms the thesis: If we share a brotherhood of man, then we also share an insanity of man. None of which is intended as a defense of either the sick joke or insanity but merely as an explanation of why the best horror films, like the best fairy tales, manage to be reactionary, anarchistic, and revolutionary all at the same time.

12   The mythic horror movie, like the sick joke, has a dirty job to do. It deliberately appeals to all that is worst in us. It is morbidity unchained, our most base instincts let free, our nastiest fantasies realized . . . and it all happens, fittingly enough, in the dark. For those reasons, good liberals often shy away from horror films. For myself, I like to see the most aggressive of them—*Dawn of the Dead,* for instance—as lifting a trap door in the civilized forebrain and throwing a basket of raw meat to the hungry alligators swimming around in that subterranean river beneath.

13   Why bother? Because it keeps them from getting out, man. It keeps them down there and me up here. It was Lennon and McCartney who said that all you need is love, and I would agree with that.

14   As long as you keep the gators fed.

WHAT DID THE WRITER SAY AND WHAT DID YOU THINK?

1. What is the thesis?
2. What are the main reasons why people like horror movies?
3. In what ways other than horror movies do we exercise our "anticivilization emotions"?
4. What is the purpose of mentioning the "sick joke" in paragraph 11?
5. Explain the last sentence.

HOW DID THE WRITER SAY IT?

1. In paragraph 1, why is "I think that we're all mentally ill" better than "I think people are all mentally ill?"
2. In paragraph 10, why is "rotten little puke of a sister" better than "irritating little sister?"
3. The author claims that horror movies urge us to "become children again." Where does the writing make use of some of the language of childhood?
4. Explain the meaning of "heh-heh-heh" in paragraph 8.

What About Your Writing?

In paragraph 9, Stephen King writes, "The potential lyncher is in almost all of us . . . and every now and then, he has to be let loose to scream and roll around in the grass." Most American publishers would strongly urge the author to rewrite this sentence—and some publishers would insist. The "potential lyncher" could just as easily be a woman as a man, after all. In fact, the sex of the person is totally irrelevant to the meaning of the sentence. Isn't the use of *he* both illogical and unfair (even though few people actually want to be a lyncher)? In a technical sense, the wording in King's sentence is grammatical, but isn't there a way of being correct without the risk of offending some readers?

Many people have charged that our language echoes the sexual discrimination of society as a whole. The ease with which jokes, sometimes good ones, can be manufactured at the expense of the feminist movement probably tends to make it too easy for some to shrug off legitimate complaints. One may feel entitled to laugh at the insanely enlightened captain of a sinking ship who yells "Person the lifeboats" instead of "Man the lifeboats." One should be more hesitant, however, about laughing at the female employee of the post office who has spent an exhausting day trudging through the snow and who resents being known as a "mailman" instead of a "mail carrier." In any event, many writers and readers have singled out for special censure the use of *he, his, him,* and *himself* when sex is unknown, mixed, or immaterial.

Whatever your personal preferences may be, publishers of books, magazines, and newspapers have responded positively to the complaints. The *he, his, him, himself* usage has all but disappeared from print. A sentence like *A driver needs to know how his car works* is already beginning to sound as outdated as words like *icebox* and *Victrola*. The best and easiest way to solve the "he problem" without damaging your style is to rephrase into plural forms whenever possible:

Original	Rephrased
A good student turns in his assignments on time.	Good students turn in their assignments on time.
Nobody wants his friends to take him for granted.	People do not want their friends to take them for granted.
Everyone at the banquet rose from his seat to give the senator an ovation.	All the guests at the banquet rose from their seats to give the senator an ovation.

(Note: *Nobody* and *everyone,* in the original sentences, always take a singular verb and pronoun in standard written English. Use of *they, them, their* in those sentences would be incorrect.)

The word *one* can also be helpful at times, though it often creates an excessively formal tone. The plural approach is generally more satisfactory:

Original	Rephrased
A person must concentrate on his own happiness first.	One must concentrate on one's own happiness first.
Anybody can break his bad habits if he only tries.	One can break one's bad habits if one only tries.

If you find yourself, for some reason, locked into a singular form, repetition or substantial revisions may be necessary. In King's complete sentence, for example, he mentions *saints* as well as the *lyncher*. Changing *lyncher* to *lynchers* would create confusion, because the nonsexist *they* could then refer to two different groups of people. When the plural form won't work, look for other possibilities:

Original	Rephrased
The potential lyncher is in almost all of us (excluding saints, past and present; but then, most saints have been crazy in their own ways), and every now and then, he has to be let loose to scream and roll around in the grass.	The potential lyncher is in almost all of us (excluding saints, past and present; but then, most saints have been crazy in their own ways), and every now and then, the lyncher has to be let loose to scream and roll around in the grass.
The reader will need to use all his attention to understand the plot.	The reader will need to be extremely attentive to understand the plot.
The best policy for someone who has been arrested is to keep his mouth shut.	The best policy for someone who has been arrested is to say as little as possible.

Now for two warnings. First, do what you can to avoid habitual reliance on the phrases *he or she, his or hers, him or her, himself or herself.* These expressions belong more to legal contracts than to ordinary writing, and when they are used repeatedly, the result is often absurd:

Poor	Better
A writer always should remember that he or she is writing for his or her audience, not just for himself or herself.	Writers always should remember that they are writing for their audience, not just for themselves.

Second, avoid artificial constructions like *s/he* or *he/she*. Many readers, and most English teachers, will view them as strained efforts to show off the writer's devotion to good causes. The devotion may deserve praise, but straining and showing off have almost never resulted in good writing.

BEYOND CHAGRIN
David Bradley

David Bradley is the author of *South Street* and *The Cheney Incident,* which won the PEN/Faulkner award. He has published articles in *Esquire, Redbook, The*

Reprinted by permission of The Wendy Weil Agency, Inc. First published by BREVITY Magazine, Issue 29. © 2009 by David Bradley.

New Yorker, New York Times Magazine, and a range of other publications. He teaches fiction writing at the University of Oregon.

✓ WORDS TO CHECK:

piecemeal (paragraph 4)	peccadilloes (6)	obtuse (8)
deluge (4)	precipitate (6)	methodology (8)
chagrin (5)	myriad (6)	unfeigned (8)
plethora (6)	gaffes (8)	

---

1   When I was in the second grade I wet my pants.

2   At a rehearsal of my grade school's pageant, just before I spoke my lines– well, *line,* but, according to the director, a fourth grade teacher who'd minored in drama, it was a crucial one. For in this version of "Little Red Riding Hood" the BIG BAD WOLF (Yours Truly) is transformed from a predator, lurking and growling (Grrr) upstage to a protector who, in the last scene, comes down-stage and to Our Heroine's defense: "Leave her alone! Grrr!"

3   I'm not sure I grasped that particular symbolism, but I did grasp that all the other speaking parts had been given to sixth graders; also that I was one of the few Negro children in the school. So I studied my line and practiced my growling, the better to be a credit to my race with, my dear.

4   I had a sixth-grade reading level, but only a second-grade bladder, and the script called for the WOLF to lurk in every scene. I managed in piecemeal rehearsals, but at the end of the first full run-through, as I stepped downstage, I experienced a release of dramatic tension. Despite the deluge I spoke my line, then exited stage left, dripping.

5   Lurking in the Boys Room, waiting for my mother to fetch fresh pants, I *grred* furiously, my belly burning with the acid of chagrin. BIG BAD WOLF? Big, bad disgrace–to myself, my Negro schoolmates, the entire Negro race. Next day the director assured me I'd do fine in performance, that delivering my line when no longer under pressure showed stage presence, but kept having flashbacks. Finally just told me, flatly, to get over it, because though now it seemed a huge event, it was probably not the most embarrassing thing I'd ever do.

6   A terrifying prophecy–and too often fulfilled. In high school, a plethora of peccadilloes, like that chemistry experiment that produced not the predicted white precipitate but a green cloud of poison gas, or that jump-shot at the buzzer that swished through the opponents' net. In college, in the city, a myriad of misdemeanors arising from my rural, culturally incompetent upbringing.

7   I did not order a ham sandwich in a kosher deli . . . but I did order a corned beef with Swiss. I did ask if I could get sashimi well done. I did whisper to a nun, one February Wednesday morning, that she'd an ash smudge on her forehead. I did amuse the few black students in the school with my abject igno-rance of What Was Happening, Where It Was At or the Usual Places to buy tickets to It. If I became (or was made) aware that I'd stepped in It, I'd insert

the same foot in my mouth in lame attempts at self-justification (Well, where *I* come from we fry our fish) but later I'd lie sleepless, haunted by the ghosts of *faux pas* present, past and future.

8   In later life I learned (the hard way) to check my facts, my pronunciations and my fly—better to be caught at that than to lecture with one's zipper down. I developed coping strategies: a deadpan affect that encouraged comic interpretations of potential gaffes; a Socratic style that made obtuse questions methodology; ironies instantly deployable if *savoir* fell behind *faire*. Still many ironies were unintended (Would your friend Bill like to join us for a drink?) many obtusities unfeigned (I really thought that working girl was a grad student doing fieldwork). And no strategy could cope with the premonition that the worst gaffe yet lay ahead.

9   But recently, listening to an old friend introduce me to a distinguished academic audience with a much-embellished account (I did *not* attempt to leap it in a single bound, I was just trying to climb the thing) of one of my Greatest Misses, it occurred to me that I am no longer vulnerable to such embarrassment; these days I couldn't even lift my leg that high. Then it struck me: at fifty-something, the most embarrassing thing I'll ever do is probably something I've already done. So I checked my fly and I took the stage, in a state of grace beyond disgrace, beyond the fear of future mortification, beyond chagrin.

WHAT DID THE WRITER SAY AND WHAT DID YOU THINK?

1. David Bradley mentions his race several times in the course of this essay. Why do you think he does this?
2. Explain the irony in paragraph 8 when Bradley asks, "Would your friend Bill like to join us for a drink?
3. Why is Bradley now "beyond chagrin"?

HOW DID THE WRITER SAY IT?

1. How does the author make sure he grabs his reader's attention?
2. Locate some examples of euphemisms and alliteration in this essay.

What About <u>Your</u> Writing?

At various places in his essay, David Bradley refers to various embarrassing mistakes he has made as: peccadilloes, misdemeanors, *faux pas,* gaffes, and obtusities. Why *peccadilloes*? Why *faux pas*? Why not just repeat *mistakes*? It's possible that Bradley, while having fun with language, also fell victim to *elegant variation*.

Too many writers worry about repeating a word in the same sentence or in sentences close to each other. This worry sometimes leads them into using synonyms—often "elegant" ones—that can be more distracting than any repetition:

- As mother brought the turkey to the table, I thought of how often that fowl had added to the joys of Thanksgiving.
- In planning your wedding, remember that nuptial ceremonies are largely a matter of individual taste.

Another "What About Your Writing?" section, while warning against monotony, discusses how repetition can often be an effective stylistic device (see pages 140–141). But even when the issue is direct communication of meaning rather than a distinguished style, straightforward repetition is preferable to elegant variation: As mother brought the turkey to the table, I thought of how often turkey has added to the joys of Thanksgiving. In planning your wedding, remember that weddings are largely a matter of individual taste.

Aside from common sense concern about monotony, the only serious danger in repetition is when the same word in the same sentence or in sentences close to each other *changes in meaning.* (This warning includes different forms of the same word: *convention-conventional,* for example.) Do, at all costs, avoid confusing repetition like:

- The heart of our medical research project is heart failure.
- The one bright spot in his report card was his brightness in math.
- I can't bear the thought of the polar bears becoming extinct.
- The plain truth is that Deborah is very plain.

COLD AUTUMN
Steve Dublanica

For four years, Steve Dublanica anonymously wrote WaiterRant.com, the uncensored true story of his life as a New York City waiter. When the blog became increasingly popular, Dublanica published *Thanks for the Tip: Confessions of a Cynical Waiter,* a collection of essays from the blog. The success of the book, which spent five weeks on the best-seller list, coupled with appearances on *Oprah* and other television shows meant he had to give up his anonymity. This essay records a moment when Dublanica's success as a writer was beginning, but his anonymity was still intact.

✓ **WORDS TO CHECK:**

hookah (paragraph 2)	schizoid (63)
anonymity (63)	scuttling (65)

1 It's Saturday night. Beth and I are drinking dirty martinis at Istanbul, a Turkish restaurant with a fun bar and live music. I'm keen on seeing some belly dancers.

"Cold Autumn" first appeared on waiterrant.net on October 16, 2006. Reprinted by permission from Steve Dublanica.

2   "Did you ever smoke a hookah?" Beth asks me, motioning to the ornate water pipes standing at attention behind the bar.

3   "Yes," I reply. "But only the ones with tobacco in it."

4   "C'mon," Beth says. "You're talking to me, remember?"

5   "No, seriously," I say. "I went to this Arab restaurant once and smoked a hookah with some friends."

6   "Nothing else?" Beth asks, her voice betraying a note of suspicion.

7   "I only smoked pot once, Beth," I say. "And that was a long time ago."

8   "How can you smoke pot once?"

9   "Never did anything for me," I reply. "But I did enough stupid things with booze to make up for it."

10   "OK," Beth says, unconvinced.

11   "You don't believe me?"

12   Beth just laughs and chases the last olive in her martini glass with a swizzle stick.

13   "Fine," I say. "Don't believe me, then."

14   I drain the last of my drink and set the glass down on the bar. Suddenly I feel a finger tap me on the shoulder. I turn around. The finger's attached to a cute blonde. Things are looking up.

15   "Remember me?" the girl asks.

16   I look at the young woman. She looks about 25 years old. I wait a moment and let the connections spiderweb in my mind. Suddenly I remember. This girl worked as a hostess at the Bistro seven years ago.

17   "Alice," I say, snapping my fingers. "My God, how long has it been?"

18   "Almost seven years," she says.

19   "How old are you now?" I ask, looking at her incredulously.

20   "Twenty-six."

21   "Wow."

22   Seven years ago, Alice was an innocent looking young girl. Now she's a shapely young woman. Seven years ago my thirty-one-year-old self wouldn't have given Alice the time of day. But now? Things are different. My pulse quickens.

23   "So what are you up to?" I ask. "Finished with school?"

24   "Not yet," Alice says. "I'm tending bar over at Club Expo while I earn my Master's at NYU."

25   "Good luck," I reply. "What are you studying?"

26   "Social work."

27   "That's great."

28   "You look really good," Alice says. "You've lost a lot of weight."

29   "Thanks," I say. "Been going to the gym and stuff."

30   "It's working."

31   "I'm trying," I say, mildly flattered. A girl hasn't complimented my appearance in a long time.

32   "So," Alice asks, "what are you doing with yourself?"

33   "I'm still over at the Bistro with Fluvio," I say.

34   A funny look passes across Alice's face.

35   "Wow," she says softly. "Has it been that long?"

36   "Can you believe it?" I say. "It's been almost seven years."

37   There's an awkward pause. While I'm wondering why there's an awkward pause, someone calls Alice's name.

38   "Well," Alice says, "my friends are calling me over. Nice to have seen you."

39   "Nice to see you too, Alice."

40   "Bye."

41   Alice disappears into the crowd. I begin to think about the look Alice gave me, why she went from giving me compliment to running away. Then it hits me.

42   Alice thinks I'm a loser.

43   "Goddammit," I mutter.

44   I pick up my empty martini glass. Suddenly I need another drink. The bartender's too busy looking cool to notice me. A violent pressure builds up inside me. The martini glass I'm holding threatens to break in my grasp. I put the glass back down on the zinc bar and take a deep breath.

45   "What's the matter?" Beth asks, putting her hand on my arm. "You look upset."

46   I can't tell Beth a girl looked at me like I was some kind of loser. How can I be sure that was the sentiment behind the look? And why do I give a shit what a 26-year-old girl thinks of me?

47   "I'm fine, Beth," I say. "Something just pissed me off."

48   "What?" Beth says. "Tell me what happened."

49   I'm not sure what happened myself. Maybe I'm projecting my own loneliness and frustration into the encounter. Experience tells me that if I don't understand what I'm feeling–say nothing.

50   "Forget it, Beth," I say. "It's nothing important."

51   "If you say so."

52   I put some money on the bar and grab my coat. "I'm done for the night," I say.

53   "You're leaving already?" Beth asks.

54   "I'm not in a drinking mood," I say. "I just want to get home."

55   "OK," Beth says. "I'll see you next week."

56   "Your boyfriend coming to get you?" I ask.

57   "He'll be here soon."

58   "OK then," I say, feeling old and out of place. "See ya."

59   "Be careful going home," Beth says.

60   "I will."

61   I walk out the door. In the brisk night air I realize I'm breathing heavily. I'm intensely angry. Being fighting mad with two martinis in your system can be a dangerous thing.

62   So instead of going home, I walk around trying to process what I'm feeling. I know I'm angry because I feel frustrated. Sexual frustration and loneliness are part of it, sure. But if I'm honest, I'm really frustrated because I didn't tell Alice I have a book deal and I'm trying to become a writer.

63   Why didn't I say that? Why didn't I tell her I've got other things going on? My anonymity? Please, I'm not that schizoid. Why do I even feel the need to tell anyone I've got "other things going on?" That sounds like pretentious horseshit. I've never used my blog as a pickup line. And I'm not about to start telling women, "Hey, babe, I've got a book deal." Besides, being a waiter at thirty-eight's an honorable profession.

64   Isn't it?

65   It's a cold autumn night. An easterly wind sends leaves scuttling across the pavement, choking storm grates with red, orange, and gold. Ahead of me a young couple walk arm in arm. I step into the street to bypass them. I notice the girl has long thick black hair. I speed up, hop back onto the sidewalk, and continue on my way.

66   I catch my reflection in the store windows as I walk along the avenue. My reflection looks tired—like he needs a vacation, like he needs to get laid, like he needs an entirely new life.

67   Disgusted, I stuff my hands in my pockets and stare at the pavement as it treadmills beneath my feet. Suddenly I start shivering. I draw the sensation around me like a cloak.

68   It's a cold I know all too well.

WHAT DID THE WRITER SAY AND WHAT DID YOU THINK?

1. Dublanica never tells us why he didn't tell Alice about his book deal and his blog. Why do you think he didn't tell her? Why doesn't he tell us the reason?
2. Why does Dublanica tell us about the young couple walking ahead of him in the street?
3. Is the author's disappointment about more than his rejection by an attractive woman?

HOW DID THE WRITER SAY IT?

1. Dublanica's essay is primarily dialogue. Why might he have chosen this format for his essay?
2. Explain the selection's title.

What About Your Writing?

There is a Haitian proverb that reminds us that "If work were nice, the rich would not have left it to the poor." If you have a job, you have something to complain about. And if you have something to complain about, you have something to write about.

Take a quick look at the table of contents for this book. James Alexander Thom's essay "The Perfect Picture" is about his work as a news photographer. "The Happiest Day of My Life" is Michael T. Smith's story of unexpected joy and friendship found in a dreary workplace. "Chores" is about Debra Marquart's work on her family farm. "The Exploding Toilet and Other Embarrassments" is Patrick Smith's essay about the worst day at work anyone has ever had. "Too Many Bananas" is about David Counts' work as an anthropologist. In this chapter, both "Cold Autumn" and "Why I Quit the Company" are about, you guessed it, work.

We didn't set out to create a mini-collection of essays about work. It just happened. It happened because there's so much to say about work—so much to praise, so much to hate, so many funny stories and so many tragic ones. It doesn't matter what your job is. You can write an essay about any kind of work and in any kind of rhetorical format.

Narration: Babysitting, Dogwalking; Lifeguarding: My Summer at Minimum Wage

A Day in the Life of a Work-Study Student

Description: Behind the Scenes at a Luxury Hotel (fancy restaurant/greasy spoon diner/bookstore)

My Uniform

Examples: Work: Boredom Punctuated by Panic

Learn Something: Every Job Is a Learning Experience

Process: How to Ask for the Day Off

How to Call in Sick

Comparison and Contrast: Best Job, Worst Job

Then and Now: My First Day and My Last Day

Cause and Effect: How Working as a (Teacher/Chef/Bank Teller/Gas Station Attendant) Changed Me

Learning to Teach: What Being a Math Tutor Taught Me

Division and Classification: Five Types of Job Interviews

The Good, the Bad, and the Ugly: Three Kinds of Coworkers

Definition: The Best Boss

Doing a Good Job

Argumentation: Experience Shouldn't Count: Why Hiring the Inexperienced Is a Great Idea

Working from Home: Bad Idea, Really Bad Idea, or Worst Idea Ever?

WHY I QUIT THE COMPANY
Tomoyuki Iwashita

Tomoyuki Iwashita is a journalist and freelance writer. His essay tells of a time before he began that career, when he was involved in the highly routinized, socially rigid, demanding Japanese corporate culture.

✓ **WORDS TO CHECK:**

prestigious (paragraph 1)	revert (9)	opt (13)
isolation (5)	fetters (11)	

1 When I tell people that I quit working for the company after only a year, most of them think I'm crazy. They can't understand why I would want to give up a prestigious and secure job. But I think I'd have been crazy to stay, and I'll try to explain why.

2   I started working for the company immediately after graduating from university. It's a big, well-known trading company with about 6,000 employees all over the world. There's a lot of competition to get into this and other similar companies, which promise young people a wealthy and successful future. I was set on course to be a Japanese "yuppie."

3   I'd been used to living independently as a student, looking after myself and organizing my own schedule. As soon as I started working all that changed. I was given a room in the company dormitory, which is like a fancy hotel, with a twenty-four-hour hot bath service and all meals laid on. Most single company employees live in a dormitory like this, and many married employees live in company apartments. The dorm system is actually a great help because living in Tokyo costs more than young people earn–but I found it stifling.

4   My life rapidly became reduced to a shuttle between the dorm and the office. The working day is officially eight hours, but you can never leave the office on time. I used to work from nine in the morning until eight or nine at night, and often midnight. Drinking with colleagues after work is part of the job; you can't say no. The company building contained cafeterias, shops, a bank, a post office, a doctor's office, a barber's. . . . I never needed to leave the building. Working, drinking, sleeping, and standing on a horribly crowded commuter train for an hour and a half each way: This was my life. I spent all my time with the same colleagues; when I wasn't involved in entertaining clients on the weekend, I was expected to play golf with my colleagues. I soon lost sight of the world outside the company.

5   This isolation is part of the brainwashing process. A personnel manager said: "We want excellent students who are active, clever, and tough. Three months is enough to train them to be devoted businessmen." I would hear

"Why I Quit the Company" by Iwashita Tomoyuki from THE NEW INTERNATIONALIST, May 1992. Reprinted by permission.

my colleagues saying: "I'm not making any profit for the company, so I'm not contributing." Very few employees claim all the overtime pay due to them. Keeping an employee costs the company 50 million yen ($400,000) a year, or so the company claims. Many employees put the company's profits before their own mental and physical well-being.

6   Overtiredness and overwork leave you little energy to analyze or criticize your situation. There are shops full of "health drinks," cocktails of caffeine and other drugs, which will keep you going even when you're exhausted. *Karoshi* (death from overwork) is increasingly common and is always being discussed in the newspapers. I myself collapsed from working too hard. My boss told me: "You should control your health; it's your own fault if you get sick." There is no paid sick leave; I used up half of my fourteen days' annual leave because of sickness.

7   We had a labor union, but it seemed to have an odd relationship with the management. A couple of times a year I was told to go home at five o'clock. The union representatives were coming around to investigate working hours; everyone knew in advance. If it was "discovered" that we were all working overtime in excess of fifty hours a month our boss might have had some problem being promoted; and our prospects would have been affected. So we all pretended to work normal hours that day.

8   The company also controls its employees' private lives. Many company employees under thirty are single. They are expected to devote all their time to the company and become good workers; they don't have time to find a girlfriend. The company offers scholarships to the most promising young employees to enable them to study abroad for a year or two. But unmarried people who are on these courses are not allowed to get married until they have completed the course! Married employees who are sent to train abroad have to leave their families in Japan for the first year.

9   In fact, the quality of married life is often determined by the husband's work. Men who have just gotten married try to go home early for a while, but soon have to revert to the norm of late-night work. They have little time to spend with their wives and even on the weekend are expected to play golf with colleagues. Fathers cannot find time to communicate with their children and child rearing is largely left to mothers. Married men posted abroad will often leave their family behind in Japan; they fear that their children will fall behind in the fiercely competitive Japanese education system.

10   Why do people put up with this? They believe this to be a normal working life or just cannot see an alternative. Many think that such personal sacrifices are necessary to keep Japan economically successful. Perhaps, saddest of all, Japan's education and socialization processes do not equip people with the intellectual and spiritual resources to question and challenge the status quo. They stamp out even the desire for a different kind of life.

11   However, there are some signs that things are changing. Although many new employees in my company were quickly brainwashed, many others, like myself, complained about life in the company and seriously considered leaving. But most of them were already in fetters—of debt. Pleased with themselves for getting into the company and anticipating a life of executive luxury, these new employees throw their money around. Every night they are out drinking. They buy smart clothes and take a taxi back to the dormitory after the last train has gone. They start borrowing money from the bank and soon they have a debt growing like a snowball rolling down a slope. The banks demand no security for loans; it's enough to be working for a well-known company. Some borrow as much as a year's salary in the first few months. They can't leave the company while they have such debts to pay off.

12   I was one of the few people in my intake of employees who didn't get into debt. I left the company dormitory after three months to share an apartment with a friend. I left the company exactly one year after I entered it. It took me a while to find a new job, but I'm working as a journalist now. My life is still busy, but it's a lot better than it was. I'm lucky because nearly all big Japanese companies are like the one I worked for, and conditions in many small companies are even worse.

13   It's not easy to opt out of a lifestyle that is generally considered to be prestigious and desirable, but more and more young people in Japan are thinking about doing it. You have to give up a lot of superficially attractive material benefits in order to preserve the quality of your life and your sanity. I don't think I was crazy to leave the company. I think I would have gone crazy if I'd stayed.

WHAT DID THE WRITER SAY AND WHAT DID YOU THINK?

1. What caused the author to leave the company?
2. Why do employees of the company generally accept the working conditions?
3. Are there any employment practices in your culture similar to what Iwashita describes?

HOW DID THE WRITER SAY IT?

1. The author describes the company's relationship with its employees as a "brainwashing process" (paragraph 5). Do his examples support this claim of brainwashing?
2. How is this essay organized?
3. Does the author play fair? Are there other possible causes for his dissatisfaction with the company?

What About <u>Your</u> Writing?

Note how many words of qualification and caution are spread through the Iwashita essay. The author is dealing with somewhat controversial material, and he has no desire to pretend that his personal experience tells him everything about life for all Japanese businessmen. He needs to demonstrate his awareness that he is extrapolating general principles from his own personal experience. He can't prove many of his points in any rigid way; he can only make them seem plausible because of his employment history.

The persuasive power of the essay depends in part on whether Iwashita strikes the reader as reliable, a sensible person studying complex phenomena and trying to draw reasonable inferences from them. Consider how careful he is throughout most of the essay to say *many* employees, not *all employees*. Notice the way that he briefly concedes in paragraph 3 that company housing is "actually a great help" with expenses in pricey Tokyo. Look at the use of *I think* and *I'll try to explain why* in paragraph 1. Iwashita establishes a tone of reason; more, he establishes himself as a person of reason, a person with a fitting hesitation about insisting on the absolute truth of his own ideas. Words and phrases of caution and qualification can help writers establish themselves as trustworthy.

Don't go overboard. Don't write *in my opinion* in every other sentence. Don't confuse being reasonable with being timid. Don't write cowardly nonsense like *I think that George Washington played an important part in the American Revolution* or *It seems to me that heroin is a dangerous drug*. Present the strongest case you can as strongly as you can. Iwashita goes all out in presenting his case, too, once he's laid the foundation. The foundations are important, however, and the wise writer will not neglect them.

THE BEST YEARS OF MY LIFE
Betty Rollin

Betty Rollin has been an editor for *Vogue* and *Look* magazines and a former news correspondent for NBC and ABC. Her best-selling book *First, You Cry* (1976) describes her operation for breast cancer. Among her other books are *Am I Getting Paid for This?* (1982), *Last Wish* (1985), and *Here's the Bright Side (of Failure, Fear, Cancer, Divorce and Other Bum Raps)* (2007). "The Best Years of My Life" analyzes the effects of her operation—and survival.

✓ WORDS TO CHECK:

intrinsically (paragraph 1)	gynecologist (8)	masochism (11)
chemotherapy (2)	orthopedist (8)	voracious (11)

harrowing (2)   parsimonious (9)
hypochondriac (7)   hedonism (10)

1 I am about to celebrate an anniversary. Not that there will be a party with
   funny hats. Nor do I expect any greetings in the mail. Hallmark, with its infinite variety of occasions about which to fashion a 50-cent card, has skipped
   this one. This, you see, is my cancer anniversary. Five years ago tomorrow, at
   Beth Israel Hospital in New York City, a malignant tumor was removed from
   my left breast and, along with the tumor, my left breast. To be alive five years
   later means something in cancer circles. There is nothing intrinsically magical about the figure five, but the numbers show that if you have survived that
   many years after cancer has been diagnosed, you have an 80 percent shot at
   living out a normal life span.

2   Still, you probably think Hallmark is right not to sell a card, and that it's
   weird to "celebrate" such a terrible thing as cancer. It's even weirder than you
   imagine. Because not only do I feel good about (probably) having escaped a
   recurrence of cancer, I also feel good about having gotten cancer in the first
   place. Here is the paradox: Although cancer was the worst thing that ever happened to me, it was also the best. Cancer (the kind I had, with no spread and
   no need of chemotherapy, with its often harrowing side effects) enriched my
   life, made me wiser, made me happier. Another paradox: although I would do
   everything possible to avoid getting cancer again, I am glad I had it.

3   There is a theory about people who have had a life-and-death scare that
   goes something like this: For about six months after surviving the scare, you
   feel shaken and grateful. Armed with a keen sense of what was almost The
   End, you begin to live your life differently. You pause during the race to notice
   the foliage, you pay more attention to the people you love—maybe you even
   move to Vermont. You have gained, as they say, a "new perspective." But then,
   according to this theory, when the six months are over, the "new perspective"
   fades, you sell the house in Vermont and go back to the same craziness that
   was your life before the car crash or whatever it was. What has happened is
   that you've stopped feeling afraid. The crash is in the past. The it-can't-happen-
   to-me feelings that were dashed by the accident re-emerge, after six months, as
   it-can't-happen-to-me-*again*.

4   It's different for people whose crash is cancer. You can stay off the free-
   ways, but you can't do much about preventing whatever went wrong in your
   own body from going wrong again. Unless your head is buried deep in the
   sand, you know damn well it *can* happen again. Even though, in my case, the
   doctors say it isn't likely, the possibility of recurrence is very real to me. Passing the five-year mark is reassuring, but I know I will be a little bit afraid for the
   rest of my life. But—ready for another paradox?—certain poisons are medicinal
   in small doses. To be a little bit afraid of dying can do wonders for your life. It
   has done wonders for mine. That's because, unlike the way most people feel,

my sense of death is not an intellectual concept. It's a lively presence in my gut. It affects me daily—for the better.

5   First, when you're even slightly afraid of death, you're less afraid of other things—e.g., bosses, spouses, plumbers, rape, bankruptcy, failure, not being liked, the flu, aging. Next to the Grim Reaper, how ferocious can even the most ferocious boss be? How dire the direst household calamity? In my own professional life, I have lost not only some big fears, but most of the small ones. I used to be nervous in front of television cameras. That kind of nervousness was a fear of not being thought attractive, smart and winning. It still pleases me greatly if someone besides my husband and mother thinks I'm attractive, smart and winning; but I am no longer afraid that someone won't. Cancer made me less worried about what people think of me, both professionally and socially. I am less concerned about where my career is going. I don't know where it's going. I don't think about that. I think about where I am and what I'm doing and whether I like it. The result is that these days I continually seem to be doing what I like. And probably I'm more successful than when I aimed to please.

6   My book *First, You Cry,* which has given me more pleasure than anything else in my professional life, is a good example of this. As a career move, leaving television for six months to write a book about a cancer operation seemed less than sensible. But as soon as I got cancer, I stopped being "sensible." I wanted to write the book. And, just in case I croaked, I wanted to write it the way that was right for me, not necessarily for the market. So I turned down the publisher who wanted it to be a "how-to" book. I like to think I would have done that, cancer or not, but had it not been for cancer, I probably wouldn't have written a book at all, because I would have been too afraid to drop out of television even for six months. And if I had written a book, I doubt that I would have been so open about my life and honest about my less-than-heroic feelings. But, as I wrote, I remember thinking, "I might die, so what does it matter what anyone thinks of me?" A lot of people write honestly and openly without having had a disease, but I don't think I would have. I hadn't done it before.

7   A touch of cancer turns you into a hypochondriac. You get a sore throat and you think you've got cancer of the throat; you get a corn from a pair of shoes that are too tight and you're sure it's a malignant tumor. But—here's the bright side—cancer hypochondria is so compelling it never occurs to you that you could get anything *else.* And, when you do, you're so glad it's not cancer that you feel like celebrating. "Goody, it's the flu!" I heard myself say to myself a couple of weeks ago.

8   Some physicians are more sensitive than others to cancer anxiety. My gynecologist prattled on once about some menstrual irregularity without noticing that, as he spoke, I had turned to stone. "Is it cancer?" I finally whispered. He looked dumbfounded and said, "Of course not!" As if to say, "How could

you think such a thing?" But an orthopedist I saw about a knee problem took an X-ray and, before saying a word about what it was (a torn cartilage), told me what it wasn't. I limped home joyously.

9   I never went to Vermont because I can't stand that much fresh air; but in my own fashion, I sop up pleasure where and when I can, sometimes at the risk of professional advancement and sometimes at the risk of bankruptcy. An exaggeration, perhaps, but there's no question about it: Since cancer, I spend more money than I used to. (True, I have more to spend, but that's mostly because of the book, which is also thanks to cancer.) I had always been parsimonious—some would say cheap—and I'm not anymore. The thinking is, "Just in case I do get a recurrence, won't I feel like a fool for having flown coach to Seattle?" (I like to think I'm more generous with others as well. It seems to me that, since having cancer, I give better presents.)

10   Cancer kills guilt. You not only take a vacation now because next year you might be dead, but you take a *better* vacation because, even if you don't die soon, after what you've been through, you feel you deserve it. In my own case, I wouldn't have expected that feeling to survive six months because, once those months passed, I realized that, compared to some people, I had not been through much at all. But my hedonism continues to flourish. Maybe it was just a question of changing a habit.

11   My girlish masochism didn't resurface, either. Most women I know go through at least a phase of needing punishment from men. Not physical punishment, just all the rest: indifference, harshness, coldness, rudeness or some neat combination. In the past, my own appetite for this sort of treatment was voracious. Conversely, if I happened to connect with a man who was nice to me, I felt like that song: "This can't be love because I feel so well." The difference was that, in the song, it really *was* love, and with me, it really *wasn't*. Only when I was miserable did I know I really cared.

12   The minute I got cancer, my taste in men improved. It's not that my first husband was a beast. I'm fond of him, but even he would admit he was very hard on me. Maybe I asked for it. Well, once you've been deftly kicked in the pants by God (or whoever distributes cancer), you stop wanting kicks from mortals. Everyone who knows the man I married a year ago thinks I'm lucky—even my mother!—and I do, too. But I know it wasn't only luck. It was that cancer made me want someone wonderful. I wasn't ready for him before. I was so struck by this apparent change in me that I checked it out with a psychoanalyst, who assured me that I was not imagining things—that the damage to my body had, indeed, done wonders for my head.

13   Happiness is probably something that shouldn't be talked about too much, but I can't help it. Anyway, I find the more I carry on about it, the better it gets. A big part of happiness is noticing it. It's trite to say, but if you've never been ill, you don't notice—or enjoy—not being ill. I even notice my husband's good health. (He doesn't, but how could he?)

14   I haven't mentioned losing that breast, have I? That's because, in spite of the fuss I made about it five years ago, that loss now seems almost not worth mentioning. Five years ago, I felt sorry for myself that I could no longer keep a strapless dress up. Today I feel that losing a breast saved my life, and wasn't I lucky. And when I think of all the other good things that have come from that loss, I just look at that flat place on my body and think: small price.

15   Most of my friends who are past 40 shudder on their birthdays. Not me. They feel a year closer to death, I suppose. I feel a year further from it.

16   O.K., what if I get a recurrence? I'm not so jolly all the time that I haven't given this some serious thought. If it happens, I'm sure I won't be a good sport about it—especially if my life is cut short. But even if it is, I will look back at the years since the surgery and know I got the best from them. And I will be forced to admit that the disease that is ending my life is the very thing that made it so good.

WHAT DID THE WRITER SAY AND WHAT DID YOU THINK?

1. What is Rollin's thesis?
2. Does the essay strike you as convincing and realistic or as too overwhelmingly cheerful?
3. Does the author deal with any unpleasant effects? What are they?
4. Do you think the author wants the essay to come through as purely personal comments or as a piece with a message that people in general can apply to their own lives?
5. Explain in your own words the change in Rollin's "taste in men."
6. How much attention does Rollin pay to the often traumatic physical and emotional effects of losing a breast (rather than surviving an operation for cancer)? What is her current attitude toward the loss?
7. Explain these lines: "Most of my friends who are past 40 shudder on their birthdays. Not me. They feel a year closer to death, I suppose. I feel a year further from it."

HOW DID THE WRITER SAY IT?

1. Point out some instances of the author's use of humor. Is the humor appropriate for the subject?
2. The writing is frequently informal, even slangy—"you know damn well," "just in case I croaked," and so on. Is this tone appropriate for the subject?
3. In paragraph 2, the author mentions the "paradox" that cancer was the worst and best thing that ever happened to her. Are there other paradoxes in the reading selection, either direct or implied?

What About Your Writing?

In paragraph 3, the author writes, "You pause during the race to notice the foliage, you pay more attention to the people you love. . . ." Two sentences later, she writes, "the 'new perspective' fades, you sell the house in Vermont. . . ."

Betty Rollin is an experienced, professional writer who has written a moving and inspirational essay, but the chances are at least fair that your instructor would have used some red ink on those sentences. (The chances are even better that your instructor would have complained about the many sentence fragments, such as the second sentence in paragraph 1, but that's another matter. See page 62) The red ink would have underlined or circled the commas in both sentences, and then above those commas or out in the margin would be the letters CS, meaning *comma splice.*

The comma splice is one of the most frequent errors in punctuation. From the point of view of many instructors, it's also more serious than most punctuation errors, because it suggests that the writer not only doesn't know about commas but also doesn't know what a sentence is. In your own writing, you need to avoid comma splices and know how to get rid of them if they do pop up. You need to know, too, about those special occasions when, like Betty Rollin, you may be able to use a comma splice deliberately—and get away with it.

A comma splice results when the writer forgets this simple rule: *A comma all by itself cannot join independent clauses.* (An independent clause is a group of words with a subject and a verb that can stand alone as a separate sentence.)

Let's look first at an old-fashioned fused sentence, sometimes called a run-on sentence:

I took an aspirin and went straight to bed I had a headache.

Few writers are likely to make this gross an error. The sentence contains two independent clauses—*I took an aspirin and went straight to bed* and *I had a headache*—with no punctuation of any kind between them.

The comma splice occurs when the writer sees that something is wrong with the fused sentence, knows precisely where it's wrong, and tries to fix the sentence like this:

I took an aspirin and went straight to bed, I had a headache.

Remember the rule: *A comma all by itself cannot join independent clauses.* The writer has created a comma splice, a kind of sophisticated fused sentence. It's a slight improvement, probably, but it's still wrong.

A comma splice can be eliminated in a variety of ways:

1. Replace the comma with a period:

    I took an aspirin and went straight to bed. I had a headache.

2. Replace the comma with a semicolon:

> I took an aspirin and went straight to bed; I had a headache.

3. Add one of the following coordinating conjunctions *after* the comma: *and, but, or, nor, for, yet, so.* Which word you choose will depend on the logical relationship between clauses:

> I took an aspirin and went straight to bed, for I had a headache.

4. Change one of the independent clauses to a dependent clause:

> Because I had a headache, I took an aspirin and went straight to bed.
> I took an aspirin and went straight to bed because I had a headache.

All four of these techniques result in correctly punctuated sentences. Which one you choose often depends on subtle issues of style, and sometimes any of the four can work well. Nevertheless, it's not always a pure matter of taste. If you've just written a string of short sentences, for example, you'd want to break the monotony with a longer sentence—and thus avoid replacing the comma with a period. Conversely, with a string of long sentences, the period would probably be your first choice.

Now what about those sentences by Betty Rollin? Why was an experienced writer guilty of comma splices? Why did this discussion begin by saying that the chances of your instructor's objecting to the comma splices were only "fair"? The answer is that rules almost always have exceptions. When the clauses are short and express activities going on at the same time or an unbroken sequence of activities, comma splices can sometimes be acceptable:

- I came, I saw, I conquered.
- Add the eggs, beat the mixture, pour it in the pan.
- The wedding was an emotional explosion. We laughed, we cried, we danced, we hugged, we kissed.
- . . . the "new perspective" fades, you sell the house in Vermont. . .

If you're tempted to use a comma splice deliberately, make certain that the writing assignment does not call for a highly formal tone, as in a scholarly research paper. If in doubt, check with your instructor.

CHAPTER 7½

Office Hours: Revision: Help from the Audience

It's all but impossible to oppose the idea of asking other people to have a look at your writing before you finally submit it to your instructor. The idea of an audience is at the heart of good writing, and suggestions from others can be extremely helpful in the revision process. Don't let yourself be carried away, however. Not all advice is good advice. You are the responsible party. When it comes to your own writing, you are what the great novelist and Nobel Prize winner William Faulkner called "the sole owner and proprietor."

Consider the problems that come with asking the advice of personal acquaintances—parents, spouses, roommates, romantic interests. Their main qualifications usually are that they like you or love you and that they have time. If they like or love you, their first inclination will be to feel the same way about what you've written. The cool, tough objectivity needed for revision and critical reading—even if you insist that's what you want—is going to be hard for them to achieve. Moreover, many of them, assuming they do see some problems, may be reluctant to speak frankly. They simply don't want to risk hurting your feelings:

"Well, what did you think?" you ask.

"I liked it."

"What did you like?"

"It was interesting."

"Did you see anything wrong?"

"I didn't notice anything."

All too often these are the sorts of comments you're most likely to get. The words of praise, heartfelt and well-intentioned as they may be, mean very little.

Another form of audience participation takes place in the classroom, often going by the name of "peer review." Under the supervision of an outstanding instructor, peer review can be valuable. Here is an audience of classmates, an audience that reads the same texts, receives the same assignments, and knows what the instructor cares most and least about. There's a sense of community: Your classmates help you, and you help them. It all sounds splendid. Too often, though, peer review can be dominated by one or two strong personalities. Too often, only weak or lazy writers get the attention and the benefits. And the continuing problem of pretending to like something—or keeping one's mouth shut—to avoid offending the writer or disagreeing with the majority is built into the system.

We believe it's possible to maximize the benefits of having an audience and minimize at least some of the difficulties. Our main suggestion is to get as far away as possible from the generalized approach. Don't say, "Read this and tell me what you think." Tell your audience, if it needs to know, what the specific assignment was. Then, after you receive the obligatory comment of "I liked it," bombard your audience with specific questions, the more specific the better. Was the concluding paragraph a bit dull? Did the introduction take too long to present the thesis statement? Should you use another clarifying example or two? You already have a sense of the parts of your work that are most bothering you. Try to do all you can to force your normally reluctant audience into making useful comments. It takes some work on your part, but that's the way barriers get broken down.

Certainly, you want and need an audience. But never fall into the tempting trap of thinking that your composition must be good merely because three out of four readers said they found nothing wrong.

Division
and Classification

8

Some topics are difficult or impossible to attack head-on. Such topics are often best approached through analysis: studying a complex subject by breaking it down into smaller units. Analysis itself calls for analysis and can be broken down into division and classification.

DIVISION

What are the moving parts of a rotary engine? What are the major characteristics of realism in literature? What are the three major divisions of the federal government? The United States is divided into fifty states. Can you name them all? Your own state is divided into counties or parishes. How many of them can you name?

In *division* (also known as *partition*), a subject commonly thought of as a single unit is reduced to its separate parts. Potential renters of an apartment rarely begin by thinking of the apartment as a whole. They mentally divide it into living room, bedroom, kitchen, and bathroom. If they think it worthwhile, they may go on to subdivisions of each room: walls, ceiling, and floor, for example. At any rate, they study each division separately before reaching any useful conclusion about the entire apartment. Soldiers use division to study a rifle; chemists use division to find out the ingredients of a compound; doctors use division in a physical checkup to examine a patient–heart, lungs, blood, and so forth.

Division is a natural, logical, and necessary form of thought. For writing purposes, however, it often tends to be more cut and dried than classification, and most English teachers generally prefer classification assignments. Besides, any students who have written a process paper (see Chapter 5) have already used a form of division to break the process into its separate steps. For these reasons, the rest of this chapter concentrates on classification.

CLASSIFICATION

Are you an introvert or an extrovert? Are you lower class, middle class, or upper class? Are you a Democrat, Republican, Libertarian, Green, or Independent? Are you a Protestant, Catholic, Jew, Muslim, Hindu, Buddhist, Sikh, atheist, agnostic, or "other"? Are you heterosexual, homosexual, or bisexual?

Are you left-handed, right-handed, or ambidextrous? Are you a nondrinker, light drinker, normal drinker, heavy drinker, or alcoholic?

No answers are necessary. The questions aren't intended to snoop. They're intended to demonstrate the universality of classification.

In *classification* we analyze a subject like apartments, not *an* apartment; engines, not *an* engine. We analyze the subject by arranging it into groups or categories rather than separate parts. We divide an apartment into rooms, but we classify apartments into high rises, garden apartments, tenements, and so on. We classify when we make out a shopping list to deal with the thousands of articles in a supermarket: dairy, meat, produce, paper goods. A business manager classifies: complaints I can ignore, complaints I have to do something about. A college catalog classifies: required courses, elective courses.

Without classification, certain kinds of systematic thought would be impossible. Biologists, for example, classify to make basic sense of the world, to be able to function at all. They classify living things into Plants and Animals. They classify animals into Vertebrates and Invertebrates. They classify Vertebrates into Mammals, Birds, Reptiles, Amphibians, and Fish. Each class has distinct characteristics, so when biologists meet some wriggly little item they haven't seen before, they have some way of at least beginning to cope with it. As another example, political leaders in presidential elections undoubtedly classify the states. Which states are Sure for Us? Which states are Sure for Them? Which states are Toss-ups? Classification here is not a parlor game or intellectual exercise. It's the only way of determining where the time and money should go.

Classification can sometimes be a game, however, and it can lead to excellent humorous papers. Members of a bad football team could be classified as Hopeless Bums, Hopeless Mediocrities, and Hopeless Physical Wrecks. Household chores could be classified as Chores I Can Put Off for a Week, Chores I Can Put Off for a Month, and Chores I Can Put Off Forever. A student once classified teachers as Fascist Pigs, Middle-of-the-Road Sheep, and Mad Dog Radicals.

The pattern of a classification—or division—paper is straightforward and pretty much self-evident. Each class or division generally represents a major section of the paper. Each is defined and described, with as many examples as are needed for clarity. Each is carefully differentiated from the others when any possibility of confusion occurs.

In writing a classification paper, keep the following elementary principles of logic in mind.

Use Only One Principle of Classification

Different classifications can apply at different times to the same subject, depending on one's interests and insights. The essential requirement is that only one basis of classification be used at a time. Cars, for instance, can be classified by size. They can also be classified by manufacturer, price, body style, country of origin, and so on. Choose the principle of classification suitable to your purpose. Something is obviously cockeyed in this arrangement of cars: subcompact, compact, intermediate, Fords, full-size.

Exercise

What are the errors in the following classification outlines?

Schools

I. Elementary schools

II. Junior high schools

III. Parochial schools

IV. High schools

V. Colleges and universities

Students

I. Bright

II. Average

III. Hardworking

IV. Dull

Teachers

I. Hard graders

II. Friendly

III. Easy graders

Crimes

I. Violent

II. Nonviolent

III. Fraud

Sections of America

I. East

II. South

III. Midwest

IV. Slums

V. Far West

Politicians

I. Good

II. Bad

III. Mediocre

IV. Honest

Be Consistent

Once you have determined a principle of classification, stick with it throughout the paper. Mixing principles invariably creates illogical overlapping of classes.

Make the Classifications as Complete as Possible

All individual units within your subject should be able to fit into one of the classes you have devised. Classifying politicians as only Good or Bad doesn't take care of the many who are neither all one nor all the other; you need another category. When you face the prospect of an endless number of classes, it's generally better to revise the subject a bit than to add a catchall class like

Miscellaneous or Others. A paper classifying religions, for example, could go on forever, whereas a paper classifying Major Religions in America would have a much simpler task.

Exercise

Point out incompleteness in the following classification outlines.

Academic Degrees

I. B.A.

II. B.S.

III. M.A.

IV. Ph.D.

Career Opportunities

I. Business

II. Government

Television Programs

I. Comedies

II. Dramas

III. Sports

IV. Quiz shows

Where to Live in America

I. Cities

II. Suburbs

Acknowledge Any Complications

Classification is logical and essential, but it's also arbitrary and artificial. It pins labels on materials that weren't born with them. It may be helpful at times to classify people as introverts or extroverts, but a good paper points out that introverts can sometimes be outgoing among close friends, and extroverts can sometimes be shy in unfamiliar or threatening circumstances. Similarly, labels such as liberal and conservative can be valuable, but a good paper will mention that few people are entirely liberal or conservative about everything.

Follow the Persuasive Principle

Finally, what of the persuasive principle? A classification paper classifies. What does it have to persuade anyone about?

In a fussy, technical sense, every classification paper has a thesis—whether the writer wants one or not. The writer asserts that there are three classes of teachers or four classes of mental illness or five classes of surgeons. By the end of the paper, sure enough, there are the three, four, or five classes, logically consistent and complete.

And there, sure enough, if that's all the writer does, is a distortion of the persuasive principle.

A good classification paper can utilize the persuasive principle in far more effective ways. To the logic and order of classification, it can add the power and bite of a forceful point of view. In some papers, the naming of classes in itself can express the writer's attitude. An introductory paragraph stating that the three kinds of teachers are Fascist Pigs, Middle-of-the-Road Sheep, and Mad Dog Radicals probably doesn't need an explicit thesis statement that all three classes are obnoxious. A paper with less dramatic labels can declare a thesis by expressing a strong preference for one class over the others. It can express scorn for all classes. It can ridicule traditional classifications. Almost all the subjects for classification brought up in this chapter invite a thesis:

- Each different kind of car has serious drawbacks.
- Good politicians in this country are vastly outnumbered by the bad and mediocre.
- Every major religion in America has a similar concept of God.
- The distinctions among normal drinkers, heavy drinkers, and alcoholics are dangerously vague.
- Only one kind of television program makes any appeal to the viewer's intelligence.

It's not hard to see the extra interest such approaches can give a paper. Don't just classify, then. Convince.

WRITING SUGGESTIONS FOR CLASSIFICATION THEMES

Use classification to analyze one of the following subjects. Narrow down any of the subjects as necessary, and remember the importance of working a thesis into your paper. With slight changes, some topics may also lend themselves to analysis by division.

1. Television doctors
2. Snobbishness
3. Drug users
4. People at a concert or sporting event
5. Methods of making excuses
6. Cashiers in supermarkets
7. Clothing
8. Parents
9. Love
10. Hate
11. Laziness
12. News programs or commentators

13. Freshman English students
14. Managers or coaches of athletic teams
15. Ambition
16. Summer jobs
17. Pessimists or optimists
18. Attitudes toward Christmas
19. Attitudes toward money
20. Attitudes toward sex

VISUAL PROMPT

Writing Prompt

In classification we analyze the subject by arranging it into groups or categories rather than separate parts. The fruits in this photograph have been organized by type—blueberries, raspberries, grapes, etc. List a few other ways they could have been arranged.

STUDENT ESSAY: BOOKWORM

Gracie Jane Watson

Thesis: I own four kinds of books.

    I. Books I read
        A. What they cost
        B. What they look like
        C. What they're about
        D. Where they are

    II. Books I want to read
        A. What they cost
        B. What they look like
        C. What they're about
        D. Where they are

    III. Books I have to read
        A. What they cost
        B. What they look like
        C. What they're about
        D. Where they are

    IV. Books I'll never read
        A. What they cost
        B. What they look like
        C. What they're about
        D. Where they are

Conclusion: No matter what library school teaches me about books, I'll always think of them in these four categories.

I have a lot of books. I have books in bookcases and books in piles in front of the bookcases. I have books stacked beside my bed on a small table, and I have books stacked beneath the table. I have some books in boxes under my bed. I have books that are still in the boxes that Amazon used to ship them to me. I have hundreds and hundreds of books. Recently I realized, though, that despite all these books, and despite all the different subjects they cover, and despite all the different ways that bookstores and libraries and book collectors might organize them, I really only have four kinds of books.

First, there are the books I read. These are, strangely enough, usually the least expensive of my books. I tend to pick them up in used bookstores, or out of the bargain bin at the big fancy bookstore at the mall. They tend to be a bit battered and bruised, and after I've read them in the bathtub, pulled them out to entertain me on the subway and the bus, thrown them into my backpack, and folded down the corners of their pages to mark my place they look even worse. The books I read are usually about murders, or passionate love affairs, or magic. Sometimes they're about adventures on distant planets. Sometimes they're even practical books that teach me to cook, to fix my bicycle, or to plant a garden. These books are in stacks all over my apartment. If you come to my place and accidentally sit on a book left open on the sofa, it will be one of these.

Next, there are the books I want to read. In hopes that I'll be inspired, I'll even spring for these in hardback. I order these on-line, or just fall in love with them at rare bookstores. These books are often really pretty. They come in sets with matching covers. They sometimes have their own cases. The books I want to read are about the same subjects as the books I do read, but they're by more famous writers, or they've won important prizes, or they've had a lot of reviews written about them by college professors and poets. Sometimes they're translated from Norwegian. These books are carefully displayed on my shelves. I always hope that their beauty and mystery will encourage me to take them off the shelves, but usually I still reach for the old familiar books from my first category.

Then, there are the books I have to read. These are my most expensive books. I get them at my college bookstore, because my professors tell me I have to. These books have austere covers from university presses, or they have carefully chosen stock photographs on the cover underneath titles like "An Introduction to Biology" and "Making Friends with Calculus" and "Shakespeare: Sources and Criticism." I keep these by my desk, and I do the assigned reading. But I keep looking at the piles of books I'd rather be reading.

The last category of all is the books I'll never read. I have no idea what these books cost. They come into my apartment as birthday presents from people who "know that I like books" but who don't know what I like. This is how I got three copies of that new book by the televangelist who wants to tell me how to run my life. This is how I got that book of baseball statistics and that other one on women's fashion through the ages. This is how I got that book of 25 ways to restyle a T-shirt. I keep these in boxes, usually labeled "to sell" or "to give away." It's nice of people to think of me, but really, a gift certificate to a bookstore would make me so much happier. I could buy more of the books I do read, or at least some of the books I want to read.

I'm hoping to go to school to be a librarian one day. I know they'll insist that I use the Dewey decimal system or the Library of Congress system to organize books. I know they'll have official established cataloguing and categorizing techniques for books. But I know that no matter what I learn, my books will always be books I read, books I want to read, books I have to read, and books I'll never read.

MOTHER-IN-LAW

Charlotte Latvala

Charlotte Latvala, a freelance writer and a correspondent for the *Beaver County Times,* has fun in this essay analyzing the many different kinds of bad mothers-in-law and longing for the one good kind.

✔ WORDS TO CHECK:

nirvana (paragraph 3)	uterus (10)	impromptu (20)
adversary (5)	precocious (15)	maxims (32)
guises (5)	harpies (16)	decadence (35)
fallopian tubes (10)	vipers (16)	liposuction (37)

1   You're in heaven. You've found a man who adores you, who makes you laugh and keeps you sane. For the first time in your life, you're thinking about a long-term commitment; in fact, you're discussing *the* long-term commitment, the June bride, till-death-do-us-part one.

2   Everything's going well; you've worked out a plan for careers, children, where you'll live, etc. Your bliss knows no bounds; your world is a sunny, positive place where birds chirp from dawn to dusk and all the movies have happy endings.

3   Sooner or later, however, you must leave nirvana for a few moments and face the one very real obstacle that women throughout the centuries have faced: You must meet his mother.

4   Never underestimate a mother's influence on her son. (If you're feeling brave, watch *The Manchurian Candidate* right before your meeting.) She was the first and most important woman in his life, and their complex relationship, good or bad, has spanned decades. She's seen him through the chicken pox, the prom and his first major heartache. You are cutting in on a dance that's been going on for years.

5   A potential mother-in-law can be a lot of things. She can be your adversary, your ally, or your critic. Once in a while she might become your friend. She is never your own mother. Here are a few of the different guises she may take.

The Naysayer

6   This woman looks at the world through dark-gray glasses; she is negativity personified. She has frequent imagined illnesses and pains no one can ease. One of her favorite lines is "No one cares about me," closely followed by "He never comes to see me anymore."

7   The Naysayer sees the world as a bleak and dreary place, full of suffering and torment. She is convinced that human nature is rotten, and that young people today are selfish and immoral. Nothing, though, looks darker to her than her son's future with you.

8   You really don't have many options here; she will assign evil motives to your most innocent actions. No matter how hard you try to please her, she will find a way to get her digs in. "I really had no idea that Frank was dating such a talented girl. I don't know whether I'd spend so much money on painting lessons, though."

9   Grit your teeth and smile. You can probably pick up tips from your future husband.

The Baby-Crazed Fanatic

10   This woman's excitement at meeting you has nothing to do with you as an individual. She looks at you and sees fallopian tubes and a uterus. You are the answer to her prayers, the woman who will provide her with a soft little bundle of joy to croon sweet nothings to.

11   Within minutes of meeting you, she has informed you that most of her friends are grandparents already. "Do you come from a large family?" she asks eagerly, and coos with delight when you tell her that your younger sister already has three children.

12   You hate to burst her bubble; you hate to tell her that you really want to get your career off to a solid start before you even consider children. You honestly don't think you should be discussing the subject with her in the first place. But, before you can say anything, she puts her arm around your shoulder and says, "Well, I'm sure it won't be long before you have one, too."

"No One's Good Enough for My Son"

13   Similar to The Naysayer, but more upbeat. At least on one subject.

14   God made one perfect man, and it is her son. He has never done anything wrong in his life. He is handsome, talented and generous. His manners are beyond reproach, and he is so intelligent he scares her.

15   She has a tendency to rattle on and on about his accomplishments throughout the years, from the precocious age at which she removed his training wheels to the ease with which he graduated from college with honors.

16   This wonderful man, however, has dated only harpies and vipers, of which you are the latest. At the slightest prompting, she will tell you much more than you want to know about the terrible women who have tried to trap her little boy into matrimonial hell. Don't bother trying to impress her with your sweet nature or good intentions. This woman would think Mother Teresa was a conniving shrew.

The Woman of the World

17   This mother-in-law has been everywhere, and she wants to make sure you know it. She's fond of saying things like, "And as you know, Paris is so lovely in the spring! You *have* been to Paris, haven't you, dear?" while you squirm on the couch and try to think of an impressive way to say that you've only been out of the Tri-State area four times in your life.

18   To her, you are a provincial little drip, and you will probably hinder her son's progress in life by making him settle down in some wretched suburb and take vacations to the Poconos.

19   There is only one way to deal with this woman. Lie. For every trip abroad, for every exotic excursion that she brags about, make up one of your own.

The Accomplished Mother-in-Law

20 It's impossible to compete with a woman who has more talents than Madonna has bras. She's a heart surgeon who also has a Ph.D. in romance poetry. She's a nationally ranked chess champion. In her spare time, she plays the violin in a string quartet, teaches blind children to ride horses and whips up impromptu four-star meals in her gourmet kitchen.

21   Just listening to her exhausts you. Your fiancé warned you about her (he said, "Oh, Mother keeps herself busy"), but you never dreamed any single human being could cram so much into a lifetime.

22   On top of it all, she's polite and charming. And when she asks you, "And what do *you* do, dear?" you would rather curl up and die than admit you're a word processor who rents a lot of movies and takes three-hour naps on Sunday afternoon.

The Experienced Mother-in-Law

23 This mother has been through it before. You are not the first woman to sit in her house and joyously proclaim that you really and truly love her son and will do everything in your power to make him happy forever and ever.

24   Divorce has a strange effect on people, and it tends to make mothers either extremely suspicious or nostalgic, depending on her opinion of Wife No. 1.

25   If she hated Wife No. 1, you're in luck, because you are the sensible decision that her son made when he was old enough for it.

26   If she was fond of Wife No. 1, you're in trouble. You will be forever compared, unfairly, to a woman who's not there to speak for herself. Little comments and asides ("Well, a lot of women these days can't cook. Of course, Freddy never could get Patrice out of the kitchen; she was always in there whipping up his favorites . . .") will forever remind you of who you're not.

The Pal

27 On the surface, this woman looks like a treat. She takes you warmly by the arm and insists that you call her Gladys. How sweet, you think. How friendly.

28   One day she wants to meet you for lunch. Next, she wants to go shopping for lingerie with you. Soon, she wants to double-date with you and her son. Her boyfriend has a tan and wears jogging shoes everywhere.

29   Before long, you start to feel as if you've inherited a younger sister. Things get bad when you get phone calls from her and she wants to talk about her sex life, or when she introduces you to the members of her jogging club as "my new best friend."

30   You will find yourself longing for the distance that your friends have from their mothers-in-law. You will find yourself plotting evil deeds that will make her despise you.

31   You find yourself saying "yes" when she asks you if you want to play tennis next weekend.

The Know-It-All

32 This woman knows more maxims than Aesop, and she won't keep any opinion to herself.

33   "All that will change when you get married," she says smugly when the two of you announce you're going out to dinner and a movie. "You won't have the money to fritter away."

34   When you get married and still fritter money away on going out, she predicts the end is near. "You won't be able to do that when you have kids."

35   You could try to shock her into silence by announcing that you aren't intending to have children, that you plan to go on throwing money away foolishly, living a life of decadence at expensive restaurants and nightclubs. However, she'll probably just nod and mumble about a fool and his money.

The Hot Tamale

36 Like The Pal, this woman sees you as a contemporary. Unlike The Pal, she sees you as competition.

37   This mother-in-law refuses to age, gracefully or not. She'll do whatever it takes to maintain her face and body; liposuction, face lifts and tummy tucks are as routine to her as a visit to the post office. She wears mini-skirts and too much mascara. Her CD rack is filled with the B-52's and Paula Abdul, not Glenn Miller.

38   She coyly asks you if you want to borrow her Victoria's Secret catalog, then says that you probably won't find anything in it that's "your style."

39   She treats her son like a bit of an old fogey, and you find yourself feeling rather prudish around her. You may as well get used to this role reversal, unless you want to begin a long uphill battle to outdo a woman who's been practicing her young and silly act longer than you've been alive.

The Mother-in-Law Who Isn't

40 Maybe you're **not** getting married. Maybe you've decided, for whatever complicated reasons people decide these things today, that you're going to live together as man and wife without the benefit of official documents, bouquet-throwing and name-changing.

41   Do you still have a mother-in-law?

42   Well, yes. That is, she has the job without the title. Call her what you like (my lover's mother, my live-in-law, the mother of my significant other),

she's still your mother-in-law, subject to all the complications that arise in legal unions.

43   You just can't call her Mom.

The Saint

44 For every hundred difficult mothers-in-law, there is one perfect one. She is as precious as she is rare.

45   She never insists that you call her "Mom-mom" or "Binky."

46   She never introduces you to her friends as "the one who finally snagged Junior."

47   She is friendly and warm without being overbearing; she doesn't plant slobbery kisses on your cheek when she hasn't seen you for a week.

48   You are comfortable talking to her about world events, shared friends and literature; neither of you feels the need to discuss your sex life or her friend's divorces.

49   She recognizes that however much she loves her son, he is a human being, complete with faults and virtues.

50   She accepts the fact that you have a career and interests of your own; she encourages and supports them.

51   She doesn't call you "that woman" when speaking to the other relatives.

52   She keeps her opinions on child-rearing to herself.

53   If you find yourself related by marriage to such a woman, cherish the connection as if she were royalty. She is.

54   So, there you have it. You may have spotted someone you know. You may be shaking your head wisely. But, before you get too carried away with yourself, remember one thing.

55   Someday, you might have a son. Someday, that son may fall in love with a woman he believes is **the one.** And someday, you may be stuck with a daughter-in-law you can't stand.

WHAT DID THE WRITER SAY AND WHAT DID YOU THINK?

1. Is there a thesis? If so, is it stated or implied?
2. Do any of the classifications overlap or repeat themselves?
3. Does the author show any sympathy for mothers-in-law? If so, where?
4. First published in a newspaper, this article provoked a number of angry letters. What would you guess the complaints were about?

HOW DID THE WRITER SAY IT?

1. Why is the introduction so much longer than usual?
2. How much of the humor is merely good-natured joking, and how much covers genuine irritation or resentment?

3. How does the description of "The Saint" help serve as a summary of the essay?

4. What stylistic features indicate this essay was first written for a newspaper?

What About Your Writing?

Charlotte Latvala begins "Mother-in-Law" with a charming two-paragraph rhapsody on romantic bliss, then devotes the rest of her essay to what pharmacists call unpleasant side effects. We'd like to suggest that the huge area of Romance, more specifically Romantic Highs and Lows, is one of those can't-miss general subjects like Work (see pages 211–212) or Nostalgia (see page 55) that everyone has plenty to write about. Consider the hundreds—the millions—of possibilities for a narration paper represented merely by titles like "My First Date," "My Last Date," "My Worst Date," and "My Best Date."

Stuck for a subject? Don't let anyone force unwanted or unworkable subjects on you, but think about the opportunities offered by Romantic Highs and Lows in all the rhetorical patterns, not just Narration.

Description? What about The Perfect Husband, Wife, In-Law, Wedding, Honeymoon? What about "My Husband the Slob" or "My Wife the Scold"—with changes in relationships and character defects as necessary?

Examples? "Frogs I Have Kissed." "Lies My Mother Told Me." "It Won't Take Much to Win My Heart."

Process? Planning a wedding—probably limited to one specific topic like choosing a photographer or caterer. Planning a romantic getaway. How to fall out of love.

Comparison and Contrast? Past-versus-present and illusion-versus-reality themes always work well: a change in your ideas, a change in your expectations, a change in your character. "Where Did All the Magic Go?"

Cause and Effect? "I Was a Teenage Idiot." "He Said He Loved Me: Confessions of an Abused Spouse." "Love Required. Luck Helps." "Our Secret Ingredient."

Division and Classification? "Boys, Guys, and Men." "The Three Kinds of Love Stories." "Styles in Relationships: No Size Fits All." "Approaches to Conflict: Ignoring, Confronting, or Solving."

Definition? Love versus Infatuation. Love versus Affection. "It Depends on What You Mean by 'Happy.'" "This Is My, Uh, Boyfriend: There Must Be a Word." "What Does He Mean, I'm His 'Woman'?"

Argumentation? Gay marriage, pro or con. "Of Course Religion Matters." "What's Wrong with Arranged Marriages?" "'In Like' Is More Important Than 'In Love.'" "First, Let's Kill All the Songwriters."

If you tell us you're not in the mood to write a paper or that you're too busy, we may be sympathetic. Just don't tell us you have nothing to write about.

―――――

TAKE A LEFT TURN ONTO NOWHERE STREET
Anne Bernays

Anne Bernays is the author of several novels, including *Trophy House* (2005) and *Professor Romeo* (1997), and the coauthor of *What If?: Writing Exercises for Fiction Writers* (1991). Fed up with the chaos created by what seem to be thousands of sets of bad directions, Bernays draws a deep breath and tries to make sense of it all.

✔ WORDS TO CHECK:

impeccably (paragraph 2)	pixies (5)	ambiguity (8)
sanguine (3)	fraught (5)	verbatim (9)

1   It's a fair bet that if you have been at the mercy of homemade directions to "our place" more than once or twice, you have also gotten lost. When this happens, your first impulse is to blame your own stupidity. Forget that. It's their fault—that sweet old guy, that nice young couple who invited you for dinner or the weekend have given you the wrong directions. Just one error can keep you driving back and forth over the same stretch of alien turf for hours, switching among panic, frustration and fury.

2   Years ago, soon after my husband, Justin, and I were married, Justin's boss, the poet and anthologist Louis Untermeyer, and his wife, Bryna, asked us over for dinner. As we drove from New York City toward rural Connecticut, we ticked off, one by one, the course changes and landmarks indicated in the impeccably typed directions, which Bryna, a freelance editor, had sent. The only trouble was that she had neglected to tell us that the road sign on the crucial turnoff had been blown away during a recent storm.

3   We arrived at their house, steaming, more than an hour late, having backtracked for miles to find a telephone. It's hard to show up sanguine and all smiles after you've been calling each other blind and stupid for the last couple of hours.

4   Soon after we moved to Cambridge, Mass., we were invited to a party in nearby Winchester. Armed with a hand-drawn map from our hostess, we drove for well over an hour before we stopped, my eyes brimming, under a bridge, hopelessly raking a flashlight beam over the map and snarling at each other. A police car drew up, and an officer stepped smartly out. "Where you folks headed?" I told him and handed him our map. He looked it over. "Holy moly," he said, "where'd you get this thing?"

5   Ever since that episode, we've tried to keep every set of directions sent to us, and now, several decades later, we have a collection of about three dozen. All but a few of these are faulty in one or more respects and all of them are proof that writing exact directions or producing a reliable map is no easy exercise. There are scores of ways in which you can lead people seriously astray, like those Olde English pixies who did it on purpose. Our collection–funny now, not so funny at the time–includes directions in assorted shapes and sizes; handwritten or typed narratives; free-form, all-too-creative maps with little stick figures, cars and houses; on colored paper and white; some photocopied, others dictated casually over the phone (probably the form most fraught with errors).

6   Occasionally the mistakes are huge such as instructing you to take a right turn when it should have been a left–and sometimes tiny, like saying six-tenths of a mile when it's really eight-tenths.

7   Breaking down the errors into categories helps to dramatize how tricky it is to compose a set of precise, clear directions that do what they're supposed to do, namely get you there in one psychic piece by the most straightforward route.

8   **Ambiguity.** By far the largest category, it includes directions studded with traps like "go west" and "cross the bridge," which could mean anything from a culvert to the Golden Gate. The "gray garage" you're looking for isn't gray at all; it's white, something you discover only after driving up and down the same stretch of road for half an hour, passing and ignoring a white garage. If you have a cell phone, you can call your hosts to find out where the heck you are, but only if they're within range. Usually, it seems, they're not.

9   Here is a verbatim example of near-fatal vagueness: "To get to Wachusett, take the Mass Pike from Cambridge to 495 North (signs say Lowell, I think)." He thinks?

10   **Too Much Explicitness.** This is most often seen on maps that are drawn by hand. All too often the imp of creativity seems to have guided the fingers of the map maker, for more detail is given than most travelers need–markers both large and small that distract the anxiety-prone (that is, most people driving somewhere for the first time). Among these are the names and locations of streets you're not supposed to turn into; items like "grass island," as incidental to the route as the clouds above, or careful renderings of a "parking lot," "school gym," and something that looks like an upside-down lollipop.

11   **Night Blindness.** This category focuses on the assumption that you, the traveler, have night vision. Here are some of the landmarks we've been instructed to look for even when our hosts knew we would be arriving after dark: "Catholic Cemetery," "big field," "statue of Charles Sumner," "library," "Methodist Church," and my favorite: "We're the pale green house."

12   **Out-of-Dateness.** The "blue" mailbox, for example, has been painted red since the directions were composed. The Sunoco station where you're supposed to turn was recently bought by Exxon.

13   **Just Plain Wrong.** As when we were told to take Exit 16 and our host was off by one digit; or when we were directed to bear right "after the boulder" and finally discovered that the jog came first, the boulder second. We were very late for lunch.

14   **Crucial Omissions.** These are the vital markers your hosts have failed to include—for instance, arrows telling you which way to go on a hand-drawn map; huge structures like gas tanks and cement factories; railroad crossings. For some reason, if the directions fail to account for the tracks you've just crossed, you automatically assume you've taken a wrong turn. And then there's the traveler's genuine nightmare: a fork in the road. It would be nice if you could follow Yogi Berra's advice: "When you come to a fork in the road, take it."

15   **Impossible to Follow.** "Go three-eighths of a mile." Likewise, complicated handwritten directions scrawled on three scraps of paper. Bad enough if you have a navigator with you, but what are you supposed to do if you're flying solo?

16   **Return-Trip Blues.** Sometimes it's impossible to turn the thing inside out for the return trip. Getting back home is often the riskiest leg of the journey, especially at night. I suggest asking your hosts if they have a spare room.

17   **Famous Last Words.** "If you have any trouble, just ask someone in the village." And "You can't miss it."

WHAT DID THE WRITER SAY AND WHAT DID YOU THINK?

1. In paragraph 5, the writer refers to "all-too-creative" maps, and in paragraph 10, she complains about "the imp of creativity." What does she have against creativity in written directions?
2. Where does the writer come closest to a direct thesis statement? State the thesis in your own words.
3. Are all the instructions as bad as the author thinks? Is the example in paragraph 9, for instance, really guilty of "near-fatal vagueness"?
4. Why is it impossible to follow the instruction to "go three-eighths of a mile?"
5. Chapter 1 of this book provides an example of bad instructions (page 15) on "How to Get from Town to Camp Wilderness." Do these bad instructions fall into one or more of the categories in this essay, or do they reveal categories of their own?

HOW DID THE WRITER SAY IT?

1. Why does the writer mention the Untermeyers by name in paragraph 2 but leave other creators of bad instructions anonymous? Is she merely showing off that she knows some famous people?
2. The names of each class generally communicate some helpful preliminary information. Are there any names that do not?

3. Explain the meaning of "Famous Last Words" (paragraph 17). Is this actually a separate category or just a different kind of concluding paragraph?

What About Your Writing?

Think of the possibilities of our interest being grabbed by a title like "Nine Kinds of Bad Directions" or "Common Errors of Direction Providers." Now consider Anne Bernays' title, "Take a Left Turn onto Nowhere Street." It arouses our curiosity if for no other reason than our desire to find out what on earth the phrase means. The apparent nonsense of the wording may also make us anticipate a touch of humor, and we are motivated to read on. A good title is worth fussing about. It usually helps identify your subject as well as your attitude toward the subject. It enables the reader to become properly oriented even before looking at your opening sentence. A good title also stimulates curiosity: It makes the reader willing to bother with your opening sentence in the first place. A good title won't save a bad piece of writing, and a bad title won't destroy good writing, but good titles help, and writers shouldn't be shy about accepting all the help they can get.

Boring Title	Better Title
The Making of the Constitution	A More Perfect Union
Bad Roommates	Pest Control: Coping with Bad Roommates
Great Vampire Movies	Fangs for the Memory
The New Father	Have a Baby, My Wife Just Had a Cigar
Problems of Medical Expenses	Your Money or Your Life

THE SEVEN-LESSON SCHOOLTEACHER
John Taylor Gatto

As John Taylor Gatto's essay makes clear, he had a lifetime career as a teacher. He was named New York City Teacher of the Year three times and retired after being named New York State Teacher of the Year. He has published three books on education and is working on a film on the topic as well.

✔ WORDS TO CHECK:

idiosyncratic (paragraph 3)	entails (5)	dogmas (7)
coherent (3)	hierarchy (6)	catechism (7)
superficial (5)	clientele (6)	exhort (11)

insinuate (11) intervene (14) promiscuous (23)
inoculate (13) ken (15) espoused (25)
predestined (14) deviants (16)

1   Call me Mr. Gatto, please. Twenty-six years ago, having nothing better to do at the time, I tried my hand at schoolteaching. The license I hold certifies that I am an instructor of English language and English literature, but that isn't what I do at all. I don't teach English, I teach school—and I win awards doing it.

2   Teaching means different things in different places, but seven lessons are universally taught from Harlem to Hollywood Hills. They constitute a national curriculum you pay for in more ways than you can imagine, so you might as well know what it is. You are at liberty, of course, to regard these lessons any way you like, but believe me when I say I intend no irony in this presentation. These are the things I teach, these are the things you pay me to teach. Make of them what you will.

1. Confusion

3   A lady named Kathy wrote this to me from Dubois, Indiana the other day: "What big ideas are important to little kids? Well, the biggest idea I think they need is that what they are learning isn't idiosyncratic—that there is some system to it all and it's not just raining down on them as they helplessly absorb. That's the task, to understand, to make coherent."

4   Kathy has it wrong. **The first lesson I teach is confusion.** Everything I teach is out of context. I teach the un-relating of everything. I teach disconnections. I teach too much: the orbiting of planets, the law of large numbers, slavery, adjectives, architectural drawing, dance, gymnasium, choral singing, assemblies, surprise guests, fire drills, computer languages, parents' nights, staff-development days, pull-out programs, guidance with strangers my students may never see again, standardized tests, age-segregation unlike anything seen in the outside world. . . .What do any of these things have to do with each other?

5   Even in the best schools a close examination of curriculum and its sequences turns up a lack of coherence, full of internal contradictions. Fortunately the children have no words to define the panic and anger they feel at constant violations of natural order and sequence fobbed off on them as quality in education. The logic of the school-mind is that it is better to leave school with a tool kit of superficial jargon derived from economics, sociology, natural science and so on than to leave with one genuine enthusiasm. But quality in education entails learning about something in depth. Confusion is thrust upon kids by too many strange adults, each working alone with only the thinnest relationship with each other, pretending for the most part, to an expertise they do not possess.

6   Meaning, not disconnected facts, is what sane human beings seek, and education is a set of codes for processing raw facts into meaning. Behind the

patchwork quilt of school sequences and the school obsession with facts and theories, the age-old human search lies well concealed. This is harder to see in elementary school where the hierarchy of school experience seems to make better sense because the good-natured simple relationship of "let's do this" and "let's do that" is just assumed to mean something and the clientele has not yet consciously discerned how little substance is behind the play and pretense.

7   Think of the great natural sequences like learning to walk and learning to talk; following the progression of light from sunrise to sunset; witnessing the ancient procedures of a farmer, a smithy, or a shoemaker; watching your mother prepare a Thanksgiving feast–all of the parts are in perfect harmony with each other, each action justifies itself and illuminates the past and the future. School sequences aren't like that, not inside a single class and not among the total menu of daily classes. School sequences are crazy. There is no particular reason for any of them, nothing that bears close scrutiny. Few teachers would dare to teach the tools whereby dogmas of a school or a teacher could be criticized since everything must be accepted. School subjects are learned, if they can be learned, like children learn the catechism or memorize the Thirty-nine Articles of Anglicanism.

8   I teach the un-relating of everything, an infinite fragmentation the opposite of cohesion; what I do is more related to television programming than to making a scheme of order. In a world where home is only a ghost, because both parents work, or because too many moves or too many job changes or too much ambition, or because something else has left everybody too confused to maintain a family relation, I teach you how to accept confusion as your destiny. That's the first lesson I teach.

2. Class Position

9   **The second lesson I teach is class position.** I teach that students must stay in the class where they belong. I don't know who decides my kids belong there but that's not my business. The children are numbered so that if any get away they can be returned to the right class. Over the years the variety of ways children are numbered by schools has increased dramatically, until it is hard to see the human beings plainly under the weight of numbers they carry. Numbering children is a big and very profitable undertaking, though what the strategy is designed to accomplish is elusive. I don't even know why parents would, without a fight, allow it to be done to their kids.

10   In any case, again, that's not my business. My job is to make them like it, being locked in together with children who bear numbers like their own. Or at the least to endure it like good sports. If I do my job well, the kids can't even imagine themselves somewhere else, because I've shown them how to envy and fear the better classes and how to have contempt for the dumb classes. Under this efficient discipline the class mostly polices itself into good marching

order. That's the real lesson of any rigged competition like school. You come to know your place.

11   In spite of the overall class blueprint, which assumes that ninety-nine percent of the kids are in their class to stay, I nevertheless make a public effort to exhort children to higher levels of test success, hinting at eventual transfer from the lower class as a reward. I frequently insinuate that the day will come when an employer will hire them on the basis of test scores and grades, even though my own experience is that employers are rightly indifferent to such things. I never lie outright, but I've come to see that truth and schoolteaching are, at bottom, incompatible just as Socrates said they were thousands of years ago. The lesson of numbered classes is that everyone has a proper place in the pyramid and that there is no way out of your class except by number magic. Failing that, you must stay where you are put.

3. Indifference

12   **The third lesson I teach kids is indifference.** I teach children not to care about anything too much, even though they want to make it appear that they do. How I do this is very subtle. I do it by demanding that they become totally involved in my lessons, jumping up and down in their seats with anticipation, competing vigorously with each other for my favor. It's heartwarming when they do that; it impresses everyone, even me. When I'm at my best I plan lessons very carefully in order to produce this show of enthusiasm. But when the bell rings I insist that they stop whatever it is that we've been working on and proceed quickly to the next work station. They must turn on and off like a light switch. Nothing important is ever finished in my class, nor in any other class I know of. Students never have a complete experience except on the installment plan.

13   Indeed, the lesson of the bells is that no work is worth finishing, so why care too deeply about anything? Years of bells will condition all but the strongest to a world that can no longer offer important work to do. Bells are the secret logic of schooltime; their logic is inexorable. Bells destroy the past and future, converting every interval into a sameness, as the abstraction of a map renders every living mountain and river the same, even though they are not. Bells inoculate each undertaking with indifference.

4. Emotional Dependency

14   **The fourth lesson I teach is emotional dependency.** By stars and red checks, smiles and frowns, prizes, honors and disgraces I teach kids to surrender their will to the predestined chain of command. Rights may be granted or withheld by any authority without appeal, because rights do not exist inside a school—not even the right of free speech, as the Supreme Court has ruled—unless school authorities say they do. As a schoolteacher, I intervene in many

personal decisions, issuing a pass for those I deem legitimate, or initiating a disciplinary confrontation for behavior that threatens my control. Individuality is constantly trying to assert itself among children and teenagers, so my judgments come thick and fast. Individuality is a contradiction of class theory, a curse to all systems of classification.

15   Here are some common ways it shows up: children sneak away for a private moment in the toilet on the pretext of moving their bowels, or they steal a private instant in the hallway on the grounds they need water. I know they don't, but I allow them to deceive me because this conditions them to depend on my favors. Sometimes free will appears right in front of me in children angry, depressed or happy about things outside my ken; rights in such matters cannot be recognized by schoolteachers, only privileges that can be withdrawn, hostages to good behavior.

5. Intellectual Dependency

16   **The fifth lesson I teach is intellectual dependency.** Good people wait for a teacher to tell them what to do. It is the most important lesson, that we must wait for other people, better trained than ourselves, to make the meanings of our lives. The expert makes all the important choices; only I, the teacher, can determine what you must study, or rather, only the people who pay me can make those decisions which I then enforce. If I'm told that evolution is a fact instead of a theory, I transmit that as ordered, punishing deviants who resist what I have been told to tell them to think. This power to control what children will think lets me separate successful students from failures very easily.

17   Successful children do the thinking I appoint them with a minimum of resistance and a decent show of enthusiasm. Of the millions of things of value to study, I decide what few we have time for, or actually it is decided by my faceless employers. The choices are theirs, why should I argue? Curiosity has no important place in my work, only conformity.

18   Bad kids fight this, of course, even though they lack the concepts to know what they are fighting, struggling to make decisions for themselves about what they will learn and when they will learn it. How can we allow that and survive as schoolteachers? Fortunately there are procedures to break the will of those who resist; it is more difficult, naturally, if the kid has respectable parents who come to his aid, but that happens less and less in spite of the bad reputation of schools. No middle-class parents I have ever met actually believe that their kid's school is one of the bad ones. Not one single parent in twenty-six years of teaching. That's amazing and probably the best testimony to what happens to families when mother and father have been well-schooled themselves, learning the seven lessons.

19   Good people wait for an expert to tell them what to do. It is hardly an exaggeration to say that our entire economy depends upon this lesson being

learned. Think of what would fall apart if kids weren't trained to be dependent: the social-service businesses could hardly survive; they would vanish, I think, into the recent historical limbo out of which they arose. Counselors and therapists would look on in horror as the supply of psychic invalids vanished. Commercial entertainment of all sorts, including television, would wither as people learned again how to make their own fun. Restaurants, prepared-food and a whole host of other assorted food services would be drastically downsized if people returned to making their own meals rather than depending on strangers to plant, pick, chop, and cook for them. Much of modern law, medicine, and engineering would go too, the clothing business and schoolteaching as well, unless a guaranteed supply of helpless people continued to pour out of our schools each year.

20   Don't be too quick to vote for radical school reform if you want to continue getting a paycheck. We've built a way of life that depends on people doing what they are told because they don't know how to tell themselves what to do. It's one of the biggest lessons I teach.

6. Provisional Self-Esteem

21 **The sixth lesson I teach is provisional self-esteem.** If you've ever tried to wrestle a kid into line whose parents have convinced him to believe they'll love him in spite of anything, you know how impossible it is to make self-confident spirits conform. Our world wouldn't survive a flood of confident people very long, so I teach that your self-respect should depend on expert opinion. My kids are constantly evaluated and judged.

22   A monthly report, impressive in its provision, is sent into students' homes to signal approval or to mark exactly, down to a single percentage point, how dissatisfied with their children parents should be. The ecology of "good" schooling depends upon perpetuating dissatisfaction just as much as the commercial economy depends on the same fertilizer. Although some people might be surprised how little time or reflection goes into making up these mathematical records, the cumulative weight of the objective-seeming documents establishes a profile that compels children to arrive at certain decisions about themselves and their futures based on the casual judgment of strangers. Self-evaluation, the staple of every major philosophical system that ever appeared on the planet, is never considered a factor. The lesson of report cards, grades, and tests is that children should not trust themselves or their parents but should instead rely on the evaluation of certified officials. People need to be told what they are worth.

7. One Can't Hide

23 **The seventh lesson I teach is that one can't hide.** I teach children they are always watched, that each is under constant surveillance by myself and my colleagues. There are no private spaces for children, there is no private time.

Class change lasts three hundred seconds to keep promiscuous fraternization at low levels. Students are encouraged to tattle on each other or even to tattle on their own parents. Of course, I encourage parents to file their own child's waywardness too. A family trained to snitch on itself isn't likely to conceal any dangerous secrets.

24   I assign a type of extended schooling called "homework," so that the effect of surveillance, if not that surveillance itself, travels into private households, where students might otherwise use free time to learn something unauthorized from a father or mother, by exploration, or by apprenticing to some wise person in the neighborhood. Disloyalty to the idea of schooling is a Devil always ready to find work for idle hands.

25   The meaning of constant surveillance and denial of privacy is that no one can be trusted, that privacy is not legitimate. Surveillance is an ancient imperative, espoused by certain influential thinkers, a central prescription set down in The Republic, in The City of God, in the Institutes of the Christian Religion, in New Atlantis, in Leviathan, and in a host of other places. All these childless men who wrote these books discovered the same thing: children must be closely watched if you want to keep a society under tight central control. Children will follow a private drummer if you can't get them into a uniformed marching band.

II

26 It is the great triumph of compulsory government monopoly mass-schooling that among even the best of my fellow teachers, and among the best of my students' parents, only a small number can imagine a different way to do things. "The kids have to know how to read and write, don't they?" "They have to know how to add and subtract, don't they?" "They have to learn to follow orders if they ever expect to keep a job."

27   Only a few lifetimes ago things were very different in the United States. Originality and variety were common currency; our freedom from regimentation made us the miracle of the world; social-class boundaries were relatively easy to cross; our citizenry was marvelously confident, inventive, and able to do much for themselves independently, and to think for themselves. We were something special, we Americans, all by ourselves, without government sticking its nose into our lives, without institutions and social agencies telling us how to think and feel. We were something special, as individuals, as Americans.

28   But we've had a society essentially under central control in the United States since just before the Civil War, and such a society requires compulsory schooling, government monopoly schooling, to maintain itself. Before this development schooling wasn't very important anywhere. We had it, but not too much of it, and only as much as an individual wanted. People learned to read, write, and do arithmetic just fine anyway; there are some studies that suggest literacy at the time of the American Revolution, at least for non-slaves on the Eastern seaboard, was close to total. Thomas Paine's *Common Sense* sold

600,000 copies to a population of 3,000,000, twenty percent of whom were slaves, and fifty percent indentured servants.

29   Were the colonists geniuses? No, the truth is that reading, writing, and arithmetic only take about one hundred hours to transmit as long as the audience is eager and willing to learn. The trick is to wait until someone asks and then move fast while the mood is on. Millions of people teach themselves these things, it really isn't very hard. Pick up a fifth-grade math or rhetoric textbook from 1850 and you'll see that the texts were pitched then on what would today be considered college level. The continuing cry for "basic skills" practice is a smoke screen behind which schools preempt the time of children for twelve years and teach them the seven lessons I've just described to you.

30   The society that has become increasingly under central control since just before the Civil War shows itself in the lives we lead, the clothes we wear, the food we eat, and the green highway signs we drive by from coast to coast, all of which are the products of this control. So, too, I think, are the epidemics of drugs, suicide, divorce, violence, cruelty, and the hardening of class into caste in the United States products of the dehumanization of our lives, the lessening of individual, family, and community importance, a diminishment that proceeds from central control. The character of large compulsory institutions is inevitable; they want more and more until there isn't any more to give. School takes our children away from any possibility of an active role in community life—in fact it destroys communities by relegating the training of children to the hands of certified experts—and by doing so it ensures our children cannot grow up fully human. Aristotle taught that without a fully active role in community life one could not hope to become a healthy human being. Surely he was right. Look around you the next time you are near a school or an old people's reservation if you wish a demonstration.

31   School as it was built is an essential support system for a vision of social engineering that condemns most people to be subordinate stones in a pyramid that narrows as it ascends to a terminal of control. School is an artifice which makes such a pyramidical social order seem inevitable, although such a premise is a fundamental betrayal of the American Revolution. From colonial days through the period of the Republic we had no schools to speak of—read Benjamin Franklin's autobiography for an example of a man who had no time to waste in school—and yet the promise of Democracy was beginning to be realized. We turned our backs on this promise by bringing to life the ancient pharaonic dream of Egypt: compulsory subordination for all. That was the secret Plato reluctantly transmitted in *The Republic* when Glaucon and Adeimantus exhorted from Socrates the plan for total state control of human life, a plan necessary to maintain a society where some people take more than their share. "I will show you," says Socrates, "how to bring about such a feverish city, but you will not like what I am going to say." And so the blueprint of the seven-lesson school was first sketched.

32   The current debate about whether we should have a national curriculum is phony. We already have a national curriculum locked up in the seven lessons I have just outlined. Such a curriculum produces physical, moral, and intellectual paralysis, and no curriculum of content will be sufficient to reverse its hideous effects. What is currently under discussion in our national school hysteria about failing academic performance misses the point. Schools teach exactly what they are intended to teach and they do it well: how to be a good Egyptian and remain in your place in the pyramid.

III

33 None of this is inevitable. None of it is impossible to overthrow. We do have choices in how we bring up young people; there is no one right way. If we broke through the power of the pyramidical illusion we would see that. There is no life-and-death international competition threatening our national existence, difficult as that idea is even to think about, let alone believe, in the face of a continual media barrage of myth to the contrary. In every important material respect our nation is self-sufficient, including in energy. I realize that idea runs counter to the most fashionable thinking of political economists, but the "profound transformation" of our economy these people talk about is neither inevitable nor irreversible. Global economics does not speak to the public need for meaningful work, affordable housing, fulfilling education, adequate medical care, a clean environment, honest and accountable government, social and cultural renewal, or simple justice. All global ambitions are based on a definition of productivity and the good life so alienated from common human reality I am convinced it is wrong and that most people would agree with me if they could perceive an alternative. We might be able to see that if we regained a hold on a philosophy that locates meaning where meaning is genuinely to be found—in families, in friends, in the passage of seasons, in nature, in simple ceremonies and rituals, in curiosity, generosity, compassion, and service to others, in a decent independence and privacy, in all the free and inexpensive things out of which real families, real friends and real communities are built—then we would be so self-sufficient we would not even need the material "sufficiency" which our global "experts" are so insistent we be concerned about.

34   How did these awful places, these "schools", come about? Well, casual schooling has always been with us in a variety of forms, a mildly useful adjunct to growing up. But "modern schooling" as we know it is a by-product of the two "Red Scares" of 1848 and 1919, when powerful interests feared a revolution among our own industrial poor. Partly, too, total schooling came about because old-line American families were appalled by the native cultures of Celtic, Slavic, and Latin immigrants of the 1840s and felt repugnance towards the Catholic religion they brought with them. Certainly a third contributing factor in creating a jail for children called school must have been the

consternation with which these same "Americans" regarded the movement of African-Americans through the society in the wake of the Civil War.

35   Look again at the seven lessons of schoolteaching: confusion, class position, indifference, emotional and intellectual dependency, provisional self-esteem, surveillance—all of these things are prime training for permanent underclasses, people deprived forever of finding the center of their own special genius. And over time this training has shaken loose from its own original logic: to regulate the poor. For since the 1920s the growth of the school bureaucracy, and the less visible growth of a horde of industries that profit from schooling exactly as it is, has enlarged this institution's original grasp to the point that it now seizes the sons and daughters of the middle classes as well.

36   Is it any wonder Socrates was outraged at the accusation that he took money to teach? Even then, philosophers saw clearly the inevitable direction the professionalization of teaching would take, preempting the teaching function, which belongs to everyone in a healthy community.

37   With lessons like the ones I teach day after day it should be little wonder we have a real national crisis, the nature of which is very different from that proclaimed by the national media. Young people are indifferent to the adult world and to the future, indifferent to almost everything except the diversion of toys and violence. Rich or poor, schoolchildren who face the twenty-first century cannot concentrate on anything for very long; they have a poor sense of time past and time to come. They are mistrustful of intimacy like the children of divorce they really are (for we have divorced them from significant parental attention); they hate solitude, are cruel, materialistic, dependent, passive, violent, timid in the face of the unexpected, addicted to distraction.

38   All the peripheral tendencies of childhood are nourished and magnified to a grotesque extent by schooling, which, through its hidden curriculum, prevents effective personality development. Indeed, without exploiting the fearfulness, selfishness, and inexperience of children, our schools could not survive at all, nor could I as a certified schoolteacher. No common school that actually dared to teach the use of critical thinking tools—like the dialectic, the heuristic, or other devices that free minds should employ—would last very long before being torn to pieces. School has become the replacement for church in our secular society, and like church it requires that its teachings must be taken on faith.

39   It is time that we squarely face the fact that institutional schoolteaching is destructive to children. Nobody survives the seven-lesson curriculum completely unscathed, not even the instructors. The method is deeply and profoundly anti-educational. No tinkering will fix it. In one of the great ironies of human affairs, the massive rethinking the schools require would cost so much less than we are spending now that powerful interests cannot afford to let it happen. You must understand that first and foremost the business I am in is a jobs project and an agency for letting contracts. We cannot afford

to save money by reducing the scope of our operation or by diversifying the product we offer, even to help children grow up right. That is the iron law of institutional schooling–it is a business, subject neither to normal accounting procedures nor to the rational scalpel of competition.

40   Some form of free-market system in public schooling is the likeliest place to look for answers, a free market where family schools and small entrepreneurial schools and religious schools and crafts schools and farm schools exist in profusion to compete with government education. I'm trying to describe a free market in schooling just exactly like the one the country had until the Civil War, one in which students volunteer for the kind of education that suits them, even if that means self-education; it didn't hurt Benjamin Franklin that I can see. These options exist now in miniature, wonderful survivals of a strong and vigorous past, but they are available only to the resourceful, the courageous, the lucky, or the rich. The near impossibility of one of these better roads opening for the shattered families of the poor or for the bewildered host camped on the fringes of the urban middle class suggests that the disaster of seven-lesson schools is going to grow unless we do something bold and decisive with the mess of government monopoly schooling.

41   After an adult lifetime spent teaching school, I believe the method of mass-schooling is its only real content. Don't be fooled into thinking that good curriculum or good equipment or good teachers are the critical determinants of your son's or daughter's education. All the pathologies we've considered come about in large measure because the lessons of school prevent children from keeping important appointments with themselves and with their families to learn lessons in self-motivation, perseverance, self-reliance, courage, dignity, and love–and lessons in service to others, too, which are among the key lessons of home and community life.

42   Thirty years ago [in the early 60s] these things could still be learned in the time left after school. But television has eaten up most of that time, and a combination of television and the stresses peculiar to two-income or single-parent families have swallowed up most of what used to be family time as well. Our kids have no time left to grow up fully human and only thin-soil wastelands to do it in.

43   A future is rushing down upon our culture which will insist all of us learn the wisdom of non-material experience; a future which will demand as the price of survival that we follow a path of natural life economical in material cost. These lessons cannot be learned in schools as they are. School is a twelve-year jail sentence where bad habits are the only curriculum truly learned. I teach school and win awards doing it. I should know.

WHAT DID THE WRITER SAY AND WHAT DID YOU THINK?

1. Why does Gatto begin his essay by asking you to call him "Mr. Gatto"?
2. The author claims that he "intends no irony." Does he mean it?

3. Gatto has harsh words for class position. Do you agree with his argument that education is designed to teach children to know and stay in their place?

4. Why does Gatto specify that the authors of the books mentioned in paragraph 25 are childless?

HOW DID THE WRITER SAY IT?

1. Which of the seven lessons seems to enrage Gatto the most? How do you know?

2. Why does the author put the first sentence of each section in boldface type? Do you think it is necessary?

3. In paragraph 4, Gatto gives a long list of things he teaches. Do any of the items in the list seem like they don't fit? Why does he include these items? Why is his list so long?

What About Your Writing?

John Taylor Gatto uses what can best be called *ironic quotation marks* in paragraph 22 when he writes, "The ecology of 'good' schooling depends upon perpetuating dissatisfaction just as the commercial economy depends on the same fertilizer." He uses them again in paragraph 24: "I assign a type of extended schooling called 'homework,' so that the effect of surveillance, if not the surveillance itself, travels into private households...." The quotation marks indicate that in some way the writer is distancing himself from the word: He disapproves of it or is amused by it or feels generally that it is inappropriate.

Be cautious with ironic quotation marks. Some instructors may advise you to avoid them entirely. Too often writers use them as a kind of cheap visual aid instead of letting the careful choice and arrangement of words do the job more effectively. When writers put the quotation marks around their own words, the results are almost always crude sarcasm:

- My high school "teacher" was a disgrace to the system.
- Eleanor's "good friend" betrayed her.
- Our family's "vacation" last summer was a catastrophe.

Closely related to this writing problem is the use of quotation marks around trite expressions and slang or other informal words and phrases:

- I suspected the other team would get the "last laugh" after all.
- He was a good-looking young man, "tall, dark, and handsome."
- The policeman continued to "hassle" us.
- The fraternity party caused many people to get "smashed."
- I don't dislike "veggies" nearly as much as I used to.

First, if you are forced to rely on a trite expression, it seems bad policy to highlight your problem. Second, effective slang should sound natural, and if it does, there's no need to call special attention to it. Third, and most important, a writer can run the risk of coming through as an offensive snob: "I'm far too cultivated to employ language like this myself, but look how cute I can be."

By and large, quotation marks are best reserved for their more common functions:

Words and Phrases Pointed to as Such

If I ever find out what the word "love" means, I won't tell you—I'll write a book.

He keeps confusing "there" and "their."

(*Note*: Italics often substitute for quotation marks here.)

Dialogue and Short Quotations

"Sit down and relax," she said.

Which Dickens novel begins with "It was the best of times, it was the worst of times"?

Titles of Short Works—Stories, Poems, Magazine Articles, Songs, and So On

"Falling into Place" was written by Jaime O'Neill.

I love that old record of Judy Garland singing "Over the Rainbow."

A BRUSH WITH REALITY: SURPRISES IN THE TUBE

David Bodanis

David Bodanis has written several best-sellers on topics ranging from history to popular science. In this selection from *The Secret House* (1986), he takes readers inside a common daily ritual to explain what's really going on, and why.

✔ **WORDS TO CHECK:**

lucrative (paragraph 2)	unduly (5)	tout (11)
Cretaceous (3)	cavernous (5)	intrudant (12)
aeons (4)	errant (5)	
abrading (4)	gustatory (11)	

1 Into the bathroom goes our male resident, and after the most pressing need is satisfied it's time to brush the teeth. The tube of toothpaste is squeezed, its pinched

metal seams are splayed, pressure waves are generated inside, and the paste begins to flow. But what's in this toothpaste, so carefully being extruded out?

2   Water mostly, 30 to 45 percent in most brands: ordinary, everyday simple tap water. It's there because people like to have a big gob of toothpaste to spread on the brush, and water is the cheapest stuff there is when it comes to making big gobs. Dripping a bit from the tap onto your brush would cost virtually nothing; whipped in with the rest of the toothpaste the manufacturers can sell it at a neat and accountant-pleasing $2 per pound equivalent. Toothpaste manufacture is a very lucrative occupation.

3   Second to water in quantity is chalk: exactly the same material that schoolteachers use to write on blackboards. It is collected from the crushed remains of long-dead ocean creatures. In the Cretaceous seas these creatures had to wrap around themselves to keep from getting chomped by all the slightly larger other ocean creatures they met. Their massed graves are our present chalk deposits.

4   The individual chalk particles—the size of the smallest mud particles in your garden—have kept their toughness over the aeons, and now on the toothbrush they'll need it. The enamel outer coating of the tooth they'll have to face is the hardest substance in the body—tougher than skull, or bone, or nail. Only the chalk particles in toothpaste can successfully grind into the teeth during brushing, ripping off the surface layers like an abrading wheel grinding down a boulder in a quarry.

5   The craters, slashes, and channels that the chalk tears into the teeth will also remove a certain amount of built-up yellow in the carnage, and it is for that polishing function that it's there. A certain amount of unduly enlarged extra-abrasive chalk fragments tear such cavernous pits into the teeth that future decay bacteria will be able to bunker down there and thrive; the quality control people find it almost impossible to screen out these errant super-chalk pieces, and government regulations allow them to stay in.

6   In case even the gouging doesn't get all the yellow off, another substance is worked into the toothpaste cream. This is titanium dioxide. It comes in tiny spheres, and it's the stuff bobbing around in white wall paint to make it come out white. Splashed around onto your teeth during the brushing it coats much of the yellow that remains. Being water soluble it leaks off in the next few hours and is swallowed, but at least for the quick glance up in the mirror after finishing it will make the user think his teeth are truly white. Some manufacturers add optical whitening dyes—the stuff more commonly found in washing machine bleach—to make extra sure that that glance in the mirror shows reassuring white.

7   These ingredients alone would not make a very attractive concoction. They would stick in the tube like a sloppy white plastic lump, hard to squeeze out as well as revolting to the touch. Few consumers would savor rubbing in a mixture of water, ground-up blackboard chalk, and the whitener from latex

paint first thing in the morning. To get around that finicky distaste the manufacturers have mixed in a host of other goodies.

8   To keep the glop from drying out, a mixture including glycerine glycol—
related to the most common car antifreeze ingredient—is whipped in with the
chalk and water, and to give *that* concoction a bit of substance (all we really
have so far is wet colored chalk) a large helping is added of gummy molecules
from the seaweed *Chondrus Crispus.* This seaweed ooze spreads in among the
chalk, paint, and antifreeze, then stretches itself in all directions to hold the
whole mass together. A bit of paraffin oil (the fuel that flickers in camping
lamps) is pumped in with it to help the moss ooze keep the whole substance
smooth.

9   With the glycol, ooze, and paraffin we're almost there. Only two major
chemicals are left to make the refreshing, cleansing substance we know as
toothpaste. The ingredients so far are fine for cleaning, but they wouldn't
make much of the satisfying foam we have come to expect in the morning
brushing.

10   To remedy that, every toothpaste on the market has a big dollop of detergent added too. You've seen the suds detergent will make in a washing machine.
The same substance added here will duplicate that inside the mouth. It's not
particularly necessary, but it sells.

11   The only problem is that by itself this ingredient tastes, well, too like detergent. It's horribly bitter and harsh. The chalk put in toothpaste is pretty foul-
tasting too for that matter. It's to get around that gustatory discomfort that the
manufacturers put in the ingredient they tout perhaps the most of all. This is
the flavoring, and it has to be strong. Double rectified peppermint oil is used—a
flavorer so powerful that chemists know better than to sniff it in the raw state
in the laboratory. Menthol crystals and saccharin or other sugar simulators are
added to complete the camouflage operation.

12   Is that it? Chalk, water, paint, seaweed, antifreeze, paraffin oil, detergent, and peppermint? Not quite. A mix like that would be irresistible to the
hundreds of thousands of individual bacteria lying on the surface of even an
immaculately cleaned bathroom sink. They would get in, float in the water
bubbles, ingest the ooze and paraffin, maybe even spray out enzymes to break
down the chalk. The result would be an uninviting mess. The way manufacturers avoid that final obstacle is by putting something in to kill the bacteria.
Something good and strong is needed, something that will zap any accidentally
intrudant bacteria into oblivion. And that something is formaldehyde—the dis-
infectant used in anatomy labs.

13   So it's chalk, water, paint, seaweed, antifreeze, paraffin oil, detergent,
peppermint, formaldehyde, and fluoride (which can go some way towards
preserving children's teeth)—that's the usual mixture raised to the mouth on
the toothbrush for a fresh morning's clean. If it sounds too unfortunate, take

heart. Studies show that thorough brushing with just plain water will often do as good a job.

WHAT DID THE WRITER SAY AND WHAT DID YOU THINK?

1. What's the thesis of this essay? Is it stated?
2. What are some of the reasons toothpaste is composed of the ingredients described here?
3. How does the author expect the audience to react to the information in this essay? How do you know?

HOW DID THE WRITER SAY IT?

1. Is this essay division or classification?
2. In paragraph 3, why does the author explain how chalk is formed?
3. The author chooses words designed to elicit an emotional reaction. What are some of these words? What emotions do they provoke?

What About Your Writing?

Most of us probably haven't spent very much time thinking about the contents of our toothpaste tubes. Most of us probably never gave our toothpaste a second thought.

David Bodanis isn't most of us.

Bodanis has specialized knowledge. He has quirky facts and unusual information that most of us don't have. More importantly, he knows how to make us care about that unusual information, even though we never thought we would. All his chemical knowledge is put to use to help persuade us that our toothpaste is filled with ingredients that are useless at best, and dangerous at worst.

Do you have an esoteric specialty that might intrigue others? If you're an enthusiastic player of video games, you have a beautiful piece on man versus machine that's waiting to be written. If you own tropical fish and have seen adult fish eating their own young, you have the potential for a powerful cruelty-of-nature essay.

In a sense, you also have a specialty in anything that has ever hit you hard. If you waited week after week as a child for a "free offer" after you sent in a box top, aren't you "one of the world's leading authorities" on what waiting can do to the soul? Don't shy away from specialties because you're afraid that people won't be interested. Show how the specialty is related to something they care about, and make them interested.

THREE KINDS OF DISCIPLINE
John Holt

John Holt (1923–1985) was one of the important voices in modern American education. His work is much admired, even by many of those who disagree with his conclusions, for his ability to identify with children and sometimes to seem to enter their minds. Too sophisticated a writer and thinker to be associated consistently with any particular party line in education, Holt is viewed as one of the influences behind experiments with open classrooms in the 1960s and early 1970s. His books include *How Children Fail* (1964), *How Children Learn* (1967), *The Underachieving School* (1969), *What Do I Do Monday?* (1970), *Escape from Childhood* (1974), and *Never Too Late* (1978). This selection is an excerpt from Holt's influential *Freedom and Beyond* (1972).

✔ **WORDS TO CHECK:**

impartial (paragraph 1)	impotent (3)	autocratic (4)
wheedled (1)	novice (4)	suppleness (4)

1   A child, in growing up, may meet and learn from three different kinds of disciplines. The first and most important is what we might call the Discipline of Nature or of Reality. When he is trying to do something real, if he does the wrong thing or doesn't do the right one, he doesn't get the result he wants. If he doesn't pile one block right on top of another, or tries to build on a slanting surface, his tower falls down. If he hits the wrong key, he hears the wrong note. If he doesn't hit the nail squarely on the head, it bends, and he has to pull it out and start with another. If he doesn't measure properly what he is trying to build, it won't open, close, fit, stand up, fly, float, whistle, or do whatever he wants it to do. If he closes his eyes when he swings, he doesn't hit the ball. A child meets this kind of discipline every time he tries to *do* something, which is why it is so important in school to give children more chances to do things, instead of just reading or listening to someone talk (or pretending to). This discipline is a great teacher. The learner never has to wait long for his answer; it usually comes quickly, often instantly. Also it is clear, and very often points toward the needed correction; from what happened he cannot only see that what he did was wrong, but also why, and what he needs to do instead. Finally, and most important, the giver of the answer, call it Nature, is impersonal, impartial, and indifferent. She does not give opinions, or make judgments; she cannot be wheedled, bullied, or fooled; she does not get angry or disappointed; she does not praise or blame; she does not remember past failures or hold grudges; with her one always gets a fresh start, this time is the one that counts.

2   The next discipline we might call the Discipline of Culture, of Society, of What People Really Do. Man is a social, a cultural animal. Children sense

around them this culture, this network of agreements, customs, habits, and rules binding the adults together. They want to understand it and be a part of it. They watch very carefully what people around them are doing and want to do the same. They want to do right, unless they become convinced they can't do right. Thus children rarely misbehave seriously in church, but sit as quietly as they can. The example of all those grownups is contagious. Some mysterious ritual is going on, and children, who like rituals, want to be part of it. In the same way, the little children that I see at concerts or operas, though they may fidget a little, or perhaps take a nap now and then, rarely make any disturbance. With all those grownups sitting there, neither moving nor talking, it is the most natural thing in the world to imitate them. Children who live among adults who are habitually courteous to each other, and to them, will soon learn to be courteous. Children who live surrounded by people who speak a certain way will speak that way, however much we may try to tell them that speaking that way is bad or wrong.

3   The third discipline is the one most people mean when they speak of discipline–the Discipline of Superior Force, of sergeant to private, of "You do what I tell you or I'll make you wish you had." There is bound to be some of this in a child's life. Living as we do, surrounded by things that can hurt children, or that children can hurt, we cannot avoid it. We can't afford to let a small child find out from experience the danger of playing in a busy street, or of fooling with the pots on the top of a stove, or of eating up the pills in the medicine cabinet. So, along with other precautions, we say to him, "Don't play in the street, or touch things on the stove, or go into the medicine cabinet, or I'll punish you." Between him and the danger too great for him to imagine we put a lesser danger, but one he can imagine and maybe therefore wants to avoid. He can have no idea of what it would be like to be hit by a car, but he can imagine being shouted at, or spanked, or sent to his room. He avoids these substitutes for the greater danger until he can understand it and avoid it for its own sake. But we ought to use this discipline only when it is necessary to protect the life, health, safety, or well-being of people or other living creatures, or to prevent destruction of things that people care about. We ought not to assume too long, as we usually do, that a child cannot understand the real nature of the danger from which we want to protect him. The sooner he avoids the danger, not to escape our punishment, but as a matter of good sense, the better. He can learn that faster than we think. In Mexico, for example, where people drive their cars with a good deal of spirit, I saw many children no older than five or four walking unattached on the streets. They understood about cars, they knew what to do. A child whose life is full of the threat and fear of punishment is locked into babyhood. There is no way for him to grow up, to learn to take responsibility for his life and acts. Most important of all, we should not assume that having to yield to the threat of our superior force is good for the child's character. It is never good for anyone's character. To bow to superior force makes us feel impotent and cowardly for not having had the strength or

courage to resist. Worse, it makes us resentful and vengeful. We can hardly wait to make someone pay for our humiliation, yield to us as we were once made to yield. No, if we cannot always avoid using the Discipline of Superior Force, we should at least use it as seldom as we can.

4   There are places where all three disciplines overlap. Any very demanding human activity combines in it the disciplines of Superior Force, of Culture, and of Nature. The novice will be told, "Do it this way, never mind asking why, just do it that way, that is the way we always do it." But it probably is just the way they always do it, and usually for the very good reason that it is a way that has been found to work. Think, for example, of ballet training. The student in a class is told to do this exercise, or that; to stand so; to do this or that with his head, arms, shoulders, abdomen, hips, legs, feet. He is constantly corrected. There is no argument. But behind these seemingly autocratic demands by the teacher lie many decades of custom and tradition, and behind that, the necessities of dancing itself. You cannot make the moves of classical ballet unless over many years you have acquired, and renewed every day, the needed strength and suppleness in scores of muscles and joints. Nor can you do the difficult motions, making them look easy, unless you have learned hundreds of easier ones first. Dance teachers may not always agree on all the details of teaching these strengths and skills. But no novice could learn them all by himself. You could not go for a night or two to watch the ballet and then, without any other knowledge at all, teach yourself how to do it. In the same way, you would be unlikely to learn any complicated and difficult human activity without drawing heavily on the experience of those who know it better. But the point is that the authority of these experts or teachers stems from, grows out of their greater competence and experience, the fact that what they do *works*, not the fact that they happen to be the teacher and as such have the power to kick a student out of the class. And the further point is that children are always and everywhere attracted to that competence, and ready and eager to submit themselves to a discipline that grows out of it. We hear constantly that children will never do anything unless compelled to by bribes or threats. But in their private lives, or in extracurricular activities in school, in sports, music, drama, art, running a newspaper, and so on, they often submit themselves willingly and wholeheartedly to very intense disciplines, simply because they want to learn to do a given thing well. Our Little-Napoleon football coaches, of whom we have too many and hear far too much, blind us to the fact that millions of children work hard every year getting better at sports and games without coaches barking and yelling at them.

WHAT DID THE WRITER SAY AND WHAT DID YOU THINK?

1. The author neatly defines and gives examples of three kinds of discipline. Where does he follow this book's advice to acknowledge the not-so-neat complications (see page 228)? What is the complication?

2. What is the single principle of classification?

3. Is there a thesis? If so, is it ever stated?

4. Which kind of discipline does the author like most, and which kind does he like least?

5. What are the dangers of the "Discipline of Superior Force"? Why is it sometimes necessary?

6. Does the author paint too cheerful a picture of the "Discipline of Nature"? What happens with the child who bends the nail, gives up, and never learns how to use a hammer? How would the author reply to these questions?

7. A parent tells a child wearing a thin T-shirt to put on a coat before the child steps outside into bitter cold weather. The child refuses. What would the author's advice be?

8. Do you think the essay as a whole diminishes or increases the importance of a teacher? Explain.

HOW DID THE WRITER SAY IT?

1. Many English instructors would probably criticize Holt for his comma splices—a frequent punctuation error of many student writers (see pages 221–222). Find at least two of the author's comma splices.

2. The description of Nature at the end of paragraph 1 presents an unstated contrast to someone or something else: "She does not give opinions, or make judgments; she cannot be wheedled, bullied, or fooled; she does not get angry or disappointed; she does not praise or blame; she does not remember past failures or hold grudges; with her one always gets a fresh start, this time is the one that counts." What is Nature being contrasted to?

3. The author has least to say about the "Discipline of Society." Would more examples have been a good idea?

4. Do the concluding observations on football coaches strike you as an effective ending or the sudden raising of a trivial side issue?

What About _Your_ Writing?

Critics make much, as they always have, about the sounds and "music" of poetry, but generally not enough is made of the sounds of prose. All readers have an inner ear that hears what they are reading, no matter how outwardly silent the act of reading may be. And the sounds can be good or bad, pleasant or unpleasant.

Apart from the rhymes and meter of poetry, the most common musical device is probably _alliteration:_ the repetition of identical sounds at the beginning of words. (Once limited to consonant sounds only, alliteration in general usage now refers to vowel sounds as well.) Holt uses alliteration effectively when he writes in paragraph 1 that Nature is "impersonal, impartial, and indifferent." The repetition of sounds is pleasing, even downright catchy, in itself. Moreover, the repetition of sounds helps to reinforce thought: The three alliterative words are all related by being qualities of nature, and the identical sounds drive home that relationship.

A few moments' consideration can turn up a host of titles and famous phrases that show the appeal of alliteration:

"Little Boy Blue"	*The Great Gatsby*
East of Eden	calm, cool, and collected
in fine fettle	*The Brady Bunch*
Sighted sub, sank same	*All Things Bright and Beautiful*
The Pride and the Passion	"Love Me or Leave Me"
Boston Bruins	dry as dust
Philadelphia Phillies	through thick and thin
wit and wisdom	*The Doctor's Dilemma*

On a humble level, Chapter 1 of this book used alliteration to describe the importance to good writing of a thesis and support of a thesis: "The Persuasive Principle." The phrase seemed more vivid and easier to remember than "The Persuasive Idea" or "The Persuasive Slant."

Like most other good things, alliteration can be abused. Beware of pouring on too many identical sounds all at once. Remember, too, that alliteration is a special stylistic touch; if your reader expects it in every sentence, it loses its impact and distracts attention from your thought. Shakespeare parodied simple-minded overindulgence in alliteration in *A Midsummer Night's Dream* as some amateur playwrights came up with these lines for "he stabbed himself":

Whereat, with blade, with bloody blameful blade, He bravely broach'd his boiling bloody breast.

CHAPTER 8½
Office Hours: Revision: The Psychology of It All

Let's face it. From time to time, some writers may contend that revision is boring drudgery. But boredom is not what makes revision such hard work. The main impediment to effective revision is that most writers, deep down, are hoping against hope that they won't find anything that needs to be revised.

Think of all the time, thought, and trouble that you put into the creation of a paper. Think of the hours of television, movies, concerts, and other excellent forms of goofing off that you had to sacrifice. Remember the exquisite pleasure of writing the last word of the last sentence? How could anyone but a sadistic troll presume to remind you that it was only the last word of the last sentence of the first draft?

A psychological challenge lies at the heart of all revision. The paper is your baby. Your painful labor has created something out of nothing, made the invisible visible. You wouldn't be human unless you felt that everything about your baby was beautiful, but the truth is that most newborn babies, like most first drafts, are raw, rough, and wrinkly. It takes still more time and trouble before they start looking as beautiful as you had imagined—but try telling that to any parent.

These psychological barriers to effective revision—vital as revision is—will always be with us, and trying to eliminate them is like waging a doomed war against human imperfection. We can learn how to live with these barriers, however, and often even profit from them.

We suggest the wisdom of one guiding principle: *If it doesn't seem right to you, it isn't.* It's not just your imagination. Trust your instincts. If you are feeling vague tremors of uneasiness—about a word choice, an intended humorous touch that now seems strained, a possible lack of clarity or logic, an organizational issue—pay attention to those tremors. You're feeling what the proud parent in you is trying not to feel, and a reader without your emotional involvement is sure to feel something, too.

What if you feel uneasy but can't find any solution? You don't know *why* an idea seems a bit unclear. You think a phrase may be awkward, but you can't think of a less awkward version. We believe that these are perfect occasions to ask your instructor for a hand. Few instructors have the time, and most surely object in principle, to going over every student's rough draft and turning it into an A paper. But most instructors welcome with enthusiasm a student who asks them to have a look at a trouble spot. "Is it all in my mind, or is this paragraph off the subject?" "I keep thinking I need to add something here, but I don't know what." Your instructors keep office hours and usually try to make themselves available after class for just such questions.

Intelligent revision is always necessary and frequently difficult. Understanding the psychology can be a big help.

Definition

One of the most frequent impediments to clear communication is the failure to define terms. Some conversations and writings aren't just impeded by that failure–they're made incomprehensible. In isolation, a catchphrase like *power to the people,* for example, can mean anything from revolution to better electric service. Far more often, failure to define or to agree on a definition can lead to hours–and years–of futile controversy, complete with name-calling and shaking fists. Think of United Nation debates on *aggression* and *human rights.* Think of the storms in American history over terms such as *free speech, due process, quotas,* and *globalization.*

A definition essay often includes a "dictionary definition" but goes far beyond it and is best thought of as providing an *extended definition.* It discusses the meaning of words and phrases to which even the best dictionaries can't do full justice.

Dictionary definitions work in two ways, both of them short and one of them extremely formal. First, a dictionary can define by giving a direct synonym: *liberty* means *freedom*; *couch* means *sofa*; *plate* means *dish*; *cry* means *weep.* Second, a dictionary can, and for many terms must, use the techniques of a formal definition: A term is placed in the class it belongs to and then is differentiated from all other members of the same class:

Term	Class	Differentiation
Convertible	a car	with a top that can be raised and lowered
Widow	a woman	whose husband has died
Martini	a cocktail	made with gin or vodka and dry vermouth

Dictionary definitions, to repeat, are often incorporated into an extended definition, but no definition paper will discuss a term for which a dictionary definition alone would be sufficient. Some definition papers, in fact, may have as their central point the inadequacy or impossibility of good dictionary definitions for the term under consideration. (The skilled writer, however, will almost always avoid starting off with such tired phrases as "According to the dictionary" or "*Webster's* says that. . . .")

What terms are promising candidates for definition papers? Here are some suggestions:

Abstract concepts: love, morality, patriotism, apathy, equality

Controversial terms: suburban sprawl, the information explosion, the glass
    ceiling, police brutality, racism, pro-choice, downsizing

Common phrases and ideas: a good movie, the ideal vacation, the perfect job

A definition paper usually turns out to be an expression of opinion, a
"What Such-and-Such Means to Me" paper. A good movie for one person will
have to stimulate the mind; for another person, it will have to give the mind a
rest. The expression of an attitude toward the term is what gives life to a definition paper and makes it more interesting to read than a dictionary. In other
words, a definition paper benefits from a thesis:

- An ideal vacation can mean snoozing in the backyard just as much as
  seeing new sights.
- Creative complaining is one of humanity's best hopes for progress.
- Love is a severe mental illness curable only by time.

Definition papers follow no set pattern. Most turn out to be combinations of
patterns that are studied separately in other chapters of this book. Which pattern
or combination of patterns is used depends on which works best, and which works
best depends on what's being defined and what the writer has to say about it.

A Definition Paper Can Compare and Contrast

A term can be made clearer and more interesting by distinguishing it from
similar terms: A paper on socialism might distinguish it from communism; a
paper on love might distinguish it from infatuation. Discussing opposites sometimes works well, too: A definition paper on a *liberal* might take the same set of
circumstances and contrast a liberal's behavior to a conservative's. These negative techniques—showing what a term is not—often lead to successful papers.

A Definition Paper Can Classify

It may be both convenient and insightful to break some terms into separate
classifications. Morality, for example, could be considered in two parts: passive morality—not doing evil, and active morality—doing good.

A Definition Paper Can Give Examples

A paper defining a good movie would naturally discuss specific examples of
good movies that fit the definition. Without the examples, the paper would
probably be abstract and dull.

A Definition Paper Can Trace a Process

A writer engaged in defining schizophrenia might make the illness more understandable with a step-by-step analysis of its progress from the first signs of mental aberration to its full development.

A Definition Paper Can Study Cause-and-Effect Relationships

Advocates or opponents of globalization, in supporting their thesis by defining the term, would need to discuss what they see as the favorable or unfavorable effects of increased or decreased globalization.

A Definition Paper Can Use Narration

Narration is the telling of a story. A paper on competition could show the good and the bad sides of the term in action by telling the story of the author's friendly and unfriendly rivalry with a fellow student during high school days.

WRITING SUGGESTIONS FOR DEFINITION ESSAYS

Any of the following terms lend themselves to extended definitions. Remember that definition papers are not tied down to any one writing pattern. Use whatever approach works best:

1. Comfort food
2. A ham actor
3. Good sportsmanship
4. Conflict of interest
5. A good teacher
6. Fad
7. Atheism
8. An intellectual
9. Courtesy
10. Worship
11. A good marriage
12. Child abuse
13. Conscience
14. The ideal college
15. A good salesperson
16. Friendship

17. Courage
18. Jealousy
19. Obscenity
20. Humanity's best friend
21. Humanity's worst enemy
22. Fear
23. Road rage
24. Frustration
25. Writer's block

VISUAL PROMPT

Writing Prompt

One of the most frequent impediments to clear communication is the failure to define terms. Write a definition essay that clarifies a term you have always found confusing.

STUDENT ESSAY: GROWING UP

Anonymous

Thesis: Being tested for HIV taught me how to be a grown-up.

    I. Grown-ups and fear
          A. Still get scared
          B. Face the fear

   II. Grown-ups and responsibility
          A. Temptation to ignore it
          B. Responsibility to others

III. Grown-ups and reality
    A. Temptation to deny it
    B. Need to accept real world

Conclusion: Although being a grown-up is difficult, we can each work to become one.

Many, many years ago, I thought that a grown-up was someone who could drive a car. But when I finally was old enough to drive, I found out that I wasn't a grown-up yet. Then, I figured that a grown-up was a person who could vote. But when I cast my first vote, I realized that I still wasn't a grown-up. A little later, I decided that a grown-up was someone who went to college. But college wasn't what helped me to become a grown-up either.

It wasn't until I decided to get tested for HIV that I learned what really made someone a grown-up. I like to think, too, that as I learned what defined a grownup, I also became one.

I had stopped by the free clinic where a friend of mine works, and while I was waiting for her, one of the other volunteers asked me if I wanted to be tested. My immediate reaction was, "Who, me?" As I thought about it for a while, though, I realized that the only reason not to be tested would be fear—fear of testing positive, fear of facing the facts. I took a deep breath, and I got tested. Grown-ups get scared, but they don't let fear keep them from doing what they need to do.

My test results, the clinic said, wouldn't come back for ten days. Those were ten very long days. I spent a lot of time thinking about what I would do if my results were positive. Who would I tell? Could I tell anyone? Was it really my problem if I had infected anyone? Would I have to change my life, or could I just pretend it wasn't true? I wrestled with those questions and many more for days, deciding that, however awful it might be, I would have to tell my "exes" if my test was positive, and that my life would have to change drastically. I owed that to anyone I had ever loved. Besides, however unpleasant it may be, a grown-up has a sense of responsibility to other people.

The day my results came back, I thought that I might try to avoid the whole problem by just not showing up to get my results. That way, I'd be no better or worse off than I had been before the test. I could just forget about it. I could go on as I had been going. When the time came, though, I knew that I had to go find out, that I couldn't ignore reality any longer. A grown-up has to learn to accept the real world.

The medical results of my test aren't important to anyone but myself and my "exes," but the mental results are important to anyone who has ever wondered what a grown-up is. I have discovered that grown-ups face fear, have a sense of responsibility, and learn to handle realities, even the grimmest ones. That's a lot to aim for, and no one can do all that all the time. Everyone, though, can do it sometimes. Whatever your age, once you find out what it means to be a grown-up, you can always work to be one.

THE REAL THING

Frankie Germany

Writers have been trying to define love since writing began. In "The Real Thing," teacher and freelance writer Frankie Germany tries to do it with one simple, or seemingly simple, narrative.

✓ **WORDS TO CHECK:**

surreptitiously (paragraph 8)   poignant (8)   eavesdropped (8)

If I know what love is, it is because of you.
–Herman Hesse

1 Cecile and I have been friends since college, for more than thirty years. Although we have never lived closer than 100 miles to each other, since we first met, our friendship has remained constant. We have seen each other through marriage, birth, divorce, the death of loved ones–all those times when you really need a friend.

2 In celebration of our friendship and our fiftieth birthday, Cecile and I took our first road trip together. We drove from my home in Texas to California and back. What a wonderful time we had!

3 The first day of our trip ended in Santa Fe, New Mexico. After the long drive, we were quite tired, so we decided to go to the restaurant near the hotel for dinner. We were seated in a rather quiet part of the dining room with only a few other patrons. We ordered our food and settled back to recount our day. As we talked, I glanced at the other people in the room. I noticed an attractive elderly couple sitting a short distance away from us. The gentleman was rather tall and athletic looking, with silver hair and a tanned complexion. The lady seated beside him was petite, well-dressed, and lovely. What caught my immediate attention was the look of adoration on the woman's face. She sat, chin resting gently on her hands, and stared into the face of the man as he talked. She reminded me of a teenager in love!

4 I called Cecile's attention to the couple. As we watched, he reached over to place a gentle kiss on her cheek. She smiled.

5 "Now that's what I call real love!" I said with a sigh. "I imagine they've been married for a long time. They look so in love!"

6 "Or maybe," remarked Cecile, "they haven't been together long. It could be they've just fallen in love."

7 "Well, whatever the case, it's obvious they care a great deal for each other. They are in love."

8 Cecile and I watched surreptitiously and unashamedly eavesdropped on their conversation. He was explaining to her about a new business investment

he was considering and asking her opinion. She smiled and agreed with whatever he said. When the waitress came to take their order, he ordered for her, reminding her that the veal was her favorite. He caressed her hand as he talked, and she listened raptly to his every word. We were enthralled by the poignant scene we were witnessing.

9   Then the scene changed. A perplexed look came over the finely wrinkled but beautiful face. She looked at the man and said in a sweet voice, "Do I know you? What is this place? Where are we?"

10   "Now, sweetheart, you know me. I'm Ralph, your husband. And we're in Santa Fe. We are going to see our son in Missouri tomorrow. Don't you remember?"

11   "Oh, I'm not sure. I seem to have forgotten," she said quietly.

12   "That's okay, sweetheart. You'll be all right. Just eat your dinner, and we'll go and get some rest." He reached over and caressed her cheek. "You sure do look pretty tonight."

13   Tears coursed down our cheeks as Cecile and I looked at each other. "We were right," she said quietly. "It is the real thing. That is love."

WHAT DID THE WRITER SAY AND WHAT DID YOU THINK?

1. When the author and her friend first see an elderly couple in a restaurant, they correctly assume that the two people are "in love." What incorrect assumptions do they make?
2. The essay ends with the author and her friend arriving at a fuller definition of love–"the real thing." What are the new elements of the definition?
3. Express the thesis in your own words.

HOW DID THE WRITER SAY IT?

1. Is the author's definition of love ever specifically stated?
2. Is the one extended example in this essay enough to provide a useful definition? Would more examples have been desirable?

What About Your Writing?

Go easy on exclamation points. We like the term *comic-book punctuation* to describe the pouring on of artificial aids like exclamation points, question marks, italics, and capital letters to create emphasis. Writers guilty of these practices almost always deliver their messages too loudly and sometimes betray a lack of confidence in their command of words and their readers' intelligence.

Most instructors will agree that whatever the merits of "The Real Thing" as a whole, the author is too fond of exclamation points. The truth is that in paragraph 2 "What a wonderful time we had!" is not a particularly exciting sentence, and the exclamation point doesn't make the sentence more power-ful. It only lets us know the author wishes it were more powerful. We feel the same about the exclamation points in paragraphs 3 and 5. Turn down the vol-ume by getting rid of the exclamation points, and the sentences gain in dignity and thoughtfulness.

When words themselves haven't done the job adequately, the words need to be changed. The only way to fix a lame sentence is to fix the language, not toss in a pushy exclamation point. And two exclamation points are twice as bad, not twice as good. If your intended sarcasm in a sentence hasn't come through effectively with your words, a pushy little question mark isn't going to help, either.

Comic-Book Punctuation	Improved
I had never seen anyone with such an ego! Never!!	Never had I seen anyone with such an ego.
Art?? The movie was filth!	The movie was not art. It was filth.
Professor Jones was a teacher (?) in Renaissance History.	Professor Jones was a poor Renaissance History teacher.

Don't assume that punctuation has suddenly been banned. All the resources of the language, including punctuation, are at your disposal. When a character in a novel is choking to death, nobody will object to the exclamation point in "Aaargh!" In a textbook, nobody will object to the italics in a sentence like "The first principle of good writing is the *persuasive principle*." The more flashy forms of punctuation, however, require extreme caution. It's a matter of taste.

WHAT IS INTELLIGENCE, ANYWAY?

Isaac Asimov

Isaac Asimov (1920–1992) wrote or edited more than 500 volumes and an estimated 90,000 letters or postcards, and he published in every major cat-egory of the Dewey decimal system except Philosophy. He was a master of the science fiction genre and may be best known for his *Foundation* series. His "Three Laws of Robotics" have become a classic part of the thinking behind most modern science fiction writing.

✓ WORDS TO CHECK:

vitals (paragraph 3)	academician (4)	arbiter (4)
oracles (3)	foist (4)	raucously (6)

1 What is intelligence, anyway? When I was in the army I received a kind of aptitude test that all soldiers took and, against a normal of 100, scored 160. No one at the base had ever seen a figure like that, and for two hours they made a big fuss over me. (It didn't mean anything. The next day I was still a buck private with KP as my highest duty.)

2 All my life I've been registering scores like that, so that I have the complacent feeling that I'm highly intelligent, and I expect other people to think so, too. Actually, though, don't such scores simply mean that I am very good at answering the type of academic questions that are considered worthy of answers by the people who make up the intelligence tests–people with intellectual bents similar to mine?

3 For instance, I had an auto-repair man once, who, on these intelligence tests, could not possibly have scored more than 80, by my estimate. I always took it for granted that I was far more intelligent than he was. Yet, when anything went wrong with my car I hastened to him with it, watched him anxiously as he explored its vitals, and listened to his pronouncements as though they were divine oracles–and he always fixed my car.

4 Well, then, suppose my auto-repair man devised questions for an intelligence test. Or suppose a carpenter did, or a farmer, or, indeed, almost anyone but an academician. By every one of those tests, I'd prove myself a moron. And I'd *be* a moron, too. In a world where I could not use my academic training and my verbal talents but had to do something intricate or hard, working with my hands, I would do poorly. My intelligence, then, is not absolute but is a function of the society I live in and of the fact that a small subsection of that society has managed to foist itself on the rest as an arbiter of such matters.

5 Consider my auto-repair man, again. He had a habit of telling me jokes whenever he saw me. One time he raised his head from under the automobile hood to say: "Doc, a deaf-and-dumb guy went into a hardware store to ask for some nails. He put two fingers together on the counter and made hammering motions with the other hand. The clerk brought him a hammer. He shook his head and pointed to the two fingers he was hammering. The clerk brought him nails. He picked out the size he wanted, and left. Well, Doc, the next guy who came in was a blind man. He wanted scissors. How do you suppose he asked for them?"

6 Indulgently, I lifted my right hand and made scissoring motions with my first two fingers. Whereupon my auto-repair man laughed raucously and said, "Why, you dumb jerk, he used his *voice* and asked for them." Then he said, smugly, "I've been trying that on all my customers today." "Did you catch many?" I asked. "Quite a few," he said, "but I knew for sure I'd catch *you*." "Why is that?" I asked. "Because you're so goddamned educated Doc, I *knew* you couldn't be very smart."

7 And I have an uneasy feeling he had something there.

WHAT DID THE WRITER SAY AND WHAT DID YOU THINK?

1. Is this essay primarily a funny anecdote, or does it have a serious point to make? What is the point, if any?
2. How does the author feel about intelligence tests?
3. What distinction does the mechanic make between "educated" and "smart"?
4. In what ways is Asimov's intelligence "tested" in this essay?

HOW DID THE WRITER SAY IT?

1. What would be the effect, if any, of removing the first sentence of this essay?
2. How and where does Asimov's exceptional intelligence show in this essay?
3. Where does the author's word choice reveal his own interest in and knowledge of science?

What About Your Writing?

Some students think that developing a thesis makes demands on intellectual powers they do not possess. Isaac Asimov's "What Is Intelligence, Anyway?" demonstrates that if you have adequately interesting material, you can view your thesis primarily as an organizational device for tying things together, not as a blazing new insight or a bold stand on an issue of current controversy. Asimov's thesis, after all, comes to little more than, "Intelligence has different definitions for different people." Don't ignore great controversial ideas when they happen to pop up, but first-rate essays have been built around theses no more profound than, "There are two sharply conflicting ways of approaching such and such a subject," "Thomas Hardy's reputation as a poet is still being debated," "Solving the problems of pollution is more complicated than it looks," and so on.

CHEAP THRILLS

Patricia Volk

Patricia Volk is the author of the memoir *Stuffed: Adventures of a Restaurant Family* (2001). She has also published a novel, collections of short stories, as well as book reviews and essays in dozens of magazines. This essay, originally published in *O: The Oprah Magazine*, explores one of her favorite subjects–her family.

Originally published in O MAGAZINE. Reprinted by permission of Patricia Volk and the Watkins/Loomis Agency.

✓ WORDS TO CHECK:

Katmandu (paragraph 4)	innately (13)
languishing (9)	pashminas (17)

1 Nana Polly hung used tinfoil up to dry. You could tell what vegetables she served during the week by what showed up in her salads. Her younger sister, Aunt Ruthie, made curtains out of shawls. Her older sister, Aunt Gertie, made shawls out of curtains. In our family, saving money has nothing to do with being cheap or stingy. It has to do with not wasting.

2 In a thrifty family, being thrifty is an art form. You get to be creative. The first year my mother was married, she had a telephone plan that included 66 calls a month. Thirty went to her mother, 15 to her grandmother, leaving only 21. Luckily, her best friend lived in the apartment next door. When Mom wanted to talk to Dorothy, she knocked on the wall. If Dorothy was free, she'd knock back and they'd meet in the hall.

3 Sometimes being thrifty entails doing without, better known as making do. Making do takes ingenuity. Anyone can go to the market and put a decent dinner together. A thrifty person checks the fridge, sees a jar of peanut butter, an onion, some leftover pineapple, and says, "If I were Julia Child, what would I do?" Then the thrifty person creates General Tso's Pineapple Szechuan Peanut Noodles, a dish she never would have tasted if she hadn't been thrifty.

4 Thrifty families make dinner thinking, How can I use the leftovers? We eat roast beef looking forward to the hash. It's like sex or heading for Katmandu: The anticipation is as thrilling as getting there. We eat turkey dinners, dreaming of sandwiches moist with mayonnaise, sprinkled with sea salt. Whether you're broke and have to or you're thrifty by nature like my family, not wasting means never having to say, "I'm sorry I wasted that. If I hadn't wasted *that,* maybe I'd have *this* now."

5 Sometimes I reverse-shop. I go into a store and say, "What *won't* I buy today? Do I really need that sequined change purse in the shape of a banana?"

6 "You already have a change purse and you love *that* change purse," the angel in me says.

7 Devil: "But this banana change purse, it doesn't cost that much. It sings to you. This is the cutest change purse you've ever seen. Buy it. It'll make you happy."

8 Angel: "And what will you do with your old change purse, the one you loved until this very minute?"

9 That's when I go to imagining the banana change purse languishing in my top drawer with a lot of other stuff I had to have. I go to opening the drawer and seeing that dumb $42 change purse and thinking of all the things you can do with $42.

10 Reverse shopping can be done at home, too: My favorite catalog comes in the mail. I fold down the pages of things I adore. The catalog disappears in the

black hole of my night table. A week goes by. In a cleaning frenzy, I find it and check out the folded pages. For the life of me, I can't figure out what looked so good. The sweater with the peplum? The blouse with the bugle beads? I toss the magazine and save a wad—not only on the ordering but also on sending back. Once you get the hang of reverse shopping, you'll open a catalog and say, "Do I really want to make UPS richer?"

11   Recently, my new three-hole punch broke. It cost $4.19 at Staples. It was only a month old. I told a friend I was taking it back.

12   "Is it worth your time to take it back?"

13   I tried to figure out what my time was worth. As a writer, 90 percent of my time is spent staring into space. When I worked full-time and had a salary, I could have figured 11 blocks to Staples, earnest discussion with manager, 11 blocks home: 45 minutes at $1,200 a week, that's $22.50 to return a $4.19 three-hole punch. But innately thrifty people don't think like that. Even if we make megabucks, it's not just about money. We can't bear waste. My father looked at carpet scraps as potential cushions for washer-dryers that bump during the spin cycle. Empty tennis ball cans were storage containers. Plastic supermarket bags? Garbage can liners.

14   In a thrifty family, you boast about buys. I never pictured myself in men's tiger-striped velvet slippers from Stubbs & Wootton, but when I checked my local cancer thrift shop there were boxes of brand-new ones reduced from $200 to $16.95. I made a discovery: A woman's size 10 is a man's size 8. Now I'm in love with my "paws." And men's shoes are made so much better than women's, they'll last forever.

15   My mother can't resist a bargain at Loehmann's. She'd never treat herself to a Moschino suit retail. But getting it for a quarter of the price from the Italian import rack, even though she has the money to buy it at Bergdorf's, only then is a Moschino suit truly desirable. When someone shows up at a family dinner in a new outfit and you say, "I love your dress!" the thrifty family's response isn't "Thank you!" it's "Do you believe? $89 at Daffy's!" People fan their hearts, they're so proud of you. You not only have an eye, you're smart. You not only found an attractive dress, you got a buy on it.

16   Thrift has nothing to do with quality. If we're buying caviar for New Year's Eve, we'd rather buy beluga and have less of it than lots of that yellow farm-raised stuff. If a herd of people is coming over, instead of skimping on the beluga, we serve hummus or chopped liver. Which brings us to the thrifty family's favorite food: chicken. If you stew chicken, you get chicken soup *and* a chicken. You also get to skim the cooled yellow fat that rises in the fridge. Called schmaltz, it can be used in place of butter. The vegetables that flavored the chicken make a wonderful side dish. And then there's the actual chicken itself. Whatever is left over can make sandwiches and chicken salad, or go in the soup. My sister's mother-in-law lives alone. Her chicken lasts a week. What makes it taste extra good is the secret ingredient: thrift. That said, we would

never put water in an almost empty ketchup bottle and shake it. Being thrifty never means sacrificing taste.

17   What's it like to have so much money you don't have to think before you spend it? I don't know and don't want to. It would mean less, be less fun. My bedroom windows overlook somebody else's bedroom windows. When this stopped being interesting, it was time for a window treatment. The local shade man wanted $600 apiece for Roman shades *plus fabric*. Excuse me, most of the time these shades would be *up*. Done right, they'd be *invisible*. $1,200 plus fabric for something I didn't want to see? Inspired by Aunt Ruthie and Aunt Gertie, I got two rods at the hardware store and four lavender pashminas from the street guy, $20 apiece. Complete cost of the two window treatments: $102. They take my breath away. Sad to say, on a trip to the Lower East Side, I saw the pashminas for $10 each. When you come from a thrifty family, don't think that doesn't hurt.

18   Thrift is our family way. That's not to say we don't have a few spend-thrifts and money oozers. Granny Ethel couldn't pass a store without going in. She'd whip out her address book and see who she could send something to. My beloved sister buys Jackie-style. If she likes it, she gets three. Nana Polly, who always used a tea bag twice, bought a new fur coat every year. Could she afford it? Of course she could afford it. Look what she saved in tinfoil, tea bags, and salads.

WHAT DID THE WRITER SAY AND WHAT DID YOU THINK?

1. What is thrift most similar to? What is it different from?
2. What does the author mean by "reverse shopping"?
3. How do the writer's family members justify impractical or unexpected purchases?
4. How would you define thrift? Does this essay match your personal understanding of the term?
5. For Volk, thrift is a cherished family trait. Is it a characteristic that is still valued in our culture?

HOW DID THE WRITER SAY IT?

1. What strategies does Volk use to define thrift?
2. How is this essay organized?
3. Which example is most effective for you? Why?

What About Your Writing?

I go into a store and say, "What *won't* I buy today? Do I really need that sequined change purse in the shape of a banana?"

"You already have a change purse and you love *that* change purse," the angel in me says.

Good dialogue, either a few lines or a lengthy conversation, can add life to almost any writing, nonfiction as well as fiction. The sense of immediacy can be remarkable. These are the words the people spoke, and readers are on their own. The author may mention a tone of voice or a gesture or may drop in an occasional *he said* or *she said* so that readers can keep track of the speaker, but essentially the author butts out. Good dialogue is direct, dramatic, persuasive. Apart from anything else, it gives the reader a pleasurable sense of recognition: "This is the way people talk," the reader says. "This is authentic."

Among the less obvious uses of dialogue could be its occasional use in original and lively introductions:

"Did you have a good time on your date, dear?"

"Aw, Mom."

"Was she a nice girl?"

"Aw, Mom."

"What does her father do?"

"Aw, Mom."

The generation gap—in my house, at least—is more than a myth.

"So what should we do about protecting the environment?" my teacher asks.

If I had the nerve, I'd like to answer, "First of all, let's stop talking about it
    every single minute. Enough is enough."

Many creative writing teachers are inclined to feel that writing good dialogue is a gift. You have it or you don't. You were born with an ear for dialogue or you weren't. Still, some elementary pointers might be helpful.

Keep Your Comments Simple

Confine yourself to *he said, she said, he asked, she answered,* and similar phrases. Avoid fancy variations like *he asserted, he expostulated, she queried, she gasped, he hissed.*

Don't Worry About Standard English

If the person who's talking would swear, say *ain't,* confuse *who* and *whom,* then make the person talk that way. Don't, whatever you do, use swear words to show off how tough and courageous and unflinchingly honest you are. Just be accurate.

Change Paragraphs with Each Speaker

You'll find violations of this advice among some of the best writers, but it seems ordinary common sense. Changing paragraphs makes the dialogue easier to follow by giving the reader a direct visual indication that there's been a change of speaker.

SICK IN THE HEAD

Jennifer Traig

Jennifer Traig has published a series of books on crafts and individual volumes on the art of autobiographical writing and work. She is the author of *Judaikitsch (2002),* and *The Devil is in the Details: Scenes from an Obsessive Girlhood.* (2004)

✓ WORDS TO CHECK:

neurological (paragraph 12)	caduceus (18)	havoc (22)
toxins (14)	heyday (19)	proliferation (24)
compile (15)	stigma (19)	alarmist (25)
litany (16)	debilitating (22)	neurotic (28)

1 I had my first heart attack when I was 18. I was striding across campus when it hit, like a bomb going off in my chest. My left arm went numb, and it got harder and harder to breathe. I was used to being sick—by the time I started college, I'd already had skin cancer, meningitis, pancreatitis and blood poisoning—but this was a whopper, and I was knocked over by the crushing pain. This was different. This could kill me, kaboom, right there on the quad.

2 I had to get to a hospital. I still don't know how I got to the student clinic, how I got across the campus and up the stairs, but I did. I staggered through the double doors and collapsed into a chair.

3 "I'm having a myocardial infarction," I gasped, when I was finally ushered into an exam room. "Heart attack," I added, when this failed to produce a crash cart.

4 "I know what a myocardial infarction is," the nurse said, casually taking my vitals. "You're not having one." She pressed a stethoscope to my chest.

5   "Well, it could be a stroke," I conceded.

6   "You're not having a stroke."

7   "I think we should run some tests."

8   "Haven't we seen you in here before?"

9   "Once or twice."

10   The nurse stood up and placed her stethoscope in her pocket. "You're fine," she said. "Your vitals are normal. You're a perfectly healthy 18-year-old girl. I promise you're fine. Go out, take a walk. It's a gorgeous day and you're not dying."

11   It was a gorgeous day, and I wasn't dying. I'd been spared, by fate or just dumb luck. This, too, had happened many times before. The skin cancer turned out to be ballpoint ink; the meningitis, hay fever; the pancreatitis, too many candy bars; the blood poisoning, ill-fitting shoes. I did not have lupus, multiple sclerosis, Huntington's disease or Hodgkin's, Crohn's disease, diabetes, myelitis or muscular dystrophy.

12   What I did have was hypochondria, which meant that every other disease was inevitable. I might have escaped the heart attack and the Hodgkin's, but surely something serious was only a matter of time. I could not leave well enough alone, and once dengue fever was ruled out I would return with malaria. There were just so many diseases out there, all strange and for the most part unavoidable. There was, for instance, foreign accent syndrome, the bizarre but real neurological condition that transformed native West Virginians into Eliza Doolittle overnight. There was pibloktoq, a seizure condition common to Greenland Eskimos that compels them do things like destroy furniture, disrobe, scream obscenities, and eat feces. There was SUDS, the mysterious disorder that claimed healthy young Asian men in their sleep, and even though I was neither, my father had been born in China, so who's to say I couldn't catch it from him.

13   You could catch lots of things. Maybe you'd get paragonimiasis, and parasites would eat you; or you'd get pica, and you'd eat them. Anything was possible.

14   It's hard to say when the hypochondria started. I'd been worried about my health for as long as I could remember, the anxiety growing like a tumor, each year introducing a new way to die. There were so many ways to go. Besides diseases there were poisons everywhere you looked. A whiff of the wrong fumes and you'd have instant brain damage. Mistake the glass cleaner for Kool-Aid, and who wouldn't, they were both blue, and you'd need a new liver. By age four I knew to avoid the skull-branded bottles under the kitchen sink, but what about natural toxins? The local landscaper had thoughtfully mined the front yards of our family-friendly neighborhood with all manner of poisonous plants. My parents had warned us to steer clear of the oleander and holly berries, but sometimes a brush was unavoidable. What if I forgot and stuck my pollen-coated fingers in my mouth? What if I sneezed,

open-mouthed, and a gust of wind blew a blossom in? It didn't seem likely, but it was possible, wasn't it?

15   The scariest plant of all, of course, was the family tree. When a fourth-grade assignment required me to compile my own I took less note of when ancestors died than what of: did we have a lot of heart disease in our family? Any lupus? MS? How about Hodgkin's?

16   There was remarkably little cancer, it turned out. Hypochondria, however, was in ample supply. The tendency to fear the worst was right there with our short legs and big feet. I had relatives who couldn't breathe, and others who couldn't swallow, and a number who suffered from vague, lingering conditions that required me to forfeit control of the television when they came to visit and to please not wear the loud shoes. There was the musician who was more adept at what doctors dryly call the "organ recital," the litany of abstract complaints that is the hallmark of the hypochondriac.

17   My favorite hypochondriac was a cousin thrice removed who was convinced she had stomach cancer. Sure she was dying, she was too afraid to go the doctor until the pain became completely unbearable. Her stomach tumor was born six hours later. He weighed seven pounds, and they named him Francis.

18   Who knew what bombs were ticking inside you? Even if you didn't inherit any of the awful genetic diseases you could always catch something: Ebola or malaria, hepatitis or TB. You could pick up a virus, an environmental disease, an infection or a parasite. And then there's the endless list of worms, thousands upon thousands, crawling in and crawling out: fluke and flatworm, beef worm and tapeworm, roundworm, pork worm, threadworm, heartworm, hookworm. Worms surpass us in both number and fortitude; several thousand nematodes aboard the Space Shuttle *Columbia* survived the crash. Worms will certainly eat you when you die and perhaps well before. Pinworms might invade your rectum; flatworms, your bladder; guinea fire worms might consume your flesh from the inside out. It could happen. It's been happening for eons. The guinea fire worm, in fact, is what you see in the caduceus, wrapped around the rod. Healers used to slit the skin open and draw the critter out with a stick. Yes. Gross.

19   Hypochondria is no less disturbing and almost as old. It has existed, in various forms, for thousands of years. Perhaps because it allows you to lie in bed without actually killing you, it has endured and flourished and was taken quite seriously for most of history, enjoying a true heyday in the 17th and 18th centuries. By the 19th century it had started to acquire the stigma it retains to this day. It had become perceived as largely untreatable. It was too physical for psychotherapists, too mental for medical doctors, and it responded poorly to treatment of either kind. What was the point in caring for a patient who wasn't sick, but who would never get better nonetheless? And who wasn't even crazy in a fun way? At least with paranoid schizophrenics you get good stories. But unless you find the symptoms of colon polyps interesting, hypochondriacs are

just a bore. There's no glamour in it, no red-carpet charity fundraisers for it, no celebrity spokespeople. And you couldn't ask for a worse poster boy: its most famous sufferer was Hitler.

20   Even doctors hate us. Most doctors would rather see a patient with suppurating genitals than a hypochondriac, and with good reason. Hypochondriacs are difficult, doubting backseat doctors who continually second-guess their physicians. Convinced that something is fundamentally, fatally wrong, they are the patients who are angry when the path report comes back benign. They are also outrageously expensive. It's estimated that they cost healthcare providers billions of dollars in unnecessary tests, care, and procedures.

21   The problem, of course, is that sometimes hypochondriacs really do get sick. I do, in fact, have about a million things wrong with me. Besides the hypochondria, which makes me think I have everything, I have a long list of very real syndromes and conditions, and the reason I'm so uncomfortable in my body is, in part, because it's such an uncomfortable place to be. I've had just about every annoying condition that doesn't actually affect your overall health: the nuisance diseases. There's the OCD and the IBS. There are the transient parasthesias, where random parts of my body go numb for no reason at all. I've been afflicted with eczema and allergies; appendicitis, gingivitis and tendonitis; carpal tunnel syndrome, Bell's palsy, essential tremor, heart irregularities, macromastia and hypoglycemia. I have skin conditions that make me prone to other skin conditions, and have been treated for scabies three times and ringworm twice in the last three years. I'm legally blind in one eye. I also have really bad hair, and cannot for the life of me understand why Japanese hair straightening isn't a covered benefit.

22   In spite of all this, I'm essentially healthy. Other hypochondriacs aren't so lucky. Some have the misfortune of being both hypochondriac and sick, and sometimes patients who get dismissed as hypochondriacs turn out to be profoundly ill. My father, a surgeon, had a patient whose endless, baseless complaints were vindicated a long time later when new technology finally revealed a well-concealed tumor. Researchers are starting to think that one of the most famous hypochondriacs, Charles Darwin, was not a hypochondriac at all, but was suffering from a never-diagnosed case of Chagas's disease, a debilitating tropical parasitic disease that wreaks havoc on the heart and nervous system. It's theorized that both Nietzsche's and Howard Hughes's hypochondria and general weirdness may have actually been caused by end-stage syphilis. In Key West, a lifelong hypochondriac got the last word when she dropped dead at age 50. Her tombstone reads, "I TOLD YOU I WAS SICK."

23   But most hypochondriacs are just whiners. It's this endearing quality that has earned us a number of unflattering nicknames. In the medical industry we are known as GOMERs (Get Out of My Emergency Room) and turkeys. Because we are also known as crocks and crackpots, physicians will sometimes order a check of our "serum porcelain level."

24   The more sensitive call hypochondriacs the "worried well." The name is apt. We do, indeed, worry extremely well. We worry consummately and constantly. Hypochondria is, in its own way, a terrible disease. The Merck manual gives it a 5 percent cure rate. This means that you are far more likely to recover from leukemia, heart failure, or necrotizing fasciitis than hypochondria. A few sufferers have even died of it, most notably the writers Sara Teasdale and Jerzy Kosinski. Both committed suicide when they feared death, by nonexistent illness, was imminent. Cancer, genetic defects, rare disorders–hypochondria makes every condition contagious. For me, transmission usually occurs through the television. They mention it on the news, and within a few hours I'm pretty sure I have it. A hypochondriac family friend was a champ in this department. Kennedy's back problems, Johnson's gallbladder disease–he had them all. When Babe Paley and Betty Ford were diagnosed with breast cancer my mother was sure he'd have his own biopsy scheduled within days. He didn't, but he did catch Nixon's shingles, and most surprising of all they turned out to be real. Recently, it's become more common for transmission to occur through the internet. The proliferation of medical websites has produced a new variant of the disease called, predictably, "cyberchondria." It's becoming increasingly prevalent, as the number of people searching for health information online has gone up dramatically. And some of us are responsible for more than our share of hits. (To qualify as a cyberchondriac, you have to visit a health site six times a month, a number I can hit easily during the commercial break of "Trauma: Life in the E.R.")

25   This new digital form of hypochondria presents new problems. The web is loaded with the sort of bad medical advice that led me to treat one rash with a diet of all orange foods and another with direct applications of toothpaste. Many sites seem designed to enflame the alarmist, with symptom finders that quickly escalate from stuffy nose to sinus tumor.

26   Today, for instance, I'm in pretty good shape. There's a weird mass inside my cheek, my finger hurts, and my hamstrings are sore. I have a rash on my feet and a mild headache. Twenty minutes on the internet revealed that I do not have deep vein thrombosis, as I suspected, but I still have plenty to worry about: it appears that I do have bacterial meningitis, and that it's too late to do anything about it. Still, this is a blessing, because it's a faster way to go than the oral cancer that would take me if that cheek lesion were allowed to run its course.

27   It would be a shame to die now, though, just when hypochondria's reputation is starting to enjoy a boost. In the past few years the stigma has eased just a bit. Perhaps driven by the outrageous costs of treating people who aren't really sick, the medical industry has begun to reevaluate the condition and has come to view hypochondria as a disease in its own right, just not one that requires MRIs, exploratory surgery and kidney donation.

28   It's hard to say what is behind the change. The web may have something to do with it, easing the exchange of information. Money is part of it, too, as HMOs look for ways to cut costs and please patients. Patients aren't patients

so much as consumers now, and the customer is always right, even if the customer is insisting that the sore muscle is end-stage liver cancer. Or it may just be greater acceptance of neurotic behavior in general. Hypochondria is, in a way, just a logical extension of a larger trend toward self-care, like taking vitamins or getting elective coffee enemas.

29   Coffee may, in fact, play a role. The last time hypochondria was taken seriously was during the Age of Enlightenment, when hypochondria was both common and chic. Then, as now, coffee was also wildly popular, and it does seem worth nothing that caffeine is a drug that induces both palpitations and manic self-examination.

30   In the last 20 years hypochondria has been renamed "somatoform disorder," which is more descriptive of the disease as it's understood today—a condition in which you translate stress, or unhappiness, or too much free time, into actual physical symptoms. The common perception of hypochondria as a condition in which a perfectly healthy person worries himself into a lather over nothing isn't quite right. He's worrying himself into a lather over something that turns out to be nothing. The pain and symptoms are real; they just have no underlying cause.

31   It sure seems like they do, however. Hypochondria is very different from faking sickness to get out of work or military service, and it's not a variation of Munchausen's, where the patient knowingly fakes illness to get attention. Hypochondriacs think they're sick because they really, really feel sick, with symptoms they can't ignore: shooting pains or numbness, hair loss and rashes, fevers and palpitations. It's amazing what the mind can produce. Expectant fathers suffering from a somatoform condition called Couvade's syndrome acquire all the symptoms of pregnancy except the actual fetus: morning sickness, weight gain, cravings, even labor pains.

32   The good news is that somatoform disorder is fairly treatable. Hypochondria is an expensive disease, but once you stop treating the phantom brain tumors and start treating the hypochondria itself it becomes very cost-effective. Recently it's become clear that cheap treatments like cognitive behavior therapy and Prozac will usually do the trick. CBT works about half the time, and SSRIs, about 75 percent. And if not more effective, they are certainly more fun than 17th- and 18th-century cures, which leaned toward enemas and worse. John Hill's 1766 I'll-give-you-something-to-cry-about prescription is particularly unpleasant: You'll stop fretting over your imaginary aches and pains, he argues, if you develop honest-to-goodness scurvy, and your bleeding hemorrhoids won't worry you at all once you catch leprosy.

33   In the past year, I've gotten much better. There was exactly one doctor visit, for a very real and completely gross sebaceous cyst. Though I still surf from time to time, I no longer have WebMD bookmarked; and while it's true that I received both a Physicians' Desk Reference and Stedman's Medical Dictionary for Hanukkah, I mostly use them to diagnose other people.

34   I'm not entirely sure why things improved. Maybe my hypochondria responded to CBT and SSRIs, or maybe it responded to HBO and MTV–I got really, really great cable, and this has proved a wonderful distraction.

35   And this, I realize, is part of it. John Hill was right: you don't notice the bleeding hemorrhoid when you get leprosy. You don't notice the boredom and depression and the fear that your life is completely off course when you have a funny twinge to preoccupy you instead. And you don't notice the funny twinge when Meredith Baxter Birney is fighting off both alcoholism and would-be kidnappers on the E! network.

36   I'm particularly fond of the medical shows. Because I'm still susceptible to infection by TV, I tend to favor shows about conditions I'm unlikely to get: dwarfism, gigantism, inguinal hernias, or that genetic anomaly where you grow a full head of hair on your face.

37   Just now I noticed a little, pinkish pocket of fluid under my eye. It could be an infection, I suppose, or maybe something deadly bit me in the night. And I could spend the rest of the morning on the Web, on the phone with my doctor or my dad, trying to figure out what it is, and how long I have left. But at eleven The Learning Channel has a special on the morbidly obese, followed by eight hours of maternity ward emergencies. After dinner, I'll watch a show about Munchausen moms and another about cataplexy, then go to sleep by the light of plastic surgery disasters.

38   I'll probably be just fine.

WHAT DID THE WRITER SAY AND WHAT DID YOU THINK?

1. How does the author follow this book's advice about getting her reader's attention?
2. Does Traig give a traditional definition of hypochondria? Why or why not? If she does, where does it appear?
3. In paragraph 21, the author lists the illnesses she suffers from, in addition to hypochondria. Are you inclined to believe her? Why or why not?
4. How can hypochondria be treated?
5. What difficulties are raised for hypochondriacs by the Internet?

HOW DID THE WRITER SAY IT?

1. Traig uses a lot of technical medical terms in her essay, most often without defining them. Why does she do this? Does it make her essay hard to understand? Is she being lazy, or is she making a point?
2. It would be easy to find the author's list of illnesses and complaints annoying. How does she keep you on her side? How effective is this technique?
3. Should we be worried about the bacterial meningitis the author says she has in paragraph 26? How do you know?

What About <u>Your</u> Writing?

In paragraph 15, when Traig talks about plant allergies and then mentions that the "scariest plant of all, of course, was the family tree" she's making a pun. She takes the standard expression, "family tree" and gives it a new twist by comparing the metaphocial tree to literal oleanders and pines. Suddenly the phrase is no longer just about tracing your family history. It's powerfully tied to Traig's fears about allergies, illnesses, and poisons. An everyday phrase has been reworked to make a special point, to fit in with a particular purpose, to acquire extra density. She does it again in paragraph 16, when she discusses the "organ recital" that her musician relative enjoyed giving. Opinions may differ, of course, on how successful this device is. Some people, too, probably still accept unthinkingly the tired old cliché that puns and word plays are the lowest form of literature. In fact, however, writers as diverse as Shakespeare and Thoreau have been entranced by the exciting stylistic possibilities of word plays.

e.e. cummings, the American poet, once wrote that poetry should do to you what the old burlesque gag does:

> Question: Would you hit a woman with a baby?
> Answer: No, I'd hit her with a brick.

cummings' view is that poetry should fool around with words, should try to astonish and delight the reader by revealing previously unnoticed possibilities of language. Although prose is ordinarily more sedate than poetry, it too can profit from the touch of originality, the fresh slant, the new twist that fooling around with words can sometimes contribute.

Most frequently, word plays provide a welcome note of humor. "The orchestra played Beethoven last night. Beethoven lost." *A Time* magazine movie review once described a wagon train under attack as being "in the Siouxp."

Word plays lend themselves to satire, too. In Shakespeare's *Henry IV, Part I,* Glendower, a braggart with mystical inclinations, is talking to Hotspur, an honest, downright soldier:

> Glendower: I can call spirits from the vasty deep.
> Hotspur: Why, so can I . . . But will they come when you do call for them?

Other word plays can be entirely serious. In *Walden,* Thoreau simply treats a common figurative expression with unexpected literalness:

> If you have built castles in the air, your work need not be lost; that is where they should be. Now put the foundations under them.

There's no compulsion to experiment with word plays. They're risky. Unsuccessful word plays are always damaging because they call attention to themselves. They should generally be used in moderation; the writer wants to give an impression of being clever, but not of being a show-off. If you have neither the temperament nor the knack for word plays, you should avoid them completely. With all these cautions, however, a distinctive style helps capture your reader's attention, and skillful fooling around with words can help create a distinctive style.

CATACHRESIS
Patricia O'Hara

Patricia O'Hara is a professor of English at Franklin and Marshall College. She has published poetry, fiction, and nonfiction, and has served as the editor of the academic journal, *Nineteenth Century Studies*.

✓ WORDS TO CHECK:

perennially (paragraph 1)	malform (4)	orthography (4)
cognitive (2)	vestigial (4)	dioramas (5)
perforce (3)	stenography (4)	empathy (9)

1 Irony: college English professor, PhD 1989, perennially (perrenially?) bad speller, conscripted to serve as judge for the Lancaster, Pennsylvania 48th Annual Intelligencer Journal Spelling Bee.

2   I've dodged this town/gown relations-building task for seventeen years by responding to the request for a volunteer by squinting and looking off into the distance, as if trying to recall a previous engagement–a really important one. I know that spelling bee judges aren't actually expected to know how to spell: you have the correct spelling of the words on a list in front of you. But so impaired is my cognitive spelling function that I worry that I'm going to be so worried about being exposed as Dr. Fraud that I might not see the words correctly or that I might develop (develope?) situational anxiety-dyslexia. Because there are certain commonly-used words–roughly seven or eight hundred of them–that I never have been able to spell and I never will be able to spell because I can't trust my spelling instincts because I don't have spelling instincts. Think: developing (developping?), relevance (relevence?), pharmaceutical (pharmacuetical?).

3   I have perforce become a spelling relativist. Brocolli or broccoli? Whatever. It's a green vegetable that's a principal ingredient in Szechuan chicken
and broccoli/brocolli.

4   I compensate for bad spelling with bad penmanship. When in doubt, I
carefully malform my letters so they appear to be written in haste by a woman
with way more interesting things to do than carefully form her letters. Bad penmanship isn't a big problem anymore given that one is so rarely called upon
to handwrite. In fact, handwriting and spelling have a lot in common: they're
both vestigial skills. The dictation machine killed stenography, the typewriter
killed Palmer penmanship drills, and spell check programs are killing orthog-
raphy. You won't catch me mourning.

5   So from the start, I'm a very bad candidate to judge a spelling bee, a competition that I find about as useful as those crafts projects my son was assigned
for homework in elementary school: the construction of dioramas illustrating
the forest's ecosystem, the baking of antebellum johnny cakes, and the sewing
of hand puppets of Roald Dahl characters. "Why can't we just order this stuff
online?" was my persistent reaction to those assignments, and it still seems a
not unreasonable question.

6   Here's another: why can't we just teach kids where to find Check Spelling
on the pop-up menu then invite them to read poetry in their spare time. Why
encourage middle-schoolers to memorize words like:*

- "aphasia" (the loss or impairment of the power to use words as symbols
  of ideas)
- "fantoccini" (puppets moved by strings or mechanical devices)
- "oculogyric" (relating to or involving circular movements of the eyeballs)

7   But I've signed on for the Bee and it's a Very Big Deal in these parts because
the winner is rewarded with an all-expenses paid trip to the Scripps National
Spelling Bee in Washington, DC. So it matters to the little memorizers. A lot.

8   And irony is not the appropriate posture for the judge.

9   Posture: a conscious mental or outward behavioral attitude. Sentence:
The professor adopted a respectful posture when she entered Conestoga Valley Middle School at 5:45 PM on March 10, 2006 to serve as judge for the
48th Annual Intelligencer Journal Spelling Bee. She did, however, experience
authentic empathy for the thirty-six contestants who "spelled down," or mis-
spelled words while standing in the spotlight on a stage at a microphone in a
large, middle-school auditorium in central Pennsylvania.

10   And in case you're curious, the winning word was "balmony": a showy
perennial herb of the marshy lands of eastern and central North America that
has flowers with the lower parts creamy white and the upper parts pale pink
to deep purple.

11   The word that knocked the runner-up out of the competition was—and this I swear is true**—"catachresis": the misuse of words.

12   Indeed.

*Actual words, selected from the © 2006 Scripps National Spelling Bee Guide.
**See Lancaster Intelligencer Journal, March 11, 2006.

WHAT DID THE WRITER SAY AND WHAT DID YOU THINK?

1. Why is it particularly embarrassing for O'Hara to be a bad speller? Do you think she's really embarrassed?
2. Why does the author argue that spelling is a vestigial skill? Do you think she is correct?
3. O'Hara seems to find the word *catachresis* an important one in relation to the spelling bee. She uses it for her title and mentions that it is the word that knocks the runner-up out of competition. What is so significant about this word for her essay topic?
4. Why does the author discuss her son's elementary school craft projects?

HOW DID THE WRITER SAY IT?

1. How does the writer demonstrate her considerable intelligence despite her difficulties with spelling?
2. Explain the "Dr. Fraud" pun in paragraph 2.
3. Paragraphs 1 and 10 are parodies of a particular kind of definition. What do they parody and why?
4. Why does O'Hara capitalize "Very Big Deal" in paragraph 7?

What About Your Writing?

The dancers in the musical *Gypsy* know that in order to succeed, "You gotta have a gimmick." Like the dancers, writers will often use a gimmick, a trick, or a bit of schtick, to keep their readers entertained and interested. O'Hara does this very skillfully as she gives multiple examples of her spelling difficulties.

Rather than just telling us that she's an English professor who is an embarrassingly bad speller, O'Hara gives lots of chances to see what a bad speller she is. In the first two paragraphs of her essay, whenever she uses a word that challenges her spelling capabilities, she invites us to struggle along with her by showing us, in parentheses, another way that she thinks the word might possibly be spelled. Is it prennially or perrenially? relevance or relevence? By the time O'Hara is done with us, we probably can't remember either.

And that's the point of her gimmick. She wants us to experience the difficulties of being a bad speller, not just hear about them.

O'Hara's gimmick works so well because she uses it with restraint. You'll notice that after the flurry of parenthetical misspellings in the first two paragraphs, they drop out of the essay entirely. O'Hara knows that the joke would have gotten old and lost its charm if she overused it. By the third paragraph she's made her point and she's made us laugh, and she can move on to the rest of her essay. O'Hara also backs up her gimmick with an interesting topic, strong writing, and good supporting detail in the rest of her essay. She's got a gimmick and she uses it well. But a gimmick isn't all she's got. If you try a gimmick of your own, make sure it's not all you have either.

CHAPTER 9½
Office Hours: Deadlines

"I had to work."

"I had a math test."

"My kids were sick."

"My kids were sick, and I was even sicker."

"My car broke down."

"I couldn't get the books I wanted from the library."

"I had computer trouble."

"I had a game . . . a performance . . . a practice . . . a rehearsal."

There are infinite reasons for not handing in a piece of writing on time. Some of them are legitimate. Some are inventive. Some of them will get you sympathy and maybe even an extension from your instructor. But no matter how true they are, no matter how valid, no matter how convincing, all these explanations do just one thing. They avoid a deadline.

Nobody likes deadlines. Everybody has them. You do. Your instructors do. Your bosses do. And every author from J.K. Rowling down to the most obscure writer of obituaries for the tiniest small town newspaper has them and has to learn how to deal with them.

The reasons for learning to deal with deadlines are obvious. While you're in school, getting material in on time helps your grade, keeps you organized, saves you from being overwhelmed at the end of the term, and shows your instructors that you care enough to be responsible about your work. It also helps keep your instructors on schedule so they're not grading your papers at 4 A.M. after a rough week. (Just imagine what that can do to your grade!) Once you're out of school, getting tasks done on time helps you develop a reputation as a competent and professional employee. It means you won't find yourself working weekends when you could be at home relaxing. It means you'll get paid. It means you'll keep your job.

Despite all these excellent reasons for learning to cope with deadlines, some of us aren't that good at it. Some of us will do anything to try to wriggle out of a deadline, and all the while the deadline just keeps coming.

Some writers invent distractions. Drop in on these folks two days before a piece is due and you'll find them cleaning closets, making roast chicken, partitioning their hard drives, doing anything but writing. They plan to write eventually, of course, but when they finally do, it's much too late to write anything good and far too late to even think about revising it.

Delayers keep just as busy. They buy stylish folders and high-bond paper. They read their source material so often they have it memorized. They make tidy stacks of note cards. They alphabetize. They too plan to write eventually, but right now they're just not ready. When they finally do get started, guess what? Too late to be any good.

And then there are those who despair. One way or another these people say they're doomed. They just weren't born to be writers. They just can't get inspired. Things aren't going well, and it's not their fault. They plan to write eventually, of course, but first they have to feel better.

Distractions, delay, and despair won't help you with a deadline. What will? A desk. A chair. And the seat of your pants.

If you're one of the many with deadline troubles, why not bribe yourself a little? Try setting intermediate deadlines before the actual piece is due. Promise yourself a night out if you have an outline and an introduction put together one week before the paper is due. See how far ahead you'll feel if you get a page or two written before you go to work or go to bed at night. Try writing a paragraph a day, every day, at lunch. Try doing your homework while your kids, or your kid sisters, do theirs.

Deadlines don't have to be your enemies. Learn to use them as a source of motivation, as a spur for your work, as the drive that pushes you to put something down on paper before the last possible moment. You'll feel better. You'll write better. You'll please your instructors and your bosses. And you'll sleep better at night, knowing that even if the kids get a rash, or you get the flu, or your car battery dies, your paper is finished and ready to go.

Argumentation

CHAPTER

10

In this chapter, argumentation does not refer to fighting or bickering. It refers to providing logical reasons in support of a particular point of view. In that sense, this whole book has been about argumentation. It has urged you from the start to form a thesis and devote your primary energies to proving or supporting it.

The argumentation readings in this chapter have two outstanding characteristics. First, they employ no particular pattern of development consistently; a paragraph that describes may be followed by a paragraph that compares and contrasts and another that explores cause-and-effect relationships. To that extent, the readings here can be viewed simply as readings that refuse to fit neatly into one of the patterns dealt with in previous chapters. This mixture of patterns is a healthy antidote to excessive rigidity of thought. Not all subjects lend themselves to only one pattern, and in such cases it's as absurd to write in only one pattern as it would be to play a round of golf with only one club.

The second characteristic of these readings is that they rely, to a far greater extent than any others studied so far, on the techniques of formal logic. Formal logic generally combines two ways of thinking: induction and deduction.

Induction is the process of arriving at general conclusions by studying individual cases. All the cats we have seen or read about have whiskers. As far as we can determine, all the cats our friends and acquaintances have seen or read about also have whiskers. We therefore conclude that all cats have whiskers. We haven't come close to surveying all the cats in the world, so to reach our conclusion, we must make an *inductive leap*. We work on the unproven assumption that what is true of some or many is true of all. Induction is often the only possible way to approach certain subjects, and it can be extremely convincing. Ultimately, however, the final step in the inductive process must be a leap, an intelligent guess, not proof in the strictest sense of the word.

Doctors use induction when, seeing a child with a fever and a particular kind of rash, they conclude that the child has chicken pox, since all the other children the doctors have known with those symptoms have turned out to have chicken pox. (The same symptoms could be those of an obscure tropical disease—just as some cats somewhere may have no whiskers—but the doctors are justified in making their inductive leap.) Customers in a supermarket use induction when they decide no longer to buy milk there. The three most recent times they shopped there, the milk they bought was sour, and by induction they conclude that milk supplies in that store are likely to be of poor quality. Readers use induction when, having been bored by three of a novelist's books, they conclude that the novelist is a boring writer.

Skillful induction is mostly a matter of seeing to it that conclusions about a group are drawn only from a study of well-chosen members of that group. Chapter 4 on examples discusses this issue in detail (page 98).

Deduction is the process of arriving at a conclusion by starting with a general premise or assumption instead of with a specific instance. The primary tool in deductive reasoning is the *syllogism,* a three-part argument consisting of two premises and a conclusion:

All Rembrandt paintings are great works of art.

The Night Watch is a Rembrandt painting.

Therefore, *The Night Watch* is a great work of art.

All doctors are quacks.

Smith is a doctor.

Therefore, Smith is a quack.

The syllogism is a tool for analyzing the validity of an argument. You'll rarely find a formal syllogism outside of textbooks on logic. Mostly, you'll find *enthymemes,* abbreviated syllogisms with one or more of the parts unstated:

The Night Watch is by Rembrandt, isn't it? And Rembrandt is a great painter, isn't he?

Look, Smith is a doctor. He must be a quack.

Translating such statements into a syllogism enables the logic to be examined more coolly and clearly than it otherwise could be. If both premises in a syllogism are true and the reasoning process from one part of the syllogism to the other is valid, the conclusions will be proven. No leap or intelligent guess will be required; the conclusion will be inescapable.

Few arguments worth going into, of course, are open-and-shut cases. The premises are often debatable, to mention just one possible source of difficulty. (*Are* all doctors quacks? Didn't Rembrandt ever have *any* off days?) Argumentation, therefore, usually combines deduction and induction. A deductive argument, for example, will often have to call on induction to establish the soundness of its premises. A reader has been bored by three books a particular novelist has written and inductively arrives at a conclusion about that novelist's work. That inductive conclusion can now serve, in turn, as the first premise of a syllogism:

Books by Marcel Proust are likely to bore me.

Swann's Way is a book by Marcel Proust.

Therefore, *Swann's Way* is likely to bore me.

In addition to relying on formal logic, good argumentation, though it usually does not limit itself to one special rhetorical pattern, does require a special pattern of manners. The readers have not yet, in theory, made up their minds and need to be convinced not only that the writer's argument is logical but also that the writer is a reasonable, fair-minded person.

GO EASY ON UNIVERSALS— QUALIFY WHEN APPROPRIATE

Reasonable people can disagree. Logic beats chaos any day, but logic cannot create total uniformity of opinions. Be moderate with sweeping generalizations that use—or imply—terms like *all, every, always, never, nobody*. Qualifying terms like *usually, often, perhaps, it seems likely, probably, seldom, rarely, almost* can be helpful in establishing a climate of reason, a sense that the writer is fully aware of the complexities and ambiguities of human experience. Don't assume from these comments that you should not express strongly held views in a strong way or that obvious truths should be expressed with mealymouthed hypocrisy. Assume only that most writers are sometimes tempted to be carried away by enthusiasm for their own ideas into making gross overstatements—and the good writer successfully resists the temptation.

GIVE CONSIDERATION TO DIFFERING OPINIONS

After starting with a cool, impartial presentation of the issue and your way of dealing with it, present any opposition to your ideas fairly. Sometimes you may even wish to begin by outlining your opponents' point of view. Refute the opposition when you can. When you can't, concede that the opposition has a good point. Argumentation that shows awareness of only one viewpoint will rarely gain a reader's respect.

BE CAUTIOUS WITH ABUSE AND RIDICULE

You may consider some of the opposition's arguments to be foolish or even dangerous. Moreover, one of the hazards built into any piece of argumentation is that it may commit itself so completely to the precision of logic that it reads as if it were written by a computer instead of by a human being. Though there's no law against introducing humor or even passion into argumentation, be careful that such elements do not sabotage the essential logical strengths of your paper. Be particularly careful that any irresistible abuse or ridicule is directed against the ideas of your opponents, not the opponents themselves.

DEVOTE MOST OF YOUR ATTENTION TO SUPPORTING YOUR VIEW, NOT ADVOCATING IT

You're trying to show that your opinion is logical. You're not trying, except in a minor way, to preach or to inspire. The introduction and conclusion will express your basic opinion. By and large, the rest of the paper will discuss your reasons for holding that opinion or for disagreeing with arguments against it.

SOME COMMON LOGICAL FALLACIES

Very briefly, here are some of the most common logical fallacies. Good argumentation depends on sound logic, and it may be valuable to have a handy guide to possible pitfalls:

- Hasty Generalization. Not enough examples or untypical examples. (See page 98)
- Post Hoc, Ergo Propter Hoc. "After this, therefore because of this." For further discussion, see pages 196–197.

  > I failed the test after I walked under the ladder; therefore, I failed the test because I walked under the ladder.

- Either/Or. A writer presents a case as if there were only two alternatives and tries to force the reader to choose between them. Life usually offers more options than that:

  > Either you're for me or against me.

  > Either we abolish automobiles or we destroy our planet through pollution.

- Non Sequitur. "It does not follow"–often the result of omitting a necessary step in the thought process or of taking wild emotional flights in which no thought process ever existed:

  > I despise Professor Jones, so I'm never going to read another book as long as I live.

  > We all want to abolish war and poverty and racism. How could we possibly care who wins the football game?

- Ignoring the Question. Instead of dealing with the topic under discussion, the writer or speaker becomes unintentionally sidetracked or deliberately creates a diversion. The question can be ignored in a number of ways. Among them are:

– *"Ad Hominem" Argument.* Arguing "to the man," attacking the person who raised the issue rather than dealing with the issue itself:

> How dare Senator Arnold advocate population control when she herself has six children?

Senator Arnold's failure to practice what she preaches has nothing to do with the merits of population control.

– *Setting Up a Straw Man.* Accusing one's opponents of saying something they never said or intended to say and then attacking them for saying it:

> You allege this movie has too much sex and violence, but people like you who want censorship are a menace to the basic constitutional rights of free American citizens.

– *Begging.* Assuming the truth of a debatable point and basing the rest of the argument on that shaky assumption:

> What prison sentence shall be given those who have systematically concealed the truth about alien invasions of our planet?

Before deciding on prison terms, the writer must first offer convincing evidence that there have been invasions and cover-ups.

– *Shifting the Burden of Proof.* As in law, "He who asserts must prove." It is not logical argument to declare:

> I believe the government is run by secret foreign agents, and nobody can prove that I'm wrong.

- **Argument by Analogy.** An analogy is an extended comparison. It can be valuable in clarifying a difficult point or dramatizing an abstract idea. *It can never prove anything.* No matter how many suggestive similarities there may be, they can never be more than suggestive, since there must also be differences.

– *Analogy Used to Clarify or Dramatize.*

> Finding a cure for cancer is much like finding a cure for inflation. The exact causes of the diseases are shrouded in mystery; medication carries the risk of unpredictable side effects, but without medication the illnesses grow beyond control; cures are increasingly difficult the longer they are delayed; and the experts always–but always–disagree.

– *Invalid Argument by Analogy: Analogy Used to Prove.*

> The Chairman has been unjustly criticized in this country for executing his political opponents in order to create a better society. Surely, one

of the oldest truths is that you can't make an omelet without breaking a few eggs.

It's too bad the beautiful shells have to be cracked open. There's a terrible mess for a little while. But the final result is well worth the effort, and only fools would waste tears over the sad fate of the poor little eggs. The Chairman has the right recipe for a greater tomorrow, and those who don't understand his techniques should stay out of the kitchen.

The second analogy assumes that a few similarities between breaking eggs and killing political opponents mean that the two actions are alike in all other respects. The writer thus attempts to prove that because one action is justified the other must be justified, too. Argument by analogy ignores all differences. Here, for example, nonhuman things are being compared to humans, nonliving things to living, breaking to killing, and so forth.

- Faultily Constructed Syllogisms.

  –*Introduction of a New Term in the Conclusion.* The two terms in the conclusion must have appeared previously in the premises. Note how the following syllogism introduces a new term in the conclusion and destroys all pretense at logic:

  > All teachers are cruel.
  >
  > Mr. Jones is a teacher.
  >
  > Therefore, Mr. Jones should be fired.

  –*Reasoning from Negative Premises.* Two negative premises can never lead to any valid conclusion:

  > No human being is free from prejudice.
  >
  > Fido is not a human being.
  >
  > Therefore . . .

  –*Shift in Meaning of a Term.* Some syllogisms are rendered invalid because a word has changed in meaning from one part of the syllogism to another:

  > Indian leaders live in India.
  >
  > Sitting Bull is an Indian leader.
  >
  > Therefore, Sitting Bull lives in India.

In the first premise, *Indian leaders* referred to leaders of the nation in Asia. In the second premise, the same term shifted meaning and referred to a leader of Native Americans.

–*Improper Relationship Between Terms.* A well-constructed syllogism establishes relationships that make a particular conclusion inevitable. The following syllogism does not:

> Sexists refuse to hire women.
>
> Jones refuses to hire women.
>
> Therefore, Jones is a sexist.

The first premise does not establish that sexists are the *only* ones who refuse to hire women. Jones could theoretically be an ardent supporter of women's rights but be under strict orders–orders he despises–to hire only men. He could be the manager of a men's professional basketball team. Jones could also be the name of a six-week-old puppy. *All* syllogisms constructed with the same relationship between terms as this one will be logically invalid. Even if the conclusion is "true," it will be true by accident, not by logic. (Jones *could* be a sexist, after all.)

> Politicians are corrupt.
>
> Simmons is corrupt.
>
> Therefore, Simmons is a politician.
>
> Baptists are not Methodists.
>
> She is not a Methodist.
>
> Therefore, she is a Baptist.

WRITING SUGGESTIONS FOR ARGUMENTATION ESSAYS

Employing the techniques of formal argumentation, attack or defend one of the following numbered statements:

1. American drivers will never renounce their cars for mass transit systems.
2. The celibacy requirement for the Roman Catholic priesthood should be eliminated.
3. Most people get married (*or divorced*) for foolish reasons.
4. The world's worst bore is _____.
5. Parents who try to impose their values on young people are the only ones young people respect.
6. The F grade should be abolished.
7. The greatest baseball (*or other sport*) player of all time is _____.
8. Elderly people should be required to take road tests before having their driving licenses renewed.
9. The greatest holiday of all is _____.

10. Life is a constant process of discovering that older people have been idiots.
11. The worst show on television is _____.
12. Required English courses should be abolished.
13. Students should have a voice in the hiring and firing of teachers.
14. Married couples should not be allowed to have more than two children.
15. Renting an apartment makes better financial sense than buying a house.
16. Cats make better pets than dogs.
17. The manufacture of cigarettes should be prohibited.
18. Automatic advancement to the next grade level must be eliminated from our schools.

VISUAL PROMPT

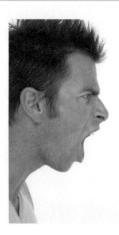

Writing Prompt

Argumentation does not refer to fighting or bickering. A good way to develop a list of topics for possible argumentation essays is to think about arguments or debates that you have had recently, no matter how trivial or important. What are a few recent debates you've engaged in? How would you restate them as thesis statements for argumentation essays?

STUDENT ESSAY: SING IT WHEN IT COUNTS
Ben Ruggiero

Thesis: "The Star-Spangled Banner" should not be sung before athletic events.

    I. No logical connection between patriotism and athletes

    II. No logical connection between patriotism and audience

III. Refutation of "Part of the Spectacle" argument
    A. National anthem is too important
    B. Other music makes more sense

Conclusion: We should restore dignity to the singing of the national anthem.

I'd like to have the singing of our national anthem saved for patriotic occasions and other serious ceremonies. I think it's stupid and offensive to sing it before athletic events.

To prevent misunderstanding, let me state right away that I love and respect our national anthem. Some people complain that it's impossible to sing. Some say the words are old-fashioned and hard to understand. Some insist that it could easily be replaced by patriotic songs with better tunes. They may be right, or partly right, but what does that have to do with love? My parents are old-fashioned and hard to understand, too, but I have no intention of trading them in. My point is that I love and respect "The Star-Spangled Banner" so much—as I know millions of others do—that I want the travesty of singing it at so many unsuitable times to stop.

What is the possible connection between patriotic pride and two boxers trying to beat each other up? The question answers itself. The more a boxer thinks about "the rockets' red glare," the more likely he is to have his lights put out by his opponent. Why pretend otherwise? Do we seriously expect—or even want—two teams of competing millionaires on the gridiron or ballpark or basketball court or hockey rink to be thinking about an old war instead of a current game? I have nothing against the athletes. They're out there to play, not to show off their patriotism, however real it may be. If their minds are on higher things instead of on using their physical skills to win the game, they are playing under false pretenses.

Well, some people may suggest, perhaps the music is for the crowd rather than the players. But check out the crowd. How often have you seen anyone accept the invitation to "join in singing" our national anthem? The last time I looked, I doubt if one in a hundred even bothered to move his or her lips, much less actually sing. How many stand at anything even approaching attention? These members of the crowd are not expressing disrespect for their country, in my opinion. They just sense the complete absence of any connection between love of country and attending a ball game. They recognize a sham, a pointless ritual, when they see one—or hear one.

I suppose it's possible to argue that the playing of the national anthem isn't directly about patriotic feelings. It's part of the entertainment, part of the spectacle. I'd reply, first, that if that's true, it's exactly what's wrong. The last thing our national anthem should be is entertainment. It should be special, should compel attention and respect. Second, if you want entertaining music of some kind to add to the occasion, let's face the realities of the event. The event is not held to glorify America but to see if the team of one city, state, or region is better than another's. We already have plenty of good music for that. College fight songs work fine, for example. If spectacle and entertainment are what we want, when the Jets play the Chiefs in football we can have the band strike up with "The Sidewalks of New York" and "Everything's Up-to-Date in Kansas City." When the Atlanta Braves play the Chicago Cubs we can cheer to the strains of "Georgia on My Mind" and "My Kind of Town."

One serious exception to what I've been advocating occurs to me. I'll readily grant that playing the national anthem is appropriate when the service academies compete against each other. Participants in those games are planning careers in which they will put their lives at risk for their country, and the music is much more than an empty formality to them.

I say let's restore some importance and dignity to the playing and singing of our national anthem. A presidential inauguration. Visits from foreign heads of state. Military parades. A veteran's funeral. People will stand at attention without being asked, and they'll sing the words, too, even if they get some of them wrong. Our national anthem should be saved for special occasions and be a source of pride, not a meaningless ritual.

THANKSGIVING'S NO TURKEY

Robert W. Gardner

Robert W. Gardner, a communications executive in Washington, DC, uses humor as well as logic to glorify one great American tradition and to denigrate another. The subject may be a matter of taste in more ways than one.

✓ Words to Check:

redemption (paragraph 2)　　　decamped (10)

1　I have never had to return a Thanksgiving gift. Of course not, you say, there are no Thanksgiving gifts. Exactly. That's just one reason I vastly prefer the coming celebration of turkey to its neighbor just down the calendar, Christmas.

2　　Don't get me wrong. I love Christmas. The joy of anticipation in little children. The warmth of gathered families. The promise of redemption and salvation embodied in the religious celebration. I just can't stand what we've done to Christmas. The traffic at the malls. The chaos. The pressure. The endless advertising urging us to give, to spend, to buy happiness. The bills.

3　　Thanksgiving is so easy. When was the last time you saw a neighbor standing in the snow trying to string Thanksgiving lights around his house? Do people shell out sixty-five bucks for a dead Thanksgiving tree for their family room? Do they sit hour after hour, addressing Thanksgiving cards they bought on sale back in May? Who, late on Thanksgiving Eve, will be driven to thoughts of suicide, murder or at least divorce upon reading the words "some assembly required"?

4　　Thanksgiving is more like an old friend come to visit. There's a knock on the door, you greet each other warmly, and soon it seems you've never been apart. Here are the complete instructions for a Happy Thanksgiving: Roast a turkey, make way too much other food, and top it off with one of three or four approved desserts. You can watch a little football, or not. Take a walk. Loaf. Whatever. No one expects you to decorate the house, make a killer table centerpiece, invite the president's entire cabinet to your cocktail party, or stroll the neighborhood singing Thanksgiving carols.

5   At work, no one gets looped at the office Thanksgiving party or chases the secretaries into the storage rooms. Working couples don't have to wrestle with which party to attend (and which boss to offend) if their office wingdings are on the same day.

6   Christmas can come any day of the week, and does. Thanksgiving is always on Thursday. Most folks get Friday off. A four-day weekend every year! No other holiday can make this offer.

7   Thanksgiving is budget-friendly. If you are invited out, bring the hosts a bottle of wine or a nice dessert. That's it. No gifts you can't afford. No endless worrying about what so-and-so got you last year or whether Grandma really wants another a) robe, b) toaster, or c) bottle of cologne.

8   There's the story one son told of giving his dad a bottle of Old Spice aftershave every year for 30-plus years, only to find half of them, unused, in a dresser drawer after his dad passed away. True story.

9   Why do you think retail chains have fiscal years that end Jan. 31? Because they do half or more of their annual sales in the days before Christmas. And who do you think buys all that stuff? You and me. Know anyone who went into debt counseling after a pre-Thanksgiving buying binge? Me neither.

10   Despite these clear advantages, Thanksgiving gets no respect. Oh sure, the kids bring home a picture they drew of the pilgrims or a one-eyed turkey. But everyone understands these are just warmups for the major Christmas art push about to follow. Thanksgiving was once the kick-off for the Christmas buying season, but even that distinction has decamped for a spot nearer to Halloween. The Thanksgiving parades can't hold a candle to the ones on Jan. 1. It's tough going for Turkey Day. So what should we do with Thanksgiving?

11   I think we should celebrate Thanksgiving as the last holiday that hasn't been taken away from us. No cute bunny. No speeches celebrating democracy. No collection of seven nearby presidential birthdays. No pressure to make this a "Thanksgiving to remember." Just four days off and one really good meal. And no kids waking you at 5 A.M. to see if some turkey's come down the chimney.

WHAT DID THE WRITER SAY AND WHAT DID YOU THINK?

1. Why are Thanksgiving and Christmas presented as rivals? Would it be as effective to write an essay on Thanksgiving versus the Fourth of July?
2. Does the author's argument rely primarily on induction or deduction? Explain.

3. Many of the author's reasons for preferring Thanksgiving to Christmas can be expressed in the sentence "Thanksgiving is so easy" (paragraph 3). Explain. Elsewhere (paragraph 11) Gardner refers to Thanksgiving as "the last holiday that hasn't been taken away from us." Explain.
4. Some readers may think that many of the author's observations about Christmas violate this book's warning to "be cautious with abuse and ridicule" (page 295). Other readers may feel personally offended by the many apparent put-downs of Christmas. Where does the author take steps to soothe the feelings of such readers?

HOW DID THE WRITER SAY IT?

1. This book's discussion of argumentation essays noted that they "employ no particular pattern of development consistently" (page 293). Still, "Thanksgiving's No Turkey" uses one pattern far more than any other. Which pattern?
2. How is the story in paragraph 8 about aftershave gifts relevant to the rest of the essay?
3. Explain the double meaning of "turkey" in the last sentence.

What About Your Writing?

Often, the most difficult part of writing an essay is trying to decide on a topic. An inexperienced writer can spend hours looking for a topic that engages his or her strongest beliefs and fiercest passions. Writers like Robert W. Gardner, however, know that sometimes the best essays come from taking a stand even when you don't really have one. Gardner, for example, probably realizes that the issue of Thanksgiving versus Christmas isn't a case of good versus evil, purity versus corruption, and the forces of light versus the forces of darkness. However, you certainly can't tell that from reading his essay.

Gardner has taken a firm stand on an issue just for the fun of it, just for the sake of producing an entertaining and original essay. He could just as easily have written an essay proving that Christmas was far better than Thanksgiving, or that cats are superior to dogs, that day is better than night, linguine better than macaroni, up better than down, or purple preferable to pink. None of these are terribly serious essay topics. None of them occupy the thoughts and emotions of the deepest thinkers. But they could all make interesting essays to write and to read.

While choosing to write an essay in support of something you don't really believe in—and may not really care about—might sound hypocritical, it is actually very good mental exercise. Debating teams, law students, and successful politicians know that it's good practice to try to structure logical and convincing arguments about seemingly outlandish topics. If you can learn to convince a reader that dark chocolate is superior to milk chocolate, you have learned the necessary techniques to convince them that the tax plan you are presenting is better than the one your opponent has suggested. The next time you have a writing assignment, rather than spending hours trying to find a deep and important subject for your essay, why not see if you can convince your instructor that beagles are better than dachshunds, or that bow ties look better than neckties? You might just find that you end up writing a livelier and more effective essay than when you take on weightier subjects.

DISTRACTING MISS DAISY

John Staddon

John Staddon is a professor of biology, neurobiology, psychological, and brain sciences at Duke University. He has written extensively on these topics. This article, which combines his professional interest in adaptive behavior and learning with a personal take on driving in America, was first published in *The Atlantic.*

✓ Words to Check:

epitomizes (paragraph 1)	innocuous (9)	engendering (19)
paradoxically (4)	overabundance (10)	correlation (22)
multitude (4)	counterproductive (11)	causation (22)
eponymous (6)	affix (12)	prevalent (22)
fatalistic (6)	optimum (19)	

1   There is a stretch of North Glebe Road, in Arlington, Virginia, that epitomizes the American approach to road safety. It's a sloping curve, beginning on a four-lane divided highway and running down to Chain Bridge, on the Potomac River. Most drivers, absent a speed limit, would probably take the curve at 30 or 35 mph in good weather. But it has a 25-mph speed limit, vigorously enforced. As you approach the curve, a sign with flashing lights suggests slowing further, to 15 mph. A little later, another sign makes the same suggestion. *Great!* the neighborhood's more cautious residents might think. *We're being protected.* But I believe policies like this in fact make us all less safe.

2   I grew up in Great Britain, and over the past five years I've split my time between England and the United States. I've long found driving in the U.S. to be both annoying and boring. Annoying because of lots of unnecessary waits at stop signs and stoplights, and because of the need to obsess over speed when not waiting. Boring, scenery apart, because to avoid speeding tickets, I feel compelled to set the cruise control on long trips, driving at the same mind-numbing rate, regardless of road conditions.

3   Relatively recently–these things take a remarkably long time to sink in–I began to notice something else. Often when I return to the U.S. (usually to a suburban area in North Carolina's Research Triangle), I see a fender bender or two within a few days. Yet I almost never see accidents in the U.K.

4   This surprised me, since the roads I drive here are generally wider, better marked, and less crowded than in the parts of England that I know best. And so I came to reflect on the mundane details of traffic-control policies in Great Britain and the United States. And I began to think that the American system of traffic control, with its many signs and stops, and with its specific rules tailored to every bend in the road, has had the unintended consequence of causing more accidents than it prevents. Paradoxically, almost every new sign put up in the U.S. probably makes drivers a little safer on the stretch of road it guards. But collectively, the forests of signs along American roadways, and the multitude of rules to look out for, are quite deadly.

5   Economists and ecologists sometimes speak of the "tragedy of the commons"–the way rational individual actions can collectively reduce the common good when resources are limited. How this applies to traffic safety may not be obvious. It's easy to understand that although it pays the selfish herdsman to add one more sheep to common grazing land, the result may be overgrazing, and less for everyone. But what is the limited resource, the commons, in the case of driving? It's attention. Attending to a sign competes with attending to the road. The more you look for signs, for police, and at your speedometer, the less attentive you will be to traffic conditions. The limits on attention are much more severe than most people imagine. And it takes only a momentary lapse, at the wrong time, to cause a serious accident.

Smeed's Law, or Why Safety Measures Don't Improve Safety

6   What matters most for road safety? The quality of the roads themselves? The engineering of the cars that travel them? The speed limit? The answer may be "none of the above." In 1949, a British statistician named R. J. Smeed, who would go on to become the first professor of traffic studies at University College London, proposed a now-eponymous law. Smeed had looked at data on traffic fatalities in many different countries, over many years. He found that deaths per year could be predicted fairly accurately by a formula that involved just two factors: the number of people and the number of cars. The physicist Freeman Dyson, who during World War II had worked for Smeed in the Operational Research Section of the Royal Air Force's Bomber Command, noted the marvelous simplicity of Smeed's formula, writing in *Technology Review* in November 2006: "It is remarkable that the number of deaths does not depend strongly on the size of the country, the quality of the roads, the rules and regulations governing traffic, or the safety equipment installed in cars." As a result of his research, Smeed developed a fatalistic view of traffic safety, Dyson wrote.

7   Smeed's Law has worked less well since the mid-1960s; traffic deaths have
been somewhat reduced by engineering features such as seat belts and air
bags. But technical improvements generally matter less than you might expect,
because they affect driver behavior. It's called "risk compensation": as cars
become safer, drivers tend to take more risks. Psychological factors, in other
words, appear to play a huge role in road safety, and they often undercut well-
intentioned safety initiatives.

8   I've spent my professional life studying adaptive behavior—how changes in
the environment lead to changes in the ways humans and animals act. I'd contend that as traffic signs have proliferated in the U.S., drivers have adapted in
profoundly unhealthy ways. We may imagine that driver training is something
that happens to 16-year-olds in small cars labeled STUDENT DRIVER. But
of course we spend a lifetime on the roads after we get our licenses, and we're
being trained by our experiences every day. Let's think about what drivers are
actually learning on the roads in America.

Driver Miseducation

9   Consider the stop sign. It seems innocuous enough; we do need to stop from
time to time. But think about how the signs are actually set up and used. For
one thing, there's the placement of the signs—off to the side of the road, often
amid trees, parked cars, and other road signs; rarely right in front of the driver,
where he or she should be looking.

10   Then there's the sheer number of them. They sit at almost every intersection in most American neighborhoods. In some, every intersection seems to
have a *four-way* stop. Stop signs are costly to drivers and bad for the environment: stop/start driving uses more gas, and vehicles pollute most when starting
up from rest. More to the point, however, the overabundance of stop signs
teaches drivers to be less observant of cross traffic and to exercise less judgment when driving—instead, they look for signs and drive according to what
the signs tell them to do.

11   The four-way stop deserves special recognition as a masterpiece of coun-
terproductive public-safety efforts. Where should the driver look? What must
he remember? State driving manuals can be surprisingly coy about exactly
what drivers should do at four-way stops. The North Carolina *Driver's Handbook*, for example, doesn't mention four-ways as a separate category at all.
Yahoo Answers imparts the following wisdom: "The rules for a four-way stop
are like those for a two-way: Stop and look for oncoming traffic, and proceed
when it is safe to do so." So far so good, but then: "You may occasionally arrive
at a four-way stop sign at the same time as another driver. In such cases the
driver to the right has the right of way. However, not all drivers know this. If
someone to your left decides to go first, let them!" Thanks! But remind me:
aside from bewildering the driver, what's the point of stopping traffic in all four
directions?

12   The four-way stop weakens the force of *all* stop signs by muddling the main question drivers need to answer, namely: Which road has priority? And indeed, American drivers have apparently become confused enough by this question that some communities are now beginning to affix *another* sign to the poles of stop signs that aren't four-way, warning CROSS TRAFFIC DOES NOT STOP.

13   Speed limits in the U.S. are perhaps a more severe safety hazard than stop signs. In many places, they change too frequently—sometimes every few hundred yards—once again training drivers to look for signs, not at the road. What's more, many speed limits in the U.S. are set in arbitrary and irrational ways. An eight-lane interstate can have a limit of 50 to 70 mph or more. What makes the difference? A necessarily imperfect guess at probable traffic conditions. The road may sometimes be busy—so the limit is set low. But sometimes the road is not busy, and the safe speed is then much higher than the limit.

14   A particularly vexing aspect of the U.S. policy is that speed limits seem to be enforced more when speeding is *safe*. As a colleague once pointed out, "An empty highway on a sunny day? You're dead meat!" A more systematic effort to train drivers to ignore road conditions can hardly be imagined. By training drivers to drive according to the signs rather than their judgment in great conditions, the American system also subtly encourages them to rely on the signs rather than judgment in poor conditions, when merely following the signs would be dangerous.

15   Which brings me back to North Glebe Road in Arlington. It turns out that the speed signs do perform an important safety function: in wet weather, many drivers had taken the curve too fast; traffic authorities have substantially reduced accidents on the curve by adding the 15-mph warning sign, and they would be foolish to remove it, absent larger changes in American traffic policy. But this is emblematic of the sort of signage arms race that has become necessary in the U.S. When you've trained people to drive according to the signs, you need to keep adding more signs to tell them exactly when and in what fashion they need to adjust their behavior. Otherwise, drivers may see no reason why they should slow down on a curve in the rain.

A Traffic Free-For-All?

16 So what am I suggesting—abolishing signs and rules? A traffic free-for-all? Actually, I wouldn't be the first to suggest that. A few European towns and neighborhoods—Drachten in Holland, fashionable Kensington High Street in London, Prince Charles's village of Poundbury, and a few others—have even gone ahead and tried it. They've taken the apparently drastic step of eliminating traffic control more or less completely in a few high-traffic and pedestrian-dense areas. The intention is to create environments in which everyone is more focused, more cautious, and more considerate. Stop signs, stoplights,

even sidewalks are mostly gone. The results, by all accounts, have been excellent: pedestrian accidents have been reduced by 40 percent or more in some places, and traffic flows no more slowly than before.

17   What I propose is more modest: the adoption of something like the British traffic system, which is free of many of the problems that plague American roads. One British alternative to the stop sign is just a dashed line on the pavement, right in front of the driver. It actually means "yield," not "stop"; it tells the driver which road has the right of way. Another alternative is the roundabout. Roundabouts in the U.S. are typically large. But as drivers get used to them—as they have in the U.K. over the past three or four decades—they can be made smaller and smaller. A "mini-roundabout" in the U.K. is essentially just a large white dot in the middle of the intersection. In this form, it amounts to no more than an instruction to give way to traffic coming from the right (that would be the left over here, of course, since the Brits drive on the left).

18   As these examples indicate, traffic signs in the U.K. are often on the road itself, where the driver should be looking. And most right-of-way signs are informational: there are almost no mandatory stops in the U.K. (The dominant motive in the U.S. traffic-control community seems to be distrust, and policies are usually designed to control drivers and reduce their discretion. The British system puts more responsibility on the drivers themselves.)

19   Speed limits in the U.K. are also simpler and better. They are set by road type, so drivers know what limits to expect on highways, rural roads, and urban roads—usually without any signs to tell them. These limits are relatively high, set assuming optimum driving conditions, in contrast to the U.S. limits, which seem to be set with something in between the best and worst conditions in mind. (Precisely where on this spectrum U.S. limits fall seems to vary from road to road, engendering mistrust of the signs in some drivers.) Nonstandard speed limits in the U.K. are rare, so you tend to take them quite seriously when they appear, and they are posted frequently—so you don't risk missing them if you're, say, watching the road ahead of you.

20   I've given several talks on traffic in the U.S. and have always found members of the audience to be highly skeptical that the U.K. traffic system could possibly be safer than the one on this side of the Atlantic. As noted, there seem to be more fender benders over here. But not all minor accidents get reported to the police, in either country, and definitions vary. So let's look at fatalities: everyone agrees on what death is, and fatalities are always reported.

21   Detailed statistics show that as of 2003, fatalities per mile traveled were 36 percent greater in the U.S. than they were in the U.K. Traffic deaths per million people show an even greater disparity through 2006, the most recent year for which full statistics are available. If the U.S. death rate were the same as the U.K.'s, roughly 6,000 fewer Americans would die each year—that's half again as many Americans as have died in Iraq in the past five years.

22   As experimentalists like to remind us, correlation isn't causation, and differences in traffic-control policies might not be the only reason for this huge difference in traffic deaths. Perhaps people drive slower in Britain? Well, no; in my experience, they usually drive faster. Are cars themselves safer in Britain? Again, probably not; they tend to be smaller, with fewer safety features. It is true that SUVs are more prevalent in the U.S., and that SUVs are often lethal when they hit smaller cars; this likely accounts for some of the difference in fatality rates. But it's also true, for instance, that when traditional intersections in the U.S. have been replaced by roundabouts, collisions have typically been reduced by about 40 percent, and fatalities by up to 90 percent. And as the U.K. has refined and simplified its traffic-control system over the past 30 years, total traffic fatalities have fallen by about 50 percent. Over the same period, fatalities in the U.S. have declined by just 20 percent; in the past several years, they haven't declined at all.

I Didn't See The Gorilla In Front Of Me

23 Conjurers and magicians have long known how to distract people so they miss a move that should be obvious. But it is only recently that social psychologists have come up with dramatic demonstrations of just how tight the limits on our attention can be. One of the most compelling is a 75-second video, by the psychologists Daniel Simons and Christopher Chabris, that shows six male and female students, in black or white T-shirts, passing basketballs to one another. The observer is asked to count the number of passes.

24   About 45 seconds in, a person in a gorilla suit walks onscreen. She strolls between passers to the center of the screen, faces the camera, beats her chest, and then exits. You can't possibly miss her—unless, that is, you've been instructed to pay attention to the basketballs. When each observer in the experiment was asked, "Did you notice anything unusual in the video?" about half said no. That's *inattentional blindness*, the effect of competition for the observer's attention: by looking for one thing, we miss another that should have been obvious.

25   The miseducation that U.S. drivers are receiving is not as explicit as the instructions to these students, but it extends over years and is in some ways more forceful: the legal penalties for failing to notice traffic signs are severe. I believe that U.S. traffic policies are inducing a form of inattentional blindness in American drivers. When so many drivers say, after an accident, "I didn't see him," they're not all lying.

WHAT DID THE WRITER SAY AND WHAT DID YOU THINK?

1. What are the author's two major complaints about driving in the United States? Do they conflict with each other?
2. Does Staddon praise anything about U.S. roads and traffic? Why might he do this?

3. What is the tragedy of the commons? How well does Staddon explain how it relates to traffic?
4. Why does the author object to four-way stops? Do you agree?
5. What is the point of the story in the final paragraphs about the person in a gorilla suit?

HOW DID THE WRITER SAY IT?

1. Why does Staddon quote Yahoo! Answers' response to his question about four-way stops instead of just telling us that the answer was confusing or unhelpful?
2. How does the author increase our shock over the number of U.S. traffic fatalities?
3. List some of the opposing arguments that Staddon discusses as possible explanations for differences in U.S. and U.K. traffic fatality rates.
4. Staddon suggests some very controversial solutions to the problems he sees with American traffic. How does he assure his readers that he's serious and that his solutions could work? How effective do you think he is?

What About Your Writing?

"Never begin a sentence with *and*." The only real problem with that rule is that it shouldn't be a rule at all. It's good enough *advice,* as far as it goes. When readers see *and* at the start of a sentence, their first thought may be that the word introduces a tacked-on idea that logically should be part of the previous sentence. More often than not, they are right.

Still, there's no rule. Precisely because most sentences don't and shouldn't begin with *and,* many good writers sometimes use the word to single out a sentence for special notice and dramatic emphasis. John Staddon does it twice in a row in paragraph 4. Abraham Lincoln does it in his "Second Inaugural Address":

> Both parties deprecated war; but one of them would make war rather than let the nation survive; and the other would accept war rather than let it perish. And the war came.

In the powerful last paragraph of Edgar Allan Poe's "The Masque of the Red Death," we find a virtual festival of *ands,* here used not only for dramatic force but to suggest the eloquence of the King James version of the Bible—many sentences of which also begin with *and*:

> And now was acknowledged the presence of the Red Death. He had come like a thief in the night. And one by one dropped the revellers in the blood-bedewed halls of their revel, and died each in the despairing posture of his

fall. And the life of the ebony clock went out with that of the last of the gay. And the flames of the tripods expired. And Darkness and Decay and the Red Death held illimitable dominion over all.

The moral is simple: Sentences shouldn't begin with *and* except in special circumstances. In special circumstances, *and* can be effective. When it is effective—clearly effective—use it.

THE SMILEY-FACE APPROACH

Albert Shanker

Albert Shanker (1928–1997) was president of the American Federation of Teachers. This reading selection is from "Where We Stand," a long-running series of weekly commentaries printed as newspaper advertisements.

✓ WORDS TO CHECK:

anomaly (paragraph 6)

1 The school board in Clark County, Nevada, has decided that its students deserve a new grading system. Now there will be no more hurt feelings—or damaged self-esteem—because somebody got a D or an F and no more swelled heads because of a straight-A report card. Here's how the system goes, according to the most recent issue of *The Quarterly Review of Doublespeak*:

> [S]tudents who earn D's or below will be characterized not as borderline passing or failing but as *emerging*. Those earning A's will no longer be commended for excellent work but will be told merely that they are *extending*, and those in between will not be described as doing adequate or mediocre work but [that] they are *developing*.

2   The people who invented the traditional grading system undoubtedly thought it was a way of providing information. The Clark County innovation is more likely to produce headaches as those concerned try to figure out what the various "grades" mean. *Emerging* from what? (What if a student is not emerging but is still stuck?) And how is *emerging* different from *developing* or *extending?*

3   If you switched the grades around, would anybody notice? Probably not, and that is probably the point. Grades used to tell a ninth grader and his parents how successful the student was in mastering algebra. They also distinguished between levels of performance, showing who was doing well and who was not cutting it. The nearly indistinguishable present participles that the Clark County board plans to substitute for A's, B's, and the rest imply that, if there

Where We Stand: The Smiley-Face Approach by Albert Shanker as appeared in NEW YORK TIMES, 06/16/96. Copyright American Federation of Teachers (1996). Reprinted with permission.

is any difference, it's not important. The new "grades" are the educational equivalent of the familiar smiley face. Their message: "You are all terrific!"

4   What will students make of them? First graders were always smart enough to see that the Bluebird reading group was for kids who were having a tough time and the Cardinal group was for those who learned to read in the first two weeks, so Clark County students will probably be able to crack this code. But they'll get another message, too: If the difference between failing and outstanding work is not significant enough to be put in words that are plain and clear, why should they make a big effort to do well?

5   Parents who want only good news about their children will be big fans of the new system. But those who are used to discussing their children's grades with the kids will be in trouble. You can say to a child who has just gotten a C, "This shows you are not trying. You have to do better next time." (Or "That B in science is great; your hard work really paid off!") What can you say about *developing*? That it won't do?

6   Of course the Clark County board could solve these problems by collapsing the three grades into one (called *breathing*). And we could sit back and enjoy a laugh—if the foolishness in Clark County were an anomaly. Unfortunately, it isn't. And until we take it on—until we have schools, families, and communities sending consistent signals that achievement counts—all our "reforms" will fail.

7   For example, officials in many school districts have become uneasy with the practice of honoring the two top-ranking students in senior classes by naming them *valedictorian* and *salutatorian*. Some have stopped the practice altogether. Others, even more mysteriously, have decided that seniors should elect classmates to those honors. It's as though a basketball team decided that the high scorer for the year should be elected.

8   Officials in a large number of school districts have also gotten rid of class ranking—even though a majority of colleges say they would like this information for the admissions process. There are some good reasons for the change. For example, a student whose grades would put him in the top 10 percent in most schools might not make the top quarter or even the top half in a high-achieving school. However, problems like this could obviously be dealt with on a case-by-case basis. The real reason school officials insist on blurring the distinctions between students is that they think it is somehow unfair to acknowledge that some students have achieved more academically than others. (This is seldom a problem when it comes to sports.)

9   If this is our attitude towards academic achievement, we will never convince students that working hard in school is worthwhile. Fortunately, a countermovement is developing. One sign is the recent "education summit" where governors and business leaders endorsed high academic standards and agreed to cooperate in working for them. Another is President Clinton's proposal to recognize hard work and good grades by giving $1000 scholarships to the top 5 percent of high school graduates and a tax credit for a second year of college

to students who get a B average the first year. But these initiatives are not enough. They will work only if we get rid of the smiley-face approach to academic achievement and attach real stakes to what students do in school when it comes to graduating from high school and getting a job or getting into college.

WHAT DID THE WRITER SAY AND WHAT DID YOU THINK?

1. Shanker recognizes and has some fun with the sillier aspects of the Clark County grading system, but he also thinks it does great harm. What is the harm?
2. The smiley-face approach in education does not apply to grades alone. What other areas are affected?
3. Does Shanker pay any attention to the reasoning of those who advocate the smiley-face approach?
4. Do you agree with Shanker that our schools value achievement in sports more than in academic areas?

HOW DID THE WRITER SAY IT?

1. Explain the comment, "If you switched the grades around, would anybody notice?"
2. Where does Shanker use ridicule? Is it justified? Is it excessive?
3. Which of the following best describes the conclusion: summary, prediction, or call for action?

What About Your Writing?

Those experienced with the horrors of bureaucracies will be amused or angered—but not, unfortunately, surprised—by the language describing Clark County's new grading system, quoted in paragraph 1 of "The Smiley-Face Approach." The entire quoted passage is written in the passive voice.

Most English sentences use the *active voice*. It sounds natural. It's what readers expect. With the active voice, the subject does the acting:

- Phillip went to the theater.
- The pitcher throws a good curve ball.
- I took the final examination.

In a sentence that uses the passive voice, the subject stands around "passively" and is acted upon:

- The theater was gone to by Phillip.
- A good curve ball is thrown by the pitcher.
- The final examination was taken by me.

The passive voice can be awkward, pompous, wordy, and downright ugly. Sometimes it can even be sinister.

Take a close look at that passage describing the new grading system. The students are being *acted upon*: they "will be characterized"; they "will no longer be commended"; they "will be told"; they "will not be described." Who is responsible for these actions? Who do we complain to if we think the grading system is stupid or pernicious? The school board? The principal? The teachers? City Hall? Use of the passive voice makes these questions difficult or impossible to answer. Perhaps we are meant to sigh, shrug, and put the blame on the impersonal forces of Fate or Change or The Authorities. The passive voice, then, can sometimes involve moral issues even though it is most often a stylistic concern. Note the evasion of responsibility in the following sentences:

- Funding was reduced for the hunger program.
- The Accounts Receivable department has been determined to be 35 percent overstaffed.
- Fred was deemed to be a disruptive influence.

In fairness, for some special situations the passive voice can be altogether acceptable. When the person or thing or group that does the acting is unknown or unimportant, the passive voice often sounds normal and natural—more so than the active voice in some cases—and there's no reason to avoid it. The passive sometimes works well, too, when the writer deliberately wants to sound formal and impersonal:

- The flight was canceled because of mechanical difficulties.
- In the Middle Ages, Aristotle was often referred to as "The Philosopher."
- Payment must be received within ten days, or legal steps will be taken.

Watch out for the passive voice, then. It shouldn't always be avoided, but most of the time the active voice works better—much better.

WORKING AT MCDONALD'S
Amitai Etzioni

A sociology professor and the founder of the Communitarian Network, Amitai Etzioni has been referred to as the "guru" of the communitarian movement. He has written more than two dozen books, is frequently heard on radio and television, and has published numerous articles in newspapers and magazines. Here, Etzioni turns these credentials toward a consideration of the seemingly innocuous topic of after-school jobs for teenagers.

✓ Words to Check:

entrepreneurship (paragraph 6)   alienation (14)   trite (18)

gumption (7)   emulate (16)   intrinsic (19)

1 McDonald's is bad for your kids. I do not mean the flat patties and the white-flour buns; I refer to the jobs teenagers undertake, mass-producing these choice items.

2   As many as two-thirds of America's high school juniors and seniors now hold down part-time paying jobs, according to studies. Many of these are in fast-food chains, of which McDonald's is the pioneer, trend-setter and symbol.

3   At first, such jobs may seem right out of the Founding Fathers' education manual for how to bring up self-reliant, work-ethic-driven, productive young-sters. But in fact, these jobs undermine school attendance and involvement, impart few skills that will be useful in later life, and simultaneously skew the values of teen-agers—especially their ideas about the worth of a dollar.

4   It has been a longstanding American tradition that youngsters ought to get paying jobs. In folklore, few pursuits are more deeply revered than the newspaper route and the sidewalk lemonade stand. Here the youngsters are to learn how sweet are the fruits of labor and self-discipline (papers are delivered early in the morning, rain or shine), and the ways of trade (if you price your lemonade too high or too low . . .).

5   Roy Rogers, Baskin Robbins, Kentucky Fried Chicken, *et al.* may at first seem nothing but a vast extension of the lemonade stand. They provide very large numbers of teen jobs, provide regular employment, pay quite well com-pared to many other teen jobs and, in the modern equivalent of toiling over a hot stove, test one's stamina.

6   Closer examination, however, finds the McDonald's kind of job highly uneducational in several ways. Far from providing opportunities for entrepre-neurship (the lemonade stand) or self-discipline, self-supervision and self-sched-uling (the paper route), most teen jobs these days are highly structured—what social scientists call "highly routinized."

7   True, you still have to have the gumption to get yourself over to the ham-burger stand, but once you don the prescribed uniform, your task is spelled out in minute detail. The franchise prescribes the shape of the coffee cups; the weight, size, shape and color of the patties; and the texture of the napkins (if any). Fresh coffee is to be made every eight minutes. And so on. There is no room for initiative, creativity, or even elementary rearrangements. These are breeding grounds for robots working for yesterday's assembly lines, not tomorrow's high-tech posts.

8   There are very few studies on the matter. One of the few is a 1984 study by Ivan Charper and Bryan Shore Fraser. The study relies mainly on what teen-agers write in response to the questionnaires rather than actual observations of fast-food jobs. The authors argue that the employees develop many skills such

has how to operate a food-preparation machine and a cash register. However, little attention is paid to how long it takes to acquire such a skill, or what its significance is.

9   What does it matter if you spend 20 minutes to learn to use a cash register, and then—"operate" it? What "skill" have you acquired? It is a long way from learning to work with a lathe or carpenter tools in the olden days or to program computers in the modern age.

10   A study by A. V. Harrell and P. W. Wirtz found that, among those students who worked at least 25 hours per week while in school, their unemployment rate four years later was half of that of seniors who did not work. This is an impressive statistic. It must be seen though, together with the finding that many who begin as part-time employees in fast-food chains drop out of high school and are gobbled up in the world of low-skill jobs.

11   Some say that while these jobs are rather unsuited for college-bound, white, middle-class youngsters, they are "ideal" for lower-class, "non-academic," minority youngsters. Indeed, minorities are "over-represented" in these jobs (21 percent of fast-food employees). While it is true that these places provide income, work and even some training to such youngsters, they also tend to perpetuate their disadvantaged status. They provide no career ladders, few marketable skills, and undermine school attendance and involvement.

12   The hours are often long. Among those 14 to 17, a third of fast-food employees (including some school dropouts) labor more than 30 hours per week, according to the Charper-Fraser study. Only 20 percent work 15 hours or less. The rest: between 15 and 30 hours.

13   Often the stores close late, and after closing one must clean up and tally up. In affluent Montgomery Count, Md., where child labor would not seem to be a widespread economic necessity, 24 percent of the seniors at one high school in 1986 worked as much as five to seven days a week; 27 percent, three to five. There is just no way such amounts of work will not interfere with school work, especially homework. In an informal survey published in the most recent yearbook of the high school, 58 percent of seniors acknowledge that their jobs interfere with their school work.

14   The Charper-Fraser study sees merit in learning teamwork and working under supervision. The authors have a point here. However, it must be noted that such learning is not automatically educational or wholesome. For example, much of the supervision in fast-food places leans toward teaching one the wrong kinds of compliance: blind obedience, or shared alienation with the "boss."

15   Supervision is often both tight and woefully inappropriate. Today, fast-food chains and other such places of work (record shops, bowling alleys) keep costs down by having teens supervise teens with often no adult on the premises.

16   There is no father or mother figure with which to identify, to emulate, to provide a role model and guidance. The work-culture varies from one place to another: Sometimes it is a tightly run shop (must keep the cash

registers ringing); sometimes a rather loose pot party interrupted by customers. However, only rarely is there a master to learn from, or much worth
learning. Indeed, far from being places where solid adult work values are
being transmitted, these are places where all too often delinquent teen values dominate. Typically, when my son Oren was dishing out ice cream for
Baskin Robbins in upper Manhattan, his fellow teen-workers considered
him a sucker for not helping himself to the till. Most youngsters felt they
were entitled to $50 severance "pay" on their last day on the job.

17   The pay, oddly, is the part of the teen work-world that is most difficult to
evaluate. The lemonade stand or paper route money was for your allowance.
In the old days, apprentices learning a trade from a master contributed most,
if not all, of their income to their parents' household. Today, the teen pay
may be low by adult standards, but it is often, especially in the middle class,
spent largely or wholly by the teens. That is, the youngsters live free at home
("after all, they are high school kids") and are left with very substantial sums
of money.

18   Where this money goes is not quite clear. Some use it to support themselves, especially among the poor. More middle-class kids set some money
aside to help pay for college, or save it for a major purchase—often a car. But
large amounts seem to flow to pay for an early introduction into the most trite
aspects of American consumerism: flimsy punk clothes, trinkets and whatever
else is the last fast-moving teen craze.

19   One may say that this is only fair and square; they are being good American consumers and spend their money on what turns them on. At least, a cynic
might add, these funds do not go into illicit drugs and booze. On the other
hand, an educator might bemoan that these young, yet unformed individuals,
so early in life driven to buy objects of no intrinsic educational, cultural or
social merit, learn so quickly the dubious merit of keeping up with the Joneses
in ever-changing fads, promoted by mass merchandising.

20   Many teens find the instant reward of money, and the youth status symbols
it buys, much more alluring than credits in calculus courses, European history
or foreign languages. No wonder quite a few would rather skip school—and
certainly homework—and instead work longer at a Burger King. Thus, most
teen work these days is not providing early lessons in the work ethic; it fosters
escape from school and responsibilities, quick gratification and a shortcut to
the consumeristic aspects of adult life.

21   Thus, parents should look at teen employment not as automatically educational. It is an activity—like sports—that can be turned into an educational
opportunity. But it can also easily be abused. Youngsters must learn to balance
the quest for income with the needs to keep growing and pursue other endeav-
ors that do not pay off instantly—above all education.

22   Go back to school.

WHAT DID THE WRITER SAY AND WHAT DID YOU THINK?

1. Why does the author say that part-time jobs are not especially educational?
2. What values are teen jobs often teaching, according to Etzioni?
3. How does Etzioni respond to the claim that these jobs "are 'ideal' for lower-class, 'non-academic,' minority youngsters" (paragraph 11)?
4. Does your experience support or refute Etzioni's argument?

HOW DID THE WRITER SAY IT?

1. Who is the audience for this argument? How can you tell?
2. How does the author address the audience's preconceptions and objections to his argument?
3. In paragraph 13, the author cites statistics about teen employment and says, "There is just no way such amounts of work will not interfere with school work, especially homework." Is this statement logically self-evident? Is the yearbook survey cited after this statement enough support for Etzioni's conclusion?
4. The essay closes with a paragraph encouraging balance between work and education followed by a single-sentence paragraph stating, "Go back to school." Are these points contradictory? Why end the essay this way?

What About Your Writing?

Inseparable from Etzioni's presentation of his own point of view about teenagers working at McDonald's is his attack on what he considers conventional attitudes. His explicit rejection of those attitudes gives his thesis a dimension that it would not otherwise have had.

Getting started is a problem for many writers, and Etzioni here demonstrates one of the most effective ways of dealing with the problem: *Many people think such and such, but. . . .* Instead of opening with a direct and sometimes flat statement of your thesis, let your thesis emerge as a response to some other people's ignorance or superstition or sentimentality or general wrongheadedness. Your thesis will then exist in a dramatic context, not an intellectual vacuum, and will have built into it the appeal of a lively argument.

Most people think such and such about jobs for teenagers, says Etzioni, *but. . . .* With a thesis that spanking small children is often the best method of handling certain difficulties, you might begin with a few satirical references to the belief that three-year-olds appreciate the fine points of logic and that the ideal family is a loosely organized debating society. With a thesis that country music is fun, you might begin by observing that respectable people

traditionally are supposed to scorn country music as trivial and commercial-
ized nonsense. Then, perhaps, you declare that you guess you're just not
respectable, *but*. . . .

For other suggestions on getting started, consult pages 134–135.

APPEASING THE GODS, WITH INSURANCE
John Tierney

John Tierney has written for *The Atlantic, Esquire, New York Magazine, Newsweek,
Reason, Rolling Stone, Playboy, Reader's Digest, Vogue,* the *Wall Street Journal,* and a
host of other publications. He has been with the *New York Times* since 1990. He
is the author of *The Best Case Scenario Handbook* (2002) and, with Christopher
Buckley, of the comic novel, *God Is My Broker: A Monk Tycoon Reveals the 7½
Laws of Spiritual and Financial Growth (1998).*

✓ WORDS TO CHECK:

efficacy (paragraph 2)	meteorology (8)	hubris (12)
litany (2)	irony (9)	dubious (16)
appeasing (7)	hedge (11)	avert (18)

1 Suppose you're preparing to travel by air. Which of these precautions do you
think is most likely to prevent your plane from crashing?

    A) Sacrificing a gilt-horned bull on an altar.
    B) Sacrificing two goats on the tarmac.
    C) Buying flight insurance.

2 I'm guessing you didn't go for the bull sacrifice. Although this preboard-
ing procedure was practiced by ancient Greek travelers, as Homer reported in
grisly detail, today there are serious doubts about its efficacy, if only because of
the litany of tourist woes in "The Odyssey."

3 The goat option was tested at Katmandu Airport in September to propiti-
ate Akash Bhairab, the Hindu sky god. Officials of Nepal Airlines told Reuters
that they had sacrificed two goats in front of a Boeing 757 whose mechanical
problems had forced the airline to suspend some flights.

4 "The snag in the plane has now been fixed, and the aircraft has resumed
its flights," one airline official reported triumphantly. Nevertheless, it is probably premature to put much faith in a single experiment that so far, to my
knowledge, has not been replicated.

5 We do, though, have abundant data regarding option C. Last year, tens of
millions of people bought life insurance for scheduled flights of airlines in the

United States. Not one of those insured passengers died in a crash–and this was not just a coincidence, at least not to many of the people who bought the insurance.

6   No, at some level they believed that their insurance helped keep the plane aloft, according to psychologists with new experimental evidence of just how weirdly superstitious people can be.

7   We buy insurance not just for peace of mind or to protect ourselves financially, but because we share the ancient Greeks' instinct for appeasing the gods.

8   We may not slaughter animals anymore to ward off a plague, but we think buying health insurance will keep us from getting sick. Our brains may understand meteorology, but in our guts we still think that not carrying an umbrella will make it rain, a belief that was demonstrated in experiments by Jane Risen of the University of Chicago and Thomas Gilovich of Cornell.

9   "It is an irony of the post-Enlightenment world," they conclude, "that so many people who don't believe in fate refuse to tempt it." The psychologists first identified this reluctance last year by reconsidering a well-known superstition about lottery tickets. Experimenters had repeatedly found that once people were given a lottery ticket, they would refuse to trade it for another ticket despite being offered a cash bonus and reassured that the other ticket was just as likely to win.

10   This superstitious behavior had been explained with the theory of "anticipated regret": Even though the people realized the odds were no different for any ticket, they anticipated feeling especially stupid if they traded away a winner, so they held on to their ticket just to avoid that regret.

11   But there's also another reason, as Risen and Gilovich reported after running a complicated lottery game with cash prizes for competing teams. If a player watched his teammate (who was secretly a confederate of the researchers) trade away a lottery number, the player actually believed the new number was less likely to win, and he would hedge his bet accordingly.

12   The fear of tempting fate showed up in further experiments with Cornell students. When told about an applicant to graduate school at Stanford who had been given a Stanford T-shirt by his mother, people assumed he would hurt his chances for admission if he had the hubris to wear it. And they believed that a professor was more likely to call on them in class if they didn't do the assigned reading.

13   Even people who consciously reject superstitions seem to have these gut feelings, says Orit Tykocinski, a professor of psychology at the Interdisciplinary Center Herzliya in Israel. She found that rationalists were just as likely as superstitious people to believe that insurance would ward off accidents.

14   In one of her experiments, players drew colored balls out of an urn and lost all their money if they picked a blue one. Some players were randomly forced to buy insurance policies that let them keep half their money if they

drew a blue one. These policies didn't diminish their risk of drawing a blue ball—but the insured players rated their risk lower than the uninsured players rated theirs.

15   That same magical thinking was evident when Tykocinski asked some people to imagine buying travel insurance before getting on a plane, and others to imagine not buying it because they ran out of time at the airport. Sure enough, the ones with insurance figured they were less likely to lose their bags, get sick or have an accident.

16   These results presumably come as no surprise to marketers of travel insurance, which is now purchased by half of American leisure travelers—a fivefold increase since 2001, according to the United States Travel Insurance Association. As a purely economic investment, some of this insurance can be dubious, particularly the flight insurance policies. (For more on this, see nytimes.com/tierneylab.)

17   A magical belief in insurance sounds crazy because at a rational level we realize that our decision to forgo an insurance policy is not going to affect pilots or mechanics. But Risen and Gilovich say that there's a logical explanation for this superstition: Because calamities are so vivid and easily brought to mind, we tend to overestimate their probability when we intuitively judge what will happen if we tempt fate.

18   So when we think about passing up flight insurance, we conjure up disaster just as easily as ancient Greeks imagined a thunderbolt from Olympus, and we too figure we can avert it through the equivalent of a bull sacrifice. Intuitively, we haven't made great strides since Homer's day. But at least our gods take credit cards.

WHAT DID THE WRITER SAY AND WHAT DID YOU THINK?

1. What are some of the common superstitions Tierney lists? Do you believe in any of them?
2. How does the experiment with the colored balls relate to travel insurance?
3. What is "anticipated regret"? How does it relate to this essay's thesis? Do you think that Tierney defines the term well enough?
4. Does the author believe that travel insurance really protected the tens of millions of people who bought it last year and traveled without incident? How do you know?

HOW DID THE WRITER SAY IT?

1. How does Tierney emphasize the oddly superstitious nature of travel insurance?
2. Why does the author reference so many scientific studies?
3. Explain the joke about credit cards in the last sentence.

What About <u>Your</u> Writing?

Countless thousands of students have been told never to write *you*. They were misinformed. *You* is a tricky word, and it's easy enough to understand how some teachers, distraught at seeing the word so frequently mismanaged, might invent a rule that outlaws it—but no such rule exists in standard English.

The tricky part is that *you* is both a pronoun of direct address, aimed at a specific person or group, and an indefinite pronoun, meaning something like *people* or *one* or *everybody*. When it's used in writing aimed at a general audience—like most freshman English writing—it can be taken in both ways and can often turn out to be unintentionally confusing, insulting, or funny. Imagine a casual reader coming across sentences like these:

- When you catch syphilis, you must consult your doctor immediately.
- Your paranoid concern with what others think of you makes you a likely candidate for suicide.
- The new night school program should give you fresh hope for overcoming your illiteracy.

Those sentences demand revision:

- Victims of syphilis must consult their doctors immediately.
- Paranoid concern with what others think increases the likelihood of suicide.
- The new night school program should give fresh hope for overcoming illiteracy.

To be fair to the inventors of imaginary rules, then, it's wise in most classroom writing to be extremely conservative with *you* as an indefinite pronoun. The assumed audience is a general one of mixed ages, sexes, backgrounds, and interests; using *you* for this audience is nearly always asking for trouble.

There is nothing wrong with using the word *you*, however, in writing that does address itself to a specific audience: the purchaser of a bike who now has to put it together, the new employee who wants information about the pension plan and hospitalization program, the person considering risks while preparing for an airplane trip, as in this reading by John Tierney. This book addresses itself to college freshmen taking a course in English composition, each of whom receives similar reading and writing assignments every day. An audience can't get much more specific than that, and therefore this book feels free to make frequent use of *you*. You must have noticed.

BLACK ATHLETES ON PARADE

Adolph Reed, Jr.

Adolph Reed, Jr., is a political science professor at the University of Pennsylvania. He is particularly interested in the complex political problems of black Americans. Here he considers the pressure on black athletes to be not only great athletes, but also great politicians.

✓ Words to Check:

canard (paragraph 1)	deportment (11)	revalorizing (20)
Jim Crow (2)	pantheon (19)	invidious (21)

1   It's difficult to be patient with the argument that the crossover popularity of Tiger Woods or Michael Jordan or Bill Cosby or Oprah Winfrey proves that racial injustice has been defeated. That reasoning is either a straight-up rightist canard or a more or less willfully naïve, ostrich-like evasion.

2   Equally frustrating is the "nothing-has-changed-since-slavery" line that seems to have gained currency in black political discourse as the realities of the Jim Crow[1] world slip out of collective memory. Recently I was on a panel with a black political scientist who insisted that things had gotten no better for black people in this country since 1619; several years ago I saw Derek Bell, then a tenured Harvard law professor, flamboyantly push a version of the same line. This is, of course, a self-discrediting argument. How many black people were on the Harvard Law School faculty or teaching in predominantly white universities thirty years ago, much less earlier?

3   But while there has been undeniable progress, racialized expectations still prevail—especially in sports.

4   Tiger Woods's Masters victory made him a social spokesman for black athletes. It's a familiar pattern. Woods was not only expected to comment on how his accomplishment, as the first black winner of the most Southern of all PGA tournaments, related to Jackie Robinson; he also was called upon to pay homage to Charlie Sifford, Lee Calvin Peete, Lee Elder, and other black trailblazers on the PGA tour.

5   Woods's responses seemed reasonable enough and genuine. His acknowledgement that he had paused on the last hole of the last Masters round to reflect that he was walking a path carved by his black predecessors was even affecting.

6   By contrast, Chicago White Sox star Frank Thomas created a bit of a media stir by admitting that he doesn't know much about Jackie Robinson or

---

[1]*Jim Crow*: Practice of segregating or discriminating against blacks (comes from the name of an early Negro minstrel song).

Reprinted by permission from THE PROGRESSIVE, 409 E. Main St., Madison, WI 53703. www.progressive.org

his sport's racial history. The ensuing controversy centered on Thomas's—and, by extension, other black athletes'—larger social and racial obligations.

7   This theme of special obligation also figured into the Tiger Woods hype. All along he has been trumpeted as a "role model" for black—and Asian American—kids. He's a clean-cut, articulate, and apparently earnest young man whose public persona isn't flamboyant or especially controversial. Nike, evoking the concluding scene from Spike Lee's *Malcolm X*, projects Woods as such a role model in an ad that quick-cuts to nonwhite kids all over the globe who proclaim, *seriatim*: "I am Tiger Woods."

8   Woods now joins Michael Jordan among the company's most visibly promoted human icons. Jordan has been the object of criticism for his silence about Nike's horrible labor practices in its off-shore production operations. (The stunning fact is that Nike pays him more than the annual payroll of its entire Indonesian workforce.) He has been criticized as well for not speaking out or being conspicuously active on behalf of black issues and causes. Woods, similarly, has been faulted by some for not being a vocal enough race man— though recent disclosures of racist threats and harassment he's received on the golf circuit give those objections a strange twist.

9   The fact that people have such expectations of athletes like Jordan and Woods is Jackie Robinson's ironic legacy. Robinson's stardom as a baseball player was inseparable from his political renown for breaking the color bar in a very visible arena of American culture. His views were solicited on all manner of political and social issues that concerned black Americans.

10   This was understandable, especially at the time: Robinson symbolically represented the goals of the burgeoning civil-rights movement and large social and political aspirations of black Americans much more broadly. At the same time, though, the spokesman status thrust onto him was both unfair to him (though he may not have bristled at it) and deeply troublesome politically. After all, Jackie Robinson had no special expertise for this role. He was a baseball player. Nor was he accountable to any particular body to speak in the name of black Americans.

11   In addition to carrying the weight of race spokesmanship, Robinson also faced constant scrutiny for deportment. Indeed, he was selected as the pathbreaker partly because of his articulate, All-American demeanor. And his agreement not to retaliate against affronts—no matter how bad—was a precondition of the whole arrangement.

12   In a racially just world, black athletes should not be expected to hold to a higher standard of behavior than whites. Nor should they be expected to shoulder the burden of racial activism. And do we really want the likes of Charles Barkley, the NBA's most prominent black Republican, or the Philadelphia 76ers' loutish rookie of the year, Alan Iverson, declaiming on social affairs in the name of black Americans?

13   Sure, it would be good and useful for Michael Jordan and Tiger Woods to exert pressure on Nike to clean up its dreadful labor practices. But the

..tion that they have some special obligation to do so because of their
as black—or in Woods's case, even Asian American—athletic icons is
g.

14 Woods and Jordan have the right to be apolitical no less than Larry Bird,
Pete Sampras, Wayne Gretzky, or Brady Anderson. Frank Thomas has the
right to have grown up playing baseball without paying much attention to the
sport's history, even the history of its desegregation, from which originates his
opportunity to become wealthy playing it. When you boil off the self-righteous
presumptions about special racial responsibility, Thomas's ignorance about
Jackie Robinson is not really different from that of many young players who
don't know much about the game's history or starts of the past. Reverence for,
or even interest in, a sport's lore isn't a condition for being able to play it well;
nor should it be.

15 The presumption that black athletes should shoulder greater social expectations at least bears a family resemblance to the persisting myth of special
black athletic prowess, which in turn, works to perpetuate the worst stereotypes and to undermine the careers of black professional athletes in general.

16 On the average, blacks in pro baseball and football perform somewhat
better statistically than their white counterparts. At first glance this fact may
seem to lend confidence to the claim that blacks are more gifted. The reality,
however, is quite the opposite: marginal black players are more likely than
comparably talented whites to get weeded out along the way.

17 The myth of black athletic superiority leads scouts and coaches to evaluate
black athletes with higher expectations in mind. So the black player needs to
exhibit a higher level of skill or performance to impress.

18 Black athletes who don't perform up to inflated expectations are more
likely to be characterized as lazy, malingering, or otherwise possessed of bad
attitudes. In 1980, for example, Houston Astros' star pitcher J. R. Richard
nearly died when he suffered a career-ending stroke on the field. He had been
complaining of weakness for some time, but when no clear medical basis for
his complaint was detected right away, the reaction of the Astros' management
and the Houston media was to attack Richard for dogging it, even though
Richard had been among the league's leaders in innings pitched for several
years. After he collapsed, a medical exam disclosed a blood clot. Earlier treatment would probably have saved his career as the most dominating pitcher in
baseball.

19 Frank Robinson and Roberto Clemente have been enshrined on the highest echelon of Major League's pantheon of heroes, and rightly so. When they
were playing, though, the story was different. The Cincinnati Reds traded
Robinson, claiming he was too old at twenty-nine, because the club considered
him to have a bad attitude. Pittsburgh Pirates management and the local media
circulated similar complaints about Clemente. Both men were rapped as surly
or moody, and both were plagued by rumors that their inevitable submission

to slumps or late-season exhaustion stemmed from being weakened by the ravages of syphilis, thereby getting the black hyper-sexuality stereotype into the picture. What prompted these judgments? Both men simply sought to conduct themselves with a measure of dignity; they presumed a right to be treated with equal respect.

20   Booker T. Washington said blacks should be "patient suffering, slow to anger," and that is the downside of Jackie Robinson's legacy, though it's hardly his fault. The public imagery of Jackie Robinson's accomplishment and ordeal has been used as a justification for preaching quiescence in the name of moral superiority. Robinson's "quiet dignity" was frequently invoked, for example, against more aggressive black radicalism in the 1960s. (Recently, even *The Nation*[2]—in its continuing drive to become the respectably liberal, loyal edge of Clintonism—published a ludicrous article exhorting blacks in South Carolina to draw on the race's legacy of demonstrated moral superiority and thus defuse the state's controversy over the public display of the Confederate battle flag by embracing the flag and revalorizing it as a symbol of a racially democratic New South.)

21   As a professional athlete and as a black person, Jackie Robinson fought to bring into existence a world in which he and others would be able to pursue their craft on an equal basis with everyone else, without the fetters of stereotypes or invidious, unfair expectations and double standards. A world, that is, in which a ballplayer would be simply a ballplayer. That quest—obviously just and proper in its own right—had much broader ramifications in 1947. Why? Because a dynamic political movement spurred it along.

22   It's not only unreasonable and unfair to expect athletes to adopt any public role other than simply as athletes; it's also a waste of time.

WHAT DID THE WRITER SAY AND WHAT DID YOU THINK?

1. Reed dismisses two claims about racial inequality—that everything is fine, and that nothing has changed—at the beginning of the essay. How does his position differ from these two arguments?
2. According to Reed, what are some of the expectations black athletes are supposed to meet?
3. Why are these expectations unreasonable?
4. What is the "downside of Jackie Robinson's legacy" (paragraph 20)?

HOW DID THE WRITER SAY IT?

1. Where does the author state his thesis?
2. How is the argument organized?
3. Does the author counter possible objections to his argument? Where?

[2] *The Nation*: Political magazine with a predominantly liberal point of view and readership.

4. Is the evidence provided in this essay adequate to convince you that this is an important issue? Does it prove that there are unreasonable expectations for black athletes?

5. Does the author provide enough background about the athletes he mentions?

What About Your Writing?

Aware that his opposition to the politicization of black athletes is liable to inspire opposition, Adolph Reed begins his essay by turning the tables on some of his opponents. He tells the story of a black Harvard professor who insists that nothing has changed for black Americans since the days of Jim Crow. Reed asks, "How many black people were on the Harvard Law School faculty or teaching in predominantly white universities thirty years ago, much less earlier?" Suddenly, arguments that suggest that black athletes need to take public, political stances because the status of black Americans hasn't changed since the old days start to sound pretty shaky.

Different readers will assess the validity of Reed's argument differently. As a writing strategy, though, his approach can lead to interesting and effective papers.

Anticipate the strongest argument of your opponents, and try to turn it against them. If they contend that your stand against a new highway is holding back progress, show how they are holding back progress in mass transit systems, ecology, and so forth. If they maintain that grades in school are artificial and should be abolished, try to show that nothing is more artificial than an environment in which good work is not rewarded and bad work is not penalized. These approaches won't prove in themselves that your own position is correct, but they put your opponents on the defensive, and that's where you want them to be.

A MODEST PROPOSAL

Jonathan Swift

Jonathan Swift (1667–1745) still has the power to inspire, to shock, and to offend. Once the dean of St. Patrick's Cathedral (Church of England) in Dublin, the politically active Swift is the master of satire in English literature, as seen in *A Tale of a Tub* (1704), *The Battle of the Books* (1704), "An Argument Against Abolishing Christianity" (1708), *Gulliver's Travels* (1726), and, in the majesty of its full title, "A Modest Proposal for Preventing the Children of

Poor People in Ireland from Being a Burden to Their Parents or Country, and for Making Them Beneficial to the Public" (1729). The fury, hatred, and cruelty in much of Swift's satire often make readers overlook his passionate and idealistic commitment to human welfare. Also too often overlooked is his spare and muscular prose style, especially remarkable in an age sometimes given to forced elegance. "A Modest Proposal" is an attack on British oppression and exploitation of Ireland. As you read, distinguish between what is said and what is meant.

✓ WORDS TO CHECK:

importuning (paragraph 1)	collateral (12)	brevity (26)
alms (1)	repine (13)	parsimony (28)
prodigious (2)	mandarins (17)	animosities (28)
dam (4)	desponding (18)	factions (28)
raiment (4)	tithes (20)	effectual (31)
proficiency (6)	curate (20)	sustenance (31)
nutriment (7)	emulation (25)	

1 It is a melancholy object to those who walk through this great town[1] or travel in the country, when they see the street, the roads, and cabin doors, crowded with beggars of the female sex, followed by three, four, or six children, all in rags, and importuning every passenger for alms. These mothers, instead of being able to work for their honest livelihood, are forced to employ all their time in strolling to beg sustenance for their helpless infants, who, as they grow up, either turn thieves for want of work or leave their dear native country, to fight for the Pretender in Spain, or sell themselves to the Barbadoes.[2]

2   I think it is agreed by all parties that this prodigious number of children in the arms, or on the backs, or at the heels of their mothers, and frequently of their fathers, is in the present deplorable state of the kingdom a very great additional grievance; and therefore whoever could find out a fair, cheap, and easy method of making these children sound and useful members of the common-wealth, would deserve so well of the public as to have his statue up for a preserver of the nation.

3   But my intention is very far from being confined to provide only for the children of professed beggars; it is of much greater extent, and shall take in the whole number of infants at a certain age, who are born of parents in effect as little able to support them, as those who demand our charity in the streets.

[1]Dublin.

[2]The Pretender was James Francis Edward Stuart (1688–1766), son of the deposed Catholic king of England, James II. He claimed the British throne and was supported by most of Catholic Ireland. Many Irish tried to escape from their poverty by hiring themselves out as indentured servants in the Barbados and other islands of the West Indies.

4   As to my own part, having turned my thoughts, for many years, upon this important subject, and maturely weighed the several schemes of other projectors, I have always found them grossly mistaken in their computation. It is true, a child just dropt from its dam, may be supported by her milk for a solar year with little other nourishment, at most not above the value of two shillings, which the mother may certainly get, or the value in scraps, by her lawful occupation of begging; and it is exactly at one year old that I propose to provide for them in such a manner, as, instead of being a charge upon their parents, or the parish, or wanting food and raiment for the rest of their lives, they shall, on the contrary, contribute to the feeding and partly to the clothing of many thousands.

5   There is likewise another great advantage in my scheme, that it will prevent those voluntary abortions, and that horrid practice of women murdering their bastard children, alas! too frequent among us—sacrificing the poor innocent babes, I doubt,[3] more to avoid the expense than the shame—which would move tears and pity in the most savage and inhuman breast.

6   The number of souls in this kingdom being usually reckoned one million and a half, of these I calculate there may be about two hundred thousand couples whose wives are breeders; from which number I subtract thirty thousand couples, who are able to maintain their own children, although I apprehend there cannot be so many, under the present distresses of the kingdom; but this being granted, there will remain an hundred and seventy thousand breeders. I again subtract fifty thousand, for those women who miscarry, or whose children die by accident or disease within the year. There only remain an hundred and twenty thousand children of poor parents annually born: The question therefore is, How this number shall be reared, and provided for: which, as I have already said, under the present situation of affairs, is utterly impossible by all the methods hitherto proposed; for we can neither employ them in handicraft or agriculture; we neither build houses (I mean in the country) nor cultivate land: They can very seldom pick up a livelihood by stealing till they arrive at six years old, except where they are of towardly parts,[4] although, I confess, they learn the rudiments much earlier; during which time they can however be properly looked upon only as probationers; as I have been informed by a principal gentleman in the country of Cavan,[5] who protested to me, that he never knew above one or two instances under the age of six, even in a part of the kingdom so renowned for the quickest proficiency in that art.

7   I am assured by our merchants, that a boy or a girl before twelve years old, is no saleable commodity, and even when they come to this age, they will not yield above three pounds, or three pounds and a half crown at most, on the

[3]I think.

[4]Advanced talents.

[5]An especially poor district of Ireland.

exchange; which cannot turn to account either to the parents or kingdom, the charge of nutriment and rags having been at least four times that value.

8   I shall now therefore humbly propose my own thoughts, which I hope will not be liable to the least objection.

9   I have been assured by a very knowing American of my acquaintance in London, that a young healthy child well nursed is at a year old a most delicious nourishing and wholesome food, whether stewed, roasted, baked, or boiled; and I make no doubt that it will equally serve in a fricassee, or a ragout.

10   I do therefore humbly offer it to publick consideration, that of the hundred and twenty thousand children, already computed, twenty thousand may be reserved for breed, whereof only one fourth part to be males; which is more than we allow to sheep, black cattle, or swine; and my reason is that these children are seldom the fruits of marriage, a circumstance not much regarded by our savages; therefore one male will be sufficient to serve four females. That the remaining hundred thousand may, at a year old, be offered in the sale to the persons of quality and fortune through the kingdom; always advising the mother to let them suck plentifully in the last month, so as to render them plump and fat for a good table. A child will make two dishes at an entertainment for friends; and when the family dines alone, the fore or hind quarter will make a reasonable dish, and seasoned with a little pepper or salt will be very good boiled on the fourth day, especially in winter.

11   I have reckoned upon a medium that a child just born will weigh 12 pounds, and in a solar year, if tolerably nursed, increaseth to 28 pounds. I grant this food will be somewhat dear,[6] and therefore very proper for land-lords, who, as they have already devoured most of the parents, seem to have the best title to the children.

12   Infant's flesh will be in season throughout the year, but more plentiful in March, and a little before and after; for we are told by a grave author, and eminent French physician,[7] that fish being a prolific diet, there are more children born in Roman Catholic countries about nine months after Lent than at any other season; therefore, reckoning a year after Lent, the markets will be more glutted than usual, because the number of popish infants is at least three to one in this kingdom: and therefore, it will have one other collateral advantage, by lessening the number of papists among us.

13   I have already computed the charge of nursing a beggar's child (in which list I reckon all cottagers, laborers, and four-fifths of the farmers) to be about two shillings per annum, rags included; and I believe no gentlemen would repine to give ten shillings for the carcass of a good fat child, which, as I have said, will make four dishes of excellent nutritive meat, when he hath only some particular

[6]Expensive.

[7]Francois Rabelais (1494–1553) in *Gargantua and Pantagruel.*

friend or his own family to dine with him. Thus the squire will learn to be a good landlord, and grow popular among his tenants; the mother will have eight shillings net profit, and be fit for work till she produces another child.

14 Those who are more thrifty (as I must confess the times require) may flay the carcass, the skin of which artificially dressed will make admirable gloves for ladies, and summer boots for fine gentlemen.

15 As to our city of Dublin, shambles[8] may be appointed for this purpose in the most convenient parts of it, and butchers we may be assured will not be wanting; although I rather recommend buying children alive and dressing them hot from the knife, as we do roasting pigs.

16 A very worthy person, a true lover of his country, and whose virtues I highly esteem, was lately pleased in discoursing on this matter to offer a refinement upon my scheme. He said that many gentlemen of this kingdom, having of late destroyed their deer, he conceived that the want of venison might be well supplied by the bodies of young lads and maidens, not exceeding fourteen years of age nor under twelve; so great a number of both sexes in every country being now ready to starve for want of work and service; and there to be disposed of by their parents if alive, or otherwise by their nearest relations. But with due deference to so excellent a friend, and so deserving a patriot, I cannot be altogether in his sentiments; for as to the males, my American acquaintance assured me from frequent experience, that their flesh was generally tough and lean, like that of our schoolboys, by continual exercise, and their taste disagreeable, and to fatten them would not answer the charge. Then as to the females, it would, I think with humble submission, be a loss to the publick, because they soon would be breeders themselves: And besides it is not improbable that some scrupulous people might be apt to censure such a practice (although indeed very unjustly) as a little bordering upon cruelty, which, I confess, hath always been with me the strongest objection against any project, how well soever intended.

17 But in order to justify my friend, he confessed, that this expedient was put into his head by the famous Psalmanazar,[9] a native of the island Formosa, who came from thence to London, about twenty years ago, and in conversation told my friend, that in his country when any young person happened to be put to death, the executioner sold the carcass to persons of quality, as prime dainty, and that, in his time, the body of a plump girl of fifteen, who was crucified for an attempt to poison the Emperor, was sold to his Imperial Majesty's prime minister of state, and other great mandarins of the court, in joints from the gibbet, at four hundred crowns. Neither indeed can I deny, that if the same use were made of several plump young girls in this town, who, without one

[8]Slaughterhouses.

[9]George Psalmanazar (c. 1679–1763) was a Frenchman who pretended to be a Formosan and wrote a popular, completely fictional account of the supposed customs of his native land.

single groat to their fortunes, cannot stir abroad without a chair, and appear at a play-house and assemblies in foreign fineries which they never will pay for, the kingdom would not be the worse.

18   Some persons of a desponding spirit are in great concern about that vast number of poor people, who are aged, diseased, or maimed, and I have been desired to employ my thoughts what course may be taken, to ease the nation of so grievous an encumbrance. But I am not in the least pain upon that matter, because it is very well known, that they are every day dying, and rotting, by cold, and famine, and filth, and vermin, as fast as can be reasonably expected. And as to the young labourers, they are now in almost as hopeful a condition. They cannot get work, and consequently pine away for want of nourishment, to a degree, that if at any time they are accidentally hired to common labour, they have not strength to perform it, and thus the country and themselves are happily delivered from the evils to come.

19   I have too long digressed, and therefore shall return to my subject. I think the advantages by the proposal which I have made are obvious and many, as well as of the highest importance.

20   For *first*, as I have already observed, it would greatly lessen the number of papists, with whom we are yearly over-run, being the principal breeders of the nation, as well as our most dangerous enemies, and who stay at home on purpose with a design to deliver the kingdom to the Pretender, hoping to take their advantage by the absence of so many good Protestants, who have chosen rather to leave their country, than stay at home, and pay tithes against their conscience to an Episcopal curate.

21   Secondly, the poorer tenants will have something valuable of their own, which by law may be made liable to distress and help to pay their landlord's rent, their corn and cattle being already seized, and money a thing unknown.

22   Thirdly, whereas the maintenance of an hundred thousand children, from two years old and upward, cannot be computed at less than ten shillings apiece per annum, the nation's stock will be thereby increased fifty thousand pounds per annum, besides the profit of a new dish introduced to the tables of all gentlemen of fortune in the kingdom who have any refinement in taste. And the money will circulate among our selves, the goods being entirely of our own growth and manufacture.

23   Fourthly, the constant breeders, beside the gain of eight shillings sterling per annum by the sale of their children will be rid of the charge of maintaining them after the first year.

24   Fifthly, this food would likewise bring great custom[10] to taverns, where the vintners will certainly be so prudent as to procure the best receipts[11] for dressing it to perfection, and consequently have their houses frequented by all the

[10]Trade.
[11]Recipes.

fine gentlemen who justly value themselves upon their knowledge in good eating; and a skillful cook, who understands how to oblige his guests, will contrive to make it as expensive as they please.

25   Sixthly, this would be a great inducement to marriage, which all wise nations have either encouraged by rewards or enforced by laws and penalties. It would increase the care and the tenderness of mothers toward their children, when they were sure of a settlement for life to the poor babes, provided in some sort by the public, to their annual profit instead of expense. We should soon see an honest emulation among the married women, which of them could bring the fattest child to the market. Men would become as fond of their wives during the time of their pregnancy as they are now of their mares in foal, their cows in calf, their sows when they are ready to farrow; nor offer to beat or kick them (as is too frequent a practice) for fear of a miscarriage.

26   Many other advantages might be enumerated. For instance, the addition of some thousand carcasses in our exportation of barreled beef, the propagation of swine's flesh, and improvement in the art of making good bacon, so much wanted among us by the great destruction of pigs, too frequent at our table; which are no way comparable in taste or magnificence to a well-grown, fat, yearling child, which roasted whole will make a considerable figure at a lord mayor's feast or any other public entertainment. But this and many others I omit, being studious of[12] brevity.

27   Supposing that one thousand families in this city would be constant customers for infants' flesh, besides others who might have it at merry-meetings, particularly at weddings and christenings, I compute that Dublin would take off annually about twenty thousand carcasses; and the rest of the kingdom (where probably they will be sold somewhat cheaper) the remaining eighty thousand.

28   I can think of no one objection that will possibly be raised against this proposal, unless it should be urged that the number of people will be thereby much lessened in the kingdom. This I freely own, and 'twas indeed one principal design in offering it to the world. I desire the reader will observe that I calculate my remedy for this one individual kingdom of Ireland, and for no other that ever was, is, or, I think, ever can be upon earth. Therefore let no man talk to me of other expedients: of taxing our absentees at five shillings a pound: of using neither clothes, nor household furniture, except what is of our own growth and manufacture: of utterly rejecting the materials and instruments that promote foreign luxury: of curing the expensiveness of pride, vanity, idleness, and gaming in our women: of introducing a vein of parsimony, prudence and temperance: of learning to love our country, wherein we differ even from Laplanders, and the inhabitants of Topinamboo[13]: of quitting our

---

[12]Concerned with.

[13]Jungle region of Brazil.

animosities, and factions, nor act any longer like the Jews, who were murdering one another at the very moment their city was taken[14]: of being a little cautious not to sell our country and consciences for nothing: of teaching landlords to have at least one degree of mercy towards their tenants. Lastly, of putting a spirit of honesty, industry, and skill into our shop-keepers, who, if a resolution could now be taken to buy only our native goods, would immediately unite to cheat and exact[15] upon us in the price, the measure, and the goodness, nor could ever yet be brought to make one fair proposal of just dealing, though often and earnestly invited to it.

29   Therefore I repeat, let no man talk to me of these and the like expedients, till he hath at least some glimpse of hope, that there will ever be some hearty and sincere attempt to put them in practice.

30   But as to myself, having been wearied out for many years with offering vain, idle, visionary thoughts, and at length utterly despairing of success, I fortunately fell upon this proposal, which as it is wholly new, so it hath something solid and real, of no expense and little trouble, full in our own power, and whereby we can incur no danger in disobliging England. For this kind of commodity will not bear exportation, the flesh being of too tender a consistence, to admit a long continuance in salt, although perhaps I could name a country, which would be glad to eat up our whole nation without it.

31   After all, I am not so violently bent upon my own opinion, as to reject any offer, proposed by wise men, which shall be found equally innocent, cheap, easy, and effectual. But before something of that kind shall be advanced in contradiction to my scheme, and offering a better, I desire the author or authors, will be pleased maturely to consider two points. *First,* as things now stand, how they will be able to find food and raiment for a hundred thousand useless mouths and backs. And *Secondly,* there being a round million of creatures in human figure throughout this kingdom, whose whole subsistence put into a common stock would leave them in debt two millions of pounds sterling, adding those who are beggars by profession, to the bulk of farmers, cottagers and labourers, with their wives and children, who are beggars in effect; I desire those politicians, who dislike my overture, and may perhaps be so bold to attempt an answer, that they will first ask the parents of these mortals, whether they would not at this day think it a great happiness to have been sold for food at a year old, in the manner I prescribe, and thereby have avoided such a perpetual scene of misfortunes as they have since gone through, by the oppression of landlords, the impossibility of paying rent without money or trade, the want of common sustenance, with neither house nor clothes to cover them from the inclemencies of the weather, and the most inevitable prospect of entailing the like or greater miseries upon their breed for ever.

[14]Reference to the fall of Jerusalem, as described in the Bible.
[15]Impose.

32   I profess, in the sincerity of my heart, that I have not the least personal interest in endeavoring to promote this necessary work, having no other motive than the public good of my country, by advancing our trade, providing for infants, relieving the poor, and giving some pleasure to the rich. I have no children by which I can propose to get a single penny; the youngest being nine years old, and my wife past childbearing.

WHAT DID THE WRITER SAY AND WHAT DID YOU THINK?

1. "A Modest Proposal" is an ironic essay: The author deliberately writes what he does not mean. What is the real thesis? Is there more than one?
2. Is the essay only an attack on something? Does Swift ever present any serious proposals for improving conditions? If so, where?
3. What is the character of the "projector" of the proposal? Don't confuse him with Swift.
4. Are there any flaws in the logic? Could you refute the proposal by using logic? What assumptions about life and morality does the projector make before the logical argument begins?
5. What people or groups are singled out as special targets for Swift's attack?
6. Are the Irish presented completely as innocent victims, or are they also to blame?
7. Where does Swift's own sense of bitterness and rage come closest to emerging from beneath the cool irony?
8. Would it be possible to read this essay as a seriously intended proposal?

HOW DID THE WRITER SAY IT?

1. When does the reader start to realize that the essay is ironic? Before or after the actual proposal is made in paragraph 10?
2. Comment on the word choice in "a child just dropt from its dam" (paragraph 4), "two hundred thousand couples whose wives are breeders" (paragraph 6), and "a boy or a girl before twelve years old, is no saleable commodity" (paragraph 7).
3. Comment on the word choice in "people might be apt to censure such a practice . . . as a little bordering upon cruelty" (paragraph 16) and "they are every day dying, and rotting, by cold, and famine, and filth, and vermin, as fast as can be reasonably expected" (paragraph 18).
4. What is the purpose of the last paragraph?

What About Your Writing?

Verbal irony in its simplest form is saying the opposite, or near opposite, of what is meant. It can be seen at a primitive level when someone says, "Nice weather we're having," during a thunderstorm–and at the level of genius in "A Modest Proposal."

Nearly any subject can lend itself to the ironic approach, and you may want to consider trying your hand at an ironic paper. Successful irony has structured into it a strong element of humor and dramatic tension—tension between the surface statement and the underlying reality. With its special slant, it can also break through an audience's resistance toward reading another piece on a frequently discussed subject. It can often present familiar ideas in a fresh and exciting way.

A writer opposing capital punishment, for example, may be concerned about being perceived as a shallow idealist who thinks that all murderers are poor misunderstood victims of society. Using irony, the writer might be able to avoid the problem by pretending to be a bloodthirsty advocate of capital punishment, urging public executions, death by torture, and any other hideous ideas that come to mind. A writer supporting capital punishment, on the other hand, concerned about being perceived as an unfeeling brute, might pretend to be a simpleminded idealist, arguing ironically that if only society had provided more playgrounds and parks, the murderer would have become a consumer activist or ecologist.

In writing an ironic essay, watch out for two pitfalls:

Don't Let the Reader Misunderstand

Exaggerate enough so that the reader knows what side you're really on.

Don't Lose the Ironic Tone

Don't let your true feelings enter directly. The worst enemy of an effective ironic paper is sincerity. Beware, in particular, of the last paragraph that introduces a "but seriously, folks" or "what I really mean to say" element. If the irony isn't clear long before that, the whole paper probably needs to be reworked.

Critics often distinguish between verbal irony and two other kinds. *Irony of fate* refers to events that turn out differently from a normal person's expectations. A man compulsively afraid of germs has his whole house sterilized, fills his medicine chest with every known drug, and dies before he's thirty by tripping over a discarded bottle of medicine and breaking his neck. Most short stories with surprise endings employ irony of fate. *Dramatic irony* occurs when a literary character says or does something without realizing its significance, but the audience or reader does realize it. The hero of a melodrama beats up some villains, turns to the audience, says "Virtue triumphs again," and does not see another villain sneaking up behind him with a club.

Sarcasm is verbal irony used in an extremely bitter and personal fashion: "You really have a big heart, don't you?"

CHAPTER 10½

Office Hours: What About the Rest of Your Writing?

Just because you've finished the class you bought this book for doesn't mean that you're finished with the lessons of this book. We're confident that the advice we've given you about the importance of the Persuasive Principle and other writing strategies and tactics will stand you in good stead every time you sit down to write. The Persuasive Principle doesn't cease to exist just because the semester or the quarter is finally over.

If you're about to move eagerly on to your next English class and begin seriously analyzing great literature, you're probably expecting to need the Persuasive Principle and all the other tools for writing that we've written about. After all, it's an English class. But even if you never take an English class again, don't forget what you've learned here. As we said in Chapter 1, every kind of writing benefits from having a thesis. Every kind of writing benefits from the Persuasive Principle. If your history professor asks for a description of the battle of Agincourt, don't just settle for turning in a collection of facts and figures. Remember the Persuasive Principle:

- The French loss at the battle of Agincourt was the result of one major tactical error.
- At the battle of Agincourt, English innovations proved superior to the French reliance on tradition.
- Agincourt is a perfect example of how to lose a battle even when you have more troops, more armor, and more experienced tacticians than your opponent does.

The continuing usefulness of the lessons in this book doesn't stop with your academic life, either. The Persuasive Principle can help give life and unity to business and professional writing as well:

- Both computer systems we are considering adopting have features that can help with our work, but one is clearly the better choice.
- The cancellation of "Casual Fridays" in this office may not please everyone, but we're doing it to help maintain a professional environment, impress our clients, and eliminate some embarrassing mishaps.
- The patient's accusations of malpractice are based on distortions, misunderstandings, and omissions.

And don't forget that we showed you throughout Chapter 1 and the rest of this book that the Persuasive Principle can enliven types of everyday writing as diverse as driving directions, personal ads, and thank-you notes.

The class may be over, but your need for the Persuasive Principle isn't. It won't ever be.

Index

A

A Brush with Reality: Surprises in the Tube, 254–257
Abuse and ridicule in argumentation essays, 295
Active voice, 314–315
A Cultural Divorce, 55–57
Ad hominem argument, 297
Adjectives, parallel, 117–119
A Few Short Words, 199–200
Agreement, pronoun, 77–78
All By Myself, 83–85
Alliteration, 261–262
Allusions, 73–74
Always Settle Scores at Noon, 104–106
A Modest Proposal, 328–336
Analogy, argument by, 297–298
"And," using at the start of sentences, 311–312
Announcement of subject, 5
Anonymous, 268–269
Anticipating arguments, turning against
 opponents, 295
Appeasing the Gods with Insurance, 320–323
Argumentation essays, 293–337
 Appeasing the Gods with Insurance,
  320–323
 Black Athletes on Parade, 324–328
 Distracting Miss Daisy, 305–311
 A Modest Proposal, 328–336
 Sing It When It Counts, 300–302
 Smiley-Face Approach, The, 312–314
 Thanksgiving's No Turkey, 302–304
 Working at McDonald's, 315–319
Arrangement
 of examples, 99
 of process groups, 126
Articles, using quotation marks in, 254
Asimov, Isaac, 272–274
Audience
 help from the, 223–224
 writing for, 134–135
Authority, citation of, 82–83

B

Begging questions, 297
Benefits of a thesis, 4
Bernays, Anne, 239–242
Best Years of My Life, The, 216–220
Beyond Chagrin, 205–207
Big Bully, 39–40

Black Athletes on Parade, 324–327
Bodanis, David, 254–257
Bookworm, 231–232
Bradley, David, 205–207
Broke and Bored, 102–103

C

Catachresis, 287–289
Cause and effect essays, 195–222
 Best Years of My Life, The, 216–220
 Beyond Chagrin, 205–207
 Cold Autumn, 208–211
 A Few Short Words, 199–200
 Why I Quit the Company, 213–215
 Why We Crave Horror Movies, 201–203
Caution, phrases of, 216
Chain of causes and effects, linking, 197
Cheap Thrills, 274–277
Chores, 112–115
Citation of authority, 82–83
Clarity, revision process, 193–194
Classification, 225–262. *See also* Division
 and classification
Cold Autumn, 208–211
Collections of quotations, 33–34
Comic-book punctuation, 271
Coming in Last, 172–173
Comma splices, 221–222
Community bulletin board, ads on the, 13
Comparison and contrast essays, 165–192
 Coming in Last, 172–173
 Dad and Dads, 174–175
 Dearly Disconnected, 182–186
 Lassie Never Chases Rabbits, 175–177
 Love Thy Playstation, Love Thyself, 189–192
 My Real Car, 179–181
  patterns, 166–169
  alternating, 168–169
  block, 166–167
  selecting, 169–170
 Speaking of Writing, 187–189
Comparisons, metaphors and similes, 86–87
Computers, uses and abuses of, 161–164
Conclusions, 178–179
Conflict in stories, 36
Contrast. *See* Comparison and contrast
Convincing realistic details, using, 36–37
Corn Bread with Character, 131–134

Counts, David R., 147–153
Couple Lies, 106–108
Cowherd, Kevin, 174–177

D
Dad and Dads, 174–175
Deadlines, 291–292
Dearly Disconnected, 182–186
Definition essays, 265–290
    Catachresis, 287–289
    Cheap Thrills, 274–277
    Growing Up, 268–269
    Real Thing, The, 270–271
    Sick in the Head, 279–285
    What is Intelligence, Anyway?, 272–274
Description essays, 65–94
    All By Myself, 83–85
    Double Take, 87–89
    I Was a Member of the Kung Fu Crew, 74–77
    Loneliness of Rose, The, 90–94
    Master of Bad Management, 69–70
    My Glove: A Biography, 79–82
    Winstead's Best Burgers, 71–74
Details
    convincing realistic, using, 36–37
    specific, 66
Dialogue, 278–279
    quotation marks in, 253–254
Dictionaries, 33–34
    definitions, 265
Directions, two sets of, 15–16
Distracting Miss Daisy, 305–311
Division and classification essays, 225–262
    Bookworm, 231–232
    A Brush with Reality: Surprises in the Tube,
        254–257
    Mother-in-Law, 232–238
    Seven-Lesson Schoolteacher, The, 242–252
    Take a Left Turn onto Nowhere Street, 239–242
    Three Kinds of Discipline, 258–261
Double Take, 87–89
Drafts, revision, 193–194
Dramatic irony, 336–337
Dublanica, Steve, 208–211

E
Eco, Umberto, 115–117
Editing
    help from the audience, 223–224
    overview of, 193–194
    psychology of it all, the, 263–264
Effects,. *See* cause and effect
Elegant variation, 207–208
Emotional appeal of description, 65
Etzioni, Amitai, 315–319

Example essays, 97–119
    Always Settle Scores at Noon, 104–106
    Broke and Bored: The Summer Job, 102–103
    Chores, 112–115
    Couple Lies, 106–108
    Fruitful Questions, 109–111
    How to Speak of Animals, 115–117
Exclamation points, 271
Exploding Toilet and Other Embarrassments, The,
    141–146

F
Fallacies, logical, 296–299
Fatsis, Stefan, 79–82
First drafts, revision, 193–194
First sentences, writing strong, 134–135
Formal tone, using "one,", 203
Foul Shots, 42–45
Fragments, sentences, 62
Frazier, Ian, 182–186
Free Tibet, Man!, 40–41
Froncek, Thomas, 58–62
Fruitful Questions, 109–111
Fulford, Robert, 104–106

G
Gardner, Robert W., 302–304
Gatto, John Taylor, 242–252
Generalizations, 295
General subject, 1–2
Germany, Frankie, 270–271
Getting even, 45
Gimmicks, 289–290
Gomez, Rogelio R., 42–45
Good thesis, definition of, 6–8
Grammar
    checkers, 161–164
    exclamation points, 271
    forms, parallel, 117–118
    revision of, 193–194
    and spelling, importance of, 120–122
Greene, Max, 129–131
Grossman, Annette P., 172–173
Growing Up, 268–269

H
Hall, Ashley, 174–175
Happiest Day of My Life, The, 49–52
"He," using, 203
Hiestand, Elizabeth, 39–40
Holt, John, 258–261
How I Spent my Summer Vacation, two essays,
    21–23
How Not to Work Out, 129–131
How to Speak of Animals, 115–117

Hughes, Langston, *52–54*
Humor, 192
  puns, 286
Hyperbole, 89

I
Imperatives, parallel, 117
Independent clauses, parallel, 117
Infinitives, parallel, 117
Intensifiers (very, really), 114
Introductions, 134–135
Irony, 336–338
"*IT,*" 135–140
I Was a Member of the Kung Fu Crew, 74–77
Iwashita, Tomoyuki, 213–215

J
Jackson, Shirley, 23–32
Jargon, 154

K
Katz, Jon, 90–94
King, Stephen, 201–203

L
Lafsky, Melissa, 87–89
Lara, Adair, 106–108
Lassie Never Chases Rabbits, 174–177
Latvala, Charlotte, 232–238
Lau, Henry Han Xi, 74–77
Length of sentences, varying, 106
Letters of complaint, two, 17–18
  Replies, 19–20
Limited subject, 2–3
Literary subject, two essays on, 23
Loneliness of Rose, The, 90–94
Lottery, The, 23–32
Love Thy Playstation, Love Thyself, 189–192
Lundy, Ronni, 131–134

M
Marquart, Debra, 112–115
Master of Bad Management, 69–70
Metaphors, comparisons, 86–87
Miller, Sarah Bryan, 71–74
Monroe, Matthew, 199–200
Moore, Dinty W., 40–41
Morris, Reid, 174–175
Mother-in-Law, 232–238
My Glove: An Autobiography, 79–82
My Real Car, 179–181

N
Narration essays, 35–62
  Big Bully, 39–40

A Cultural Divorce, 55–57
Foul Shots, 42–45
Free Tibet, Man! 40–41
Happiest Day of my Life, The, 49–52
Perfect Picture, The, 46–48
Salvation, 52–55
Sitting Duck, 58–62
Non sequitur, 296
Nostalgia, 55
Notebooks, the writer's savings account, 95–96
Nouns, parallel, 117

O
O'Hara, Patricia, 287–289
"One," using, 203
One-sentence transitional paragraphs, 41
Onomatopoeia, 182
Overwriting, 48–49

P
Paragraphs
  conclusions, 178–179
  dialogue, 278
  introductions, 134–135
  one-sentence transitional, 41
Parallelism, 117
Partition, *See also* Division and classification
Passive voice, 314–315
Patrick, Robynn, 69–70
Pearl-McPhee, Stephanie, 135–140
Peer review, 223–224
Perfect Picture, The, 46–48
Personals, 14–15
Persuasive Principle, The, 1–23
Petrunkevitch, Alexander, 155–159
Phrases, using repetition for emphasis,
  140–141
Post hoc ergo propter hoc fallacy, 296
Prepositions
  at the end of sentences, 52
  parallel prepositional phrases, 117
Process essays
  Corn Bread with Character, 131–134
  Exploding Toilet and Other Embarrassments, The,
    141–146
  "*IT,*" 135–140
  Spider and the Wasp, The, 155–159
  Too Many Bananas, 147–153
Pronoun agreement, 77
Proofreading, 193–194
Puns, 286

Q
Qualification, phrases of, 216
Quotation marks, misused, 253

R

Readers. *See* Audience
Reading around, 63–63
"Really," using, 114
Real Thing, The, 270–271
Reed, Jr., Adolph, 324–327
Repetition
  alliteration, 261
  for emphasis, 140
  words, repeating in the same sentence, 207
Research tools, computers, 161–164
Restricted thesis, 6
Revision
  help from the audience, 223–224
  overview of, 193–194
  psychology of it all, the, 263–264
Reynolds, Tom, 83–95
Ridicule in argumentation essays, 295
Rollin, Betty, 216–220
Ruggiero, Ben, 300–302

S

Salam, Reihan, 189–192
Salvation, 52–54
Selection
  of examples, 98
  of patterns, 169
  of subjects, 1–3
  of titles, 242,
  of topics, 1–3
Sentences
  "And", using at the start of, 311
  comma splices, 221
  first, writing strong, 134
  fragments, 62
  length, 106
  prepositions, at the end of, 52
  words, repeating the same in a sentence, 207
Sexism, using "he," 303
Shanker, Albert, 312–314
Sick in the Head, 279–285
Similes, comparisons, 86–87
Sing it When it Counts, 300–302
Smiley-Face Approach, The, 312–314
Smith, Michael T., 49–52
Smith, Patrick, 141–146
Sollisch, James, 109–111
Speaking of Writing, 187–189
Specialties of the author, as subject matter, 257
Specific details, 66–67
Specific language, using, 66
Specific thesis, 7–8
Spelling
  and grammar, importance of, 120–122
  revision of, 263–264

Spider and the Wasp, The, 155–159
Story
  conflict in, 36
  stress the, 36
Straddon, John, 305–311
Straw man, setting up, 296
Subjects
  announcement of, 159
  general, 1–2
  limited, 2–3
  literary subject, two essays on, 23
  romantic highs and lows, as subject matter, 238
  specialties of the author, as subject matter, 257
  topicality, 186
  work, as subject matter, 211
Swift, Jonathan, 328–335

T

Take a Left Turn onto Nowhere Street, 239–242
Taking Sides, 304
Thanksgiving's No Turkey, 302–404
Thank-you notes, 16–17
Thesaurus, 33–34, 207
Thesis
  absolute fact, statement of, 5
  announcement of subject, 5
  benefits of a, 3
  good, definition of, 6–8
  overview of, 3–4
  restrictions of, 6
  specific, 7–9
  statements, 3–4
  titles, 4–5
  unified, 7
  unstated, 94
  at work in the paper, 10–14
Thom, James Alexander, 46–48
Three Kinds of Discipline, 258–261
Tierney, John, 305–311
Titles, 4–5
  selecting, 242
Too Many Bananas, 147–153
Tools for writers, basic, 33–34
Topicality, 186
Traig, Jennifer, 279–285
Turning Tables, 328
Types of conclusions, 178–179

U

Unfamiliar terms, defining, 127
Unified thesis, 6
Unstated thesis, 94
Usage, levels of, 146

V
"Very," using, 114
Volk, Patricia, 274–277

W
Watson, Gracie Jane, 231–232
What is Intelligence, Anyway?, 272–273
White, Bailey, 179–182
"Why didn't I say that?",108
Why I Quit the Company, 213–215
Why We Crave Horror Movies, 201–203

Wilkinson, Will, 189–192
Winstead's Best Burgers, 71–74
Wong, Elizabeth, 55–57
Working at McDonald's, 315–319

Y
"You," using in an essay, 323

Z
Zinsser, William, 187–189